Later Victorian Britain, 1867–1900

Each volume in the 'Problems in Focus' series is designed to make available to students important new work on key historical problems and periods that they encounter in their courses. Each volume is devoted to a central topic or theme, and the most important aspects of this are dealt with by specially commissioned essays from scholars in the relevant field. The editorial Introduction reviews the problem or period as a whole, and each essay provides an assessment of the particular aspect, pointing out the areas of development and controversy, and indicating where conclusions can be drawn or where further work is necessary. An annotated bibliography serves as a guide for further reading.

PROBLEMS IN FOCUS SERIES

FURTHER TITLES ARE IN PREPARATION

Later Victorian Britain, 1867–1900

EDITED BY

T. R. GOURVISH and ALAN O'DAY

MACMILLAN
EDUCATION

First published 1988

Published by
MACMILLAN EDUCATION LTD
Houndmills, Basingstoke, Hampshire RG21 2XS
and London
Companies and representatives
throughout the world

Typeset by Wessex Typesetters
(Division of The Eastern Press Ltd)
Frome, Somerset
Printed in Hong Kong

Later Victorian Britain, 1867–1900.—
(Problems in focus series).
1. Great Britain—History—Victoria,
1837–1900
I. Gourvish, T. R. II. O'Day, Alan
III. Series
941.081   DA560
ISBN 0–333–42494–8
ISBN 0–333–42495–6 Pbk

Contents

Preface

LATER *Victorian Britain* is similar to other volumes in the 'Problems in Focus' series in examining a limited number of important themes concerned with a specific problem or period. The book does not pretend to treat all the issues of the later Victorian era or to present a unified view of the age. In one way or another each contributor has stressed vital elements of the period but the various articles do not always propose identical or even necessarily consistent views. Ultimately the essays are the product of individual outlooks.

The editors are grateful to the contributors, who submitted their articles on schedule, accepted our criticisms with good grace and humour, and also offered searching comments on other sections of the volume. We both had the benefit of other contributors' appraisals of our own essays. This has been a genuine 'team' effort with the editors serving as convenors. We wish to express our appreciation to Vanessa Couchman and Vanessa Graham, our editors at Macmillan, who encouraged the enterprise and acted as willing mentors; also to Judy Marshall for copy-editing and Margaret Purcell for assistance with proof-reading.

T.R.G.
A.O'D.

1. Later Victorian Britain

T. R. GOURVISH AND ALAN O'DAY

BETWEEN the second Reform Act and 1900 Britain experienced a crucial transformation. By the turn of the century the country had become a mass democracy, though not one founded on universal suffrage; it was a heavily urbanised community based increasingly on distribution and professional services for economic success; and some 4.7 million square miles and 88 million people had been added to what was an already immense empire. Contrary to the fears of many people at the outset of the period, change had taken place gradually and without sparking a serious upheaval. To outsiders and also to many at home Britain appeared a model community capable of resolving internal conflict without resort to excessive force or revolution. Britain, by the norms of other nations, enjoyed high degrees of social cohesion and national unity built on consent and co-operation between the governed and the ruling order. This sense of community survived despite the economic difficulties of the period, troubles in Ireland, labour unrest, imperial problems, religious tensions and a hard-fought political contest between competing factions. Later Victorian Britain was pre-eminently a stable society in which disputes were conducted within understood guidelines. Public disturbances such as the Trafalgar Square riots of February 1886 and November 1887 were rare.

The eleven essays in this volume examine aspects of British society in the late nineteenth century giving particular emphasis to how demands for change were articulated by those who sought reform, how these claims were received by the governing order and the community in general, and why Britain was so evidently a stable nation. If anything, there were many indicators in the pre-1867 heritage to suggest that change in Britain would generate more turbulence than was experienced by the late Victorians. In a larger number of respects the period is remarkable. Yet it is apparent that few people at the time saw themselves as living in a unique or self-contained era. Indeed, the very Whiggish outlook of the time naturally regarded the late Victorian years as part of the continuum of progress. Historians, too, have found difficulty in attaching specific dates or hypotheses to the period. There is no single great controversy, such as Dangerfield's 'Strange Death of Liberal England' thesis for the last Edwardian years, to command attention. Perhaps the closest approximation is the recent search by intellectual and economic historians for the point at which there was an irreversible decline in Britain's 'industrial spirit', part of a broader debate about the features and causes of industrial decline. But so far at least the notion of a 'decline of the industrial spirit' has remained both a contentious and a parochial issue; it has certainly failed to draw other kinds of historian into the argument. Thus, the very idea of 'Later Victorian Britain' must be regarded as somewhat amorphous. The originating and terminal dates recommended by the editors – 1867 and 1900 – are partly a matter of convenience. Few would start the period much earlier than 1867, though some, and particularly economic and social historians, might choose another date, such as 1873, which marked the beginning of a period of falling prices, often characterised by the term 'Great Depression'. Nevertheless, the year 1867 forms a useful start if not a sharp divide in Victorian history. Marking the end of W. L. Burns's *Age of Equipoise*, it was, according to Geoffrey Kitson Clark, the point at which 'the old regime began to break'. The concluding date may also be debated. The death of Victoria in 1901 is an obvious choice, though some might prefer the outbreak of the Boer War in 1899. While the general election of 1900 is not itself a significant turning-point, there is some measure of agreement that events in Britain began to move in new directions around the turn of the century, and it therefore seemed reasonable to end the volume there.

Stability in Britain rested on the twin pillars of a belief in – and respect for – the Constitution and the ability of the economy to produce a satisfactory standard of living. The first could not function without a stable institutional framework, while the latter required an effective economic structure. Although few could define closely what the 'Constitution' was it did imply a set of values as much as a list of precise rules and regulations. At the cornerstone of the 'Constitution' were the monarchy, Parliament and an avowedly impartial judiciary. Parliament, and especially the House of Commons and Cabinet, were the centre of government – the places where change was discussed, formulated and presented to the nation at large. Possibly at no other time did the House of Commons play so central a role in the political system – it was at this time a focus of public attention, the chief forum for argument and the legitimate instrument to initiate reforms. Outsiders like Irish nationalists, nonconformists, trade unionists and women accepted that the House of Commons was the appropriate forum to air grievances and demands. That concurrence helps explain the stability of the nation – though it was a consensus which could only be maintained so long as the whole community through the House of Commons showed itself responsive to people's aspirations. The attention given to politics and institutional reforms in the late Victorian age is warranted.

Walter Bagehot's *The English Constitution*, first published at the beginning of the period, remains one of the prime documents of later Victorian Britain. His vital insight was to draw attention to the 'dignified' and the 'efficient' portions of the country's institutions. He argued that neither could function successfully alone. Dignified organs such as the monarchy and the House of Lords were essential because they enjoyed recognition and legitimacy. Under the cloak of the dignified elements, the efficient instruments of governance – the House of Commons and Cabinet – were able to conduct the affairs of state. Bagehot's analysis contains exaggerations and archaic features but he continues to provide a useful tool of social as well as political understanding of the period. He sought to explain how British society amalgamated new with old elements – persons, institutions and classes – without upsetting the existing balance. The essays in this volume address the theme raised by Bagehot. The aim is threefold: to treat certain key issues in fuller perspective than can be done in general accounts or survey books; to reassess some of the historical literature about the period; and to offer different appraisals of selected problems. The volume attempts to balance economic, social and political approaches. Not all topics have been covered – space limitations precluded further material – but most of the important issues are highlighted.

The first three chapters consider the fusion of the new with the old elite in Britain from differing perspectives. Terry Gourvish examines the swift expansion of the professions, Martin Daunton assesses the implications of further rapid urbanisation, and Roland Quinault traces the career of Joseph Chamberlain, who epitomised many of the characteristics outlined by Bagehot. Terry Gourvish shows the critical role of the professions in the period and his analysis reveals the intimate connection between social and economic trends on the one hand and political matters on the other. As he notes, the professions expanded their numbers and economic influence and came to dominate the economic, social and political life of the country. They achieved their exalted station because the state lent them authority, specialist services being deemed essential to the efficient running of society. Areas of increased state responsibility such as public health required specialised knowledge. In turn the state permitted individual professions to manage their own internal affairs, to control entry and enforce standards of competence and behaviour. The professions, for their part, posited claims to privileged status on the possession of exceptional responsibility and respectability as evidenced by the requirements of training, qualifying examinations and obedience to the canons of controlling bodies. Gourvish sees the professions providing the vital bridge between the dignified and efficient sections of the community. They formed the cornerstone of a refashioned social and political hierarchy, a new elite which managed the state effectively. And, in Britain, potential dissidents found themselves deprived of the support and leadership of the bulk of the professional middle class, which preferred its position as a group accorded financial and occupational recognition by the existing state. This chapter offers a clue to an understanding of the exceptional stability of later Victorian Britain.

Martin Daunton extends the discussion in his examination of the single greatest demographic change of the period – the continued rapid growth of urban centres and the absolute decline of Britain's rural population. Whereas the old elite had retained firm roots in the countryside, the new elite, and particularly members of the professions, were clustered in the towns. Urban growth, Daunton observes, was especially evident in some of the already sizeable cities – London, Glasgow, Birmingham, Liverpool and Manchester – which all enlarged their proportion of the national population. By 1891 London contained 14.5 per cent of the people of England and Wales; Glasgow was even more dominant in Scotland, having 19.4 per cent of that country's population. But the urban landscape was not, Daunton notes, static or uniform but changed over the period and varied between places. Scotland notably had features which resulted from the peculiar legal traditions of that country and distinguished development there from that which took place elsewhere in the United Kingdom. Daunton draws attention to the ability of municipalities to meet their problems by · large-scale investment in infrastructures such as gasworks, drainage schemes, reservoirs and tramways. Extension of responsibility required more professional and bureaucratic forms of local government. City councils became the focus of interest of the professional classes – a forum where their expertise was invaluable. These remodelled urban institutions were intended to be respectable and responsiole – to reflect the ethos of the emergent town elites. Daunton's article complements Gourvish's, showing how and why the expanding professional elite came to dominate many aspects of late Victorian life.

Perhaps no major figure exemplified the reshaped late Victorian elite better than Joseph Chamberlain. He was the one national leader who had made his initial mark in municipal government, having proved a dynamic mayor of Birmingham. Throughout his political career Chamberlain was closely identified with that city. Roland Quinault gives texture to this career, suggesting that it has been tempting to overestimate his provincial status at the expense of his metropolitan interests. Chamberlain was a Nonconformist and industrialist who had been born and attended school in London prior to migrating to Birmingham. As his political interests developed, he spent greater amounts of time in the capital and with passing years seldom resided in his Birmingham home. Indeed, his business and political involvements increasingly reflected a London environment. Chamberlain's financial interests came to be concentrated on City of London investments, particularly speculation in overseas ventures, and his withdrawal from industry was virtually complete. National, even international politics, rather than provincial affairs, became his forte. Chamberlain sent his sons to traditional English public schools. Thus, as Quinault demonstrates, Birmingham Joe was a man of many faces but most of all characterised the fusion of the new with the old elite. Chamberlain represented the efficient rather than the dignified element of society but he in effect transformed himself into a hybrid of the two. In a later chapter certain of the characteristics Quinault identifies in Chamberlain are extended to the Victorian elite as a whole by Keith Burgess. As Quinault usefully shows, Chamberlain both made and reflected opinion and also personified the strengths and the contradictions apparent in later nineteenth-century British life.

The following three chapters – John Dunbabin's on electoral reform and its effects; John Garrard's on parties and political integration; and Paul Hayes's on the making and purposes of foreign policy – consider vital aspects of the late Victorian political system. As John Dunbabin illustrates, there was an intense debate about who was allowed to vote and how the franchise was to be exercised. In what is probably the most comprehensive brief analysis of the subject ever made he examines the many facets of the electoral system and concludes that it succeeded in satisfying both the aspirations of the 'responsible' working classes for political recognition and the desire of the governing classes for stability. Many people on the eve of the Reform Act of 1867 had doubted that the two aims could be reconciled. Dunbabin suggests that the electoral system which emerged provided a formula for expression of strong feelings while containing safeguards to ensure continuity and stability. It succeeded because major groups were not alienated from British institutions and the working class was united with its superiors in wanting a system that functioned smoothly, efficiently and most of all economically. Britain, in consequence, was able to maintain an electoral apparatus which was relatively cheap and enjoyed public confidence. He also observes that stability was possible because the remodelled political elite chose to limit public competition for the favour of the masses and sought instead to ensure that the voters were incorporated into the existing political framework. Thus there was little attempt to exploit potential discontent for partisan ends. Indeed, much of the animosity directed at Gladstone arose from a belief that he threatened to use the masses against the middle class. For the reasons Dunbabin describes, Britain was able to move from limited to household suffrage during these years without fundamentally disrupting the political fabric. His analysis assists us in interpreting how the efficient and dignified sections of the community were bound together.

John Garrard approaches the question of the stability of the political system from a local perspective. From his examination of Lancashire – that cockpit of late nineteenth-century politics – he contends that both the Liberal and the Conservative parties adapted rapidly to the challenge of enfranchisement. They created powerful and all-encompassing organisations to produce acceptable political behaviour in the new voters. Parties were, he suggests, an instrument of social cohesion for they built up a total culture which met many of the social and psychological requirements of the community. Garrard argues that the development of a complete political culture was apparent in the Liberal and Conservative parties of the late Victorian era and did not have to await the coming of a Labour party. Moreover, he shows how quickly and appropriately local leaders reacted to the prospect of an enlarged electorate. These leaders used political activity to enlarge and consolidate their own standing in society while at the same time contributing organisation and respectability to the electoral process. Garrard's treatment links national and local political activity and demonstrates once more the vital place which an urban, disproportionately professional, elite came to occupy in late Victorian life. Political parties were an important element in the rise of urban elites. Through parties the working class was persuaded of the legitimacy and responsiveness of existing British institutions.

A third investigation of the political system is undertaken in

Paul Hayes's assessment of the formation of foreign policy. The men who were responsible for foreign affairs were drawn primarily from the 'dignified' portions of society but, as Hayes observes, they acted in a responsible and efficient way. He points out that foreign policy was reflective of the nation's cultural assumptions and was used as a sort of great moral teaching machine. It was a means by which the elite demonstrated the moral and practical worth of British institutions and mores to people at home and abroad. John Dunbabin notes the high level of consensus in Britain and Hayes extends this observation. British foreign policy, he suggests, was characterised by genuine continuity which, however, did not exclude an intense and sometimes heated debate about its objectives and methods. Thus strong emotions could be expressed within an agreed framework. One of Hayes's most acute points is his insistence that the makers of foreign policy, though drawn from the traditional order, proved sensitive to the opinions of other groups in Britain and adaptive to changing circumstances. As the era closed, foreign policy priorities shifted to meet different national needs. His article throws light not only on the dignified element in government but also on how the old elite was able to prolong, even enhance, its utility and legitimacy in the democratic age.

The next three contributions consider the claims and strategies of Victorian outsiders. Pat Thane looks at the growth of feminism, Stuart Mews looks at the Salvation Army as a case-study in religious attitudes, while Alan O'Day offers a differing perspective on that old chestnut, the Irish dilemma. Each essay, in some measure, assesses how the dominant elements in late Victorian society met the challenge of unsatisfied groups. Women and their difficulties, as Pat Thane indicates, provide an opportunity to test many assumptions about late Victorian society. In an arresting and original contribution she takes issue with the widely held view that the period saw women in an increasingly passive role as a prelude to Edwardian militancy. She notes that many aspects of women's lives were being altered, often as a consequence of the demographic and economic changes of the period. The decline in family size and growing prospects for female employment had very substantial implications. Using much new information, Thane argues that middle-class women were not the exclusive harbingers of female self-assertiveness and that working-class women played a vital part in trades unions and other activities. Within the confines of Victorian law, ideology and social arrangements women in impressive numbers from all classes pressed for equity and recognition. They may have been far from united on beliefs and aspirations but their very diversity of outlook was a source of strength. She maintains that although women were not alienated from society, 'never in history had male predominance been challenged simultaneously on so many fronts'. For her, then, the period is something immensely more profound than a mere backdrop to the exciting women's suffrage battle of the Edwardian years. Her treatment also adds a dimension to the understanding of the working class as a whole. She disputes the standard view of labour historians that women were marginal to the growth of trades unions and the struggle for better wages and conditions, demonstrating that many displayed assertive, indeed, militant tendencies. Although women, like many men, had only a restricted scope of activity they proved adept at seizing opportunities for enhancing their status.

Religion had an important function in late Victorian life. For centuries clergymen had been vested with responsibility for instilling social cohesion but the census of 1851 revealed that in England and Wales less than half of churchgoers subscribed to the national church. In the expanding towns there were sections of the population who fell outside all clerical influence. Stuart Mews examines the means by which William Booth and the Salvation Army sought to meet the challenge of de-christianisation. Booth used sensationalist methods and adopted uniforms, brass bands, a flag and other devices to capture the attention of the urban masses. Essentially, the Salvation Army was a movement of religious outsiders aimed at the lower ranks of society. As Mews notes, in the early days some of the bishops of the Church of England were anxious to give Booth encouragement or at least benevolent neutrality. However, that attitude soon passed. Mews dissects the change in outlook within the establishment. His article is a con-tribution to religious history but pertinently he identifies some of the limits of Victorian tolerance. The Salvation Army worried many people because of its techniques and the role accorded to women. But most of all, Mews observes, the movement violated accepted conventions of respectability and responsibility. In doing so it lost support among the Anglican bishops. Mews's argument is a potent reminder of the ability of outsiders to make an impression but only when they confined themselves to acceptable modes of conduct.

Alan O'Day looks at an entirely different sort of outsider, the Catholics of Ireland. It is generally acknowledged that the Irish problem was one, perhaps even the, principal difficulty of the age. Commentators usually stress the political aspect of the Irish question. O'Day re-examines the traditional position and places the issue in a wider context. In contrast to the received view, he insists that the Irish were not exceptionally politicised and that the policies of both British political parties were impressive, if not always successful. Why then did Britain fail to win the minds and hearts of the Irish people? O'Day's explanation shifts the focus to the inability of successive governments to tamper with the natural laws of the economy in ways which would make Ireland prosperous. Without an end to the haemorrhage of enforced emigration the Irish problem could only elude resolution. The flow of people out of the country both showed the weakness of Ireland's economy and stood as a symbol of the failure of the Union. But British leaders, he asserts, were never able to treat the real cancer in Irish society because of entrenched beliefs and from a recognition that Ireland's needs could never be treated wholly separately from wider policy considerations. What the Irish received today must be granted to the rest of Britain tomorrow. Ireland gained a measure of special treatment but did not always receive the right remedies. O'Day's essay throws further light on the constraints upon change in later Victorian Britain.

The final two articles expand upon the theme of the limitations of late nineteenth-century Britain. Keith Burgess's discussion relates directly to the current controversy about whether and why the nation lost its industrial ethos. Peter Alter assesses policy towards scientific development at a time when it was becoming clear that economic and political success depended on the innovations of a new technology. These two pieces provide a fitting conclusion for the volume since they point to some of the less favourable features of the age and lead, in both cases, towards those disputes which animated the Edwardian years.

Burgess's analysis considers the ways in which the blending of old and new elites shaped attitudes and expectations. He demonstrates that the result was an adaptive elite though perhaps not in quite the right way for industry. Economic development was notably less industrial than commercial with the influences of the City of London pervading both politics and society. Burgess poses an important reminder that the expansion of an economy is very much a product of its past. Britain, he rightly observes, was never so much a workshop as a commercial nation. The constraints and rigidities which afflicted industry in the last third of the century had been present earlier but were less noticeable during an era when competition was largely absent. Relative industrial retardation was not, he suggests, a consequence of an altered 'spirit' or attitude but the perhaps predictable outcome of changed circumstances in which British deficiencies were exposed. Burgess offers a subtle interplay of economic, political, social and cultural forces showing that both the historical legacy and the contemporary reality of City influence were crucial in determining economic policy. His article is a significant caveat to easy assumptions about a 'decline of the industrial spirit'.

Peter Alter takes up a similar theme from a different angle. He explores the hesitant emergence of a public science policy despite the apparent relevance of technology for industry. Although these years were not wholly barren Alter observes that the British mixture of *laissez-faire* and state interventionism dictated a slow rather than a swift pace. Public policy was generally to encourage private initiative except when some outstanding urgency made state action imperative. As Alter comments, British leaders and the nation at large simply did not feel sufficiently threatened during the late Victorian era. His contribution makes a fitting conclusion to the period as he goes on to contrast it with the rapid growth of interest in, and support for, science during the Edwardian years. The motivation in the latter period was the rise of a powerful and potentially hostile Germany. Alter's article is a contribution to the discussion of why Britain did or did not react in particular ways. He demonstrates that when a challenge emerged British leaders proved adaptable once again. In vital respects, as he notes, the period immediately prior to the Great War offered different possibilities from those of the late Victorian years.

Later Victorian Britain was a critical epoch. It contained many aspects, most of which have been considered in the contributions to this volume. Above all there was a concerted attempt to establish a stable community. That search necessarily roused tensions and anxieties. In many areas the Victorians successfully tamed new forces and ideas, integrating them into the existing pattern while in other cases that goal remained elusive. At its best the age saw a blending of the 'dignified' and 'efficient' elements of society into an effective community. It is hoped that the present collection identifies the vital ingredients of the late Victorian age and will stimulate further discussion about the period.

2. The Rise of the Professions

T. R. GOURVISH

I

THE emergence of a substantial and powerful professional group – class, perhaps, is not quite the right word – within the British middle class was a phenomenon which gathered considerable pace in the later Victorian period. Yet it is a process which is rather difficult to summarise effectively. There are many problems inherent in defining the term 'profession' and in measuring the extent of professional development. In this chapter attention is given to these, after which an examination is made of the several paths to professional status in the period to 1900; the impact of professions on the economy; and, briefly, the role of professional people in stimulating social change and, in particular, social reform. By way of introduction, it should be noted that the emergence of a larger group of professional occupations was naturally a function of more global developments in nineteenth-century Britain: the growth and maturation of the world's first modern capitalist economy; an increasing, and an increasingly prosperous, population, together with its concentration in urban settlements; and the diversification of the industrial structure, with an increased emphasis upon the service sectors. The statistical summary in Table 2.1 provides an indication of the scale of these changes since 1841, and an opportunity to compare change in the thirty years before and after 1871.

The UK population grew by almost a third in the last three decades of the century, a higher growth rate than for 1841–71, though here the rate is influenced by the Irish famine and its aftermath. The growth of real GNP was impressively high in

TABLE 2.1   UK economic and social indicators, 1841–1901

Year	Population (m)	GNP^a (m)	GNP per capita	Population living in urban areas^b (%)	Service sectors' share of NI^c (%)
1841	26.7	£489.9	£18.34	48	44
1871	31.5	£1050.4	£33.36	65	48
1901	41.7	£1925.8	£46.18	78	54
Growth rates (%):					
1841–71	17.9	114.4	81.9	35.4	9.1
1871–1901	32.5	83.3	38.4	20.0	12.5

Source: B. R. Mitchell and P. Deane, *Abstract of British Historical Statistics* (Cambridge, 1962) pp. 6–7; P. Deane, 'New Estimates of Gross National Product for the United Kingdom 1830–1914', *Review of Income and Wealth*, xiv (June 1968) 106–7; P. Deane and W. A. Cole, *British Economic Growth, 1688–1959* (Cambridge, 1967), data summarised in F. Crouzet, *The Victorian Economy* (1982) pp. 67, 70, 90.

Notes:
^aGross National Product at factor cost, constant 1900 prices.
^bPercentage of population of England and Wales [n.b.] living in areas with a population of 2500 and above.
^cService sectors = trade and transport, domestic and personal, housing, income from abroad, and public and professional, etc. Data are for Great Britain.

both periods. It more than doubled in the period to 1871 and, in spite of growing anxieties about Britain's weakening competitive position it nevertheless managed an 83 per cent increase to 1901. Consequently, national product per capita also exhibited a steady growth, although this was more modest after 1871 than in the mid-Victorian boom years. A larger and more affluent society, whatever the inequalities in the class structure, had obvious implications for the demand for professional services. So too did the intensifying urbanisation of Britain, impressive by international standards, which not only concentrated demand for professional services but also created new opportunities for specialists in local government bureaucracies strengthened by the expanding role of local authorities in the late nineteenth century. In 1871 65 per cent of the population of England and Wales lived in settlements of

2500 people and more; thirty years later the proportion had increased to 78 per cent, by which time the service sectors in the economy represented over half of the national income (Table 2.1). It was in the towns and cities that the middle classes burgeoned. The search for a precise growth rate founders on the rock of elusive definition, but as a very rough approximation we may take those with incomes in excess of £150 a year. Here, numbers in Britain increased by about 170 per cent, from around 307,000 in 1860–1 to about 833,000 in 1894–5.[1] From the ranks of this expanding group came not only those who retained the non-industrial tasks of the traditional professional occupations – religion, law, medicine and education (the civil service and armed forces may also be considered part of the traditional professions but, equally, they may be seen as part of 'government') – but also those who helped to 'professionalise' other occupations connected with the demands of the post-industrial world: accounting, surveying, civil and mechanical engineering, and so on. The 'rise of the professions', then, is very much part, and a key part, of the growth of the middle class and the emergence of what has been termed the 'service class'. In Harold Perkin's well-known formulation, the professions constituted a 'forgotten middle-class', temporarily ignored in the early stages of industrial revolution as the aristocratic, entrepreneurial and working-class ideals vied for supremacy. This neglected group nevertheless benefited from the expanded opportunities provided by industrialisation. Whether closely related to the entrepreneurial classes, as Perkin implies, or not, the professions gave the entrepreneurial ideal a non-industrial expression. The result was a bourgeois culture emphasising gentlemanly respectability, a culture developed by a new, urban gentry far removed from cotton, coal, iron and steel, and shipbuilding.[2]

When we try to venture beyond these straightforward, perhaps even rather trite, observations we run into considerable difficulties. What *is* a profession? Who *were* the professional groups in the late Victorian economy? How did they emerge? What were the implications for society of an expanded professional sector? These questions are by no means easy to answer satisfactorily. Sociologists from Talcott

Parsons to Freidson and Larson, from Millerson to Johnson and Rueschemeyer, have been engaged in a lengthy and discursive debate, searching for a definition of the term 'profession' and the attributes of professional status; causal factors in the process of professionalising occupations; the relevance of this process for post-industrial societies and, in particular, the professions' relationship with the state. Above all, the sociologists seek an adequate theory of the professions.[3] Some of this work has only a limited application for the historian looking for empirical evidence for the mid–late nineteenth century and a satisfactory framework for the facts he is able to unearth. Recently, Shortt went so far as to accuse sociologists of presenting the uninitiated with a 'taxonomic quagmire', their theoretical constructs 'quite at odds with the historian's principal concerns'.[4] On the other hand, we are still some way from a complete economic and social history of the professions. While there have been some notable contributions on individual occupations, for a broad introduction to the subject one is compelled to turn to two works of relatively modest pretensions, Carr-Saunders and Wilson's *The Professions*, first published as long ago as 1933, and Reader's *Professional Men* of 1966. No historian has managed to go beyond these useful surveys and, drawing upon the best of recent sociology, present a new history of professional development.

In these circumstances we must be cautious. Many of the recent sociological interventions, for example, have been keen to establish the special characteristics of professional status in the United Kingdom and USA, and this leads them, *inter alia*, to pooh-pooh the 'attributes' or 'traits' approach to a definition of 'profession' favoured by Millerson.[5] But by restricting our inquiry to the UK we may use the attributes approach to provide some useful insights into what we are trying to measure and explain. By the middle of the nineteenth century certain occupations had acquired a fairly high social status by mastering a core of esoteric knowledge and offering it to society for financial reward. However, it was the notion of service to the community which was held to justify a privileged position of trust. As an official parliamentary paper put it: 'This great class includes those persons who are rendering direct service to mankind, and satisfying their intellectual, moral, and devotional wants.'[6] A promise of integrity and codes of conduct, identified with the established professions of religion, law, medicine and education, differentiated 'professional' from 'non-professional' occupations, and in return the state permitted the former to license and regulate themselves, a process which was organised increasingly through specific institutions or, in Millerson's formulation, 'qualifying associations'. The late nineteenth century saw a considerable competition for professional status as emerging occupations tried to join their more established colleagues. In order to do so they had to combine an ideology of service with the mastery of a differentiated body of knowledge. The great extension of the existing market for professional services was satisfied, in the main, by the private sector, by individual practitioners espousing professional ideals but operating under the umbrella of a protective occupational organisation.

Whether the above account fully captures the concept of 'profession' is, of course, a matter for argument. Some scholars, having found the search for satisfactory definitions fruitless – Freidson, for example, has referred to the concept as an 'intrinsically ambiguous, multifaceted' one[7] – have turned instead to a study of occupational change as a whole. Following on from the work of Everett Hughes, the process of professionalisation may be viewed as merely part of the division of labour, wherein certain groups, by exploiting the opportunities presented by industrialisation, urbanisation and an expanding market, sought a degree of monopoly power via restrictive practices and what has been dubbed 'exclusionary market shelters'. Here the emphasis is not upon service and legitimacy but upon the struggle for power in society, a struggle in which all occupations were engaged. The professions used their control of knowledge and collective organisation to establish a mandate to define the parameters of the work to be performed. A distinction is made here between the myth or ideal of professional service and aloofness from income and the reality of income-maximisation and the sharing of power with the landed and entrepreneurial elites.[8] How much of this actually applies to the period 1860–1900 is something to be carefully considered, although the approach offers useful insights in relation to the rise of the new, industry-based professions.

To summarise, sociologists have done a great deal to focus our thoughts on the reality of professional status and the processes of professionalisation, but we must be cautious in applying recent analyses to a particular historical period. The debate on definitions and attributes is best left to others since the term 'profession' was used loosely and with changing emphasis in the nineteenth century. Modern definitions embracing higher education and training, for example, would rule out many considered to be professionals in 1860–1900, and it would be sensible to leave the term imprecise. What we are essentially concerned with is the way in which existing professional occupations cemented their position in late Victorian society, and at the same time others coalesced to form new, distinct professional groups. In the next section we look at the problem of measuring the extent of professional development in the period to 1900.

II

The counting of professional heads is naturally as difficult a task as that of defining professional status. The main source for the historian is, of course, the decennial census of population, which exhibits numerous adjustments to the occupational classification. These reflect not only the structural changes in the economy but also shifting contemporary perceptions of what constituted a 'professional' in Victorian society (and subsequently). Thus, for example, the 'professional class' isolated in 1851 embraced not only those in the 'learned professions' plus 'literature, art and science' but also those engaged in government and defence. On this basis, Queen Victoria and the royal family were listed as professionals. On the other hand, notable omissions from the class were accountants, architects and surveyors, who were included in the industrial occupations, though the latter two were reclassified as professional in the general revision of occupations in 1881. If government and military personnel are excluded from the inquiry, we are left with the order subsequently entitled 'professional occupations and their subordinate services'. Taking the last forty years of the century, numbers in this group in the United Kingdom are found to rise from about 345,000 in 1861 to 515,000 in 1881 and 735,000 in 1901, an increase of 113 per cent, 1861–1901. Expressed as a percentage of the occupied population, the professional elements in society increased from about 2.5 per cent of the total in 1861 to 4.0 per cent in 1901.[9]

However, such calculations do not really tell us a great deal. As the census reports were keen to point out, to combine 'professional occupations' and 'their subordinate services' was to produce a rag-bag of occupations. In 1901, for example, it was emphasised that 'this heterogeneous order, considered as a whole, is of very little value, comprising as it does – not only the Barristers, Solicitors and Doctors, but also the Lawyer's Clerks and the Sick Nurses – not only the Painters, Musicians and Actors, but also many of their subordinates, whom it would be absurd to class as professional persons according to the ordinary acceptation of that term'. The next report, in 1911, was keen to point out that the category had 'little value for statistical purposes'.[10] Certainly, there was much to criticise in a classification which excluded accountants but included organ-grinders and street musicians; which in 1861, for example, deemed betting men, 'turfites' and billiard-table keepers and markers to be professional under the heading 'actors, actresses'; which included chemists and druggists in the medical suborder until 1881 and then, having excluded them, added sick nurses and midwives (though by no means all nurses, since those working in hospitals, workhouses and other institutions were included elsewhere). On top of this, there was a notable vagueness in the handling of art and literature, while Edward Higgs has recently drawn our attention to the ambiguities and pitfalls in using the census treatment of scientists and engineers. Indeed, so many alterations were made to the decennial listings that, even if we were agreed on which occupations were truly professional in the late Victorian period, we would not be able to establish a satisfactory global aggregate.[11]

Under these circumstances, the best that can be attempted is to follow the example of Musgrove, Perkin, Reader et al. and

TABLE 2.2   Approximate growth of selected 'professional' occupations (males and females, England and Wales), 1861–1901

Occupation	Numbers			Growth rates[k]	
				1861–1901 (%)	1881–1901 (%)
	1861	1881	1901		
Clergy[a]	19,195	21,663	25,235	31	16
Barristers and solicitors[b]	14,457	17,386	20,998	45	21
Physicians and surgeons	14,415	15,116	22,698	57	50
Midwives	1,913	2,646	3,055	60	15
Dentists[c]	1,584	3,583	5,309	235	48
Teachers[d]	110,364	168,920	230,345	109	36
Authors, editors[e]	2,315	6,111	11,060	378	81
Actors[f]	2,202	4,565	12,487	467	174
Artists[g]	10,819	11,059	13,949	29	26
Musicians[h]	15,191	25,546	43,249	185	69
Architects	3,843	6,898	10,781	181	56
Surveyors	1,843	5,394	6,414	248	19
Civil and mining engineers[i]	4,400	9,415	11,052	151	17
Accountants[j]	6,273	11,606	9,028	44	−22

Source: Census data, 1861, 1881, 1901.

Notes:

[a]Established church only.

[b]Not separated in 1901. 1861 figure excludes 70 parliamentary agents and 60 judges.

[c]1901 figure excludes makers of artificial teeth, dental apparatus and so on.

[d]Broad category including university lecturers, etc. but excluding music teachers (see musicians).

[e]Includes writers, journalists, shorthand writers. Shorthand clerks excluded in 1901.

[f]Actors and actresses only.

[g]Painters, engravers and sculptors only.

[h]Includes music teachers. Organ-grinders excluded in 1901.

[i]Mining engineers not distinguished in 1861. Figure estimated for 1861 on the basis of civil:mining ratio in 1881.

[j]1861 and 1881 figures include all those so described; 1901 figure eliminates book-keepers and clerks.

[k]Retired persons are included in occupational groups in 1861, then excluded, except for clergy and physicians and surgeons.

provide numbers for some of the main occupational categories. This is done, for England and Wales only, in Table 2.2. Notwithstanding the difficulties of interpretation which still remain with the disaggregated data, it is possible to discern considerable variations in the growth rates of the several occupations. For 1861–1901, the growth of the established professions was fairly modest. Numbers in religion, law and medicine rose by 30–60 per cent, compared with an overall increase in the population of 61 per cent and an increase of 170 per cent in those with incomes over £150 a year. It was findings like these which led Frank Musgrove to assert, in a notable short article in 1959, that middle-class employment opportunities lagged behind the expansion of educational opportunities, producing something of a crisis for middle-class men seeking lucrative work.[12] On the other hand, some occupations exhibited much higher growth rates: dentistry, which established itself as a recognised activity after the Medical Act of 1858 and the Dentists Act of 1878;[13] writing and journalism; music and entertainment, indicative of the expansion of leisure pursuits and their commercial exploitation in the late nineteenth-century; teaching, stimulated by the expansion of both public and state schools; and the 'industrial professions' – architecture, surveying and engineering.

After 1881, it is true, the expansion of most professional occupations was more modest. However, we should note that changes in the census classification usually served to understate growth, a point stressed by Harold Perkin in an attack on Musgrove's thesis. An extreme case is that of accounting, where a much tighter definition of 'accountant', encouraged by the formation in 1880 of the Institute of Chartered Accountants of England and Wales, eliminated 'book-keepers' and clerks and produced a fall in numbers of 22 per cent, 1881–1901 (Table 2.2). Two occupations experienced considerable growth. Most of the increase in the numbers of physicians and surgeons after 1861 was concentrated in the period after 1881, although this may be interpreted as compensation for the earlier decline in numbers produced by the weeding out of amateurs and 'quacks' by the Medical Act of 1858. And acting continued to exhibit above-average growth, its 174 per cent increase in 1881–1901 receiving special attention in the Census Report of 1901. This occupation may have failed to acquire the patina of respectability before the establishment of the Royal Academy of Dramatic Art (1904) and the Central School of Speech and Drama (1906), but it received considerable encouragement from royal patronage and from university support, as well as from the expansion of both the legitimate theatre and the music hall. By 1901 there were more actors and actresses than civil and mining engineers. It has also been suggested that the increased popularity of acting as a career among the middle class – the 'gentrification of the stage' – was in part a product of the perceived 'overcrowding' of the traditional professions.[14] Musgrove may be in error when he asserts that 'professional men constituted a diminishing proportion of the nation's population', and the possibilities in Britain's growing empire should not be ignored, but it remains true that domestic opportunities in the church and in law were not expanding in line with middle-class demand for jobs, and that employment prospects in other prestige occupations were dimmer in the period 1881–1901 than in 1861–81. As Musgrove rightly points out, the qualifying associations were as much about restricting entry as about raising standards, and although employment in the professions as a whole expanded, licensing and the increased attention to educational qualifications often worked in the opposite direction, at least in the short run.[15]

For women, employment opportunities remained limited. The global census data are misleading, since the increase in the proportion of females in the UK 'professional class' – from a third in 1861 to just under half in 1901 – is largely explained by the inclusion of 'sick nurses' after 1861. Penetration of the major professions and, within them, the more prestigious posts was meagre. In the main, women took part in more subordinate activities and dominated three occupations, teaching, midwifery and nursing, where status was usually low. Of the 230,000 teachers listed in Table 2.2 for 1901, 172,000 or 75 per cent were women. In the same year 64,200 sick nurses were listed in the medical category, while elsewhere in the census 26,300 women were shown to be employed in hospitals and other private institutions, and another 10,400 in local authority jobs, most of them in workhouse infirmaries. Nevertheless, women did make some progress in the late Victorian period, supported by access, albeit limited, to secondary and higher education. On a standardised basis the female participation rate in professional occupations increased from 43 to 48 per cent, 1881–1901.[16] In the arts there were occupations in which women could establish an entrée more easily. By 1901 there were 3700 female artists in England and Wales (27 per cent of the total), 6400 actresses (52 per cent), and 22,600 musicians (also 52 per cent). Elsewhere, representation was very much that of a few pioneers: 212 physicians and surgeons, 140 in dentistry, 6 architects, 2 accountants and 3 vets. And many male preserves remained unbreached. There were as yet no female barristers, solicitors, engineers or surveyors.

III

The years 1860–1900 were notable for a clear demonstration of the organising ability of these predominantly male professionalising occupations. New, protective organisations were established, and there was a considerable increase in educational and training initiatives, though we must recognise that for several occupations the process was certainly not confined to this period. Many important landmarks lay outside it, for example, the establishment of a new Law Society for solicitors in the 1820s, the creation of the Institution of Civil Engineers in 1818 and a similar body for Mechanical Engineers in 1847, the appearance of the Institute of British Architects in 1834 and the British Medical Association in 1856.[17]

In the late Victorian period earlier advances were strengthened. Disparate local and provincial bodies coalesced to form national associations; royal charters were conferred upon existing institutions; and other elements of enhanced status were evident in statutory recognition, regulation, and privilege. Table 2.3 merely provides a brief list of some of the dozens of new institutions and legal changes affecting the leading occupations. In the law, the separation of English barristers from the subordinate branch of solicitors and attorneys remained, and educational reforms were limited. But

TABLE 2.3 Professionalising activity, c. 1860–1900

Law	Medicine	Education	Engineering	Accountancy	Surveying
Supreme Court of Judicature Act 1873	British Medical Association 1856	Education Code 1862	Institution of Naval Architects 1860	Institute of Chartered Accountants of England & Wales 1880	Institute of Surveyors 1868 (Royal Charter 1881)
Solicitors Act 1888	Medical Act 1858	Education Act 1870	Iron & Steel Institute 1869 (Royal Charter 1899)	Incorporated Society of Accountants and Auditors 1885	
Bar Council 1894	Dentists Act 1878	National Union of Elementary Teachers 1870	Society of Telegraph Engineers 1871 (Institution of Electrical Engineers 1888)		
London Law School 1903	Medical Act 1886	Oxbridge Reforms 1880–3	Institution of Mining Engineers 1889		
	British Nurses' Association 1887				
	Midwives Act 1902				

while the essence of barristers' training – pupillage – was retained, the senior branch did establish examinations in 1852, making them compulsory for new entrants twenty years later. It also tooks steps to defend restrictive practices through a Bar Committee of 1883, reorganised in 1894 as the Bar Council. The solicitors, who already enjoyed a monopoly of conveyancing (since 1804), obtained more work with the establishment of the county courts in 1846. Their association, the 'Incorporated Law Society', was entrusted with the registration of attorneys and solicitors from 1843. Strengthened by the granting of a new charter in 1845, the Society encouraged a number of education reforms which culminated in the right to conduct its own examinations in 1877 and the founding of its own Law School in London in 1903. Solicitors fought a long battle to preserve their conveyancing monopoly, although in the end they were unable to prevent the first breach in the wall made by the land registration reformers, the Land Transfer Act of 1897. On the other hand, an Act of 1888 gave the Law Society the right to investigate complaints against solicitors and to strike off wrongdoers. And the most important change in our period, the establishment of a single superior court following the Supreme Court of Judicature Act of 1873, also created the modern solicitor by merging the occupations of solicitor (chancery court), attorney (common law) and proctor (ecclesiastical court). All this brought more status to the junior branch of the law. The number of members of the Law Society increased fourfold after 1861 to reach 7700 by 1901, and the number of practising solicitors rose by 60 per cent to 16,300 over the same period. In the words of a legal historian, 'the concept of the profession was sharpened considerably'.[18]

Medicine had pointed the way for others such as law to follow, although its status remained comparatively low. Once a fragmented group dominated by the educated gentlemen physicians of the Royal College in London (founded in 1518), the surgeons and apothecaries had made great strides by 1860. The Apothecaries Act of 1815 may have disappointed reformers who wished to break the physicians' dominance, but it did give the Society of Apothecaries authority to examine and licence all those who wished to dispense and prescribe medicines under the name in England and Wales, and was thus a forerunner of modern, state-sponsored qualification and registration. The Act also stimulated the rise of the 'general practitioner' (GP), a combination of surgeon and apothecary, since it became customary for doctors to hold both the apothecary's licence and the diploma of the Royal College of Surgeons.[19] The next step in the professionalising process was the establishment of a formidable medical pressure group. Beginning life in Worcester in 1832 as the Provincial Medical and Surgical Association, the British Medical Association of 1856 was merely one, though ultimately the most successful, of a number of associations formed to promote the interests of doctors outside London's medical elite. Their demand for control of registration was given legislative expression in the Medical Act of 1858, which in establishing a General Medical Council brought together representatives of the several licensing bodies and gave them authority to validate qualifications and create a single medical register for UK practitioners. A national procedure for separating the qualified from the unqualified was thus instituted, and registered persons secured the right to practise anywhere in the country and to obtain employment in public service.[20]

The Act did little to disturb the dominance of the medical colleges, however. The General Medical Council was not representative of the GPs, and nothing was done to prevent the unqualified from practising. The medical colleges may have ceded some of their old monopoly powers to Liberal free trade sentiments, but they continued to control licensing, and were able to use state recognition to enhance their position in the medical market-place. After 1860, in fact, a new hierarchy began to emerge, led by the consultant in teaching hospitals. The change was advanced by the growing importance of hospital treatment in health care, the rise of anatomy, physiology and pathology in medicine, and the extension of medical education based upon university and hospital training, notably in London, Glasgow and Edinburgh. Recognition of the new order and, in particular, the integration of medicine, surgery and midwifery came in 1884 with the establishment of a conjoint examining board of physicians and surgeons. Two years later a further Medical Act required qualification in all three branches of medicine. It also extended representation on the General Medical Council to the GPs. The late nineteenth-century saw a strengthening of the profession within this framework. Both the Council and the British Medical Association grew in stature, the latter not only expanding in the UK but also establishing a prominent position in the Empire. By 1900 there were 35,650 registered medical practitioners, including 3875 working abroad, and 2705 in naval, military and the Indian service.[21] At the same time, the process of occupational differentiation continued, with new bodies created for dentists, midwives, nurses and physiotherapists, although these found the road to effective registration a long and tortuous one.[22] By 1900 medicine, like law, had made considerable progress in its quest for recognition, and some of the 'intra-professional uncertainty and conflict' had been eliminated.[23] On the other hand, there was now a conflict between the doctor as gentleman and the doctor as scientist and this undoubtedly affected the occupation's social status. The medical elite had exploited the nation's faith in science – in Shortt's words they had 'forced the rhetoric of science into the social vocabulary of the period'[24] – but there was still much support for the concept of the unscientific, cultivated man in clinical practice, a by-product of the physician's earlier dependence on the aristocracy. The trail was a false one. For most doctors, and for the provincial GP and doctor in public employment in particular, the failure to exert authority in the workplace, whether hospital or workhouse, lay at the root of the problem of social status. The solution was to increase autonomy within an expanded public sector, and although changes were stimulated by the expansion of Poor Law infirmaries from the 1870s, the task was very much one for the twentieth century.[25]

It is more difficult to provide a constructive précis of the other 'liberal professions', although some developments should be noted. The clergy experienced considerable growth in the nineteenth century, but this occurred within a context of intensifying religious division and increasing secularity in society. The Anglican Church expanded in physical terms (churches and chapels) by about 20 per cent in the forty years to 1901, but its growth was more than matched by a revived Roman Catholicism and an ever more diverse nonconformity.

At the same time, church attendance fell away and, as one historian puts it, 'religion was well on the way to becoming an entirely voluntary aspect of social behaviour'.[26] In consequence the clerical profession, 'the highest avocation one can be called upon to pursue',[27] experienced low economic rewards and a diminished social status. The greater emphasis on occupational competence seen in law and medicine had its counterpart in the performance of clerical duties. Non-residence and pluralism virtually disappeared, and lay control was weakened. But this did not raise the profession's profile. Education, which underpinned so many of the aspirations of the professionalising occupations, could scarcely be called a true profession in the nineteenth century. A fragmented collection of services ranged from the elite universities of Oxford and Cambridge to the emerging civic colleges, precursors of the red-brick universities; from the public schools to the grammar schools; and in elementary education from the state-run 'board schools' established under the Education Act of 1870 to the multiplicity of private institutions. Teaching at any of these levels remained an occupation with a relatively low status. There are clear signs of this in the large presence of women in its ranks, while for men the position was redeemed only partially by the presence of clergymen, who took up Oxbridge fellowships or public school appointments as a stepping stone to a successful clerical career.

Nevertheless, there were some significant changes in education in late Victorian Britain, even if their professional implications were initially limited. At the top, university education was both reformed and expanded. Oxford and Cambridge experienced two periods of major reform, the 1850s and the 1870s–1880s, with degrees and fellowships opened to dissenters, provision for female students, and the reorganisation of the curriculum to embrace science. These moves were in part a response to the success of the colleges of the University of London – University (1828) and King's (1831) – as examining bodies. Degrees were opened to women in 1878, and the university's external degree, introduced in 1858, helped to spawn a number of civic colleges in the provinces, no less than 11 of them in the period 1871–84, including Leeds (1874), Bristol (1876), and Birmingham

(1880). Institutions such as Owen's College, Manchester, and Liverpool University College flourished as a result of the patronage of local businessmen.[28] At the same time, public school provision was both improved and expanded following the government's Clarendon and Taunton Commissions in the 1860s. That decade saw the establishment of new schools such as Clifton and Haileybury (both in 1862), Cranleigh and Malvern (both in 1865). There then followed the successful reorganisation of schools such as Repton, Sherborne, Uppingham and Oundle. By 1900 over 100 schools belonged to the Headmasters' Conference, a loosely-defined body established in 1869 as a defensive measure against the threat of restrictive legislation. At elementary level there was a considerable expansion in the wake of 'Payment by Results' and the Education Code of 1862, and the Education Act of 1870. Further Acts of 1876, 1880 and 1891 secured free, compulsory education for about 4.5 million children in England and Wales, 2.5 million in the private sector.[29] For teachers there were some moves towards a more professional stature. The clergyman-don gave way to the career graduate; celibacy restrictions on Oxbridge fellows were removed in the early 1880s; and there was more emphasis on the teaching role – in Oxford 58 per cent of fellows were engaged in teaching in 1900, compared with only 18 per cent in 1858.[30] In the public and grammar schools also there was a trend towards graduate recruitment, and in the primary schools higher standards were encouraged, partly as a result of lobbying by new associations, including the National Union of Elementary Teachers of 1870 (from 1889 the National Union of Teachers), and bodies representing headmasters and headmistresses. The National Union, 44,000-strong by 1900, secured an end to 'Payment by Results' in 1895 and fought for state-aided pensions (first provided in an Act of 1898). But the teachers lacked unity, registration remained an elusive goal, and there were only limited improvements in training before the Act of 1902. As Reader notes, a largely unreformed public school education was the breeding ground of the late Victorian professional man.[31]

The creation of the 'industrial professions' was emphatically a nineteenth-century development, with considerable growth and consolidation evident in several occupations in the late Victorian period. The railways acted as a major stimulus, encouraging change in engineering, accounting, surveying and architecture as well as in specialist branches of the law (note the emergence of the 'parliamentary agent', who handled the railways' private bill submissions). These large-scale businesses produced a range of problems concerning occupational competence and control which demanded institutional solutions. They also acted as a training ground, both for the engineer via the apprenticeships of the railway workshops, and for the business executive with the traffic apprenticeship schemes introduced by the major companies.[32]

In engineering, the railways were particularly important in the 1840s and 1860s, but that occupation's remarkable advance was also the product of more generalised industrial activity. Two notable organisations were founded before 1860, the Institution of Civil Engineers (1818) and the Institution of Mechanical Engineers (1847). But in the period 1860–1900 a dozen more bodies were established, six in 1860–73 and six more in 1889–97 (the Civil Engineers were invariably recognised as a parent body, however). Membership of engineering institutions grew from about 1700 in 1860 to over 23,000 forty years later. Differentiation was based mainly upon the staple industries of the Industrial Revolution, for example naval architecture (1860), iron and steel (1869), marine engineering and mining (both 1889). But there were also bodies representing the newer technologies of the Second Industrial Revolution, among them the Society of Telegraph Engineers of 1881, which became the Institution of Electrical Engineers in 1888, and the British Association of Gas Managers (1863), which became the Institution of Gas Engineers in 1902. Urban development provided the arena for municipal, sanitary, and heating and ventilating engineers.[33] These associations used an aspiration to gentlemanly status to raise their social esteem, part of an attempt to differentiate themselves from the 'trade' aspects of their work. University chairs in civil engineering were created in 1840, courses in engineering from mid-century, but the institutes showed little interest in university qualifications. The Institution of Civil Engineers was quite happy to rely on conventional apprenticeship until the strategy came under pressure in the wake of German and American competition, and did not establish its own examinations until 1897. As Buchanan notes, 'the profession appeared to maintain itself without the conventional requirements of educational qualifications and examination achievements'.[34]

More than one authority suggests that it was the railways which created accountancy in the modern sense.[35] Although other factors were at work, of course, including the development of industry and commerce and the extension of limited liability after the legislation of 1855–62, it is clear that the auditing of railway accounts, in Jones's words, 'played an important part in the development of the accountancy profession, both as a source of work and as a proving ground for new accounting techniques'.[36] Accountants benefited directly from the railway companies' financial difficulties following the collapse of the great investment 'mania' of 1845–7. A desire to protect the small investor from losses arising from abuse of the railways' joint-stock and limited liability status lay behind a demand for improved auditing, boosted by enabling legislation in the 1840s and the recommendations of a Select Committee of 1849. In 1868 the Regulation of Railways Act required the companies to publish a standardised set of annual accounts; similar obligations were placed on gas (in 1871) and electric lighting (1882). The leading accounting firms, such as Deloitte, Coleman, Quilter Ball and Price, Holyland & Waterhouse, owed their rise to advice given to the shareholders of railways in difficulties from the late 1840s. But it was the regular half-yearly audit of these large-scale businesses, who pioneered the use of the double-account system, that helped to transform an occupation formerly associated primarily with broking and auctioneering. In the late nineteenth century the growth of public companies – there were over 30,000 registrations in England and Wales, 1856–89 – encouraged both specialisation and a diversity of performance in accounting. The creation of qualifying associations to regulate entry and protect standards began in Scotland in the mid-1850s. In England a number of provincial bodies were formed in the 1870s, but a more unified aspiration for accountancy found expression in the establishment of the Institute of Chartered Accountants of England and Wales in 1880. This organisation, with its tight rules for admission, including compulsory examinations and five-year articles, and a defined code of conduct, was a bold attempt to raise the status of an occupation which was not held to be unambiguously 'professional' (it remained outside the professional classification in the census). Even so, many accountants found the Institute's rules too restrictive, and a rival body, the Incorporated Society of Accountants and Auditors, was formed in 1885. Other bodies followed, including the Corporation of Accountants (Glasgow), 1891 and the Institution of Public Accountants, 1903.[37]

Surveying was also transformed by the needs of the Victorian railways. This occupation left its land-measuring roots to specialise in valuation and arbitration, work which was enhanced by the railway companies' compulsory purchase of land. The sudden demands of the railways, first in the 1840s and again in the 1860s, attracted both the unscrupulous and the incompetent into surveying, encouraging mechanisms for self-regulation and the formulation of ground-rules for specialisation. It is no coincidence that fifteen of the twenty founding fathers of the Institute of Surveyors of 1868 were railway engineers. Chartered status was obtained in 1881.[38] Similar accounts of growth and the establishment of protective associations can be told of other occupations too, ranging from those who, like the architects, pharmacists and vets, organised at a comparatively early date, to others, such as the musicians, writers and journalists, whose efforts came later, and were often more tentative.[39]

This survey of professionalising activity has isolated several common features. Whether members of occupations organised themselves in clubs, study groups, qualifying or non-qualifying associations, all had broadly similar aims. The intention was to raise status, financial rewards and occupational security by means of differentiation, regulation and an emphasis on the gentlemanly virtues of education and a middle-class morality. Both the transformation of the older professions and the emergence of the new 'lower branches' were part of the general process of socio-political change in Britain, with the middle class 'striving for an idealized and organizing image of itself'.[40] Professionalising activity, whether stimulated by internal occupational factors (e.g. pressure from below, new knowledge) or by external changes (e.g. industrial growth, urbanisation, imperial expansion, the railways), was a major element in the process by which the middle-class elites established and protected their position in industrial society. This involved both a separation from the working classes and a power-sharing (and therefore partial identification) with the old aristocratic order. The origins of this process may lie in the period before 1860, but there is no doubt at all that its core was cemented in the late Victorian years.

IV

What were the implications for Britain of the rise of a 'professional culture'? As we have noted, the professions, though growing, remained numerically small, about 4 per cent of the labour force by 1900. But there is abundant evidence to suggest that this group wielded a disproportionate amount of influence in late Victorian society. Professionals, by espousing the ideal of the educated gentleman, helped to perpetuate the pre-industrial distinction between the gentlemen and the players, in Donald Coleman's formulation, and with the former predominating, this encouraged the incorporation of industrialists into a refashioned elite.[41] Although the competitive examination became an important strategic device for aspiring occupations, it is clear that a successful drive for enhanced status owed as much to the use of the conventional education of public school and university as to specialised training and competitive endeavour. But the precise efforts of this 'professional ideal', in Perkin's phrase, are difficult to pin down. How important it was, for example, in contributing to Britain's apparent decline in industrial performance in the late nineteenth century is a challenging question. The alleged failure of the late Victorian economy raises very complex issues, as another chapter in this book makes clear. That chapter isolates two factors in which professionalising activity may have had an impact – the regulatory emphasis on the state, and the failure to restructure education for the Second Industrial Revolution.[42] Professions also figure in Martin Wiener's recent hypothesis that Britain experienced a 'decline of the industrial spirit', in which a general distaste for manufacturing and trade became part of an 'English culture', and socio-economic advance was expected to involve families in a move *from*, not *to*, industrial endeavour. For Wiener, the 'gentrification of the Victorian middle classes' was closely connected with the rise of the modern professions, and 'the existence of a powerful aristocracy . . . reinforced the anticapitalist tendencies within professionalization'.[43]

Wiener's thesis is superficially persuasive, but appears much weaker when examined from a business viewpoint. As Donald Coleman and Christine Macleod argue, the emphasis should be placed not upon any decline of industrial spirit but upon a continuity. They suggest that the industrial spirit of the Industrial Revolution, with its hesitant response to innovation, persisted for far too long.[44] Nevertheless, it is certainly true that non-economic factors deserve more attention than that customarily accorded them by economic historians in explaining Britain's faltering industrial record in the twentieth century. Structural and institutional rigidities require close examination, as Elbaum and Lazonick's recent book demonstrates.[45] And it is here that the professionalising process contributed to Britain's difficulties. The strengthening of professional occupations with continuing sympathies for aristocratic pretension helped to discourage entry into business and to place limits on the extent of educational reform. At the same time, the growth of natural science and the rise of the university don intensified anti-bourgeois attitudes within a self-conscious intellectual elite, and this encouraged a separation of the 'intellectual' and 'commercial' or 'industrial' professions.[46] The professional ideal was contradictory in that it embraced both a support for and an attack upon the entrepreneurial ideal of competition and competence, a support for and an attack upon the status of industrial endeavour. In its latter manifestations it certainly encouraged the legitimisation of occupational monopolies and semi-monopolies and thus bolstered the political processes of state regulation. After all, professions were valued, as Escott noted, 'according to their stability, their remunerativeness, their influence, and *their recognition by the state* [emphasis added]'.[47] In addition, the urban gentry of professionals were activists in the broader arena of state intervention and social reform. It is no surprise to find doctors, lawyers and even engineers at the centre of the public health debate, for example, since the outcome often promised greater employment opportunities and the enhancement of status for interested occupational groups. Professional people were also active in the policy debates about the poverty problem, and were prominent in such organisations as the Society for the Relief of Distress and the Charity Organisation Society. Thus, the rise of the professions pointed both backwards and forwards: backwards in that professionalisation failed to shake off the trappings of aristocratic values; forwards in that it encourged a greater degree of government intervention in the economy, the hallmark of the modern twentieth-century state.

3. Urban Britain

M. J. DAUNTON

ALTHOUGH the census of 1851 had for the first time recorded over half of the population living in towns, as yet the population of the countryside had fallen only proportionately, with an absolute decline so far confined to Wiltshire and Montgomeryshire. By 1870 this had changed, and rural depopulation had started with a vengeance: between 1871 and 1881, nine rural counties in England had a falling population.[1] The formation of new towns was virtually over by 1870, and continued urban growth came not by the sudden appearance of upstarts so much as by the increasing dominance of the largest of the existing towns. Suburbs sprang up around these towns, and conurbations – a word coined by Patrick Geddes for a new phenomenon – emerged which linked together settlements in continuous built-up areas of Greater London and 'Midlandton' or Tyne–Wear–Tees. Adna Weber, in his *The Growth of Cities in the Nineteenth Century* which appeared in 1899, showed that London had increased its share of the population of England and Wales from 9.7 per cent in 1801 to 14.3 per cent in 1871 and 14.5 per cent in 1891; even more striking was the increase in the other 'great cities' with a population over 100,000, which rose from nothing in 1801 to 11.5 per cent in 1871 and 17.3 per cent in 1891. In Scotland, the same trend was apparent, and the population of Glasgow rose from 5.1 per cent of the population of Scotland in 1801 to 19.4 per cent in 1891.[2]

What was at stake, it seemed to many contemporaries, was not simply the growth of cities but the destruction of rural society and the creation of a top-heavy urban system, dominated by London and the great cities of Glasgow, Birmingham, Liverpool and Manchester. Here, it seemed to many, was a threat to the future of Britain: towns led to the degeneration of their inhabitants, both physically and morally;

and they were kept buoyant only by the continued migration of sturdy stock from the country. What – it was wondered with trepidation – would happen when pools of healthy and moral country-dwellers no longer existed to replenish the cities?[3]

Such fears informed much of the debate on urban social problems in the 1870s and 1880s. The poor of the great cities should perhaps be removed, sent to colonies in the country to be rescued from sloth and immorality, with the expectation that the wages of those who remained behind in the urban labour market might increase once the overstocking had been ended. There was a feeling, then, that London and the great cities were overpopulated by the wrong sort of people, and that in the capital above all greater control was needed in order to prevent the creation of a mass of casual and sweated labour. These were not the notions of isolated and marginal figures, but may be found in the writings of such central commentators as Charles Booth, author of *Life and Labour of the People of London*, and Alfred Marshall, professor of economics at Cambridge.[4] In a recent provocative paper, Tony Sutcliffe has indeed suggested that contemporaries saw Britain as facing an intrinsically *urban* crisis, most obviously in London but also in the other large towns, from which grew the Liberal welfare reforms of 1906 to 1914. In his view, urban conditions were seen as independent variables in the debate over social conditions, and this was, he feels, a perfectly plausible case. He accepts that the great cities had a mounting labour surplus in the late nineteenth century, and that at the same time rising land costs forced industry out of the towns and drove up house rents, creating a serious crisis in the urban economy. Both the social problems of late Victorian Britain and the solutions devised by the Liberal government were, he believes, distinctly urban.[5] Is this a notion which should be accepted as a key to understanding British society and politics?

It would seem that after 1900 the more apocalyptic ideas of urban degeneration and the draconian solutions which had been propounded in the 1880s were in retreat. One turning point might be identified in the report of the Inter-Departmental Committee on Physical Deterioration, which reported in 1904. This had grown out of alarms about the fitness of recruits of the Boer War, and the consequent concern which had been expressed about the stunted and feeble products of Manchester and London. However, the Report rejected the notion of deterioration in the racial stock, and even pointed to an improvement; it was rather that the army had raised its standards than that the fitness of the race was in decline. There was more emphasis upon the piecemeal amelioration of the worst urban problems, and by the early twentieth century root-and-branch responses were giving way to pragmatic solutions: the creation of labour exchanges to break down the imperfections of the labour market; the establishment of minimum wages in the sweated trades; the creation of maternity services, and so on.

The analysis upon which such reforms were based was not, on the whole, hostile to cities, and it must be doubted whether the 'urban variable' was viewed as an independent explanation of the problems which these policies were designed to tackle. Charles Booth in the 1880s had wanted to remove people from London which, he felt, was sapping their moral and physical strength, but when William Beveridge came to write his book on unemployment in London, this was seen as a problem arising from the organisation of the labour market which needed to be reformed so as to operate in a more efficient way in bringing men who were in search of jobs into touch with employers. Although the subtitle of Seebohm Rowntree's *Poverty* was *A Study of Town Life*, it is interesting that he did not blame urbanisation itself for the social problems he laid bare, but rather concentrated on such issues as the low wages paid by employers and the death of the main wage-earner. Most of the problems which were tackled in the early twentieth century were seen as being *in* the towns but not *of* them.[6]

It does also seem implausible that there was an *increasing* urban labour surplus. Much evidence in fact runs in the opposite direction towards a greater stability of employment as production of goods moved into factories in response to rising consumer demand with the improvements in working-class living standards over the last quarter of the nineteenth century. Indeed, a radical change was taking place in the healthiness of urban life by the early twentieth century.[7] It might be argued that one of the trends of the late nineteenth and early twentieth centuries was a greater sense of competence in the face of the great cities, rather than the fears and alarms with which the period had opened. This was in part the result of the growth of a professional expertise within councils which had medical officers and borough engineers aware of the dimensions of urban disease and sanitation. A significant achievement of the decades after 1870 was rather the mounting large-scale investment in the infrastructure of towns – gasworks, drainage schemes, reservoirs, tramways – whether by private companies or local authorities.

Some writers would indeed suggest that there was a cycle in urban growth based upon the development of transport technology. The American economist W. Isard pointed in the 1940s to the link between the expansion of the city and the development of tramways, both horse and electric, and the coming of the subway systems and elevated railways.[8] British historians have, however, been more sceptical about the impact of developments in transport, which in this country followed rather than led the expansion of cities. In American cities, tramways often went beyond the existing built-up area into the open fields, leading the process of development; the companies could often share in the increase in the land values created by their presence. In British cities, tramways lagged behind the built-up area, and were inserted into the existing fabric; they did not share in the increase in land values and derived their profit entirely from the fares charged for journeys. British developments in urban transport lagged behind America. Horse trams had been running in New York since 1832, and were generally replacing omnibuses in American cities by 1860, whereas in British cities major developments were delayed until after 1870. Significantly, it was an American entrepreneur, G. F. Train, who introduced the first horse tram in Britain, at Birkenhead in 1860. Equally significant was the fact that he did not inspire many to follow his example for a decade. Similarly, electrification did not really start until the late 1890s, although in America it had commenced in the 1880s. In the United States, 84 per cent of lines were electrified by the end of 1895, by which time the level in Britain was only 6 per cent, rising to 12 per cent by the end of 1898 and 38 per cent by the end of 1902. It might also be noted that when the building of the underground started in London at the end of the nineteenth century, it owed its technology and capital to American firms.

The explanation of the British lag behind America has been located by some historians in the inadequacies of the political system which distorted investment decisions: the Tramways Act of 1870 which gave private companies power to lay lines in the streets provided that they could be purchased by local authorities after 21 years at scrap value. This, it is argued, made the companies reluctant to invest, particularly in the conversion of the horse tram system to electricity. However, care is needed with this argument: would investment in the new technology in fact have been profitable at an earlier date? This is doubtful. In Britain, the growth of urban population was slackening as it accelerated in America, so the market was different, even leaving aside contrasts in income. Conversion to electric operation only became economically feasible when the existing lines, which had to be rebuilt for heavy electric cars, had been fully depreciated. This did not apply until the end of the century. The intervention of local authorities which then occurred in most cities pushed the process ahead faster than it otherwise would have gone, for a larger investment was made than would have been feasible for the private companies with their low profitability. Electrification and municipalisation went together, and both contributed to a reduction in fares. In Leeds, at the beginning of this century, a horse tram cost 10d. a mile to operate and an electric tram 6½d. The lower costs assisted the municipal undertakings to reduce fares, and in 1903 14 out of 16 charged less than their private predecessors. In Bradford, for example, fares fell from 1d. per mile to 1d. for two miles. Urban transport was for the first time brought within the reach of the bulk of the population. Technological change therefore seemed to offer an escape from the congestion of the inner city, suggesting a suburban solution to the problems which had led to such despondency in the 1870s and 1880s. Charles Booth, for example, the erstwhile advocate of labour colonies, could in 1901 publish a pamphlet on *Improved Means of Communication as a Cure for the Housing Difficulties of London*. Here was one way of off-setting high urban land costs, by extending the available area.[9]

The expansion of urban transport was not the only capital-intensive development in the late Victorian and Edwardian city. This was also the time when most houses were connected to drains, piped water and gas. Each involved a large capital investment, often by the local authority rather than a private company. The construction of the main drains was of course a public responsibility, and there was never any suggestion that this should be left to the private market. This was also a time in which 'gas and water socialism' became of increasing significance. In 1909, of 74 county boroughs in England and Wales, 53 owned their water undertakings, 33 the gas supply, 65 the generation of electricity, and 50 the tramways.[10] Whoever owned these facilities, there was a need for major investments in this period. The provision of clean water in every household often meant the construction of large reservoirs at a distance from the town, which entailed the raising of large sums of money in advance of any income. Birmingham council, for example, took over the water company in 1875 and subsequently embarked on the construction of the Elan valley reservoirs in mid-Wales. The municipalisation of the water companies was usually a response to issues of public health, and there was no intention to make a profit.

Gas was a different matter: when the gas company in Birmingham was acquired in 1875 for £2m the intention was to make a profit which could then be used to supplement the rates and to provide facilities for the city: the art gallery, for example, was housed in the offices of the gas undertaking. Indeed, in the first year the profit was £34,000, far exceeding the anticipated £14,800. 'Municipal capitalism' might be a more accurate description, and these publicly owned gas works were run on strictly commercial lines with similar prices and operating costs to private companies, so that it is doubtful whether the change in ownership which marked many towns in the late nineteenth century had much effect upon investment.[11]

The most important development was the extension of gas supply from the lighting of the streets and middle-class homes into cooking facilities and the working-class districts. This involved a large investment by the gas undertakings in laying pipes in the streets, and also within the houses of the new consumers: the undertakings were willing to incur the capital cost in order to increase their market. This was associated with the introduction of slot meters which allowed working-class consumers to pay for the gas in small sums in advance rather than in large amounts in arrears. The South Metropolitan Company started to instal slot meters in 1892, and the number had reached 80,115 at the end of 1898. Another London company, the Gas Light and Coke Co., had invested £½m over the same period in extending supply to working-class customers. In Birmingham, the number of consumers rose from 63,339 in 1898 to 172,985 in 1914, and the proportion using slot meters from 8.2 to 54.6 per cent. At the same time, the majority of houses had been connected to both the water supply and main drainage. In Manchester, for example, 26.4 per cent of sanitary conveniences were water closets in 1899 but 97.8 per cent in 1913.[12] The late nineteenth and early twentieth centuries were, then, a period of major investment in the urban infrastructure which both reduced the urban death rate, and imposed severe strain upon municipal finances. It is here, in the financial impact of these changes, that an urban crisis might legitimately be located.

The improvement of the infrastructure of the late Victorian city had a beneficial effect on the quality of urban life, most obviously in the fall in the death rate. The 1890s marked a change from high to low urban mortality. In 1891, the death rate in Manchester was 26.0 per 1000, and had fallen to 18.0 per 1000 by 1905.[13] But the changes also led to tensions, for much of the investment came from public bodies relying upon a limited and inflexible source of income: the local property rate. The 1870s were a turning point in the relationship between the cost of urban government and the rate base. Between 1873/4 and 1878/9, the rateable value in England and Wales rose by 16.6 per cent, and the income from the rates by 15.3 per cent, so that there was no need for the rate in the pound to mount. In the next five-year period, this was not the case: between 1878/9 and 1883/4, the rateable value increased by 9.3 per cent and the income from the rates by 14.4 per cent. This remained the case right up to the First World War as the rate in the pound rose inexorably, a factor which lay at the heart of urban politics.[14]

The lack of buoyancy in the rateable value may be easily explained. The most rapid period of urbanisation was over by

1880, and continued urban growth was often outside the limits of the existing municipal boundaries. Suburbs with low rates would, of course, jealousy guard their independence from towns eager to incorporate them. At the same time, the cost of urban government mounted. This was in part the result of central government directives which imposed minimum standards on schools or police, so that the scope for economy was reduced. It was also, however, a response to the fact that much local expenditure was now 'lumpy', requiring the issue of bonds which had then to be paid regardless of both the changing political complexion of the council and the financial consequences. In 1874/5, local authority borrowing stood at 12 per cent of the total national debt; in 1896/7 it was 39 per cent. Manchester, for example, had a debt of £23m in 1909, of which 71 per cent was accounted for by 'reproductive undertakings', that is municipal trading.[15] Expenditure was more capital-intensive, and once the decision to build a new reservoir or tramway had been taken and the bonds issued, the payment of interest was inevitable, however much future councils might regret the consequences.

This changed the nature of the urban political process. In the mid-Victorian period, it was quite possible to reverse an upward trend of the rates. Expenditure was not dominated to the same extent by capital projects and the servicing of debt, so that retrenchment was more feasible. In any case, the underlying buoyancy of the rate base meant that the rate in the pound could be allowed to fall. A characteristic feature of the towns of mid-Victorian Britain was indeed a ratepayers' backlash as a party of 'economists' took over the council from the authors of schemes which had increased the rates. This alternation followed a local pattern, depending on the circumstances in each town. In the case of Birmingham, for example, the 'economists' came to the fore in the mid-1850s, and were only finally overturned in the early 1870s when professional men and large businessmen inaugurated a new phase of expansiveness, most obviously during the mayoralty of Joseph Chamberlain between 1873 and 1876. The chronology in Leeds was different. There the 'economists' started to emerge in the 1870s, epitomised by Archie Scarr, a market trader as renowned for his old, greasy clothes as Chamberlain was for his elegance. They gained control of the council in the 1880s and persisted until the 1890s. The election of Scarr as mayor in 1887 marked the apotheosis of the 'monarch of the market', contrasting with the national political status which Chamberlain had attained by this time. By the end of the century, however, the scope for the continuation of this cycle of periods of expenditure succeeded by long periods of retrenchment was much reduced.[16]

Quite apart from changing financial circumstances, the ratepayers' interest of small tradesmen and houseowners was no longer so powerful by the late nineteenth century. Although most towns had a ratepayers' organisation, which often united with the interests threatened by the extension of municipal trading, they remained somewhat peripheral. The Cardiff Ratepayers' Association, for example, brought together the Taff Vale Railway Co. (which was a leading anti-union bastion) with the Cardiff Railway Co. (another opponent of unions and an offshoot of the Bute estate which was the major landowner in the city), under the leadership of Sam Hern, a local estate agent with an interest in the tramway company which was threatened with municipalisation.[17] This might seem to be a formidable combination, but in fact it never attracted support even from its natural constituency of small property owners, let alone from the electorate in general. Why should this be?

In part, it was because the ratepayers' association adopted an extreme ideological position, often in tandem with the Liberty and Property Defence League, which was somewhat isolated in its emphasis upon individualism. In the case of Cardiff, there was greater willingness to use the power of the municipality as an adjunct to civic consciousness in building a new civic centre, and as a means of constructing new facilities. The claims of Hern seemed to be special pleading, while the railway companies in their extreme opposition to trade unions were running against the general trend of thought, seeming to threaten the city with disorder. The association with the Bute estate might not help in Liberal and Nonconformist circles, for this was a supporter of the Catholic Church and of Conservatism. To many Liberals, the real reason for high rates was the avoidance by ground landlords of their fair contribution to local taxation, so that the campaigns of the ratepayers' association might appear to be a diversionary tactic.[18] What is certainly clear in relation to earlier periods is the emergence of other interests which counteracted the claims of the ratepayers.

One was the appearance of a more professional and bureaucratic form of local government. At the beginning of the period, it was still common for councillors to fulfil executive functions; by the early twentieth century, most councils had well-paid and highly qualified professional staff who certainly took over executive functions and might also influence policy. The Medical Officer of Health and City Engineer might, for example, impel the council to a more consistent and coherent approach towards slum housing or insanitary conditions. Councillors might also need to take into account a wider range of interests. The local Trades Council might have a greater political clout than the ratepayers' association, so that the council might, for example, be forced to pay union rates to its own staff and to award contracts only to employers agreeing to union terms. The alternation of professional men and large merchants taking a long-term view of the needs of the town, and small traders looking for immediate financial savings, might possibly be an adequate description of the mid-Victorian council, but by the end of the nineteenth century it was more complicated. The adherents of expensive urban government might themselves be members of the lower middle class or working class, forming a progressive wing to the Liberal Party and seeing the development of municipal socialism as the beginning of a wider change in society. This was most obvious in the progressive group on the London County Council, but it was an attitude which could be found in many provincial cities.[19]

There is, however, no doubt that the ratepayers' associations had a valid point: the costs of urban government *were* mounting, and the narrow and inflexible base of local taxation meant that it was the owners of house property who had to pay. As a result, they were facing a serious crisis by the early years of the twentieth century. In England, rates were in theory paid by the occupier and not by the owner; in Scotland they were divided between the two parties who made separate payments to the council. In practice, the owner of most working-class housing in England 'compounded', that is paid the rates in return for a commission, hoping to cover himself for the balance due to the council by adjusting the weekly payment by the tenant. However, as rates mounted in the early twentieth century at a time of overbuilding and stagnation in working-class income, it was not possible to pass the increased burden of rates on to the tenants. Landlords consequently faced a serious erosion of their profit margins, and also of the capital value of the houses. The situation was even worse in those areas where the councils, in an attempt to increase the yield from the rates, cast a jealous eye on the allowances paid to the landlords and tried to reduce the commission. In Scotland, the problem was slightly different. Until 1911, it was very rare for landlords to pay rates on behalf of the tenants and both parties paid their contribution directly to the council; the pressure on the landlord's profit margin was accordingly less. This changed in 1911 when the English system of compounding was introduced. The allowance offered to the landlords was low, less than they paid their own agents for collection, and in future they might face a serious erosion of their profit margin if they could not pass increases in the rates to the tenants – as was indeed the case between 1911 and 1914. The structure of local taxation was therefore creating serious problems for investors in the urban fabric, and this, it is argued, created a crisis in the towns and cities of Edwardian Britain.[20]

A major issue in urban politics from the late nineteenth century was how to solve this problem of the increasing cost of local government and a narrow tax base. There seemed to be a number of possibilities. One was to bring other sources of income into contribution. Property owners complained, for example, that merchants in Liverpool with ships riding in the docks might make no contribution to local taxation beyond the rates on their office, despite a high turnover and healthy profits. Was this fair when their cargoes passed through the municipally maintained streets, were protected by the police, and the burdens of the underemployment of waterside labour fell on the poor rates? This led some to argue for a local income tax so that all sources of wealth would contribute. More realistic was the attempt to distinguish between purely local expenditure and 'imperial' expenditure. The building of a park or the improvement of the drains was a local interest which benefited property owners; education and poor relief, it was argued, were national concerns for which all should pay out of national taxation. One element in the Liberal welfare reforms was indeed to reduce the contribution of local government to social services: relief of the unemployed, for example, was slowly moved from the Poor Law to the national insurance scheme. There was, however, a disinclination to increase central government grants-in-aid to the local councils. In 1868, grants-in-aid amounted to only 3.8 per cent of local government expenditure, and although this had risen to 14.2 per cent in 1890/1 it was not enough to prevent a mounting rate in the pound. The structure of central government assistance had indeed become more inflexible in 1888. Until then, grants-in-aid were voted annually, appropriated to a particular service and related to expenditure. In 1888, a new system of 'assigned revenues' was created. The revenue from various licences – for dogs, house agents and so on – and a share of the probate duty was given to the council. This increased the grant-in-aid in the short term, but in the longer term it created serious problems of lack of buoyancy and flexibility. The contribution of the central government in fact started to fall as a proportion of total local expenditure. It seemed clear to the Royal Commission on Local Taxation which reported in 1901 that the system was grossly inadequate, creating inequity in the incidence of taxation. The answer was obvious to many commentators: assigned revenues should be replaced by direct Exchequer subventions in order to reduce the burden on house property. In fact, the system was not reformed before the First World War.[21]

This was in part because such a solution seemed to be most undesirable to many within the Liberal Party. There had long been hostility in radical circles to the aristocratic landowners and their leasehold estates, with a demand for the 'enfranchisement' of leases, that is the right to buy the freehold. In the 1880s this became a more general demand, arising from the analysis of Henry George's *Progress and Poverty*. The argument was that land received an 'unearned increment' because its price did not rise from any effort of the owner but rather through the endeavours of the rest of society. Since land was in fixed supply it could achieve a high price, and therefore – so the argument ran – act as a drain on productive groups. Since the community created this increment in value, it should be expropriated by a tax on land values. It was hoped that this would have two consequences. One was a reduction in land prices, since the owners would now have no incentive to hold out for high prices. The other was a shift in the incidence of taxation away from the building and towards the land upon which it was erected. Indeed, George went so far as to argue that this could replace all other taxes.

The Liberal Party did not go to the full extent of this 'single tax' position, but Lloyd George did see in the attack upon landowners a solution to the crisis in local government finance. The attempt to reduce land prices was also seen as a solution to the problem of urban housing, and the use of cheap land on the suburban fringe was part of the policy proposed by the garden city movement. Low fares on municipal trams could decant the poor of the inner city to cheap suburban land, whose price had been reduced by taxation designed to force it on to the market. Booth's pamphlet on improved communications was complemented by a second in 1904 on *Rates and the Housing Question: An Argument for the Rating of Site Values*. The land campaign connected with the emergence of the lower-density styles of layout which were being proposed before the First World War. At Birmingham, for example, J. S. Nettlefold, the chairman of the housing committee, was an advocate of land taxation, extension planning, and garden city layout through tenant co-operatives. Although the aesthetic of this movement did triumph, it was to be through the very different means of the council estate; the strategy of Henry George and Lloyd George was to come to nothing. It was simply not practicable to define land as a reprehensible form of property apart from the house erected upon it; after all, in the majority of cases, the owner of the house also owned the freehold of the land and the sense of conflict upon which the policy was based was unreal. Land was in any case too small a proportion of the total national income to bear the weight of consequences put upon it, particularly with the opening of new agricultural areas in the Americas and Australasia, which led to falling land prices and a reduction in

the share of rent in the national income. The urban crisis did
not arise from the *reality* of the land question, as Sutcliffe has it;
rather, it was the mistaken belief that this was the main issue
which meant that attention was diverted from more realistic
solutions to the problems of local government finance.[22]

The most controversial aspects of the government of British
cities in this period were the fiscal problems which arose from
the increasing cost of services, and the extension of the scope of
municipal trading. Less important at this stage was the
question of the structure of urban authorities, which had been a
major issue in the early Victorian period. The framework laid
down by the Municipal Corporations Act of 1835 remained
more or less intact, the major area of doubt and dissension
being the question of the government of London. In provincial
towns and cities, the change in structure was relatively slight.
The creation of the School Boards in 1870 marked the
culmination of the policy of separate bodies for each service
within an administrative area. Already by 1870 most town
councils had taken over the powers of the Boards of Health and
improvement commissions, so that power was becoming more
concentrated in the hands of one body. The School Boards
seemed to be a step away from this consolidation of functions,
and in 1902 they were indeed abolished and the borough
councils became the local education authorities. This left the
Boards of Guardians as the remaining base of power within
British towns and cities. The most important changes in the
provinces were, however, less in terms of structure than in the
changing balance between councillors and executive officers,
the emergence of a wider range of interests, and the increase in
pressure from central government which reduced the range of
variation between towns.[23]

Fundamental reform in the constitution of urban
government was confined to London. In 1867, the government
of London was based upon a two-tier system created in 1855 by
the Metropolis Management Act. At the lower level there were
23 parish vestries, 15 district boards amalgamating the smaller
vestries, and the unreformed Corporation of the City of
London. For London as a whole, the Metropolitan Board of
Works provided some wider view of needs. The MBW was not
directly elected but was composed of nominees of the local

bodies, with a consequent reluctance to encroach on their powers. It was, said one cynic, 'a Vestry, vestrified to the nth power'. Nevertheless, the MBW had been able to carry through some major works of civil engineering such as the construction of the Embankment and a main drainage system. The Act of 1855 had been an uneasy compromise: to some, there should be a centralist solution based on unification under a directly elected, London-wide, authority; to others a localist solution was preferable, based on the creation of municipal boroughs on the provincial model for each of the ten parliamentary constituencies. In the 1880s, notions of centralism were in the ascendant in Liberal and radical circles, while the Conservatives came to the support of the City Corporation; the structure of London's government had become a party political issue. Pardoxically, it was the Conservatives who were responsible for the creation in 1888 of a single London authority, the London County Council. This was part of a wider reform in local government, with the creation of elected county councils, and the initial intention of the measure was to create an elected body in place of the MBW in association with relatively powerful district councils. However, the reform of the lower tier was dropped from the Bill, perhaps because of pressure from the Liberal Unionists such as Chamberlain who were coming over to support Salisbury's government.

The structure of London's government was not to be permanently settled by this measure. Although London was dominated by the Conservatives in parliament, the new LCC was at once captured by the Progressives who adopted a radical posture on many issues which had national ramifications, such as the taxation of ground rents. In 1899, the Conservatives' original intention was fulfilled and 28 borough councils were created, not so much because of the power of the vestries and City than as a way of limiting the influence of the Progressives and reviving Conservatism. What some Conservatives wanted was a further extensive devolution of power from the LCC to the boroughs, while amongst Progressives there was pressure in the opposite direction for a 'greater London' authority. Lines were drawn around the turn of the century in a debate which is still current on the proper government of London.[24]

In considering the problems of local government, it is

important not to lose sight of the fact that towns and cities are, most obviously, collections of buildings: houses, shops, factories, offices, railway stations, hotels. This might seem to be a trite point, but the nature and method of provision of the physical environment remains one of the key concerns of urban historians. Housing might, after all, take a variety of forms: it might be supplied through the subdivision of existing property and the tighter packing of the built-up area, or by the expansion of new, purpose-built housing on to land in the suburbs; areas might be clearly differentiated in terms of social status or might contain a variety of social classes; the physical form might vary widely from the self-contained terraced house to the tenement block. These features of the housing stock varied over time and between areas, and this provides one focus of debate on the nature of urban Britain. New types of buildings might also appear: shopping might be transformed by the emergence of the department store and suburban shopping parades and the decline of itinerant traders and market stalls; the changing patterns of leisure might produce music halls, theatres and sport stadia in place of occasional fairs and entertainment related to the consumption of alcohol. The changing nature of commerce might produce specialised office buildings in the central business district in place of the earlier counting-house which united residence and office. The urban environment at any time was the sum of these various buildings, depending upon the way they related to each other in order to create a physical setting for urban social life. This is not to say that urban social life was *determined* by its material setting. The buildings themselves must be seen as the products of social forces, and once they had been provided they could be experienced in a variety of ways depending upon the expectations of the users. The physical environment was not simply *provided* as a setting which determined urban social life, for it had to be *interpreted* by its users. A crucial concern of urban historians is, then, why cities took the physical form they did, and how this interacted with social life.[25]

At the beginning of the period, a large part of the working-class housing stock was based upon subdivision of older property and the cramming of new houses into the limits of the existing built-up area. The result could be a dense, confused urban fabric of dead-ends, courts and cellar-dwellings in which space was used in common, facilities shared, and privacy given low priority. Although this was to remain true of many inner city districts up to the First World War and beyond, there was a clear trend away from such a pattern during the period. There was a change in the layout of towns so that streets formed a grid in which dead-ends were anathema, and individual houses were self-contained with their own separate back-yards and facilities. A high priority was given to privacy. The physical environment changed, and along with it the texture of social life.[26]

This change came about in part as the result of intervention by the government. At first at a local level, and subsequently through national legislation, steps were taken both to clear away the worst of the existing 'rookeries' and to control the layout of the new developments. There was a deliberate attempt to open up the dense central areas by driving new roads through the worst slums. Chamberlain's grand design of clearing 93 acres in central Birmingham and constructing Corporation Street as a new thoroughfare and shopping area is simply one example. It could go as far as the destruction of entire districts, such as the clearance scheme in Glasgow which was authorised by the local act of 1866 and which led to the sweeping away of the old medieval heart of the city in the next decades. By the Artisans' and Labourers' Dwellings Improvement Act of 1875 (Cross Act) councils were given powers to demolish whole areas. The concern was, of course, for public health and also for public order: the areas were seen as locations of both fever and crime, needing to be opened to inspection.

The Cross Act was indeed based upon a particular view of slums: they were 'plague spots' clearly distinguished from the remainder of the urban fabric, and could be cut out by public action. They were special areas requiring special treatment, the product of past mistakes before the creation of adequate building regulations, and slums therefore need not exist in the future since they had – so it was argued – no necessary connection with the structure of the modern city. The owner of the slum was not to be treated punitively, for improvement of conditions was beyond the scope of any individual; he was the prisoner of past errors in the design of cities, and should be compensated at full market values. Implementation of the Cross Act was soon to bring these assumptions into doubt. The slum areas were not so clearly defined as the notion of 'plague spots' assumed, and it became apparent that destruction of one area simply intensified the problem as the displaced population moved to adjacent property. The schemes were also costly as a result of the generous compensation paid to the owners. At least to some commentators, it was in any case becoming clear that slums *did* connect with the modern city, arising from the nature of the casual labour market and low wages.

The role of the council under the Cross Act was essentially destructive, to clear away the slums and to provide sites. Replacement housing was expected to be supplied by private builders or by the endeavours of the so-called '5 per cent philanthropy', bodies such as the Peabody Trust which took up the cleared land and built model dwellings which earned a limited return. Outright charity, it was believed, demoralised the poor and it was expected that architectural innovation, allied with the education of the tenants into regular payment of rent and care of the property, would raise the standards of housing and self-reliance. A somewhat similar approach was developed by Octavia Hill, who aimed to manage run-down housing, and raise the standards of the tenants through the educative role of 'lady rent collectors', reinvesting profits in improvements in the property. However, the expensive sites cleared under the Cross Act were often not taken, and even when the philanthropic trusts *did* step in, their rents were usually higher than the displaced population could afford. The result was to create a pressure for the municipality to build where private enterprise and philanthropy would not, which was usually undertaken only with reluctance, and on the condition laid down by the Cross Act that the houses were sold within 10 years.

Certainly, it was most unusual for a local authority to move beyond the provision of replacement housing as an extension of its role as the destroyer of slums, to the construction of additional accommodation. Powers were, it is true, given by Part III of the Housing Act of 1890, but this was an approach which did not commend itself to all housing reformers.

Although the London Progressives were shortly before the First World War to press towards a new policy of building additional houses in the suburbs, this was an approach which did not win universal assent even from the staunchest critics of the existing policy of slum clearance, such as Nettlefold. The councils' role as builder was to triumph after 1918, but it was generally accepted in the late Victorian and Edwardian period that the building of additional housing should be left to private enterprise, with the role of government limited to the destruction of the worst abuses of the past and the enforcement of minimum standards of construction and layout.[27]

The imposition of regulations over the form of new building dated from the seventeenth century in London, where there was concern to prevent fire. In provincial cities, the beginnings of regulations concerned with public health dated from the 1840s, when some cities such as Liverpool imposed restrictions on the construction of courts and the use of cellars. Some attempt at central guidance was made in the Public Health Act of 1858 and the issue by the new Local Government Act Office of a 'Form of Bye-laws' to assist local authorities. However, the most important measure dated from the same year as the Cross Act: the Public Health Act of 1875, which formed the second main strand of the late Victorian approach to urban housing. This Act allowed all sanitary authorities to impose bye-laws governing the construction of streets, the structure of buildings, the provision of space around buildings, and drainage. The Local Government Board set out model regulations in 1877. These required, for example, that streets over 100 feet in length should be at least 36 feet wide, and that each house was to have at the rear an open space for its exclusive use of at least 150 square feet. The model bye-laws provided, as Martin Gaskell has remarked, 'the first truly effective set of national building regulations'. Although the Act was still permissive rather than compulsory, the model bye-laws were widely adopted, and by 1882, 1000 urban districts had their building bye-laws in force.

The building of towns during the late Victorian period followed these principles, and this may be termed the bye-law phase of development. It was very much a rejection of the earlier phase of construction, and was by the end of the century itself under criticism from those who felt that it led to a sterile uniformity of development. It produced an urban landscape of straight, wide roads intersecting at right angles. To the proponents of the garden city and the architects associated with this movement such as Raymond Unwin and Barry Parker, this was an expensive and unsatisfactory form of development. Why not instead have narrower, winding roads, with houses grouped in short terraces in an irregular way, with greater respect for site and orientation, with a higher proportion of the land devoted to open space than to the provision of roads? The building bye-laws were already in the early twentieth century being seen as barriers to change and as anachronisms.[28]

There was, then, doubt by the close of the nineteenth century about both strands of policy which had been laid down in the legislation of 1875, the destruction of slums and the control over the new building which would, so it was thought, prevent the repeat of the mistakes of the past. The bye-laws seemed to some to be far too limited, and there was a growing awareness of the virtues of a more systematic planning of the growth of cities. The German example of controls over the extension of cities had impressed British commentators, most notably Nettlefold at Birmingham. This notion of 'town extension' planning coincided with other concerns at the turn of the century. One was the belief that the origin of urban problems of poor housing arose from high land prices, which should be tackled by an attack upon the great landowners; the other was the garden city movement which dated from Ebenezer Howard's *Tomorrow: A Peaceful Path to Real Reform* of 1898. These impulses together suggested that the future of cities should be the construction of self-contained garden cities or garden suburbs built on cheap land, owned and run on co-operative principles, and designed on new low-density lines which allowed the inhabitants to secure the best of both town and country. In 1903, the First Garden City Ltd was launched and the building of Letchworth started; soon after, Hampstead Garden Suburb in north London was commenced. Such strategies were to form the basis of the urban policy of the Liberal government which came to power in 1906: an attack upon landowners in Lloyd George's land campaign; and the granting of powers to councils in the Town Planning Act of 1909 to implement plans for town extension. The layouts which were drafted by Raymond Unwin and Barry Parker for the pre-war schemes at Letchworth and Hampstead were to provide the model for both council estates and speculative building in the inter-war period: the style survived although the Edwardian stress upon co-operative ownership was to disappear in the different circumstances of the 1920s and 1930s. The solutions of 1875 were therefore under attack, but it was not clear that the outcome would be the construction of council housing as the London Progressives were advocating, and starting to implement at the White Hart Lane estate at Tottenham. In the view of Dame Henrietta Barnett, one of the leading sponsors of Hampstead, council housing was anathema, and the correct response was the construction of housing in the suburbs on co-partnership lines. Where the advocates of both White Hart Lane and Hampstead were in agreement was in the changed aesthetic, which led to the rejection of the bye-laws.[29]

The 'visible hand' of public regulation helped to shape the urban environment, and this might in part explain not only the trend over time but also the variation between areas. Leeds council, for example, was very reluctant to follow the example of other authorities in banning the construction of back-to-back houses, which were only finally outlawed by national legislation in 1909. In considering these regulations, it is also important to remember that they contain what one historian has called a 'hidden social agenda': they were not simply about the size of windows or the width of streets but contained assumptions about the nature of urban society. These regulations were in fact as much about the fostering of notions of privacy within self-contained families as about public health.[30]

Is this to say that we are dealing with the imposition from above of a particular urban environment upon members of the working class? This would surely be an extreme view. For a start, working-class families might use the houses in ways which ran counter to the expectations of middle-class observers. In some cities, there was a high level of sharing of housing as a result of families taking in subtenants, and lodgers were also a feature of stages of the family life-cycle. Again, tenants might decide to set aside one room, the parlour at the front of the house, for special occasions, withdrawing it from everyday use in a way which seemed irrational to outsiders. The imposition of a sense of privacy might in any case coincide with changes *within* working-class society. It has been suggested that there was a movement towards a culture of domesticity within working-class families, which was in part a retreat into the home in the face of the erosion of work-based culture, and in part a response to the improvement in the standard of living which allowed greater expenditure both upon housing and upon the consumer goods with which it could be furnished. Housing indeed took the bulk of the gains in working-class income in the last quarter of the nineteenth century. The standard of living of the working class had risen sharply up to about 1900, largely as a result of the fall in the price of both food and manufactures. House rents, it is true, moved against this trend, rising from an index of 100 in 1870 to 123 in 1898, whereas prices in general fell from 100 to 71. However, Robert Giffen was more optimistic about this than Sutcliffe's stress upon an urban crisis would allow; he remarked in 1884 'that the houses are better, and that the increased house rent is merely the higher price for a superior article which the workman can afford'. In Scotland, for example, the proportion of the population living in one-roomed houses fell from 23.7 per cent in 1871 to 11.0 per cent in 1901. Much of the improvement in working-class housing and the urban environment must be understood in terms of the invisible hand of the market rather than the visible hand of public regulation.[31]

This conclusion that market forces were more important than regulations is confirmed when attention is turned from change over time to the variation between English towns at a point in time. In 1911, the level of overcrowding of housing was 33.7 per cent in Gateshead and 1.1 per cent in Leicester, which was paralleled by a variation in house-style: in Gateshead, 62.5 per cent of families lived in two-storied 'Tyneside flats' of two to four rooms, whereas in Leicester most families had five-roomed houses. This divergence cannot be adequately explained by the impact of regulations, but can be understood if it is noted that rents in Gateshead were 38 per cent above Leicester, while wages were 4 per cent below. The question of *why* rents varied so much remains a matter for further research.[32]

The nature of the urban environment in English cities

therefore changed over time, and as we have seen it also varied between cities. The Tyneside flats of Newcastle and Gateshead, the back-to-backs of Leeds, the terraced houses of the north without back extensions, and of the midlands and the south with back extensions, created a difference between English towns. These were, however, all variations on a single theme: the two-storied terraced house. In Scottish cities, the urban environment had a very different texture, for housing was dominated by the tenement block. This physical divergence clearly had an effect upon social life. The tenement block had communal space on the stairs and corridors, common facilities such as drying greens and washing facilities, and generated greater problems in maintaining the physical fabric. This led in turn to a greater concern for the control and management of the property, both by the owners and the local government, which was less apparent in England where property was more self-contained. Furthermore, there was a less marked trend towards privacy within the individual flats. Whereas English houses tended to assign rooms to specific functions, in Scottish tenements there were a few, larger, multipurpose rooms. The kitchen, for example, would be used not only for cooking and everyday living but also contained a bed-recess. It is quite clear that the physical form of the accommodation did have an effect upon social life; the question remains of why the difference existed between England and Scotland.[33]

The explanation would seem to be that the general level of rents in Scottish cities was high in relation to wages. The answer to the divergence might therefore be expected to be found in the operation of the invisible hand of the market, until it is noted that legal and institutional factors played a large role in increasing the level of rents. The market was shaped by non-economic forces. Scotland, of course, retained its own distinctive legal system after the Union of 1707, and one of the most obvious peculiarities which resulted was the system of land law. In English towns, most building land was made available either freehold or on short lease. In the case of freehold, the landowner received a lump sum which could then be invested to secure income and capital growth; in the case of leasehold, ownership of the land was retained and it was let for a period of 99 years at an annual rent, with the reversion of the land and the buildings erected on it at the end of the term. In Scotland, the original owner of the land – the 'superior' – would sell it to a purchaser or 'vassal' who would pay a lump sum and in addition make an annual payment or 'feu duty' in perpetuity. This acted to increase land prices. The vassal, as in England, paid the full price for obtaining the freehold, and the superior parted with this without any reversionary right; but in addition the vassal paid an annual sum which the superior wished to maximise since he could not follow the English lease-holder in offsetting short-term income by the long-term appreciation of the land and buildings which would revert to him. Furthermore, Scottish building regulations, imposed by the Dean of Guild Courts which had no counterpart in England, were much stricter than south of the border. The higher cost of Scottish housing therefore rested upon legal and institutional features which extended far beyond the limits of the city.[34]

The discussion has so far focused upon the form of housing, and the way in which this changed over time and varied between areas. It should also be noted that the building of this housing – both in England and Scotland – was marked by very intense cycles. There were two major building booms after 1870, with a somewhat different chronology depending upon which town is considered. In Glasgow, to take one example, the index of house-building (where 1900–9=100) rose to a peak of 228 in 1877, collapsing to 51 in 1878 and reaching a trough of 20 in 1883. The next boom was in the later 1890s, with twin peaks of 168 in 1897 and 197 in 1902; in 1913 the index stood at 27. There was, then, a cycle of about 20 years duration with a wide range of fluctuation. Why should this be?[35]

One influential interpretation has been that it reflected the operations of an Atlantic economy: when migration to America was high, this reduced the demand for housing and at the same time the flow of capital from Britain drove up interest rates, so checking the ability of builders to borrow money. When migration was low, population moved from the country to towns within Britain, so increasing demand; and capital was available for investment at home. Such a view would now receive little support. There were far too many variations between towns to permit such a neat argument to work, and the very wide range of fluctuations suggests that we are dealing with an industry which was highly insensitive both to the marginal changes in demand arising from migration, and to the impact of changes in interest rates. What happened was that builders continued to construct property even after effective demand had been met, so that there was a glut of houses which took a decade or more to remove. In 1871, before the boom started, 2.1 per cent of houses in Glasgow were vacant; in 1882, this figure had risen to 9.8 per cent. By 1896, this had fallen to 2.9 per cent; after the boom vacancies returned to 11 per cent in 1910–11. It would seem that the building industry was more sensitive to the level of empties in the town than to minor variations in costs or demand, and even so the responsiveness was not great. There was usually a period of overbuilding before the boom collapsed, and a period of shortage before activity recommenced. There is no sign that building was ever frustrated by capital shortages, and most historians would now stress that the building cycle should be explained largely in terms of the internal structure of the industry. This was based upon small-scale firms building houses on a speculative basis, relying upon short-term credit from builders' merchants and loans from solicitors, in the hope that a buyer would be found before payment was due. Once the process was started, it was difficult for a builder to stop without facing bankruptcy; but if everyone acted in the same way, the result was that demand was exceeded and the boom collapsed in a flurry of failures. Confidence was lost, and it was a long time before the glut of houses was removed and the onset of pressure in the housing market tempted builders to repeat the process.[36]

The course of the building cycle influenced the balance of power between landlords and tenants. Approximately 90 per cent of housing at this period was rented, and it was commented that in Glasgow a 'normal' level of vacancies of 5 or 6 per cent meant that the market was in equilibrium; below this level, rents would rise and the 'economic pull' was with the landlord; above it, the owner might be tempted to cut rents and the 'economic pull' was with the tenant. The general trend in rents was, we have seen, upwards but there were fluctuations according to the stage of the building cycle. The overbuilding in Glasgow in the early 1870s meant that property prices fell from a peak of 17 years' purchase (that is, multiples of the annual rent) to 12.8 years' purchase in 1886, with rents themselves falling by 7.9 per cent. As the level of vacant property fell, so property prices rose to 14.9 years' purchase in 1901, from which they fell precipitously after the building boom at the turn of the century, to a low of 9.5 years' purchase in 1912. Rents had increased by 7.4 per cent between the mid-1890s and early 1900s, and then fell by 2 per cent up to 1912. This does not, however, indicate the full consequences of overbuilding for the owners of property, for at the same time interest rates and local taxation were rising. Profit margins and capital values were seriously eroded in the early twentieth century. This was all the more the case because working-class real income was stagnating after the late 1890s, and it was increasingly difficult to pass higher costs to the tenants even when the property market did become tighter. The potential for landlord–tenant conflict was therefore present before 1914. This must, however, be understood in a wider context than simply the relative market position of the two sides, for the balance of advantage and the possibilities of conflict were influenced as well by the legal system.[37]

Alongside the divergences in the style of housing there were other, less visible, variations in the social relations which arose from the ownership and management of house property. The built environment did not affect urban social life simply through the impact of architectural form on the daily pattern of existence, but also produced a pattern of relationships between owners and managers, landlords and tenants. This is clear if we consider the major divergences between England and Scotland in the way in which property was owned and managed.

In Scotland, property was let on annual tenancies which expired on a single date (28 May) except for a minority of accommodation at the bottom of the market which was let on monthly tenancies. In England, accommodation was let by the week, except for the middle class where tenancies were longer. Furthermore, it was expected in Scottish cities that tenants would take the decision to remain or remove in February, so that there was a grave discrepancy between the inflexibilities of the housing market and the short-term contracts in the labour market. This produced political pressure to reform the housing market which succeeded in 1911 when there was legislation to introduce short lets. Further, in Scotland the landlords had much stricter legal powers against defaulting tenants and were much more likely to use them than in the case of English cities. Generally, housing had become a source of tension in urban social life to a much greater extent in Scotland than in England. This reflected the divergence between Scottish and English legal systems as much as the physical form of the housing, although the two variables did come together in influencing the pattern of management. Tenements imposed greater management responsibilities than self-contained houses, as did the greater tension in landlord–tenant relations. For both reasons, Scottish landlords were more inclined than their English counterparts to leave the management of property to a class of professional agents, the house factors. There was much more likely to be a division between ownership and control in Scotland than in England.[38]

There was, then, simmering discontent in the Scottish urban housing market by 1914, which was to explode in the Clydeside rent strike in 1915. In England, there was less tension over the length of tenancies, for short lets fitted better with the labour market and the working-class economy, and landlords were less able to take legal action against defaulters. Even so, there were some early examples of anti-landlord feeling in English cities. These arose in part from concerted attempts to force up rents, such as the resolution of the Wolverhampton and District Property Owners' Association to raise rents in 1913, which led to the formation of a Tenants' Defence League and a rent strike. They also arose in part from threats to the compounding allowance from councils eager to increase the yield from the rates. Landlords were loath to accept a lower commission at a time when their profit margins were being reduced, and might well refuse to co-operate. When Southwark attempted to reduce the allowance in 1901, the landlords forced the council to collect the rates direct from the occupiers, who responded by forming a Tenants' Protection League. Attention in some groups, and most obviously the Workmen's National Housing Council, was turning in the direction of 'fair rents' established by tribunals rather than the market. Of course, it is possible to read too much into isolated incidents of landlord–tenant conflict before 1914, for it must be remembered that they were by no means normal. However, what is clear is that landlords were not receiving much support from any political party. The Liberal emphasis upon land seemed irrelevant to their concerns, the Conservatives were turning attention towards owner-occupation, and the Labour Party was moving towards 'fair rents'. Private landlords, faced by a serious erosion of property values and profits in the early twentieth century, had genuine cause for concern.[39]

A major concern of urban historical geographers has been to trace the development of patterns of social segregation within cities. They have meticulously measured the sorting of areas according to their social status, so that we can agree that there was a move away from the 'walking city' with its intermixing of classes in the early nineteenth century, to the segregated city of the later nineteenth century with its single-class suburbs on the outskirts, the working-class districts in the next band, followed by the inner-city areas of the casual poor, and the central business districts of offices and shops. It would be fair to say that, until recently, the focus of historical geographers has been upon the extent to which the pattern in Britain matched the idealised description of American cities provided by Burgess and Hoyt. Historians have always been sceptical of the virtue of such an approach, and now many geographers are in agreement. What was left out of account was an explanation of why the process took the form it did. After all, a process of sifting into single-class areas did not take place in all societies. Paris in the nineteenth century did not have a district given over entirely to business as did London in the area around the Bank of England and Mansion House. Indeed, it was quite common in continental cities for the well-to-do middle class to remain in the city centre. It might even be the case that families of very different income and status might live within the same block of flats, with the most wealthy on the first floor and the poorest in the attics. The pattern of social segregation in British cities is not something simply to be measured and then compared with models of American cities; it has to be explained, in comparison with European cities as well as American.[40]

Of course, the structure of the housing market is of

importance in this process of sifting. The owners and agents had to decide to whom to offer tenancies, and this might affect the character of a street. They were, however, more likely to be responding to broader factors which determined who was willing to live in a particular area. Until recently, the factor which was stressed by urban historians was the operation of the land market. Considerable attention was paid by the first generation of urban historians to the large leasehold estates owned by aristocratic families or corporate bodies, not least because they left extensive records. It was easy to assume, after a period of immersion in their papers, that the decisions of the Bedford estate or Bute estate did in fact determine the layout and character of Bloomsbury and Cardiff, and that they acted as a sort of proto-planning department. More recently, historians have expressed scepticism. The great leasehold estates could not go against the dictates of the market. The Calthorpe estate in Birmingham, for example, could develop Edgbaston as a high-status leasehold suburb, but similar results were found at Headingley in Leeds on freehold land. The important consideration at any location was what the market would bear, and although a leaseholder might fight against this it was only rarely that he could succeed. The issue therefore returns to the structure of the market.[41]

In part, this was simply a response to prices: land and housing were cheaper in English cities than in most of Europe, with the possible exception of Belgium. This made suburban residence more feasible for a larger proportion of the population. In America, land was still cheaper and the transport system more likely to extend the urban fringe, so that suburban living was even more extensive there. The other important consideration was cultural preference, although here we are on difficult ground. In English cities, as in American, there had not been a long experience of closely packed urban life. European cities were more tightly constricted by town walls, in some cases right up to the 1870s, and they also tended to be larger than English cities in the pre-industrial period, with the obvious exception of London. The suggestion is that when the period of rapid urbanisation commenced in the nineteenth century, it was within the context of different expectations of urban life. Certainly, both

British and American historians have interpreted the growth of suburbs in cultural terms, as a flight by the middle class from the complexities of the inner cities, in order to create a haven of order and privacy which not only separated the city in terms of class, but equally removed residence from work and the sphere of the woman from that of the man.[42]

The counterpart of the creation of residential suburbs was the emergence of a non-residential central business district. This is something which has only recently started to attract the detailed attention of urban historians. This was the period in which department stores emerged, such as Selfridges or Whiteleys. Less obvious was the change in patterns of refreshment; women coming to town from the suburbs needed suitable places to have lunch unlike the public houses or chop houses for a male market, and the emergence of the Lyons Corner House responded to this new demand. The business districts were also transformed as counting houses in dwelling houses gave way to purpose-built offices. The first purpose-built office block in London was erected in 1823, but it was another 20 years before this became at all common. It was in the early 1860s that property companies started to enter the business, erecting offices in which merchants could rent rooms as needed. Of course, large companies were also constructing their impressive head offices such as the Prudential Insurance Co. with its massive building on Holborn Road designed by Waterhouse. In these buildings an army of clerks – at first men, but by the late nineteenth century, with the development of the typewriter, also women – came to work from the suburbs, carried by the railways, trams, buses and underground.[43]

The physical appearance of the towns of Britain had changed in important respects between 1870 and 1900. The new areas of bye-law housing formed a larger proportion of the total environment, producing an open grid of streets with a high premium upon privacy, a firm distinction between what was the private space of the house and the public and neutral space of the street. This contrasted with the older areas which had still been dominant in 1870, in which the threshold was less certain, and in which the public spaces were still used extensively for recreation and social life. Between 1870 and 1900, there was a sterilisation of public space as activities moved into specialised and purpose-built locations: the music hall, sports ground, department store. Streets were not used in the same way as they had been in the past in British cities, or as they continued to be used in most European cities. The urban environment of British cities looked different, and was also used in a particular way.

The urbanisation of Britain did not, of course, create a single type of town. The comments in this chapter have brought out some general trends, with some remarks on a broad distinction in the style of building and legal system between England and Scotland. The variations were, however, much wider than simply in architectural style and the pattern of landlord–tenant relations. There was little in common, after all, between one of the most rapidly growing urban types of this period – the seaside resort – and the heavy industrial towns on the coalfields. Even within a single urban type, there were variations in development. Blackpool was a working-class resort catering for the textile workers of Lancashire who were freed from the mills during the wakes weeks; it was therefore intimately linked with the economy of Blackburn or Bolton. It had a very different social and economic structure from Eastbourne which catered for the wealthy middle class, who might be retired from the industrial districts, or form part of the metropolitan circuit of Society and the Season. An industrial town of the East Midlands, based on the hosiery or lace trade, might be dominated by small workshops, whereas the wool or cotton towns of Lancashire or Yorkshire had large factories. All ports might appear to have a similar experience of a shifting world of sailors and a casual waterfront labour market, but even this breaks down when it is remembered that some ports were based upon exports and some on imports, some dominated by tramp shipping and some by liners. There were many urban Britains and not one.[44] Still, it is possible to talk in general terms about a late Victorian city before the impact of the automobile changed patterns of work and residence, before the collapse of the private rental market and the appearance of mass owner-occupation and the council estate fundamentally changed the housing market. Much as the cities differed between themselves at the end of the nineteenth century, this was a distinctive phase in the urbanisation of Britain.

4. Joseph Chamberlain: a Reassessment

ROLAND QUINAULT

I

THERE is a widespread belief that Joseph Chamberlain was the most significant and representative politician of the late Victorian era. For the two main party leaders, Gladstone and Salisbury, were survivals from an earlier age and their principal lieutenants, such as Harcourt and Balfour, remained under their shadow. Furthermore, other younger leaders who were more independent, such as Dilke and Churchill, failed to fulfil their early promise. But Chamberlain's prominence can be explained in personal as well as relative terms. He was undoubtedly an exceptionally energetic and incisive politician. 'I like to keep the story moving', he observed in 1876 at the start of his parliamentary career.[1] Twenty years later, the young Winston Churchill thought Chamberlain 'was incomparably the most live, sparkling, insurgent, compulsive figure in British affairs'. Though Salisbury was prime minister and Balfour was Leader of the House of Commons, 'Joe was the one who made the weather'.[2] Chamberlain's career seems, in retrospect, to have been as richly thematic as it was dynamic. He was closely associated with many of the growing developments of the era such as mass production, nonconformist radicalism, municipal socialism and imperialism. Consequently Chamberlain seems to embody the spirit of the late Victorian age more fully than any other politician.

This view of Chamberlain has been endorsed by many historians and particularly by his biographers. J. L. Garvin, who published the first volume of the official life in 1932, regarded Chamberlain as 'an extraordinary man of action' who 'introduced the modern age of British politics'. Garvin's portrait of Chamberlain as a dynamic imperialist was completed by Julian Amery, who portrayed him as a crusading tariff reformer.[3] Recently, Richard Jay has adopted a more critical approach in some respects, but he still acknowledges Chamberlain's 'sheer originality and creativity as a political actor'.[4] Whereas Jay regards Chamberlain as a grandmaster of the 'high politics' game, Michael Balfour has presented Chamberlain as the central figure in the scenario which led to Britain's decline as a major power.[5] These biographies and other studies of Chamberlain differ in many respects, yet they all concur in their belief in his central importance. But this premise cannot be simply assumed: it has to be empirically demonstrated.

The importance of Chamberlain's role in late Victorian politics has generally been exaggerated. Certainly his ministerial career was rather second-rate. He was only a junior member of Gladstone's Liberal Cabinets from 1880 to 1886 and he was then out of office for nine years. Though he became colonial secretary in 1895, he declined at the time the offer of two more senior posts. Neither was his position as a party leader much more authoritative. Throughout the 1880s and 1890s he was only a junior leader of a junior faction or party. Before 1886 he was only one of several national leaders of the radical Liberals. Indeed his prestige amongst these men was markedly inferior to that of another relic from the early Victorian period – John Bright. He also had less influence on the policy of the Gladstone government than did his younger contemporary, Dilke. The Liberal division over Irish home rule in 1886 also undermined his national authority in the short run. For example, his offspring, the National Liberal Federation, sided not with him, but with Gladstone on the home rule issue. Until 1904 Chamberlain remained second to Hartington as a leader of the Liberal Unionists, though he did lead them in the Commons after Hartington went to the Lords in 1891. But the great majority of Unionist MPs were Tories who followed Balfour and over whom Chamberlain had no formal authority.

It is true, of course, that Chamberlain's influence often transcended the limits of his official position. But though Chamberlain was endowed with great ability and vigour, he

could not on his own transform the political scene. If
Gladstone, in his third term as premier, could not effect home
rule, it is implausible to suggest that Chamberlain was more
able to model British politics in his own mould. In fact,
Chamberlain did not 'make the weather', but dressed to suit it.
He usually followed, rather than created, a political trend. He
was a product, rather than a progenitor, of urban radicalism
and a relatively late convert to the unionist alliance, imperial
federation and fiscal reform. On these and other issues
Chamberlain displayed a prolonged indecisiveness which
conflicts with his reputation as a daring innovator. Moreover
many of his policies were borrowed from other people.
Chamberlain's views on liberalism, local government and land
tenure were deeply influenced by John Stuart Mill. He took his
policy on education from George Dixon and his views on
imperial federation derived from Dilke, Forster, Froude and
Seeley. Above all, he modelled his whole career and many of his
campaigns on the example set by John Bright.[6] Chamberlain
can only be properly understood if he is placed in the wider
context of the era and the environment from which he sprang.

II

Chamberlain was born and brought up in London, the city in
which he lived for at least half his adult life and where he died.
Yet his links with London have been largely neglected by
historians who have not appreciated their wider significance in
shaping Chamberlain's career. This association went far
beyond mere accident of birth and subsequent political
convenience. The Chamberlains were prosperous bespoke
shoemakers in the City of London for a century before Joseph's
birth in 1836. His great-grandfather, grandfather and father
were all Masters of the Cordwainers Company and Joseph and
his sons became liverymen of the company in their turn. Joseph
made his first public speech at the Cordwainers Hall and he
returned there in 1896 when he spoke proudly of his family's
links with the company and with London. His close personal
relations with the old order in the City helps to account for his
unradical stance on local government reform in London. In the

early 1880s he opposed Harcourt's attempt to create a unitary authority for London and in 1895 he linked his own plan for separate London municipalities with a defence of the City Corporation.[7] The City was further pleased by Chamberlain's defence of its interests in South Africa during the Boer War and the Corporation presented him with commendatory addresses in 1902 and 1903. Chamberlain returned to the City in the following year to argue the case for tariff reform. He expressed the hope that 'coming to you as I do, as one of yourselves, born . . . a freeman by inheritance, having learnt the rudiments of commerce in the heart of the City . . . I might count upon a friendly hearing.' He claimed that tariff reform would benefit London more generally since it was both the capital of the empire and 'the greatest manufacturing city in the world'.[8] Though many bankers had doubts about tariff reform, Chamberlain did not oppose free trade in capital, as Jay has pointed out.[9]

Chamberlain's business links with London played a large role in generating the considerable wealth which enabled him to become a prominent professional politician. He acquired his business training working for the family firm in the City and it was profit from the firm which enabled him to become a partner in the screw-manufacturing business of his uncle, who had formerly been a London ironmonger. Thus it was London money and expertise which underlay the Chamberlain & Nettlefold business in Birmingham. Though Chamberlain sold his share of the business for £120,000 in 1876, he was able to treble his wealth over the next 12 years by judicious investments on the London stock market. These gains were partly lost in the 1890s, but Chamberlain was still a wealthy man when he died in 1914.[10]

London retained its hold on Chamberlain in a personal sense as well. Although he moved to Birmingham in 1854, at the age of 18, his family did not join him there until 1863. Despite Joseph's rapid financial and political success in Birmingham he remained nostalgic about his early life in London. When he was elected to Parliament he revisited his old London home in Highbury Fields 'and came away miserable'.[11] When Chamberlain built himself a new house in Birmingham in 1880 he named it 'Highbury'. In the same year he also acquired a house in London in Prince's Gardens, near Hyde Park. This became his home for most of the year and was where he entertained politicians. His younger brother Herbert later moved in round the corner and another brother lived not far away. By then, the family was based as much on London as on Birmingham.

Chamberlain's close connections with London assisted his emergence as a radical leader. The Chamberlain family were Unitarians and radical Liberals long before they went to Birmingham. Joseph was educated, like his cousins, at University College School, an offshoot of the famous 'godless college' largely founded by the Utilitarian radicals. This training left its mark on Chamberlain's political outlook, such as his belief in 'the greatest happiness of the greatest number' and his support for secular education. It was also reflected in his reverence for the views of John Stuart Mill, whose grave at Avignon he visited in 1875. Chamberlain's rise to national prominence owed much to his close ties with two London-based radicals: Charles Dilke and John Morley. He first met them in London in the early 1870s when they were all under the influence of Mill. Morley was the editor of the *Fortnightly Review* and invited Chamberlain to contribute to it. He wrote several articles, advocating an advanced Liberal programme, which were as important as his activities in Birmingham in gaining him a national reputation. Chamberlain's subsequent parliamentary career was centred on Birmingham, but he retained links with London liberalism. In 1885, his younger brother Richard became Liberal MP for Central Islington – the old homeland of the Chamberlain family. In a speech at Lambeth, Joseph pointed out that the 1885 Redistribution Act had awarded London a tenth of the seats in the House of Commons. Consequently he predicted that, in future, London would determine national policy and act as the centre and van of liberalism in the country at large.[12] This was a significant comment from a man nicknamed 'Brummagem Joe'. In the event, however, the Liberals did poorly in London in 1885. Richard Chamberlain became one of only three London Liberal Unionist MPs in 1886, but lost his seat in 1892. Thereafter, Joseph had no direct parliamentary connection with London.

While historians have neglected Chamberlain's links with London they have exaggerated his ties to Birmingham. It is widely assumed that Chamberlain's national position was based on his local position in Birmingham. Yet Chamberlain only acquired an assured parliamentary ascendancy in Birmingham owed much to the parallel growth of his national direct participation in the business and municipal life of the city. In fact, the growth of Chamberlain's authority in Birminghan owed much to the parallel growth of his national reputation. In this respect, Chamberlain followed a precedent set by John Bright, who was the senior MP for Birmingham until his death in 1889. Bright enjoyed enormous prestige and popularity in Birmingham – thanks to his achievements as a Liberal reformer – though he paid only occasional visits to the city. Chamberlain's personal links with Birmingham were much stronger than Bright's but these declined after the death of his second wife and his retirement from business and the mayoralty in 1876. Thereafter, though Chamberlain was an MP for Birmingham, his parliamentary and official duties kept him increasingly in London. Moreover he spent much of the parliamentary recess not in Birmingham but travelling abroad, and it was on one of these trips that he met his third wife in 1888. By 1900, Chamberlain used his Birmingham house as a quiet second home in the country, since 'Highbury' was three miles from the city centre and its large grounds included a small dairy farm. Most of the year the house was closed up, with the exception of one room used by Joseph's younger bachelor son, Neville.[13]

Historians have tended to present Chamberlain as essentially a municipal politician. In this respect they have followed the lead of some of his contemporary detractors. For example, Harcourt complained, in 1884, that Chamberlain 'thinks the universe is only a replica of a provincial town'.[14] Certainly Chamberlain had a strong interest in local government, yet his own municipal career was short-lived. He became a Birmingham borough councillor in 1869, was elected mayor in 1873 and retired for good in 1876. His rapid success reflected not only his ability, but also his Unitarian connections since his co-religionists had held the mayoralty almost continuously since the town was incorporated in 1839.[15] This

Unitarian tradition was continued when Chamberlain was succeeded by his brother-in-law, William Kenrick, and later on by his younger brother, Richard. But although Chamberlain belonged to a municipal elite he was never a mere municipalist. He was an active member of the Birmingham Liberal Association and a senior member of the National Education League before he became a town councillor. He was also a nationally known radical before he became mayor of Birmingham. Chamberlain did not progress from municipal to national politics, but had a concurrent and complementary interest in both local and national affairs. Thus he campaigned against Forster's Education Act while he was chairman of the Birmingham School Board and sought a seat in Parliament while he was mayor of Birmingham.

Chamberlain's achievements as a dynamic mayor of Birmingham have been put in perspective by several historians in recent years. His reforms were inspired by the writings of Mill and the example of other industrial cities. They were facilitated by the economic prosperity of the mid-1870s and the permissive legislation passed by Disraeli's Tory government.[16] But it would be a mistake to regard Chamberlain's reforms as a complete break with the old economical order in Birmingham. When Chamberlain boasted in 1876 that the city had, in three years, been 'parked, paved, assized, marketed, gas & watered and improved' he also added that this had been done 'with the general approval of the great bulk of the ratepayers'.[17] Indeed he justified the municipalisation of the gasworks on the grounds that it would reduce the burden placed on ratepayers by the other municipal improvements.[18] Chamberlain always advocated economical as well as efficient local services. In 1892 he warned 'the ambitious members of the new school of municipal politicians that it is possible to kill the goose that lays the golden eggs'. He then attacked the London County Council for paying their workers over the commercial rate and thus offending the ratepayers.[19] But then Chamberlain was neither a sponsor nor a member of the largest local authority in the country, but only one of its suffering ratepayers.

J. L. Garvin believed that it was Chamberlain's municipal record which ensured that he retained the loyalty of his Birmingham electors from 1876 until his death in 1914.[20] But it is improbable that 6 years service on the council guaranteed Chamberlain a safe parliamentary seat for 38 years. After his death, a local paper declared, more perceptively, that: 'The people of Birmingham followed him because he led them whither they would go.'[21] It was general concordance of outlook, rather than personal deference or gratitude, which ensured Chamberlain's tenure of the representation. For Birmingham's loyalty to Chamberlain was in no sense exceptional. Between 1832 and 1914 there were only two occasions when a sitting Birmingham MP was defeated at an election and one of those was a Tory who had had a chance victory at a by-election. This tradition of fidelity reflected the dominant influence which Nonconformist Liberalism exerted over the city. It was because this influence was so strong that Birmingham became the impregnable citadel first of Bright and then of Chamberlain. At a personal level, Chamberlain's long association with Birmingham was partly accidental since he made several attempts to represent other boroughs in Parliament before an unexpected vacancy arose at Birmingham. Since Chamberlain was well endowed with wealth, ability and connections, he could easily have pursued a successful parliamentary career away from home as did Bright, Gladstone, Harcourt and Morley.

III

Since Chamberlain has been regarded as the uncrowned king of Birmingham his policies have been interpreted as schemes to benefit urban and industrial interest groups. However, Chamberlain was often preoccupied with rural, rather than with urban issues. This was not surprising since the land question was the most emotive and most widely discussed issue for radical and other politicians in the later Victorian period. Unlike industrial cities such as Birmingham, the rural areas were the traditional stronghold of the Church of England and the Conservative Party unless they were located in the 'Celtic fringe'. Therefore English radicals took up agrarian issues in an attempt to spread liberal attitudes in the countryside. Chamberlain continued a tradition which, as he acknowledged, had been pioneered by the Chartists and the Anti-Corn Law League in the 1840s.[22] But Chamberlain's rise coincided with a period when one aspect of the land question assumed novel political importance. This was the condition of the agricultural labourers who formed the largest occupational group in the national workforce.

Chamberlain's concern with the plight of the labourers was apparent from the start of his career. In 1870 he feared that Forster's Education Bill would deny effective elementary education for children in country areas. Yet this was essential, he argued, if child labour in the fields was to be abolished and the low wages of farm workers were to be raised. He was an early supporter of Joseph Arch, the Warwickshire labourer who formed the National Agricultural Labourers Union at Wellesbourne, not far from Birmingham, in 1872. Chamberlain believed that the labourers endured conditions worse than any in the civilised world and he praised their strike for higher wages as 'the noblest event of the present century'. At the same time he urged that they should be given the vote and a stake in the soil.[23] Thus in 1884 he welcomed the extension of the franchise to the rural labourers but complained that they had been robbed of their land. Consequently, the first objective of Chamberlain's 'unauthorised programme' of 1885 was to restore 'the labourer to the soil'. D. A. Hamer has argued that Chamberlain viewed the land question merely in relation to urban problems and needs. But although he did point out that rural depopulation led to urban overcrowding and low wages he was also concerned with the plight of rural labourers as an autonomous issue. 'The agricultural labourer is the most pathetic figure in our whole social system . . . and now he will have to be reckoned with.'[24] This was an allusion to the new electoral power of the labourers and Chamberlain hoped to harness it by providing them with allotments. This policy, pioneered by his Birmingham friend, Jesse Collings, was popularly known as 'three acres and a cow'. It helped the Liberals to win many county seats from the Tories at the 1885 general election. Soon afterwards, Chamberlain saw a silver cow on a dinner table and remarked 'Oh, you blessed animal! Where should we have been without you?'[25] After the elections, Chamberlain helped Collings to draft an amendment deploring the lack of allotment provision from the government's programme which occasioned the defeat and resignation of Salisbury's Tory ministry in January 1886. In the subsequent Liberal government Chamberlain was appointed president of the Local Government Board by Gladstone with Collings as his under-secretary. They were thus in a position to pressurise local authorities to provide labourers' allotments. But within a few weeks Chamberlain had resigned his office because he opposed Gladstone's Irish Land Bill.

The Irish crisis obliged Chamberlain to switch his attention from the land question in Britain to the land question in Ireland. But he remained interested in the plight of the labourers in Britain despite the decision of Arch and most of their other leaders to support Gladstone on the home rule question. He helped Collings found the Unionist Rural Labourers League which, through its organ, *The Rural World*, had considerable influence in the 1890s. He also prepared the ground for Chaplin's 1892 Small Holdings Act. Chamberlain likewise sympathised with the plight of the crofters in the Scottish Highlands and Islands. He toured the crofting districts in 1885 and 1887, after which he introduced a Crofters' Relief Bill. His interest in agrarian reform in Britain helps to account for his animosity to Irish home rule. In 1887 he complained that 'poor little Wales', the Scottish crofters and the English agricultural labourers would have to wait for attention until Parnell had been satisfied. 'Thirty millions of people must go without much-needed legislation because three million are disloyal.'[26] This was a misleading comment since the agrarian reforms he wanted would not have directly benefited all the 30 million people of Britain. After 1895 Chamberlain was preoccupied with imperial issues, yet he remained concerned with the plight of the rural poor. In 1904 he declared:

The problem of the agricultural labourer remains, in my judgement, the greatest social problem of our time. I am one of a small band of politicians who, from the first moment we entered political life, can claim that we gave special attention to this question and did our best . . . to improve the condition of the labourer. We have gained for him free education and compensation for injuries and above all facilities for . . . becoming himself the holder of an allotment, or even a small proprietor.[27]

IV

Ireland exercised a profound influence on Chamberlain's career which has been rather neglected by those historians who have emphasised his radical or imperial credentials. Yet Ireland was the most persistent and complex problem during the whole of Chamberlain's political career from the late 1860s to 1914. Furthermore the Irish home rule crisis of 1886 decisively altered the course of Chamberlain's career. It cut him off from the Gladstonian Liberal Party and obliged him, as a Liberal Unionist, to come to terms with both the Whigs and the Tories. Why did Chamberlain apparently abandon his old friends for his old enemies? Historians have tried to resolve this problem by closely examining his conduct in the spring of 1886. But Chamberlain's course at that juncture can only be fully understood if it is set in a broader perspective.

When Chamberlain opposed the Home Rule Bill in 1886 he declared: 'I have always held the same language on this Irish question that I hold today.'[28] As a keen advocate of local government, he favoured the creation of democratic local authorities in Ireland. In 1874 he favoured Irish devolution provided the imperial link was retained. In 1885 he advocated a National Council for Ireland which 'will only be the Metropolitan Board of Works on a larger and more important scale'.[29] In 1886 it was not the principle of devolution but the proposed end to the parliamentary union between Britain and Ireland which Chamberlain opposed. Yet there was also a more negative aspect to Chamberlain's opposition to home rule which reflected his Nonconformist roots. He had come to the fore as an opponent of Forster's 1870 Education Bill which, he feared, would pave the way for Catholic denominational education in Ireland. As a representative of the National Education League at the Birmingham School elections in 1870, he campaigned against the local Irish Catholic supporters of denominational education.[30] This set a precedent for his attacks on 'Rome rule' which were features of his later Unionist speeches.

Chamberlain also had little sympathy for Irish nationalist MPs. In 1877 he wrote that: 'The Irishmen in the House are a scurvy lot and a most embarrassing element in all party politics.' In 1880 he told Dilke that the conduct of Parnell and his supporters was alienating them from English radicals and workmen.[31] Chamberlain was never intimate with Parnell. Their well-known negotiations which led up to the 'Kilmainham Treaty' in 1882 were via an intermediary, O'Shea, who initiated the correspondence. O'Shea had had previous dealings with Gladstone, but not with Chamberlain who was a junior Cabinet minister unconcerned with Ireland. This was in contrast to the direct experience of the Irish problem which many of his contemporaries in the Liberal government – Spencer, Forster, Trevelyan, Campbell-Bannerman and Morley – gained in the years 1880–6. For most of that period Chamberlain was content to echo the Irish policy of his senior radical partner, Bright. This consisted of two strands: coercion to suppress disorder and land reform to sap the roots of rural discontent. When Gladstone took up home rule in 1886 Chamberlain's response was to revive Bright's proposals for tenant purchase as a preferable panacea. Although Chamberlain opposed Gladstone's 1886 Land Bill as an expensive landlord-relief measure, he continued to argue the case for tenant purchase for many years. Indeed he hoped that British as well as Irish farmers should be enabled to become owner occupiers.[32]

Chamberlain's break with Gladstone in 1886 has been interpreted as a struggle between a radical who wanted social reform in Britain and a conservative who wanted justice for Ireland. But too much weight should not be placed on the events of 1885–6, for Chamberlain's decision to oppose Gladstone's policy was the culmination of a much longer period of mistrust. Chamberlain had first emerged into the political limelight as a critic of the policies of Gladstone's first government in the early 1870s. So he shed no tears when Gladstone resigned the party leadership in 1875 and continued to regard him as unreliable thereafter. His entry into the Liberal Cabinet in 1880 owed more to Bright's pleading than to

Chamberlain's links with Gladstone. Relations between the two men were frequently strained before the Liberals left office in 1885 and when Gladstone returned to power in 1886 he gave Chamberlain an even more junior Cabinet post than he had received in 1880. Thus Chamberlain was in no sense Gladstone's heir-apparent before their rupture over Ireland.

By contrast, Chamberlain had a much more satisfactory relationship with his near contemporary, Hartington. It has been too readily assumed that Chamberlain, the representative bourgeois radical, was opposed to Hartington, the archetypal aristocratic Whig. In fact Chamberlain admired the man he once described as 'the serious son of a respectable duke'. Hartington was the leader of the Liberal Party when Chamberlain first became an MP and the two men co-operated over the organisation of the National Liberal Federation in 1877. In 1878 Chamberlain refused to support a move to oust Hartington from the party leadership 'as I really think he keeps the place out of worse hands'.[33] At the height of his radical campaign in 1885 Chamberlain sought an alliance with Hartington based on a non-Gladstonian compromise. Both men were imperialists as well as unionists. They both supported the Egyptian intervention in 1882; the annexation of Bechuanaland in 1884 and imperial federation in the 1890s. Therefore their long partnership as leaders of the Liberal Unionist Party from 1886 to 1904 is understandable.

However, in 1886 it was the influence of Bright above all which persuaded Chamberlain openly to rebel against Gladstone. Chamberlain followed Bright in his decision to vote against the second reading of the Home Rule Bill and this proved fatal to that measure. Chamberlain was not yet opposed to the principle of home rule, but the dissolution of Parliament forced him to come off the fence. When Bright denounced home rule at Birmingham, Chamberlain soon followed suit. He had little alternative, for few Birmingham Liberals were keen on home rule. Only one of the city's seven sitting Liberal MPs stood as a home ruler and he was defeated, while both the leading Liberal papers were Unionist. Thus Birmingham Liberal Unionism was in no sense simply Chamberlain's creation. The Gladstonians did not mount a serious challenge in the city until 1892. Then Chamberlain was helped by

Bright's posthumous reputation and a strong swing to the Unionists throughout the West Midlands even in areas where Chamberlain had no influence. This swing mirrored a wider trend as the Unionists won a majority of all English borough seats from 1886 to 1906. Thus Chamberlain inherited, rather than created, what has been termed his 'West Midlands duchy'.[34]

Chamberlain had a natural sympathy with the Non-conformist Liberal Unionists of Ulster. He visited Belfast in 1887 and made the Ulster question the central theme of his 1892 general election campaign. By then, Unionism dominated Chamberlain's entire political outlook. The defeat of the Second Home Rule Bill was confirmed by the defeat of the Liberals at the polls in 1895 and Chamberlain was left with 'nothing but personal ambition to keep me in harness'. Nevertheless he remained much concerned with the defence of the Union throughout the rest of his political career. This was understandable since the Irish Nationalists formed a third of the parliamentary opposition to the Unionist government between 1895 and 1906. Moreover they were vehement opponents of Chamberlain's imperial policy and openly sympathised with the Boers' militant opposition to Britain. Winston Churchill remembered that the Nationalists were Chamberlain's most persistent foes in the Commons: 'the malignity of their resentment was unsurpassed by anything I have ever seen.'[35] Chamberlain repaid their animosity with interest and linked his campaign for tariff reform with opposition to home rule. He pointed out that home rule would disrupt the empire as well as the United Kingdom and launched his tariff campaign in Unionist strongholds such as Birmingham, Glasgow and Liverpool. In his last public speech, made in 1906, just before a stroke forced him to retire from active politics, Chamberlain observed that the conversion of the Liberal Party to home rule in 1886 had been 'the great event in our generation'. For it had 'altered the whole course of our political history, revolutionized our political relations, destroyed the Liberal Party as we knew it.'[36] He remained a determined Unionist until he died in 1914.

V

Chamberlain's period as colonial secretary from 1895 to 1903 was overshadowed by events in South Africa. Soon after his appointment Jameson's raid on the Transvaal took place and thereafter Anglo-Boer relations deteriorated up to the outbreak of war in 1899. When peace returned in 1902, Chamberlain paid a long visit to South Africa in an attempt to sow the seeds of reconciliation between Britons and Boers. The long South African crisis ensured that Chamberlain played a more central role in Salisbury's government than he might otherwise have done. It also enhanced his popularity and prestige amongst many Conservatives who had previously regarded him with suspicion because of his radical past. Yet it was largely fortuitous that Chamberlain became so associated with the crisis in South Africa. He had first wanted to become colonial secretary in 1886 at a time when Anglo-Boer relations were pacific. While he held that position Chamberlain spent much of his time dealing with colonies which were far from South Africa. It was Alfred Milner, the British high commissioner at the Cape, who was directly responsible for relations with the Boer republics. Milner's determination in 1898–9 to enforce change on the Transvaal contrasted with the more vacillating policy of Chamberlain, his remote overlord in London. Milner was only one of number of Liberal Unionists who helped Chamberlain to resolve the South African crisis. They included Selborne, Chamberlain's under-secretary; Lansdowne at the War Office; Goschen at the Admiralty and Lyttelton, who succeeded Chamberlain at the Colonial Office in 1903. Thus Chamberlain was only part of a wider Liberal Unionist group who advocated imperial unity at the turn of the century.

Chamberlain's general imperial policy was determined less by the situation in South Africa than by developments in North America. He never regarded South Africa as Britain's most important colony, yet he was well aware of the growing importance of North America in world affairs. The rapid development of the United States convinced Chamberlain that the world would soon be dominated by large territorial states which could command great resources. Hence Britain would have to exploit its own 'undeveloped estates' abroad if it was to remain a great power. Chamberlain admired the democratic and secular constitution of the USA and it was alleged that he, like Bright, wanted to Americanise British institutions. Chamberlain denied that he wanted to import the American caucus system of party organisation, but he did wish to imitate the federal character of the American constitution. Indeed this provided him with a model in the 1880s for both Irish devolution and imperial federation. In 1888 Chamberlain studied American institutions at first hand and married the daughter of the American secretary of state for war who became 'my best and truest counsel'. In the 1890s he paid two more visits to the United States; wrote articles for American journals and then called for an Anglo-American alliance. However, Chamberlain disliked some aspects of American society and government, while his unionist and imperialist convictions aroused the antipathy of groups like the Irish-Americans. Hence he was particularly interested in the British half of North America – Canada.

Chamberlain's unionist and imperial policies in the late Victorian period were specifically inspired by the example of Canada. In 1886, during the debate on the Home Rule Bill, Chamberlain rejected Gladstone's proposal that Ireland should be given the same autonomy as Canada, but he suggested, as an alternative model, the relationship between the provinces of Canada and the Dominion Parliament.[37] At the 1887 Round Table conference between the Gladstonian and Unionist Liberals, Chamberlain declared that the 1867 Act which had created the union of Canada was a 'very suggestive basis of discussion' for a compromise home rule scheme, but his idea was rejected by Bright and Hartington.[38] Chamberlain's interest in Canada at this time was encouraged by personal ties. Both his younger brothers married Canadian women and one of them, Mrs Herbert Chamberlain, became president of the Birmingham Women's Liberal Unionist Association. Chamberlain's faith in the economic potential of Canada was reflected in his purchase of shares in the Canadian Pacific Railway, but he was obliged to sell these before they rose rapidly in value. In 1887 he visited Canada as the British commissioner responsible for settling the Newfoundland fisheries dispute and he made two further visits to the

Dominion in the 1890s. On these occasions he became friends with politicians like Denison who wanted closer ties between Britain and Canada.

Chamberlain's growing interest in imperial federation owed much to his awareness of Canadian development. At Belfast, in 1887, Chamberlain declared that the ties between Britain and her colonies would have to be strengthened by federation or else they would disintegrate. He pointed out that there was already an agitation in Canada for commercial union with the United States and a tariff against Britain. Two months later, at Toronto, Chamberlain suggested that the confederation of Canada 'might be the lamp to light our path to the confederation of the British Empire'.[39] This theme was Chamberlain's *leitmotiv* when he went to the Colonial Office in 1895. In his first official speech, Chamberlain advocated a Canadian-style federation of the British and Boer states of South Africa. He next suggested that the Australian colonies should imitate Canada's wise example and join a federal union.[40] He realised this aim when the Commonwealth of Australia was created in 1901.

Chamberlain regarded local colonial federation as a necessary preliminary to a general federation of the whole empire. To achieve this higher aim he again looked to Canada to lead the way. He considered Canada the most important of the colonies and the easiest one to deal with since it was a unified Dominion. In 1896 Chamberlain welcomed Canadian support for imperial preference schemes designed to benefit colonial foodstuffs and British manufacturers. In private he expressed the hope that Canada would lead the way in creating an imperial tariff union on the lines of the German *zollverein*.[41] Yet in public, Chamberlain was reluctant to screw his courage to the sticking-place of tariff reform. Until 1903 he merely repeated the stance he adopted in 1896: a cautiously vague support for Canadian preference initiatives. In 1897 Canada gave Britain a unilateral tariff preference of 25 per cent, but Chamberlain offered no reciprocal concession – to the dismay of young imperialists like Amery. Chamberlain realised that the government was reluctant to upset the free trade system merely to please Canada which had for decades imposed duties on British goods. Moreover he appreciated that Canadian enthusiasm for imperial preference was not matched by a complementary enthusiasm for imperial defence. Although volunteers from Canada fought with British troops in the Boer War, few Canadians wanted a comprehensive military pact with Britain. In 1901 Chamberlain told Parkin, an influential Canadian imperialist, that 'he was prepared to go just as far in the direction of imperial federation as Canada and Australia will go, but that he and his colleagues feared to spoil all by appearing to drive the colonies into taking a share of the burdens of empire.'[42]

Nevertheless, British America was primarily responsible for the gradual change in Chamberlain's fiscal outlook. Chamberlain's interest in Canada led him to take a close interest in the other part of British America: the West Indies. On a visit to Montreal in 1890 he met the governor of the Bahamas, Sir Ambrose Shea, who encouraged him to invest in sisal production in those islands. Chamberlain spent £50,000 creating a sisal plantation which was managed by his son Neville. But the project was beset with problems and the venture had to be abandoned. However, when Chamberlain became colonial secretary he continued to take a close interest in the economic development of the West Indies. The prosperity of the islands depended on sugar cane but this was undermined when several continental countries granted bounties to their sugar beet producers to encourage exports. By 1898 Chamberlain had concluded that only countervailing duties would restore the prosperity of the British West Indies. This was an early example of his move away from the rigid free trade outlook which he had adopted as president of the Board of Trade in the early 1880s. However, his conversion was not put to the test because the European sugar bounties were abolished by convention in 1902. But Canadian pressure for tariff reform continued to mount, fed by the conversion of the western prairies into vast wheatfields. By 1902 Winnipeg was receiving more wheat than Chicago and Canada's wheat production doubled in a few years. Britain was the obvious market for this produce since it grew only one-sixth of its own wheat consumption.[43]

For the coronation of Edward VII in 1902, the Canadian government erected a huge arch across Whitehall with the inscription 'Canada Britain's Granary'. In July, Chamberlain's cab horse shied when it approached this arch and he suffered a bad accident. This kept him out of action at a critical time. While he was in hospital, his local option clause was deleted from the government's Education Bill by Anglican Tory MPs. This upset Chamberlain's Nonconformist supporters in Birmingham and may have encouraged him to look for a new electoral rallying cry: tariff reform. While Chamberlain was convalescing, Salisbury resigned the premiership and was succeeded by his nephew Balfour. Chamberlain, as a Liberal-Unionist, had no claim to the succession, but he might have had more influence on the composition of Balfour's government if he had not been ill at the time. Thus Canadian corn had a literal impact on Chamberlain's career.

Chamberlain, as colonial secretary, was in any case more susceptible than other members of the government to Canadian pressure. For the Colonial Office, unlike the Foreign Office or War Office, was generally a loyal and determined defender of Canadian interests. Chamberlain was also influenced by the personal outlook of Lord Minto, who became governor-general of Canada in 1898. By 1902, Minto was plying Chamberlain with Canadian literature in favour of imperial preference and assuring him that Canada would welcome a British initiative on this issue. Minto feared that if Britain postponed such action Canada would soon become part of the United States.[44] The trilateral relationship between Britain, Canada and the USA had been Chamberlain's concern when he dealt with the Newfoundland fisheries dispute in 1887 and it also concerned him when he was colonial secretary. In 1897 he had to deal with the Behring Sea seal fisheries dispute with the USA and in 1898 with the Alaskan boundary dispute which was prompted by the Yukon gold rush. Britain appeased the United States on that question and thus annoyed Canada. This made Chamberlain more anxious to accommodate Canada on the tariff question.

When Chamberlain finally declared his support for tariff reform in 1903, he made it clear that Canada had influenced his thinking. In his famous Birmingham speech he stated that imperial preference was 'not a policy inaugurated by us, but

. . . a policy which comes to us from our children abroad.' He noted that the most important colony was the one most in favour of preference – Canada, which was currently 'in the full swing of an enormous prosperity'.[45] Chamberlain was anxious to know how his speech was received in Canada. Although it was hailed enthusiastically by Borden, the leader of the Conservative opposition, it elicited only a cautious response from Laurier, the Liberal premier, who wanted Chamberlain to come up with more specific proposals. So Chamberlain, urged on by Minto, took the plunge and called for food taxes. In practice, this meant a corn tax which would primarily benefit Canadian producers. Even then, however, Chamberlain failed to elicit the extent of support from Canada that Minto had led him to expect. Nevertheless he still remained convinced that the response of Canada was crucial to the success of tariff reform. In 1911, for example, he hailed the victory of Borden in the Canadian general election as 'the most important incident in our long campaign for tariff reform and imperial preference'.[46] Clearly, the Canadian dimension to tariff reform deserves more attention than the incidental reference which it has received from many historians of the subject such as Alan Sykes.[47]

Chamberlain's conversion to tariff reform was only marginally affected by domestic economic concerns. He endorsed the idea of a corn tax even though he realised it would be unpopular with the British electorate. He told Chaplin, the leader of the English agrarian protectionists, that food taxes were only needed for preference with the colonies. Neither did Chamberlain believe that other sectors of the British economy needed protection since in 1903 he thought that Britain was: 'Richer, more comfortable, the working classes getting higher wages, consuming more food and luxuries, its capital increasing more rapidly than at any previous period of our history.'[48] Chamberlain saw tariff reform as a means of strengthening the British empire rather than the British economy. He observed in 1904: 'I am a fiscal reformer mainly because I am an Imperialist.'[49]

VI

'Once on a time there was a Man' declaimed Rudyard Kipling when he compared Joseph Chamberlain's imperial vision with the dream of Joseph in Genesis. But imperial Joseph, like his biblical namesake, wore a coat of many colours. Historians have focused on the primary rather than the secondary colours of Chamberlain's career and have thus tended to oversimplify what he stood for. In fact there was often an ambiguity about Chamberlain which makes it difficult to label him as a typical representative of any particular group or movement. He was bourgeois, yet his wealth and leisure made him a typical member of the political elite. He began his career by flirting with republicanism and attacking the aristocracy, but he soon established good relations with the royal family and his aristocratic colleagues. He represented Birmingham yet he was largely a Londoner by upbringing, education and domicile. He made his first fortune as a Midland manufacturer, but he was an international rentier in later life. He was a Nonconformist, but belonged to the small, wealthy and powerful Unitarian sect. He made his name by championing nonconformity but he abandoned sectarianism when he became an MP. He lauded local government, but preferred the House of Commons to the council chamber. He pressed for votes for rural householders, but not for urban lodgers. He was dynamic by temperament, yet he was often indecisive. He was by upbringing a radical, yet he spent half his career opposing changes such as two Education Acts and three Irish Home Rule Bills. He was a staunch free trader who eventually became a tariff reformer, but he continued to regard himself as the true heir of Cobden and Bright. Chamberlain's complexity reflected not only his character, but also the changing moods of the age in which he lived.

As a reformer and legislator, Chamberlain was in many respects a failure. He consciously followed in the footsteps of Bright, but with markedly less success. Many reforms he supported – such as disestablishment of the Church of England and municipal licensing – proved stillborn, while others – such as the Merchant Shipping Bill of 1884 – failed to reach the statute book. Those reforms he endorsed which were implemented, such as free elementary education, representative county government and old age pensions, were both originated and enacted by other hands. Chamberlain was not directly responsible for any major domestic reforms, although he certainly provided influential support for many of them. At the Colonial Office Chamberlain presided over the creation of the Commonwealth of Australia, but he neither initiated nor consummated the movement for imperial federation. A generation elapsed before his policy of imperial preference was generally adopted. Chamberlain's failure to implement most of his reform policies can be explained partly by his lack of prescience (or even realism at times) and partly by a lack of opportunity. Since he never held one of the top Cabinet posts he often had to exert his influence from outside the inner circle of decision-makers. His influence over party policy was similarly restricted by his junior status. Nevertheless, the 'duke of Birmingham' has been regarded as a kingmaker who toppled Gladstone, crowned Salisbury and then undermined Balfour. Thus Henry Lucy, the parliamentary journalist, thought that Chamberlain had the unique distinction of having rent both parties in two: the Liberals in 1886 and the Unionists in 1903.[50] But the belief that Chamberlain single-handedly broke the mould of British politics owes more to his retrospective reputation than to his actual influence at those times. In 1886, the Liberal secession was led by Hartington, then endorsed by Bright, while Chamberlain remained anxious for compromise until the last moment. In 1903, Chamberlain responded, rather belatedly, to pressure for tariff reform which had been generated by developments in Canada and the South African war. It was Devonshire, not Chamberlain, who initiated the subsequent rupture in the Unionist Party.

Nevertheless, it would be folly to deny that Chamberlain's political influence grew steadily in the late Victorian period. Since his record as a reformer was not particularly impressive, how should we account for his growing reputation? Historians have stressed his role as a grass-roots politician based on his own local organisations and platform speeches. Yet Chamberlain used these agencies as vehicles for policies such as unionism or imperial preference which had very little connection with local issues. From the start of his career he was preoccupied with national (and later supra-national) policies which were determined at Westminster. But historians have tended to play down the specifically parliamentary character of Chamberlain's career. Richard Jay, for example, has argued that Chamberlain had small sympathy with 'liberal parliamentarianism' and cared little about parliamentary speeches or management.[51] However, Henry Lucy, who was in a good position to judge, thought that Chamberlain was masterly at conducting parliamentary business and considered him the most powerful parliamentary debater of the age.[52] Sir Richard Temple, a contemporary Tory MP, thought Chamberlain was a consistently good persuader and second only to Gladstone as a speaker.[53] It was Chamberlain's rhetorical skill, rather than his skill at intrigue or the size of his personal following, which made him so useful to Salisbury and Balfour. As Lucy noted in 1891: 'Mr Chamberlain's personality is so strong, his ability so conspicuous and his generalship so brilliant, that his influence accumulates though his party decays.'[54]

In some respects, Chamberlain's influence reached its apogee, not at the turn of the century, but after his death in 1914. Many of the new Conservative leaders – such as Bonar Law, Baldwin, Smith and Amery – had been inspired by Chamberlain's career and policies. Moreover both of Chamberlain's sons, Austen and Neville, became leaders of the Conservative party and held between them, at different times, all the highest Cabinet posts. Their prominence owed much to the continuing lustre of their father's name and they carried on his social and imperial policies. When Neville Chamberlain, as chancellor of the exchequer, signed the Ottawa imperial preference agreements in 1932 he pointed out that they were the 'direct and legitimate descendants' of his father's tariff proposals of 1903.[55] Joseph's faith in tariff reform and Canada had finally been rewarded. In the same year, J. L. Garvin, one of the most influential journalists of the era, published the first volume of his authoritative life of Joseph Chamberlain, which attracted wide interest. Winston Churchill observed that: 'All our British affairs today are tangled, biassed or inspired by his actions.'[56] Chamberlain, who had always been a rather late starter (he did not become an MP until he was 40), had finally made his mark. Thus in more senses than one, Joseph Chamberlain was a late Victorian figure.

5. Electoral Reforms and their Outcome in the United Kingdom, 1865–1900

J. P. D. DUNBABIN

I

IN the nineteenth century, as now, Parliament consisted of Queen, Lords and Commons. Electoral reforms naturally had repercussions on the inter-relationships of all three, but they only directly affected the Commons. To understand the reforms it is necessary to look briefly at the mid-century electoral system. MPs were chosen on the basis of a bewildering variety of franchises, whose details were so technical as sometimes even to elude the comprehension of ministers. To simplify, English MPs (there were slight differences in Wales and Scotland, greater ones in Ireland) sat for either *boroughs* or *counties*. The basic borough franchise was the ownership or occupation of premises worth £10 p.a. rent plus the payment of local property taxes (*rates*). Boroughs returned some two-thirds of all MPs. But though some rationalisation had been effected by the 1832 Reform Act, the distribution was basically the product of Tudor and Stuart history – with a corresponding bias towards small southern country towns often dominated by the local landed gentry. Virtually all other MPs sat for the more prestigious county constituencies; here the basic franchise was the traditional freehold ownership of land or premises worth forty shillings (£2) a year, to which the 1832 Act had added various other types of owners, and tenants of land or premises rented at £50 p.a. (mostly farmers). Everywhere voting was open, and confined to men; as today, a simple plurality of votes sufficed for election, but most constituencies then returned two members regardless of their enormous disparities in size. In any given constituency each voter had only as many votes as the constituency returned members. But one could vote in all the constituencies in which one had qualifications – Chamberlain had six votes in 1885 – subject to the important constraint that one could not vote in a county for a property that entitled one to a borough vote. Ownership of a borough property worth more than £2 and less than £10 p.a. would, however, confer a county vote; and such urban freeholders assumed considerable salience in discussion of the electoral system.

Elections could revolve around national issues. Public opinion did exist; it was clearly voiced in the elections of 1832 (in favour of parliamentary reform), probably in those that brought Peel to office in 1841, certainly in Palmerston's triumphs of 1857 and 1865; and both Wellington and Cobden thought Peel could have mobilised it by dissolving in 1846, though he preferred not to. But recent writers have preferred to focus on the equally influential mosaic of local forces and influences. A model has come into vogue that sees elections essentially as the struggle between local groups, the return of one's chosen candidate being the symbol of success and his subsequent behaviour at Westminster fairly unimportant. These groups would certainly cut across classes, though they might correspond closely to religious denomination. And they were frequently territorial in their incidence: of the South Lincolnshire parishes entirely owned by a single proprietor, three-quarters voted unanimously in 1841, over half in 1868 – while: 'In some of the [Lancashire] factory districts they vote by mills and wards in the spirit in which schoolboys play cricket or football by "houses" or "forms".' In such an environment people's politics were generally known, and electoral success was gained most simply by seeing that one's own supporters were placed on the electoral register while doing one's best to strike off one's opponents by showing that they lacked the requisite qualifications for the franchise. This was in fact the chief occupation of party organisers until well after the turn of the century; and it could be claimed that: 'In the long run, the party that gives the most regular, patient and systematic attention to the register will control the election.'

The parliamentary franchise, and the system of electoral registration, had been established by the 1832 Reform Act. A natural corollary had been the subsequent reform of local government, more especially by the Municipal Corporations Act, 1835, and the Poor Law Amendment Act, 1834. The former made municipal corporations elective; but the Whigs showed no disposition to deal with county government, which continued for another half-century to be run by the in practice self-selected justices of the peace (drawn mostly from the landed gentry). For the Poor Law, however, an elective machinery was set up, the Guardians being chosen by a heavily property-weighted franchise. By the 1860s neither county government nor the administration of the Poor Law was particularly controversial. But changes in the parliamentary franchise might, and by the end of our period did, entail their alteration.

II

The 1832 Reform Act had been meant to prove permanent, and its chief framer, Lord John Russell, earned the nickname of 'Finality Jack' by insisting on this. But by 1848 he had come round to the view that, though further reform might bring on revolution, in the long run inaction certainly would. Next year, in the belief that the best time was when the country was quiet, he began to press reform on his Cabinet, then in 1851 took advantage of an awkward parliamentary situation to promise, without prior consultation, to bring in a government measure. Palmerston ensured (by destroying the government) that it got nowhere, but Russell had succeeded in re-establishing parliamentary reform on the political agenda. Official measures were introduced in 1854, 1859 and 1860 – that of 1859 being noteworthy as coming from the Conservatives, who recognised dangers in appearing hostile to progress and saw no reason why they should not improve an electoral system they regarded as rigged against them. Liberals could not allow this and voted the Bill down: but in the reconciliation that followed the subsequent election, Palmerston had to concede to Russell the right to bring in another measure. Perhaps, though, it now looked too much as if something might really happen, and substantial opposition emerged within the Liberal parliamentary party. So the issue was postponed, at first temporarily, but soon by tacit consent for the remainder of Palmerston's life.

On Palmerston's death Russell took over, fully committed to reform and strongly backed by Gladstone. But in 1866 his Bill was overcome by hostile amendments in the Commons and he resigned. Two points have a bearing on subsequent developments. First, Russell had extreme difficulty in settling on his course of action. His initial impulse was to have a lengthy Commission of Enquiry to appease his more reluctant supporters and acquire statistical knowledge. When he could not construct an administration on this basis, he promised an immediate measure; the government then dithered between a £6 rating and a £7 rental franchise for so long that at least one copy of the Bill was printed and published with the wrong figures. Secondly, the government had not wanted to combine the enfranchisement of electors with the redistribution of seats; but it was compelled to do so, and the result was a hastily scrambled measure.

Actually Russell's Bill was a moderate one, but it still proved too much for the Commons where the opponents of 'democracy' had a field day. Lowe, in particular, secured oratorical triumphs at the cost of insulting the unenfranchised:

> If you want venality, if you want ignorance, if you want drunkenness and facility for being intimidated. . . . Do you go to the top or the bottom?

There would, no doubt, have been protests against the rejection of the 1866 Reform Bill in any case. But such rhetoric added fuel to the flames, and was warmly denounced that autumn by major demonstrations throughout the great northern cities.

1867 brought a settlement. The Conservatives had intended to buy time by proposing only abstract resolutions in the Commons, followed by a Royal Commission to gather information for a definitive measure; in particular it was to look at the new idea of a householders' suffrage (in the boroughs) off-set by extra votes for those possessed of property or education. The Liberal opposition seemed impatient, and Disraeli suddenly promised to bring in a Bill at once. The discovery of defects in his arithmetic enabled diehards in the Cabinet to swing the government back to proposing a £6 rating franchise (which would have been slightly more restrictive than Russell's £7 rental one). But this was badly received and soon reversed by a Conservative backbench revolt (probably abetted by Disraeli). Cranborne and other diehards resigned, but did not succeed in destroying the government. This then proceeded on the basis of a nominal household suffrage, limited by two provisions adapted from municipal corporations' elections – viz. that only those who had resided for two years and paid their rates *in person* should qualify for the vote – and also by introducing dual voting for the better off. However, as the measure went through the Commons, these safeguards were successively defeated or dropped. And the House that in 1866 had declined to add 200,000 to the English borough electorate found itself adding 700,000 (or nearly 140 per cent).

Few historians would wish to plump for a single cause of this *volte face*. But four types of explanation can be isolated.

First, the British working class 'had attained precisely that level of development at which it was safe to concede enfranchisement and dangerous to withhold it.' 'It was surely the presence of the Reform League which stopped the players crying off' in 1867 'as they had done so often in the past'. In particular the League's 6 May 1867 defiance of a ban on holding a meeting in Hyde Park placed the government in a position where it could prevent them only by military force. In the short run this would have been quite feasible. But it would have broken the unwritten social contract whereby British radicals were reformers not revolutionaries while the upper classes governed, in Gladstone's words, by 'good will' rather than force or fraud. Finding themselves in such an untenable position, in May government and Parliament rapidly dropped the safeguards that had recently seemed so vital, and finished up with a simple household (and lodger) franchise. (Royden Harrison, *Before the Socialists* (1965) pp. 132, 133 and Chap. III.)

Second, external agitation (especially in late 1866) may well

have convinced most politicians that the reform question would
have to be settled but did not determine the nature of the
settlement. What did was a combination of the Conservatives'
minority position in the Commons, which forced them to
accept any amendment on which they did not think they could
split the Liberals; the extreme complexity of the subject once
one went beyond first principles; and the mixture of
incompetence, exasperated impatience, and general levity to
which government and Parliament were alike reduced by these
difficulties. Lord Derby initially suggested household suffrage
as a *delaying* tactic: 'Of all possible Hares to start I do not know
a better'. Disraeli then inexplicably promised immediate
legislation. Nevertheless the combination of household suffrage
and full personal payment of rates appeared ideal. Household
suffrage would outbid the Liberals and settle the agitation by
giving it what it demanded. Personal payment of rates was
desirable in principle. But its chief recommendation was that
most occupiers of the cheaper urban houses did *not* pay rates
directly: landlords 'compounded' with the local authorities,
recouping themselves indirectly through the rent; so most
householders (occupiers) would not in fact be entitled to vote.
Alas, things were not so simple. £10 householders whose
landlords had compounded were already enfranchised; so their
rights had to be preserved, which destroyed the principle of
personal payment and introduced an anomaly as between the
old and the prospective new voters. Then the incidence of
compounding was so arbitrary that some streets would have
had a wide, others a narrow, franchise. Neither could one
always determine from the ratebooks who had and who had not
paid personally. And though nobody much minded using the
force of inertia to keep the electorate small, people agonised
over the problem of the enthusiastic householder who wished,
although a 'compounder', personally to tender payment of
rates and vote. The simplest solution was to draw a fixed line,
say at £5 rental, and demand that all occupiers above it pay
their rates personally, while all below should 'compound' and
so not come on to the electoral register. But this was
Gladstone's scheme, so Disraeli could not accept it. Instead he
suddenly adopted Hodgkinson's amendment – which he could
probably have defeated – abolishing compounding altogether.

This saved the principle of personal payment of rates, but made the enfranchisement far greater than had originally been intended. (F. B. Smith, *The Making of the Second Reform Bill* (1966); Robert Blake, *Disraeli* (1966), Chap. XXI.)

Third, Maurice Cowling starts from the assumption that politics is simply a matter of jockeying for position by parliamentary leaders for whom proposals and policies are only weapons. All players were alike, but Disraeli was the most skilled. He could not know in advance which part of the Liberal majority he 'would be able most successfully to detach'. Initially, he sought to draw off Adullamite support,[1] and to construct a 'Cave/Conservative combination' that would disrupt the Liberal Party and hopefully enable the Conservatives to fight a general election as defenders of the constitution. Cranborne's refusal to go along with these tactics, and the Cave's temporary return to Gladstone, forced Disraeli 'to shift from one line of policy to another' and seek to detach Radicals as well. Cranborne's failure effectively to organise resistance was one condition for Disraeli's final success; another was 'loss of confidence in Gladstone's leadership and fear of a runaway public agitation' which 'drove Adullamites and Liberals back into his arms at the same time as the Radicals began to respond to him also.' (*1867, Disraeli, Gladstone and Revolution* (Cambridge, 1967), esp. pp. 302, 311–12.)

This interpretation is based on a detailed examination of the speeches and writings of the politicians of the day, but also on a distinct scepticism as to whether these always mean what they say – after all politicians sought to deceive each other, so they may also have deceived us. This bears particularly on Disraeli's behaviour, which was clearly not straightforward – thus he officially opposed Laing's first redistribution amendment but actually urged his backbenchers to vote it through. And though Cowling is sure Disraeli could not have planned the outcome in advance, his approach leaves more scope for believing part at least of Disraeli's own retrospective interpretation – that he deliberately 'educated' his party to what he had come to see as necessary – than does Smith's view that Disraeli was at the mercy of the technicalities of rating and of his minority position in Parliament. Thus the written evidence clearly shows that it was Derby, not Disraeli, who first proposed household suffrage in December 1866. But the idea was in the air, and Disraeli was as likely as Derby to be aware of its Conservative advocates. Perhaps, as Cowling half-suggests (pp. 326–7), he was following the technique of surfacing his more daring schemes through other and sounder people.

Fourth, perhaps we devote too much attention to the level of the borough franchise. In 1867 the Cabinet certainly played the numbers game: each £1 drop in the rental qualification was supposed to swell the electoral register by about 70,000 people. But the sums involved were not large, £6 p.a. rental meant about 11½p. per week, £7 p.a., 13½p; the average urban working-class cottage already cost more, and rents were rising steadily. D. C. Moore does not dispute that contemporaries focused chiefly on the level of the urban franchise, but he prefers another perspective. Liberals:

> were almost inevitably compelled to urge the removal of those limitations which initially hedged the proposal of household suffrage. Indeed, their relative concern for these limitations [and unconcern for other important parts of the Bill] would almost lead one to conclude that these limitations had been placed on the Bill to divert the Liberals' attention [from its provisions for 'redistribution' and electoral geometry].

> (*The Politics of Deference*, pp. 387–8 and Chap. IX)

Redistribution had two aspects, the transfer of seats from some constituencies to others, and Moore's chief concern, the transfer of voters from county to other constituencies. Any legislation would necessarily proceed on the basis of taking seats from small borough constituencies and dividing them between growing towns and the larger counties. But the details were traditionally settled in a partisan fashion, the Liberal Bill of 1866 being no exception. If reform had to come, therefore, it was well worth the Tories' while ensuring that *they* passed it. In fact, their disfranchisements were, on party-political criteria, remarkably even-handed; and they were only slightly more prone than the Liberals to assign the seats thus vacated to counties rather than large boroughs. But whereas Liberals were concerned to preserve the rights of urban voters to vote in county constituencies, Conservatives sought to corral them in boroughs. Their aim, an opponent charged, was 'to take away voters from the country and place them in the towns, thus eliminating [from the county constituencies] the town voters who were really the Liberal voters'. The 1866 Liberal Bill would have inhibited the expansion of borough boundaries *and* preserved the right of everybody currently possessed of a vote to exercise it for the rest of his life; the 1867 Act ensured that premises entitling *anybody* (owner or occupier) to a borough vote could *not* confer a county one, so that urban enfranchisement *reduced* the county electorate. (The Conservatives also sought to redraw borough boundaries to incorporate actual or potential overspill, but in 1868 a last-minute parliamentary revolt rejected the schemes for the fifteen largest boroughs.)

The net effect is not easy to quantify. But the creation of new parliamentary boroughs and the redrawing of some existing borough boundaries perhaps removed from English county constituencies some 100,000 voters.[2] Still the phenomenon of borough residents entitled to county votes was not eliminated – they seem to have been at least as numerous (*c.* 110,000) in 1884 as in 1865. Rather clearer is the party-political effect of Disraeli's redrawing of English constituency boundaries, a net Tory gain of 22 seats – though we cannot, of course, be sure how much of this was due to the boundary changes, how much to enfranchisement, and how much to the electoral issues.

Some aspects of these approaches to the Second Reform Act are controversial: few people ascribe as much importance as Royden Harrison to the Reform League's May 1867 Hyde Park meeting, while Moore underplays the importance many Tories attached to the small boroughs. But most of the views reproduced here are compatible. There was a widespread feeling in 1867 that some reform could no longer be safely delayed and that it would therefore be wise to enact a measure large enough to prove durable – larger, that is, than most of the political class would ideally have wished. But the details of that measure depended on the interplay of forces within Parliament. The Conservative Cabinet went for 'household suffrage' in the hope that it would prove durable, but initially only in the belief that it could be largely off-set by other safeguards. Once committed, they pressed on despite the collapse of many of these safeguards. This collapse was due partly to governmental incompetence (though, to judge by the previous Russell administration, no more than was par for the course), and partly to the inherent complexity of the rating system to which the electoral register was inevitably tied. But some, though not all, of what Smith sees as irresponsible incompetence may have been skilful and deliberate manoeuvring by Disraeli, as described by Cowling. And, as Moore reminds us, one of the rewards of passing a Bill, any Bill, was that the details of redistribution would be biased in a Conservative not a Liberal direction; here Disraeli did not get all he wanted, but he was able to work the legal technicalities in his favour.

Less commonly underlined is that, though the borough provisions of the 1867 Reform Act went far further than had originally been intended, they were remarkably successful in securing what Carnarvon once called 'a ledge on which to rest'. Nobody then in Parliament wished to extend the franchise down beyond the respectable working class, however defined, to the 'residuum'; and even the Reform League was prepared (unlike its Chartist predecessors) to restrict its demands to household suffrage plus a token facility for superior lodgers. Disraeli had to concede a lodger franchise, but at a level (£10 rateable value, equivalent to nearly £15 p.a. rental) so high and subject to so many other conditions of registration that it never amounted to much in practice. Effectively, therefore, the borough franchise was household, *not* manhood. To exercise it one needed prior residence: the government had initially wanted two years' residence; and though it was forced to reduce this to one, the electoral register did not come into force until six months after compilation, so the minimum residence necessary before voting was really eighteen months, the average apparently twenty-five. But some 20–30 per cent of the potential electorate are supposed each year to have moved across constituency boundaries in the boroughs *c.* 1900, some 5 per cent across county constituency boundaries. The effect was to deny even many householders the vote. Probably the best guess is that in 1911, 59 per cent of the UK adult male population had the vote – distinctly more in the counties, rather fewer in the boroughs. The exclusion of the remainder may have been important; some historians claim that it was their enfranchisement in 1918 that enabled the Labour Party to break through to displace the Liberals. But it gave rise to virtually no protest; what *did* eventually bring the resumption of extra-parliamentary agitation was the continued total disfranchisement of women (which had indeed been debated in parliament in 1867 and 1884, but not very seriously). As far as the borough franchise is concerned, then, the politicians of 1867 secured some 40 years of quiet, 50 years of stability. They were, as we shall see shortly, less successful in their attempt to draw a firm line between household suffrage in the boroughs and a more restrictive and rural franchise in the counties.

But before discussing the collapse of this attempt we must first look at two important changes in the manner of voting and campaigning: the advent of the secret ballot in 1872 and the Corrupt Practices Act, 1883. In the 1859 general election as many as 60 per cent of MPs had been returned unopposed. In 1865 the figure fell to 48 per cent. And the changes in constituency and electorate effected by the Second Reform Act, plus the controversial election issue of Irish Disestablishment, further reduced it in 1868 to 33 per cent. More contests meant greater opportunity for disturbance; and the management of an expanded electorate entailed more bribery – 22 successful petitions, as against 13 in 1865 – and possibly more coercion. Also in parts of rural Wales a challenge to the establishment Anglican gentry, detectable since 1859, now for the first time succeeded at the polls; some landlords responded by evicting tenant farmers who had voted the wrong way.

Experience of the 1868 election converted many people to the secret ballot, and one of the first acts of the new government was to establish a Select Committee to look into the conduct of elections; in due course it recommended the ballot, albeit lukewarmly. Building on this, perhaps also seeking to console advanced Liberals for disappointments elsewhere, the government introduced legislation in 1871. But a filibuster by Conservative backbenchers so delayed the measure that the House of Lords could reject it for want of time. There is no sign that the question excited the country; but the Bill was reintroduced in 1872 and seemed likely to precipitate a clash between the two Houses of Parliament. (It encountered four main objections: the vote was a trust to be exercised openly; the ballot would diminish the 'legimate influence' of character and social station; its introduction was only the precursor to the reopening of the whole franchise question; and, though it would have little effect in England, the ballot would produce a majority of Irish MPs pledged to secession. Also, doubt was expressed as to whether the secrecy of the ballot would not *encourage* bribery by making it harder to detect.) Eventually independent Conservative peers prevented their leaders from making the secret ballot optional (as it is today in Russia), and the Commons accepted that it be introduced for an experimental period only. Actually the new system worked very smoothly and, together with the simultaneous abolition of the traditional public nomination of candidates, greatly reduced the rowdiness accompanying electoral contests.

It is less clear how far the ballot reduced bribery: for one might still be confident that the bribed would keep their contracts even under conditions of secrecy. The number of electoral petitions did fall from the 1865-8 level, but 10 were successful in 1874, 16 in 1880. The real watershed is the Corrupt Practices Act, 1883. This was fairly uncontroversial: after all, where corruption prevailed, it was MPs who had to foot the bill; and (morality apart) they were worried that the continued increase in the number of contests, and the foreseeable expansion in the size of constituencies, would increase even the legitimate costs of representing them, which have been put, for this period, at an average of £850 p.a. for county and £423 p.a. for borough constituencies. There had, of course, been earlier legislation. But the 1883 Act was so drafted as to make it an offence for anybody other than the candidate's agent to incur expenses during a contest, to insist on a full declaration of authorised expenses, and to impose a ceiling. Breach of these conditions invalidated the election and therefore was to be detected on one's opponents' part, avoided on one's own. A second factor restricting corruption was the very widespread redistribution of constituencies in 1885; for in some seats bribery had become a long-standing tradition, even a minor economic resource, and their disappearance (whether through penal disfranchisement or redistribution) facilitated the emergence of a more sober political future. This is, of course, not to say that money suddenly ceased to be a recommendation.[3] But whereas the four elections before 1883 had occasioned 61 successful election petitions, the next four produced only 9. And the limitation of election spending (most of which was then local, not central) has in the long run proved one of the factors making British politics, by international standards, remarkably cheap.

The Second Reform Act, as we saw above, adopted household suffrage in the boroughs but a more restrictive one (£12 p.a. occupation, plus various ownership provisions), in the counties. This dichotomy seemed quite acceptable even to radicals like John Bright. For the general Liberal assumption was that the rural population was hopelessly apathetic, and that were it enfranchised, it would only vote for the landlords. However, in the early 1870s Northumberland and Durham miners, most of whom lived in county constituencies, started demonstrating for the vote; they campaigned enthusiastically for the Liberals at the 1874 general election, and their leader, Thomas Burt, took over the representation of Morpeth (a borough they numerically dominated) on the retirement of a long-serving Whig. Meanwhile large agricultural labourers' trades unions had grown up in southern England, with the franchise as an important demand. Finally the Liberal defeat in 1874 may have removed inhibitions about reopening the question. G. O. Trevelyan started to produce annual motions for the assimilation of the county to the borough franchise; in 1877–8 he was endorsed by the Liberals' leader, Lord Hartington, and virtually all the parliamentary party; and in 1880 G. J. Goschen refused to serve in the new Liberal Cabinet because of his opposition to county franchise extension. The only questions now related to timing, the relationship between franchise extension and redistribution of seats, and the treatment of Ireland – should the Irish county franchise be extended *pari passu* with the British, and should Ireland's parliamentary over-representation (in relation to its population) be reduced?

Ireland was in fact rather generously treated. Its county franchise had differed from the English ever since 1829. But the view prevailed that to refuse Ireland what was granted to

Britain would be unjust and counter-productive. On the number of MPs, however, equal treatment was not followed. Scotland's representation was increased by 12 to reflect its growing population and wealth, but Ireland's was not reduced. One might have expected otherwise. For Parnell had calculated in 1882, as a Conservative later reminded the House, that under the existing franchise he would win 65 to 70 seats. But to 'secure National Self-Government' he needed 80–90 MPs, which he could not hope for except on 'the basis of county suffrage'.

The chief Cabinet opponent of so liberal a treatment was Hartington, Gladstone's presumptive successor. Probably he allowed himself to be over-ridden because he attached more importance to the relationship between franchise and redistribution in England, and because he was convinced by Gladstone's strong assertion 'of the utter impossibility of the English and Scotch majority assenting to the legislative separation of the two countries'. Other ministers were impressed by the progress the Irish National League was already making by 'working' the existing electoral register, or even hopeful that a lowering of the franchise from tenant farmers to agricultural labourers would cause problems for Parnell. Gladstone was also able to produce a cloud of arguments against reducing Ireland's parliamentary representation.[4] More surprising is that the Conservatives did not press the matter strongly. The chief advocate of a firm line was Sir Stafford Northcote, who was deliberately pushed aside by Lord Salisbury in his orchestration of Conservative tactics. Salisbury himself may have been looking to destroy the government with the aid of Parnellite MPs; like Hartington, he certainly ascribed more importance to the nature of English redistribution.

Salisbury seems to have had two alternative policies, to force an election or to negotiate a compromise. He would have preferred an election, and had been trying to use the Conservative majority in the House of Lords to force one ever since he took over its leadership from Disraeli. For he believed a new Parliament would be 'more nearly balanced', whereas the existing one would so frame a reform bill 'as to *secure* the mass of electoral power to the party which is now dominant'. But

Salisbury's colleagues had been too wise, or too timid, to go to such lengths. Parliamentary reform provided more respectable ground on which to take a stand. As Disraeli had observed in 1880, if the government combined franchise and redistribution in one Bill, it would be too large to pass (as legislation must) in a single parliamentary session; but if the two topics were separated the Lords could seize on this as an excuse to throw out the franchise. In 1884 Gladstone's government, like Russell's in 1866, sought first to pass a simple Franchise Bill and only then to proceed to the more difficult question of redistribution. Russell's attempt had been defeated in the Commons; this time the Commons accepted the Franchise Bill, but the Lords declined to consider it until it was accompanied by a redistribution measure. Salisbury wrote that he hoped this would bring on an election, and much of the Cabinet privately sympathised with his fears and wished to oblige.

Gladstone and the majority, however, thought such a forced dissolution would establish a most unfortunate precedent and raise grave constitutional issues. Instead they sought first to intimidate the Lords by prompting a plethora of public demonstrations on the theme of 'mend them or end them', then to strike a compromise in the autumn. Gladstone did so the more readily because, while he disliked being crossed, his intended redistribution was not extreme and he had already promised Hartington to stay on in office to see it safely through before the next election. In October Salisbury publicly edged towards a compromise, acceptance of enfranchisement in exchange for satisfactory redistribution. Much sparring followed, but the upshot was an agreed redistribution, negotiated in outline between the party leaders and implemented by genuinely bypartisan Boundary Commissioners. This constituted a marked departure from earlier behaviour, and it set a precedent for the treatment of redistribution after subsequent Franchise Acts. Indeed considerations of electoral geometry largely subsided below the surface of ordinary political consciousness, at least until the later 1960s.

The 1885 redistribution constituted an important watershed in other ways too. Ever since Derby and Disraeli had sold the pass on the borough franchise, Salisbury (or Cranborne as he then was) had concentrated on the protection of the minority. In 1867 he had contended that the change had ruined the value of the small boroughs; instead of conserving these, third seats should be given to the large towns, with each elector limited to two votes so as to afford representation to a minority that would consist of 'the more intelligent classes'. Such a system of minority representation was actually introduced into the Bill by the House of Lords. Since it extended also to some counties, it benefited the Liberals. But they (and more especially Chamberlain, whose Birmingham seat it endangered) disliked it. And though Salisbury was still theoretically attracted, in 1884 he pushed instead for single-member constituencies (which Randolph Churchill termed 'the only working form of minority representation'). If delineated 'with special regard . . . to the pursuits of the population', these would both permit the representation of the new suburban 'Villa Toryism' and make easier the traditional Conservative goal of dividing town from country. They would also please Tory MPs who were apprehensive of the likely costs of representing county seats under a household franchise that would demand the cultivation of every village in the constituency; the smaller the area the easier the old amateur country-gentleman class would find things. Liberals did not like single-member constituencies; but they accepted them as the norm in exchange for concessions over Ireland, extra members for Scotland, and extra seats for the conurbations. Providing these extra seats meant more disfranchisement of small boroughs; and though the outcome was not the dreaded equal electoral districts, it did represent a considerable step towards them: the largest electorate was now 8, not 250, times the smallest, the usual spread much less.

The choice of single-member constituencies to secure minority representation may seem ironic, as we now usually seek this end by abandoning the 'simple plurality' (or 'first-past-the-post') method of translating votes into seats. Even in the mid-nineteenth century 'simple plurality' had its critics, but they did not serve their cause well. The unfortunately-named Hare floated a quite impracticable scheme of voluntary constituencies on a national basis; unsurprisingly the 1867 Parliament preferred to experiment with the limited vote in three-member constituencies; this sought to confirm in law arrangements that had often operated in practice to preserve 'the peace of the county' by according some minority representation. Experience between 1868 and 1880 discredited the limited vote, though perhaps unjustly. Equally unfortunate was the cumulative vote,[5] introduced in 1870 for School Board elections. Again this worked quite reasonably in the long run, but its reputation never recovered from the initial débâcle in Birmingham where the anti-clerical majority ran too many candidates and so lost the first elections. No other PR devices for *minority* representation had really penetrated politicians' consciousness. PR was pressed chiefly as a safeguard for moderate opinion in Ireland; but Gladstone was determined to make no concessions, while Sir Charles Dilke argued the incongruity of introducing minority representation there but at the same time eliminating it in Great Britain. So simple plurality it was, in single-member seats. And this is not an easy system to adapt. One cannot proportionally divide units of a single member, but only (at most) adopt the alternative vote. This was admittedly pushed strongly in 1917–18 at the time of the next franchise extension, and nearly enacted as a result of the 1930–1 Lib/Lab pact. But the 1884–5 solution did much to settle elections into a mould that has, so far, proved very difficult to break.

The First Reform Act of 1832 had been followed by reform of municipal corporations and the Poor Law. The Second led to consequential legislation on the municipal franchise. Everybody agreed that the Third Reform Act would be followed by a recasting of county government. This would bear directly on the role of the landed gentry, whose continued involvement in local affairs most politicians, Liberal as well as Conservative, wished to secure if at all decently possible. As late as 1881 the Liberal Cabinet had inclined towards the *ex officio* representation of JPs on the reformed authorities; but had the Liberals had the handling of the matter after 1885, they would certainly have opted for purely elective councils. The Conservatives agonised more, but came to the same conclusion: direct election on the new parliamentary franchise was the only politically acceptable solution, though the landed gentry's position might be indirectly buttressed in a number of ways. Legislation along these lines went through for Great

Britain in 1888–9 and Ireland in 1898. In most of England and Scotland the effect was slight; those previously active in county business proved surprisingly popular and either themselves won election to the new authorities or were co-opted as aldermen by those who had. But the London County Council was initially controlled by left Liberals until the area's natural Conservative majority was mobilised in 1907. And in Wales and Ireland the landed gentry were largely pushed aside. Salisbury had been resigned to worse. What he had not been willing to touch was the system of property-weighted voting for the Poor Law Guardians, on the grounds that to have the potential recipients of relief elect them would be 'rather like leaving the cat in charge of the cream jug'. In 1894 the Liberals did just this. The immediate results were slight – the Victorian lower classes were much less prone to vote themselves money at the expense of the rich than Salisbury's rather mechanical analysis of self-interest led him to anticipate. But in the long run *some* Boards of Guardians (notably Poplar in East London) did follow a policy of relief regardless of cost, and attempts to control them underlay the next major reform of local government in 1929.

We have now recounted the advent of household suffrage as the basic franchise throughout the UK, and also the move in 1885 from a constituency distribution based on tradition and a wish to represent 'interests' to one based (albeit loosely) on *numbers*. Explanations of these changes tend to be rather insular – agitation outside Parliament, shifts in the climate of opinion, politicians' aims and interests, and the not inconsiderable problem of drafting coherent legislation. There were, of course, wider forces at work; indeed there was a general European tendency towards the extension of the franchise and the diffusion of political activity. This took very different forms in different countries, but only Russia stood resolutely against the general trend (with ultimately disastrous results). Contemporaries could not deploy so broad a perspective. But even they did not operate in a vacuum. The American Civil War had occasioned much hardship in Lancashire; and the restraint with which this was borne convinced politicians like Gladstone, and possibly Derby, both that the Lancashire operatives were morally fit for the franchise and that it could be safely entrusted to them. Neither were MPs unaware of developments overseas: the Australian experience, in particular, was much debated in 1866–7. But this does not seem to have converted people, merely to have furnished arguments for positions they already held. Neither was there any conscious adoption of parliamentary reform for the sake of keeping up with other countries. In the 1850s and 1860s when reform first returned to the political agenda, no major European country was as far advanced as the UK along the road to popularly elected representative government, while conditions in America and Australia were thought to be largely *sui generis*. In the 1870s France overtook Britain, with government responsible to a chamber elected on the basis of *manhood* suffrage (albeit with unequal electoral districts and an imperfectly secret ballot). But the demand of British reformers was not to keep pace with France, only that the *household* suffrage of the boroughs be extended to the counties. Politicians *were* insular.

III

At the time of the Second Reform Act there was talk of a journey into the unknown, of 'shooting Niagara'. But one cannot point to any fundamental changes in British politics that resulted solely and directly from the electoral reforms discussed above. Even Lowe did not expect immediate consequences; it was, he said, natural for county MPs to worry more about the cattle plague than about the Reform Bill since the former threatened to ruin them, the latter only their children. And certainly the extra-parliamentary agitation of the Reform League allowed itself with remarkable docility to be absorbed into support for Gladstone at the 1868 elections.[6] Gladstone's 1868–74 government may in some respects have been disillusioning. If so, disillusion was contained by Joseph Chamberlain, one of whose chief political aims was to prevent the ultimate emergence of an independent and anti-capitalist working class by enrolling the politically active in a new radicalism firmly controlled by himself and his provincial middle-class allies. And the Liberal coalition was soon restored by Gladstone's re-emergence first to take charge of the anti-Turkish agitation and then to mount his celebrated Midlothian public-speaking campaign against Disraeli.

That 'working-class' urban radicals were content with such a subordinate role says a lot about their attitude to the franchise. Earlier in the century demands for parliamentary reform had often been instrumental, the direct product of economic difficulties and depressions. These the new *laissez-faire* House of Commons was no longer prepared to alleviate (or let JPs alleviate) in the traditional way by controlling prices and earnings. Therefore radicals felt that it must be corrupt and its reform a prelude to all improvement. It would be too much to say that 'working-class' organisations ever fully accepted classical Liberal economics. But by the 1860s they did not look for state intervention on their own behalf; if anything they wanted the state (which they saw as aristocratic, hence expensive) off their backs. (Trade unionists, in particular, wanted an end to the legal regulation of industrial relations as being inevitably biased in favour of the employers.) Many working-class leaders had already assimilated to the advanced Liberals, working for them at elections as 'non-voters' and being rewarded by middle-class acceptance and advocacy of their right to vote. This right they valued – as, probably, did the last major West European group to be enfranchised, Swiss women in the 1960s and 1970s – not as a tool to enable a new majority to force through fundamental changes in society, but as a recognition of their intrinsic worth and 'respectability'.

'Working-class' organisations were not, of course, necessarily politically progressive. Easily the largest were the friendly societies, which provided social insurance through self-help, and which mostly chose for themselves monarchist, loyal and patriotic names. *Much* smaller were their offshoot, the trades unions. But a section of these can be viewed as providing the cutting edge of working-class political activism. Gladstone would not make major concessions to their demands for improved legal status. In 1875 Disraeli outbid him, only to find that the removal of this source of friction enabled the unions to settle back smoothly into a Lib/Lab alliance. Similarly Disraeli thought it helpful, in and after 1872, to stress sanitary reform (on which Conservatives were slightly more progressive than

Liberals). That he should have done so is interesting: but the bid for the allegiance of the newly enfranchised urban classes, if such it was, can only be regarded as a small one, less important than his simultaneous attempt to pick up middle-class ex-Liberals now alienated by Gladstonian activism.

The county voters enfranchised in 1884–5 were rather more deliberately targeted. Chamberlain was told that the question that aroused them: 'is the land. The labourers will vote for the party which they think will better their condition – it is a matter with them not of sentiment but of bread and cheese.' As a hitherto urban leader, he now sought to broaden his base by cultivating rural support, pitching strongly for allotments and smallholdings in the Radical Programme and establishing connections with the Scottish crofters' movement. In and after 1886 the Conservatives, for their part, legislated in this direction, while Chamberlain (who had moved towards them as a result of home rule) had a protégé establish a 'Rural Labourers League' to work the counties in their interest. Liberals naturally denounced Conservative legislation as a sham; and both sides went into the 1892 elections supported by propaganda conferences on the English rural question. I myself think this competition did stimulate the provision of rural allotments (though not smallholdings). But it was not anything like as central to politics as the issues that headed the Liberal programme, Irish home rule and Welsh disestablishment.[7]

It is in Ireland that one would expect electoral changes to have their greatest effect – by aligning the *pays légale* more closely with the *pays réel*. Indeed it used to be thought that the advent of the secret ballot 'had revolutionary consequences' there; without it the whole of Parnell's 'meteoric career . . . might never have occurred'. More recently it has been argued that nationalists were quite capable of winning elections under open voting – cf. the Fenian dynamiter O'Donovan Rossa's 1869 return for County Tipperary – and that the advent of the ballot may even had protected anti-nationalist voters against popular pressure.[8] Theodore Hoppen takes a longer view. Before 1850, rating and registration peculiarities had produced an electorate that varied wildly and capriciously from one seat to another, no group being 'sufficiently powerful to provide a reliable constituency. . . . Out of such disparate forces even

O'Connell had not been able to fashion . . . cohesion.' 1850 saw the rationalisation of the franchise, the product partly of a reaction to the Famine and partly of a systematic revision of the rating system; its major component was now the middling farmers. There were no immediate effects, the 1850s and 1860s being marked by localism and a revival of landlord power. But:

> it was precisely this kind of electorate – compact, [increasingly well off and] politically aware, shorn . . . of the most bribable, . . fickle, and . . . subservient, slowly expanding but still a recognizable elite – which gave particular prominence to those elements most likely to respond with enthusiasm and steadiness to the campaigns of the 1870s and 1880s.

These campaigns, and notably the 'New Departure's' fusion of agrarian and national discontent, enabled Parnell to achieve: 'During the four years after 1880 . . . a real control over Irish politics, and the by-election victories of this period show that franchise changes were not a necessary prerequisite for success' as they ante-date the 1885 reforms. Politicians had, indeed, been unsure in 1884 whether the extension of the Irish electorate (from 200,000 to 700,000) would help or hinder Parnell. Clearly it did not hinder him – the Land League appears to have gained support from labourers as well as from the more numerous farmers. But it seems the 1885 reforms were only really important in the north. Here, D. C. Savage contends: 'The enfranchisement of the agricultural labourer provided the basis for both a conservative and a nationalist resurgence in Ulster. The Liberals were too committed to the tenant farmers, too narrowly based, and were submerged in the new electorate' – though poor organisation and the defection of the Catholic vote also contributed greatly to their downfall.[9] The consequences of this division of Ireland between Nationalism and an increasingly populist and Orange Northern conservatism were immense, far greater than those that followed directly from any of the British electoral reforms we have examined. But, for the most part, they had other roots.

Turning now from the agenda to the style of politics, we may trace repercussions from our electoral reforms both at the constituency level and at Westminster. Even after the upheavals of the Second Reform Act one could seek to continue with the same style of electioneering. (After all many small constituencies survived – seats with an average 1881 electorate of 1311 returned almost exactly half the UK borough MPs.) Thus much of the increase in the English electorate between 1868 and 1874 is thought to represent the competitive efforts of the two parties to 'work' the register in the old style; and it was apparently worth reissuing E. W. Cox's election manual, written in 1847 and expanded in 1868, at frequent intervals until 1885. But the new environment also encouraged two more modern responses, machine politics and the proliferation of appeals to opinion by public speaking.

The normal mid-nineteenth-century electoral organisation consisted, between elections, of an informal committee of the MP/candidate and other large subscribers that hired a solicitor to 'work' the electoral register. During contests this expanded into a central committee to supervise his management of the campaign, supported (where appropriate) by ward committees and secretaries. Such organisation was both ephemeral and candidate-centred; candidates from the same political party were often also competitors and might find it desirable to maintain separate committees. But at times, especially in large cities, such *ad hoc* arrangements crystallised into more permanent structures, based on a central committee, ward committees that chose delegates, and occasional general meetings. The revival of party controversy, and of the parliamentary reform question, in the 1860s led to the formation or reformation of a number of such Liberal associations. That in Birmingham came to have two special characteristics. Its concern for detailed campaign management (admittedly the prime purpose of all associations) was heightened by the local determination to overcome the 1867 Reform Act's minority representation provisions and by the débâcle of the first School Board elections in the city. This detailed management of the Liberal electorate ('Vote as you are told'), together with its monopolisation of municipal employment and patronage, earned the association the title of the 'caucus'. The caucus was also the heir to a long local tradition of co-operation between middle- and working-class politicians to press for franchise extension. Its income, and ultimate control, lay with a few large subscribers; but anybody (elector or otherwise) prepared to pay a shilling a year could join and participate at all levels. The Birmingham caucus soon became famous and inspired imitators. And in 1877 Joseph Chamberlain amalgamated it with those of other English provincial centres (60 had joined by 1880) to form a 'National Liberal Federation' that would represent extra-parliamentary Liberal supporters while at the same time remaining under his own control. He then sought to use the NLF as a power-base for a political career at the highest level. It would generate demands for radical policies hitherto muffled by the aristocratic and Whig parliamentary party, ginger up back-sliding MPs, and (hopefully) restrict contests between rival Liberals, mobilise voters and win seats.

These ideas were overambitious. The NLF spoke only for a section (though perhaps a hitherto neglected section) of the party; some 'caucus' seats were actually lost in 1880; and Chamberlain's *bête noire*, W. E. Forster, managed to defy the Bradford caucus both then and in 1885. So the caucus's grip over both nominations and elections was much weaker than that achieved in 1885 by the National League in Ireland. Above all, when it came to the point over home rule in 1886, the NLF preferred to follow Gladstone, the official party leader, rather than its previous mentor, Chamberlain. Its offices then moved from Birmingham to London, where it merged with the Liberal Central Association to gain improved national coverage at the expense of becoming increasingly an adjunct of the party leadership. Chamberlain's unprecedented attempt to use the extra-parliamentary to conquer the parliamentary party had failed.

But his successes should not be underestimated. Throughout his career as a Liberal the caucus/NLF enjoyed a high political profile. In 1891, after Chamberlain's departure but at a time when Gladstone seemed to be losing momentum, the NLF re-emerged to wish on him, as a supplement to home rule, the 'Newcastle Programme'. This was a somewhat ill-advised collection of the demands of special interests (such as temperance) well represented in the party; as such it was badly received by the country at large and therefore did a good deal to discredit policy-making by conference. Nevertheless when in the next decade Chamberlain failed to win the Cabinet to tariff reform, he reverted to public campaigning and machine politics within the Conservative Party. This time he eventually brought the party, and thus its leader Balfour, over; only the electorate remained obdurate.

More generally the age was one of expanding party organisation. The NLF survived Chamberlain's defection, though in time its participatory element waned and it became increasingly a collection of notables. The breakaway Liberal Unionists automatically formed their own organisations. Neither were the Conservatives behind. After the Second Reform Act Conservative associations had come spontaneously into existence in a number of provincial cities, partly to provide social reassurance to a self-conscious minority, and partly to exclude interference in their elections from the party's parliamentary whips, whose ideas of campaigning tended to be archaic and rural. In the 1880s Lord Randolph Churchill sought to imitate Chamberlain and use them to further his own career. 1884 saw first a struggle over the National Union of Conservative Associations, then a compromise. Churchill entered the inner circle of party leadership; but the National Union accepted central control by the whips and principal agent (who soon became Salisbury's men). It did not wholly eschew policy – conferences often passed resolutions favouring tariffs – but, unlike the NLF, it did not aspire to coerce the party leadership and its associations concentrated on local electoral and propaganda activity. Building on them, Salisbury and his agent Middleton proceeded to fashion an electoral machine, serviced by professional provincial agents, that was distinctly more effective than its Liberal counterpart. It was aided by two types of satellite, Conservative Working Men's Clubs (whose amenities were largely alcoholic), and the Primrose League (originally founded as an organisation of Tory Democracy, but, after 1884, primarily a vehicle for the mobilisation of rural deference through social condescension and decorous entertainment). The League was remarkable for its enormous membership, over a million in 1891, and for the part *women* played in its activities.

If the refinement of party organisation was one way of

handling an expanded electorate, the proliferation of public speaking was another. The convention that a politician did not speak outside his own constituency had been steadily relaxed since 1832, but at the beginning of our period politicians still professed to regret the need to do so. Such professions were soon abandoned and political speeches in Parliament, or at great party meetings, came to dominate the media. In part the reason was technical – arrangements for syndicating the prepared texts to newspapers were much improved. It was, too, a verbose age with copious non-political speeches delivered at public occasions of all kinds. But political speeches did represent a new style in keeping with an electorate now often too large to be 'influenced' in the old ways, but which had come to follow politics as a spectator sport. The high point, perhaps, was Gladstone's 'Midlothian Campaign', which incorporated whistle-stop tours and torchlight processions: techniques deliberately borrowed from the United States. Their effectiveness is unclear. In Midlothian itself the contest was in fact determined by the older tactics of creating dependent ('faggot') voters. But the campaign appeared to have enormous influence in the country at large, and it re-established Gladstone as leader of the Liberal Party. Certainly no party could allow its opponents a monopoly of public speaking. The prominence this assumed served to focus attention on major politicians, and more especially on the party leaders. Politics was to a considerable extent represented as a duel, Gladstone against Disraeli, Gladstone against Salisbury. On occasion Salisbury was smothered in primroses by his admirers. And Liberals more consistently developed a cult of their 'Grand Old Man', organising excursions to his country seat and collecting chips from oaks he had felled. Accordingly Gladstone's eminence was such that most even of Chamberlain's section of the party decided to follow him when he suddenly declared for home rule – despite that policy's intrinsic unpopularity.

The penchant for public speaking, Gladstone's deliberate appeals to 'the people', to 'the masses against the classes' and his preference for concentrating at any one time on a single issue (such as Irish Church Disestablishment – 1868, or the abolition of income tax – 1874), encouraged the view that the funcion of elections was to put questions to the country to decide. And decide them in a sense it did, since most elections produced clear-cut results, often with large 'swings of the pendulum'.[10] One consequence was that the power of choosing the government began to pass from the House of Commons to the electorate. Disraeli acknowledged his 1868 general election defeat by resigning before he met Parliament, a novel precedent but one which was generally (though not invariably) followed. Also the frequency with which governments were brought down in Parliament started to diminish. Liberal administrations were still vulnerable: Gladstone offered his resignation after a parliamentary defeat in 1873 and resigned after one in 1885, as did Rosebery in 1895; Gladstone was also defeated over home rule in 1886 and forced to call an election. But Disraeli's 1874–80 and (with difficulty) Salisbury's 1886–92 governments lasted until without compulsion they chose their own moment for a dissolution; and since 1895 it has been most unusual, though not unknown, for a government to be brought down by parliamentary vote. Lastly, whereas in 1841–68 the same Parliament generally supported successive governments of opposed politics, after the Second Reform Act this became rare: the *only* peacetime examples come with Salisbury's caretaker government in 1885 and in the genuinely hung Parliament that resulted from the 1885 elections. Of course all this does *not* mean that the House of Commons suddenly became of no account. But party votes there, the exception in the mid-nineteenth century, became the norm after the home rule crisis.[11] And the truer it was that 'They've got to leave their brains outside/And vote just as their leaders tell them to', the more important the electoral process that determined the party makeup of the House in the first place.

For this process was itself becoming increasingly party-dominated. One illustration is the distinct divergences before the Third (and still more the Second) Reform Act in post-election estimates of MPs' party affiliations, and the much closer agreement reached on subsequent election results. Another is W. S. Gilbert's celebrated 1882 tag:

> That every boy and every gal,
> That's born into this world alive,
> Is either a little Liberal
> Or else a little Conservative.

Many of the explanations we have already encountered: the growth in the size of the electorate and, as a response, in political organisation and public speaking, and the destruction of old constituencies and 'corrupt' localist methods of campaigning, leaving a gap most easily filled on the basis of national party alignment. But this, of course, presupposes that there was a national cleavage on the basis of party. A sharp clash of issues between fairly evenly matched sets of politicians had already produced a two-party system once before, in the 1830s. Gladstone and Disraeli deliberately recreated it. Gladstone recovered from his 1866–7 discomfiture with remarkable verve to reunite the Liberals around the clerical issue (the abolition of church rates and the disestablishment of the Church of Ireland), win the 1868 election and preside over an activist government. By the 1860s the Conservatives were already recovering from their 1846 Corn Law split; Derby and Disraeli further established their credibility by settling the parliamentary reform question. And though Disraeli was initially routed in and after 1868, he rallied in 1872, capitalised on dissatisfaction with Gladstone's activism, won the 1874 election and, in his turn, went on to give Gladstone scope to attack 'Beaconsfieldism', blame it for the economic troubles of the late 1870s, and sweep back to office in 1880. Reform did not operate in a vacuum, and the new electoral systems were as much influenced by, as decisive of, the politics of the day.

All three of these trends, the return of divisive political issues, the growing strength of the Conservative Party, and the new tendency to see elections as an appeal to the people, combined to raise the question of the proper status of the other House of Parliament, the Lords. In 1868 Conservatives hoped to profit electorally from Gladstone's choice of Irish Church Disestablishment as the chief political issue. Unable to prevent him using the underlying Liberal majority to pass a preliminary bill through the Commons, they rejected it in the Lords on the grounds that the issues had 'yet to be presented to the country in the great appeal to its enlarged constituencies'. The Conservatives lost that appeal, and enough Conservative peers accepted this for the Disestablishment Bill to pass. Prominent among them was Lord Salisbury. But he made clear his view that the inherent prerogatives of the two Houses were equal, and that the Lords should only concede when they felt the Commons to 'represent the full, the deliberate, the substained convictions of the nation'. Later, over the Ballot Bill, he refined this position, suggesting that they yield 'only when the judgement of the nation has been challenged at the polls and decidedly expressed' (as, over the ballot, it had not). Salisbury thus evolved a coherent doctrine on which to rest the powers of the Upper House in an age that would not have accepted a simple claim from hierarchical status: the nation, not the Commons, was the master; the Lords might be better able to divine the nation's true wishes than a party-bound House of Commons ('servile to the minister, servile to the caucus'); and they were amply justified in referring questions to the considered judgement of the nation in a general election.

But the Lords would probably not have acted on this doctrine but for the new strength of the Conservative Party. They did not reject the Ballot Bill in 1872. After his electoral defeat of 1880, Disraeli was only prepared to fight on parliamentary reform, and on 'subjects of great national interest' where 'you will be supported by the sympathy of the great body of the people'. When Salisbury succeeded to the leadership he found himself unable to hold out and precipitate elections, though he did use the Lords to secure a compromise over constituency redistribution. In the early 1880s the Conservatives still saw themselves as the weaker party, liable to lose further ground with the predictable expansion of the county franchise. The home rule crisis and Salisbury's successful 1886–92 government changed this perception. And during the weak 1892–5 Liberal administrations the Lords felt much freer to use their powers.

Two further factors may have been relevant. After 1886 the Liberals had resorted to obstruction in the Commons, for a *major* party a novel and very effective parliamentary weapon; now they could be repaid with interest. And, since the Liberal Party was a coalition of minorities, many of their policies (especially those of the NLF's Newcastle Programme) were unpopular – which reinforced the Lords' claim to be the better interpreters of the national mood. Quite how assertive the Lords were is difficult to say; they certainly rejected home rule,[12] amended other measures, and reduced the government to a feeling of apathetic depression. But it was a Liberal interest to erect (as in Gladstone's celebrated retirement speech) an exaggerated myth of the Lords' obstructionism that historians have not examined closely. Be that as it may, the Lords' behaviour appeared to be retrospectively sanctioned by the crushing Conservative electoral victory of 1895. Following their next electoral defeat in 1906, the Conservatives reverted automatically to a similar policy. Their tactics (very much those of Peel in the later 1830s) worked well enough to begin with; but in rejecting the budget in 1909 they went too far, and forced a definite settlement of the constitutional relationship between the two Houses – a problem the later nineteenth-century franchise reforms had raised but not solved.

The Conservative recovery noted above poses the problem of the party-political effects of electoral reform. This can be briefly stated. At the time everybody expected the Liberals to gain from franchise extension, Conservatives hoping at best to limit the inevitable damage by their framing of reform measures. But *post hoc ergo propter hoc* argument might suggest that it was the Conservatives who actually benefited. Personally I would regard the direct party-political effects as limited. The 1868 elections certainly saw more contests and changes of seats than any since 1832. Both parties made important gains, some of which (like the Conservative breakthrough in Lancashire) may have been facilitated by enfranchisement or boundary changes. But the net effect in England (to which most attention had been devoted in the reform debates) was neutral, Conservative gains from the increased number of county constituencies off-setting Liberal ones in the boroughs. Gladstone's enhancement of Palmerston's 1865 majority came from the 'Celtic fringe': a net gain of about 20 in Ireland, which was almost untouched by the Second Reform Act but much influenced by his choice of election issue; of 15 in Scotland, where reform was of some importance (though chiefly by adding 7 seats to an already Liberal country); and of 7 in Wales, due more to a change in political mood already in evidence in 1865 than to the direct workings of the Act. In any case the important difference between Gladstone's administration and Russell's lay not in the size of Gladstone's majority but in his ability to use it for several years before it splintered.

The next election, 1874, saw the first Conservative majority since 1841. Psephologically the most interesting development was their gains in suburban (and especially south-eastern suburban areas).[13] This was largely unexpected – some observers had indeed forecast that parliamentary reform would be followed by a defection of moderate 'constitutional' Liberals, but Conservative tactics during the Bill's passage had aimed rather at insulating the counties from such urban or suburban voters. However, the 1874 swing was very broad: only Welsh boroughs and Ireland went the other way. It is natural to ascribe both this and the 1880 Liberal recovery chiefly to shifts in opinion. The 1885 elections after the Third Reform Act saw much change in detail, less in aggregate. Despite a generally unsuccessful administration and the failure to relieve General Gordon, the potential Liberal plus Irish majority fell only slightly. But the Irish were now an independent party who could, until Gladstone committed the Liberals to home rule, well have continued their tactical alliance with the Conservatives. In Wales there was no net change, in Scotland a further Liberal advance (though equal only to half that country's net gain in seats). In England the Liberal majority fell. Here franchise extension certainly helped them to some 96 gains in the counties (their first county majority since 1835). But in return the Conservatives gained their first post-1832 borough majority. This represented a continuation of the suburban turn to the right, which Salisbury had provided for in the redistribution negotiations, but also the appeal of protection ('Fair Trade') at a time of depression and the unpopularity with his own Nonconformist supporters of Chamberlain's advocacy of free education. On balance the immediate effects of the Third Reform Act probably benefited the Liberals. But their county victories proved more transient than Conservative gains in the boroughs; and they could certainly not afford the luxury of splitting in 1886.[14]

Of the broader working of the electoral system in our period

124   LATER VICTORIAN BRITAIN 1867–1900

much has naturally been written. Here we can do no more than
note that, where there were communities with really strong and
distinctive feelings, the electoral system permitted their
expression (though what happened at Westminster is another
matter). The obvious example is Ireland (which would have
been far easier to govern had it been a Crown Colony without
parliamentary representation). But it was true also in Wales
(and crofting Scotland) that *Trech gwlad nag arglwydd*, 'the land
is mightier than its lord'. But if the electoral system permitted
such strong feelings of expression, it nevertheless contained
many elements of inertia that biased the outcome towards the
pattern of politics on offer at Westminster. One was simply that
government was conducted at Westminster. Chamberlain was
able to mobilise provincial urban liberalism and gain rapid
admission to the Cabinet; here he was deservedly an influential
figure, but he soon learnt he could not simply dictate to his
colleagues. At a different level the Irish and Welsh both found
that true political independence was a chimera – to get
anywhere they had to work with the Liberal party. Another
constraint was the cost of politics. MPs were unpaid and, even
after the Corrupt Practices Act, 1883, they had to meet many
expenses: in 1911–13 (not election years) the average
Conservative MP/candidate had personally to find some £200
p.a. Of course cost did not exclude all poor men. But in default
of paymasters it limited their number. There were two
principal paymasters, the Irish Americans (who in 1885–9
provided £102,000 for Parnell's parliamentary fund), and
(especially after 1900) trades unions. But it is clear that, given
more money, the Liberals would have run more working men
as candidates – before the 1892 election they appealed to
Andrew Carnegie to fund forty to fifty of them.[15] Money,
though, was not the only bar to working-class candidates;
Liberal constituency associations (like Conservative and even
Labour ones since) were reluctant to adopt them, partly for
reasons of self-interest but partly in the often justified belief that
they had better candidates available. For though there was a
feeling among the new electorate in favour of labour
representation, it was not strong. Mostly people were happy to
leave leadership to the established political class. This was
certainly broadening – by 1885–6 only 50 per cent of MPs (as

against 75 per cent in 1865) came from landed families, and the economic interests best represented in the Commons were commerce, industry and the professions. But the changes can only be described as gradual and limited.

One reason for the new electorate's general docility was that the lower classes as such did not look for much in the way of remedial action from the state and so were happy to accept the pattern of politics on offer. Admittedly *laissez-faire* ideologies were perceptibly receding in our period, and public expenditure started to rise as a proportion of GNP from about 1891. But between the Second and Third Reform Acts major pressures centred around moral and religious rather than class issues. Though not all were successful, the political system was well able to address them, passing a number of measures such as the Burials Act, 1880 (to secure Nonconformist ministers the right to conduct funerals in Anglican churchyards), the invocation of which in the Llanfrothen burial case launched Lloyd George on his political career. Given that over half the population did not attend church there is a certain irony in this prominence of religious issues; this may be one of the areas where the exclusion from the franchise of some 40 per cent of adult males was most important. By the end of the period the electoral salience of religious issues was starting to decline, though unevenly in different parts of the country. They were not simply replaced by class issues – there were, after all, plenty of others, ranging from the personal appeal of particular leaders to 'ethnic' politics in Lancashire and West Scotland and to imperial affairs. But, to the extent that class did become a primary electoral determinant, it did so first at the middle-class level and on the *status quo* side. The growing middle-class shift to the Conservatives was the move of people who no longer felt themselves outsiders, and by the 1890s members of the middle classes were more likely to vote Conservative than were members of the working classes to vote anti-Conservative, a situation that has lasted almost to the present day.

6. Parties, Members and Voters after 1867

JOHN GARRARD

I

THIS essay[1] focuses on a distinction often made in political science between different sorts of political parties. In casting doubt upon the assumptions flowing from that concept, at least as it concerns British experience, it is intended to throw light upon political parties as they evolved in the decades after 1867, and upon their response to working-class enfranchisement. Although the focus will be on the towns of South Lancashire, particularly Salford, the conclusions are assumed to have a more general application. In any case, Lancashire – as a major urban and industrial area – was one of the key points where the party political response to the 1867 Reform Act was forged.

The distinction relates primarily to the participation demanded of party members. It has been variously described, but the version most effectively encapsulating the ideas involved is Neumann's contrast between *parties of individual representation*, and *parties of social integration*. Of these, the former are usually informally, and intermittently organised, and tend to galvanise themselves solely at elections. They demand from their members only a few hours monthly of purely political activity – canvassing and the like. Otherwise they leave them alone. The party of social integration, meanwhile, moves far beyond the political sphere. More continuously organised, and organised for much more than just elections, it mounts a wide variety of activities permeating the individual member's whole life – educating him, entertaining him, looking after his children, and perhaps even burying him. As a result, the party can demand far higher commitment; in Neumann's words, 'it can count on its adherents; it has taken over a good part of their social existence'.[2] Meanwhile, such attitudes to the member flow naturally from this kind of party's emphasis upon high levels of government intervention – to ensure the individual's share in society, and his incorporation into the community.

This dichotomy is generally seen as corresponding to an evolutionary development. Parties of individual representation were normally also 'caucus' or 'cadre' parties of notables; they originated in a property-based political system, and recruited a strictly limited membership based on socio-economic prominence, and contributions to party funds. With franchise extension, these normally middle-class-dominated parties steadily became outdated, and were superseded by parties of social integration: 'mass parties' relying upon the recruitment of a large, unlimited membership for finance, and for the mobilisation of electoral support.[3]

Most writers agree that the pioneers of the new pattern were the socialists. Only for them – particularly for the continental socialists – was the new wider pattern of activity both natural and appropriate. As D. A. Chalmers has argued in his history of the German SPD,[4] the attempt to provide a total environment was the natural response of a party seeking radical alternatives to the capitalist order, yet whose members were surrounded by that order, and dependent upon it for economic survival. Meanwhile, for the more ideological socialists, it was part of a wider attempt to supply their members with a total and alternative explanation of the world: in a situation where ideology explained everything, the various ancillary activities provided a variety of situations – leisure, sporting etc. – where members could experiment with their new explanatory powers.[5]

Few analysts regard the old middle-class parties as capable of producing genuine parties of social integration. Even Duverger recognises in the Birmingham caucus only an artificial version of the mass party, and sees the ancillary organisations of these older parties (like the Primrose League) as half-hearted middle-class attempts to maintain the commitment of lukewarm working-class supporters – attempts moreover ultimately doomed to failure.

In this essay, it will be argued that, at least in South

Lancashire towns, the leaders of the old parties attempted to move beyond the political sphere – and did so in ways that were much more than half-hearted. Indeed they tried to provide an environment at least as total as that provided later by the SDF and ILP. Moreover, they did so, at least partly, for motives entirely 'natural' and appropriate to members of the nineteenth-century urban middle class – motives connected amongst other things with the 'fitness' of the new voter, and with a more general desire to 'improve' him.

It is not proposed here to undertake any detailed analysis of the organisational response to franchise reform, or of the resulting internal power structure. We need simply note that after, and some would argue well before,[6] 1867, both parties became organisationally more formal and more permanent. Thus, by the early 1870s, Salford's parties each possessed a central association and a fairly complete network of polling district associations. We should also note that, for all the lower-class character of the electorate in South Lancashire towns, both parties remained firmly controlled by their wealthy middle-class members. Each party formulated complex machinery of consultation, and undertook elaborate rituals of mass participation over important decisions.[7] Nevertheless, the main local party officers remained drawn from the manufacturing, mercantile and professional elite, and there were few proletarians amongst nominees for local authority office, still less amongst parliamentary candidates. Even local political clubs, for all their claims to be 'not "artificial creations" but the *bona fide* expressions of the feeling in the districts in which they were opened',[8] seem usually to have been heavily dependent upon liberal endowments from 'the leading gentry of the district'.[9] Thus, in analysing party responses to franchise extension in the 30-odd years after 1867, we are primarily analysing the response of local middle-class politicians.

Given where power lay, it is unsurprising that, in one sense, both parties were apparently fairly passive. Although government policies were often discussed in wards and constituencies, there was little open criticism – except, of course, where the opposite party was in charge. Even the Liberal caucus – with its ostentatiously democratic internal electoral processes subject to the quiet counterweight of co-option[10] – hardly seems adapted to the upward transmission of grass roots activist opinion in the twentieth-century manner. Hope might occasionally be expressed that:

> the obstruction of public business by the Tories will not deter [the government] from carrying to a successful issue the measures announced . . . for the widening of the electoral basis of the Constitution, and developing . . . municipal institutions.[11]

This aside, however, both organisations largely contented themselves with resolutions expressing unlimited confidence in the national leadership. Meanwhile, though subject to outside criticism, the continuing reticence about working-class candidates apparently provoked little controversy within either party before the late 1880s.

In fact, the really important work of local parties lay elsewhere. Firstly, of course, it lay in electoral activity. This meant persuading the voter ('whenever he met a Tory, he tried to turn him into a Liberal'[12]), and distributing propaganda, often on a massive scale. In what it seemed to regard as a fairly thin year, the South Salford Liberal Association reported the disposal in 1904 of some 35,000 leaflets, 'though more might have been done.'[13] It also meant canvassing and registration. Local parties had always played crucial roles in the registration process, getting their own supporters on to the electoral roll and objecting to the presence of voters predisposed to the other side. However, parties were even busier after 1867, massive work being required simply to keep up with manual workers, perpetually on the move in search of work. Women members, particularly, were urged to become 'vigilant sentinels in their particular districts, to keep their eyes on those who remove out of their neighbourhood and on those who come into it and . . . let . . . their registration agent know.'[14] More generally, both parties, in Salford at least, soon came to believe that 'there was a huge mass of floating opinion which was neither exactly Conservative, nor exactly Liberal, but which was generally swayed over to that side which had the best organization.'[15] Partly as a result, some branches could aspire to (and partially reach) levels of organisation whereby a district might be 'mapped out in blocks and a captain and a lieutenant appointed to look after each block, and under these a band of willing workers.'[16]

However, these were not just electoral parties. They were active throughout the year, and in spheres extending far beyond the merely party-political. Here we must turn our attention to the political clubs. These were established at constituency and township level by the mid-1870s and, by the end of that decade, most branches possessed at least a couple of rooms passing muster as 'a club'. Annual subscriptions were normally low, and memberships were apparently large. Indeed, as early as November 1874, Henry Rawlinson, Salford's ex-parliamentary Liberal candidate, was sufficiently impressed by the spread of these institutions, as well as by some inaugural junkctings in Pendleton, to predict that 'they were developing into the age of clubs.'[17]

Amongst other things, the clubs were 'political education', centres. Every winter, they mounted extensive programmes of lectures and debates, both on current issues, and on matters of more general interest. In Salford, the latter included presumably riveting items such as 'John Hamden and the Struggle for Liberty in the 17th Century', 'Milton and His Times', 'Money', 'George Washington', 'Napoleon', 'The British Constitution', along with mind-stretching syntheses such as 'History'. Meanwhile, most clubs boasted some sort of 'library and reading room' wherein resided a variously sized collection of books, together with national and local newspapers – mostly partisan, but sometimes including other publications 'in order to know what the enemy does'.[18]

Rivalling such earnest activity was 'the social side'. Even the most humble club generally possessed facilities for cards, draughts, billiards, dancing and the like. Many went much further. In February 1872, Broughton Liberals staged their second AGM in their new club, and the association's secretary described both future and present facilities in noting that they hoped:

> to erect a commodious billiard-room . . . replete with every convenience, and containing a full-sized table. This,

combined with a reading room, smoke room, chess, draughts, a good supply of papers and periodicals, and opportunity for obtaining tea, coffee, cigars etc . . . would, it was hoped, induce all the Liberals of the district to enrol themselves as members.[19]

The Broughton Club's annual subscription was possibly a little high for many working-class Liberals. Not so, however, the Oldfield Road branch of the Salford Constitutional Association which was inaugurated 'by a tea meeting' in January 1869. Here 'the Islington (Conservative) Glee Party . . . by their rendering of several popular and patriotic compositions, greatly enhanced the enjoyment of the company which numbered between 400 and 500.'[20] Equally proletarian was the Regent Liberal Club which, in March 1888, held 'another successful smoking concert' at which 'many artists' performed, and 'Mr Jules Keene, of the Wild West Show, gave several impersonations . . . causing intense merriment'.[21] However, had there been a jollification prize, it might have gone to the Greengate Liberal Club which, in 1879, proclaimed its inauguration to one of Salford's poorest and dirtiest districts with a meeting after which:

dancing and other amusements were indulged in until a late hour. Mr Wooley provided an electric battery, and, by permission of the patentee, a splendid telephone; Mr William Leach exhibited a polariscope, a microscope etc.; Mr Arthur Shafto amused the people vastly by a series of electric shocks administered to the audience by his battery. There was a large and varied display of botanical and rare geological specimens.[22]

Yet, although club efforts at entertainment were both frequent and impressive, the high point of the parties' 'social side' was the annual picnic. Every summer, members of constituency and township associations and sometimes even ward branches – along with their families and friends – would board special buses or trains, and descend upon a local park, or more frequently, the mansion and grounds of some regional party dignatory. Here they feasted, listened to speeches, danced, or otherwise disported themselves. Everything about these occasions was impressive. In July 1873, during festivities at Lyme Park, 2000 Tories performed 'a New Conservative Gallop' invented specially for the occasion.[23] In June 1875, 1600 Stockport Conservatives made off to sample the thoroughly non-political joys of Southport in 'two lengthy trains of 25 carriages each'.[24] Four years later, Manchester and Salford Liberals held a joint 'demonstration' at Mandley Park, Salford. In previewing the entertainments, the *Salford Weekly News* predicted a 'glee party', numerous recitations, brass bands, a cricket match, archery, gymnastics, conjuring, marionettes, Punch and Judy, and performing dogs. In the evening 'there will be dancing, and a grand ascent of Montgolfier Balloons'. Almost apologetically, the paper announced that 'during the afternoon, pleasure seekers will be asked to . . . give their attention to a few short political addresses'.[25] However, undeterred by this threat, some 50,000 people apparently attended the demonstration.

Although attracting smaller numbers, the most spectacular occasion of all was perhaps the journey by some 600 North Salford Liberals to Matlock Bath in Derbyshire in 1900. The picnic took place at the home of J. E. Lawton, North Salford's parliamentary candidate. Lawton was chairman of Matlock's urban district council, and seems, to judge by the festivities laid on, almost to have owned the town:

> By a public subscription, a festooned archway had been erected on the parade . . . gaily decorated and bearing the words 'Welcome North Salford'. . . . The mere fact of having made the journey secured the 'open sesame' to every place of entertainment, and a free inspection of all things interesting. . . . At night, a special Venetian fete was held (on the river) . . . the wooded heights of the Derwent were covered with myriads of coloured lamps, Chinese lanterns, and other illuminations . . . the footbridge over the river was also plentifully studded with lights, and the waterway itself was crowded with brilliantly illuminated boats of the most novel designs . . . 13,000 Chinese lanterns were used in the decorations.[26]

Finally, but equally indicative of the scope of party ambitions in relation to the lives of their working-class supporters are the party-based burial and co-operative societies. In December 1868, in an apparent attempt to counter the all-pervasive and Liberally-inclined influence of the Rochdale Pioneers, 'a very influential meeting of . . . Conservatives' began moves to found the Rochdale Conservative Industrial Co-operative Society.[27] By its 'first Annual General Meeting' in March 1871, it reportedly had 1150 members.[28] By 1877 it claimed 1410, was paying a dividend of 2s.9d., had capital of £13,170 and had constructed several cottages.[29] The Bolton Conservative Sick and Burial Society, like others of its kind, was an earlier creation, dating from 1848. However, it greatly expanded its operations after 1867, such that it constituted Bolton's only working-class conservative electoral organisation. With 17 lodges by 1870, the society had 'three objects . . .: the maintenance of Conservative principles; . . . the relief of their members during sickness, and . . . the respectable interment of their members after their decease.'[30]

II

Thus far, we have provided evidence that local political parties were continuously organised and, more important, that they were more than just *electoral*, or even *political*, organisations. However, this extended activity might simply indicate a desire to maintain the flagging interest of working-class supporters. If we are to demonstrate that they were, in some sense, 'total' organisations, we must go further, and examine some of the motives behind all this activity – particularly those of the local middle-class leaders who controlled the parties, and financed much of what has been described.

In some ways, they were acting for reasons common to any party at almost any time, at least since the growth of a mass electorate. At both constituency and ward levels it was crucial to have some centre for electoral organisation – which the clubs provided. They were 'rallying centre[s], where they could meet and . . . organize their forces for victory, and [where] . . .

they might rally after temporary defeat, and . . . prepare to renew the struggle with yet greater zeal.'[31] Moreover, as this implies, the clubs were also centres for longer term comradeship building. After all, it was 'in the time between [elections] that their strength was developed . . . by that communion of sentiment with each other.'[32] Benjamin Armitage believed that 'the object' of the Liberal Association 'was that the electors might see more of each other . . . the more they knew of each other, the better they would come to like each other.'[33] Some Tories rather dangerously suggested that their tea parties would unite working men in 'a firm bond of love, and if brotherly love was the groundwork of their union, they could not fail to succeed'. . .[34] Meanwhile, many Liberals believed that 'those annual picnics would have only one effect upon them as workers in the Liberal cause . . . they would be cemented more closely together . . . attached more firmly to their principles'.[35] Overall, the desired result for both parties, perhaps, was 'a numerous and happy family'.[36]

The mixture of activities was also aimed at two specific groups: the party activists, and the apolitical. If the latter could be seduced into the party through the tempting social delights offered in the clubs, political interest might creep upon them unawares. Sir William Agnew believed:

> There was a great number of people in Salford who appeared to stand between two opinions – they were neither milk nor water, but were sufficiently numerous to turn an election . . . they were more likely to be attracted by clubs than by any other means. . . . If they came to the clubs they would acquire an interest in political matters which they did not at present possess.[37]

Others agreed, and felt also that the social side of club life was the means by which, 'a non-reading element might be drawn under the influence of the more earnest, and thoughtful of [club] members'.[38] Meanwhile, as this implies, some party leaders were beginning to realise that an important element in proletarian conversion was the recruitment and care of working-class opinion leaders. Here again, club facilities were important: they allowed the politically committed to extend 'their influence amongst their own class'.[39] They also enabled 'the influential working man' to be 'looked after by the party. If a working man who was a Liberal entered a workshop where his fellow workmen were undecided upon their politics, he could talk to them, and would soon make them all Liberals.'[40]

There is a sense here of middle-class reticence in the face of an unknown proletarian quantity – a sense suggesting that there were limits to all-embracing factory culture.[41] We also get the first hint that the attempt to provide a more than political environment for party supporters amongst the new electors was born of concerns particular to a particular time, perhaps to a particular class. This emerges more clearly if we take our analysis further.

Firstly, many local middle-class party leaders were transposing their economic and philanthropic experience into politics. The role of wealthy businessmen and professionals within the locality was akin to that of an urban squirearchy.[42] The years after 1867 were still the age of the owner-manager and, even with the coming of the limited company, the age of the family firm. The owner's power amongst his workers and their families, though it can be exaggerated, was clearly great – resting, as it did, not just on the factory but upon the network of social and other institutions surrounding it.[43] Within the wider town, men of substance were expected to participate in widely ranging philanthropic activity, including local charities and the 'duties and burdens' of local government. In return, industrial towns were sufficiently autonomous to provide those men with considerable popular visibility and esteem. Thus, in financing political clubs and picnics, middle-class leaders were simply extending their squirearchical roles – fulfilling philanthropic expectations and reinforcing the deference due to them as social and economic notables.

The idea of Victorian middle-class men acting as came most naturally also emerges in a second, more important, way – in the concern of local parties about 'political education'. Partly, of course, the phrase was simply a euphemism for propaganda, and for attempts to equip their members with the 'facts' necessary to combat opponents' arguments, and with a clear sense of their party's view of the world. In Rawtenstall in 1869, the Constitutional Association was claimed to 'resemble, in some respects, the Mechanics Institutes, except that it would teach a much more sound and healthy literature than had, of late, been promulgated by the former.'[44] Yet, even here, we get a hint of broader concerns, of the fact that the numerous lectures, debates and other facilities provided by the parties were equally aimed at ensuring that those recently brought within the constitutional pale were 'politically fit' to be there.

The parliamentary debates about enfranchisement in the late 1850s and 1860s had been importantly concerned with precisely this problem.[45] The champions of franchise extension had argued – and others had ultimately come to admit – that large sections of the working class were fitted, by education, attitude and life-style, to exercise the voting privilege responsibly. Quite apart from other evidence, the widespread participation in friendly societies, and especially the co-ops, was taken to show that many workers were acquiring both self-reliance and a substantial stake in the existing community. Thus, whatever else they did with the vote, they would neither try to overthrow the political and economic system nor be open to illegitimate influences.

However, the crucial problem had always concerned the location of the line between 'respectable' working men who were fit, and 'the residuum' who were not. Norman McCord has argued that contemporary estimates mostly resulted either from guesswork or from profound optimism, and that many were enfranchised whose fitness, within the terms set, was debatable.[46] This perhaps was unsurprising, particularly given the chaotic horse-trading that helped shape the 1867 Act.

What I now want to argue is that the parties' attempt to provide a more than political environment was motivated to a considerable extent by a desire to ensure that the prophecies about fitness, if not true already, very soon would be. They were deliberately trying to impinge upon the individual's wider life in the hope of improving him. Perhaps what primarily distinguishes these parties from their present-day counterparts is their consciousness of being, in important ways, in at the beginning of some very significant integrative processes.

It is this that partly explains both parties' emphasis upon getting to the young, particularly to 'intelligent and enquiring young men'.[47] By such efforts, 'the young of the present generation, the fathers and mothers of the future, would be informed in those things necessary to a sound understanding of the political ground upon which they stood.'[48]

Such concerns also explain the emphasis upon 'political education'. Here again, the clubs were crucial. They were seen as 'political schools',[49] and the lectures, essay competitions, 'libraries' and newspapers they provided were an important part of the educational process. At its second Annual Meeting, the Salford Liberal Association reviewed the past year's lectures, and suggested that they 'cannot but have a good effect on the political education of the members. . .'.[50] Many local middle-class leaders agreed and, although they liked to stress that working men ran the clubs themselves, were ever ready with advice about what should happen in them. Daniel Hall urged Greengate Constitutional Club members to 'use the reading rooms, and get themselves educated thoroughly in political matters'.[51] C. E. Cawley, wealthy civil engineer and Conservative MP, advised another group of proletarian Tories: 'Do not let [the clubs] be mere places to idle, and lounge in, but where papers shall be read, and where conversation can take place on various subjects.'[52] In Rochdale, Councillor S. Tweedale urged the Liberal 'young men' before him 'to spend their time well in reading, and to very carefully study that which they read'. Then Rochdale's mayor was rolled forth to drive the message home:

> He trusted that, with the aid of the books and newspapers . . . at their command, they might be better able to discharge those important and responsible duties which the Government . . . had placed in their hands.[53]

However, most forthcoming of all in the foregoing respect was Arthur Arnold, Liberal candidate for Salford. He told Greengate Liberals about:

> the prime object of Liberal Clubs . . . in institutions of this sort the opinions of the people should, by reading and discussion, be formed and guided upon a good basis, and towards satisfactory and useful ends. He urged them all to interest themselves in politics, and to do so early in life. . . .

They had admirable newspapers; read them, not carelessly, but critically, especially in those points which concerned the welfare of themselves and their neighbours. Take notes sometimes, preserve cuttings.[54]

Opinions varied slightly about what should result from the educative process, but all were stated in ways signifying that speakers meant much more than just the inculcation of party doctrine – important though this might be. Some saw the desired end as a general process of enlightenment. In announcing an essay competition to the Broughton Liberal Club, Thomas Lee suggested that it 'would undoubtedly do a great amount of good in educating working-men in the history of their time'.[55] William Mather, one of Salford's wealthiest sons, expressed a similar idea almost as a call to arms: 'There was a magnificent work before them . . . that of enlightening the great mass of the public, and educating the nation.'[56] Salford's Liberal Association was equally firm, in emphasising the 'valuable educational work [these organisations] accomplish'. Party propaganda naturally figured as part of this 'work' but so equally did the promotion of 'a due appreciation of the principles of good government, the results of which will inevitably be for the public good'.[57]

Others, meanwhile, believed that the clubs were in the education business partly to make people think. In Bolton in 1870, Councillor Richardson told West Ward Conservatives that 'those associations were calculated to bring forth man's intellectuality'.[58] In 1871, in the same town, Jacob Bright advised a ward Liberal association, 'to do all they could . . . to get people into the schools, and to establish clubs for political instruction . . . and to greatly improve the mental tone of the people at the bottom of the social order.'[59] In Salford in 1876, Henry Lee expressed benevolent and customary pleasure at 'the large numbers of young men' he found in the St Stephen's Liberal Club. Then, while musing about the rising democratic tide, he was struck by 'how desirable it was that those who formed the great masses of the people should be intelligent, and well-educated . . . able to think clearly on all subjects.'[60] In a similar spirit, William Stephens linked the objects of Salford's Crescent Ward Liberal Club, of which he was wealthy chairman, to a cheerily pessimistic estimate of the voters' mental state.

> Well, they felt that . . . there were a great many voters who did not exactly know how to make use of the franchise, and the members . . . had determined to teach them. They did not much care whether a man called himself a Liberal or a Tory, if they could only get him to think, and read, and be above taking a glass of beer for his vote. In order to do this, they freely distributed political literature, and gave interesting lectures.[61]

Finally, some observers saw the clubs' educational activities as aimed at political training – training both voters and potential proletarian politicians. For these, the club's 'best object . . . is to make people competent for the wise control by their votes of the . . . business of the country'.[62] They told younger club members in particular that:

> they ought to get information so that their opinions of great questions may be formed by debating with each other, and trying to do what they can . . . to become public speakers and leaders amongst their fellow-men. There is nothing grander . . . than for a man to be standing before a large audience, like John Bright, for example.[63]

William Horrocks thought it 'a wise thing to open a Liberal club in Lower Broughton for there were a lot of people who required looking after, and the members . . . would receive a good political training.' In voicing the thought, he touched on one of the basic worries of many of those whom we have been quoting:

> It was important that working men should become well acquainted with the politics of the country because the progress of the nation depended on the opinions formed by the great mass of the constituencies which consisted of people who were working day by day.[64]

None of this should suggest that practice always followed

theory – still less that practice always achieved desired ends. Indeed, many feared that educational efforts were becoming overlaid by 'the social side'. In one club, it was actually discovered that, while the essay competition had attracted seven competitors, the billiard handicap had been overwhelmed by sixty. As the decades passed, there were increasingly well-grounded fears that 'all . . . political clubs had fallen short in the objects for which they were established . . . Social matters had . . . leavened the whole lump.'[65]

It is evident here that, like all other attempts at middle-class influence, those directed through political parties had ultimately to make their peace with the priorities of working-class culture.[66] Yet such priorities, in their turn, were still reconcilable with other broader middle-class intentions. For it could still be argued that, even in their truncated form, the clubs were important agents for the generation of political fitness. Here, the idea tended to merge into a much more general desire to improve – a concern with political fitness in its widest sense, the sense indicated by references to working-class participation in the co-operative movement. And here, parties clearly shared preoccupations common to all of Victorian middle- and upper-class society.

We begin to sense these broader concerns by examining some of the lectures delivered in the clubs. Many were about famous men, and some of these read like moral homilies on the rewards available to the suitably virtuous. Thus Richard Cobden was sometimes exhibited as an example of what could be achieved by 'the son of a small farmer of moderate means' through the exercise of 'diligence, and aptitude for business'.[67] On the other side of the political fence, a leading Salford Conservative, speaking to 'young men who are just embarking on the sea of life' could find no more 'encouraging example than Benjamin Disraeli' who commenced life 'the son of an outcast, with but a small fortune', and rose to the top 'by his genius, force of intellect, untiring energy, his marvellous patience under defeat'.[68]

However, it is in the justifications for their social activities that we get the clearest indication of the improving role the clubs were supposed to possess. For they were often seen as 'the means of saving many a young man from becoming prey to evil influences'.[69] The influence most frequently mentioned was the beerhouse – and the clubs were seen as important allies of the temperance movement. W. H. Bailey, manufacturer, chief benefactor of Salford's Regent Liberal Club, and employer of many of its members, thought that:

> Both Liberal, and Conservative Clubs had done a great deal for the promotion of temperance. A man must have the opportunity for the use of his physical, mental, and social faculties, and must have some sort of social enjoyment. These clubs offered . . . the opportunity of having that social intercourse without drinking . . . and enjoying themselves in a rational way.[70]

Similarly, Alderman William McKerrow, never one to let moral possibilities blush unseen, identified 'two valuable purposes' for the institutions. The first was the dissemination of party propaganda, while the second, 'not least important', function lay in 'affording to intelligent and enquiring young men opportunities for gaining recreation, and political instruction free from the endangering and contaminating influence of the bar parlour'.[71] Such hopes were emphasised even more prominently by William Hough who claimed that: '*the object* of the committee who had got up [Salford's Crescent Liberal] club was to take working men from the beer shops, and provide them with healthy literature . . . a healthy atmosphere'.[72] Meanwhile, in Rochdale in 1873, the Smallbridge Liberal Association purchased a billiard table:

> which has not only tended to increase our strength, but also enables the members to spend a quiet evening where the temptations to what is bad are not so numerous as at places where these things are provided for public use.[73]

In the same year, John Milne laid the national drunkenness statistics before the town's Cutgate Liberal Club, predicting:

> By such institutions . . . with the means [they] afforded for improvement and rational amusement, by keeping young men from the public house, and teaching them to respect

themselves, to put their money into their own pockets instead
of those of publicans, they would accomplish a very great
good.

At the same meeting, Rochdale's mayor speculated
imaginatively about the 'great deal of leisure time at [the]
disposal' of 'the labouring classes' implying that the clubs
would finally terminate 'those old fashioned ways . . . cock-
fighting, race running and so forth'.[74]

The Tories, if only because of their brewing constituency,
were less sanguine about their ability to 'dry out' the working
classes. But even they established a 'Salford Band of Hope and
Temperance Society' which held its first 'tea meeting' in
January 1875.[75] Meanwhile, Romaine Callendar had told
Manchester's New Cross Ward Working Men's Constitutional
Association in 1870 about 'the value of [such] associations . . .
they afforded . . . recreation [and] counteracted the evils of
meeting in public houses'.[76]

None of this was necessarily any more successful than was
the temperance movement itself. Many clubs succumbed to
proletarian demands for alcohol. But more important from our
viewpoint is the breadth of ambition. Furthermore, the desire
to control working-class leisure time went far beyond drinking.
Tories and Liberals alike insisted on the clubs being 'places
where you shall improve yourselves'.[77] The hope frequently
emerged that what happened there would permeate the
individual's whole life. Thus H. Birley felt clubs were valuable
'in . . . promoting orderly habits'.[78] C. E. Cawley agreed,
adding that they 'would have a tendency to improve the moral
[and] the social conditions of young men'.[79] Later, he further
argued that they would 'lead directly to improve the condition
of the working man's home'.[80] One suggestion helpful to this
end was provided at the Pendleton Constitutional Club in
1875:

The new premises were . . . comfortable, and convenient, . . .
such that a working man, and a gentleman could spend a
comfortable evening, and afterwards go home to their
firesides, and enjoy the company of their wives, and
sweethearts . . . what they learned at that club would have

the effect of making young men good husbands in the future.[81]

Other Conservatives advised 'the necessity of attending Church' where apart from 'being strengthened in the cause' working men 'would receive good'.[82]

Liberals too were convinced of the clubs' civilising potential. They believed they had 'a refining influence on [members'] manners . . . because the discipline of life is always best taught in crowds'.[83] Liberals declared themselves 'deeply impressed with the civilizing influence' of club meetings on 'the amenities of life'. Some felt that club life:

> promised well for the future. Some of them worked . . . in the Sunday schools, and in other ways to bring about social reform, and those clubs might be . . . a very important factor in the correction of many of the evils affecting society. (Hear, hear!). If they could get clubs . . . established where they could enjoy billiards or cards . . . in the absence of beer (applause) . . . they were doing very important work in [that] direction.[84]

Moreover, like the Conservatives, Liberals saw this civilising battle being carried into the home. Consequently, their leaders hastened to assure the ladies that they would not lose their husbands to a surfeit of billiards. Rather (and the bizarre mixture of language was not intended to alarm), 'they wanted to make the grumbling husbands into good-tempered men, and they thought that, by meeting with kindred spirits, and having friendly intercourse, that consummation would be arrived at'.[85] Some Liberals even assured wives that 'a social and political club was necessary to the well-being of their families, and . . . the state . . . they would find [their husbands] pleasanter companions when they returned to the domestic circle'.[86]

III

We have so far argued that local party leaders sought to provide

a more than political environment for working-class supporters
– and tried to influence more than political opinion. We have
also argued that more was involved here than just a wish to save
their supporters from boredom. Leading Liberals and
Conservatives made these attempts partly for reasons entirely
natural to them as partisans, as mid-Victorians, and as
members of the middle classes.

Here, we may return to our opening themes. For it now
seems obvious that the middle-class-dominated parties we
have been reviewing show similarities to what others have
argued to be uniquely the motivations and behaviour of
socialist parties. It is revealing to push comparisons somewhat
further.

Firstly, neither the middle-class-dominated parties after
1867, nor the later socialist bodies, were entirely new in these
respects.[87] Historians have increasingly highlighted the ways
in which both Liberals and Conservatives attempted to attract
working-class support well before 1867[88] – if only because
'non-electors' were useful as means of terrorising electors. Here
too, parties often ventured beyond the merely political.
Significantly, the 'Conservative Operative Friendly and Burial
societies', though greatly expanding their activities after 1867,
actually originated in the 1830s and 1840s. Furthermore, their
aims too went beyond partisan calculation, spreading into a
desire to facilitate more general social integration. Thus, as
early as 1839 and at the height of Chartist disturbances, John
Bennett told the Blackburn Operative Conservative
Association, of which he was temporary president, that:

a great portion of the lower classes . . . in our manufacturing
districts are democratic . . . if we take into view the constant
influx of population . . . the breaking up of the old framework
of society . . . the reduction in wages, the poverty and
discontent, the innumerable temptations to improvidence
. . ., we need seek no further for the present . . . reckless
desire for change and for the facility . . . presented to every
political agitator amongst these classes . . . [To improve this]
perilous situation . . ., it is the duty of every wealthy
conservative to contribute . . . to the diffusion of conservative
principles . . . It is the duty of every operative Conservative

to . . . encourage his poorer neighbour to become a member of our Association, to attend our reading room, and thereby learn to be content in that station of life which providence has pleased to call him.[89]

Secondly, political parties – whether Liberal, Conservative or Socialist – were not the only bodies attempting to create a complete environment for their working-class adherents. Irish nationalist organisations in British urban areas provided a range of ancillary activities.[90] So too did any church that was serious about attracting or retaining urban working-class adherents. Catholic churches in particular, in the poorest areas, provided a panoply of sociable and social welfare facilities in order to prevent 'leakage', and to insulate their followers against the surrounding non-Catholic and increasingly pagan slums.[91] For similar reasons, temperance, and particularly teetotal, organisations provided equally broad supportive activities for those taking the pledge and thus isolating themselves from the mores of their neighbours.[92] Indeed any middle- or upper-class body seeking influence with the urban working classes had arguably to undertake activities that, at once, catered for working-class tastes and needs, and insulated their adherents from working-class mores. Furthermore, the social welfare end of such activities was natural in a society where government intervened so minimally.

Thirdly, we should obviously be wary of assuming that most socialist bodies, in Britain anyway, totally rejected the surrounding society. Local organisations undoubtedly provided a formidable range of activities, as this account of recent achievements by the Salford ILP amply testifies:

The Socialist movement was not only a political one but . . . also had its educational and social side. . . . The clubroom had been furnished with billiard tables, chess, draughts etc. Wednesday and Saturday dances had been held each week, members' 'At Homes' had been held monthly, and swimming, cycle and football clubs had been inaugurated. . . . There were also lectures every Sunday evening. . . . The Manchester Socialist Choir occasionally rendered excellent assistance with glees. . . . A socialist Sunday School had been commenced.[93]

However, one may doubt the invariable linkage between all this and any aim of social transformation. Britain, unlike mainland Europe, never produced a Marxist mass party. Recent historians of British socialism – particularly of the ILP – have emphasised its links with much longer-term radical traditions,[94] and the way its willingness to play the rules of the electoral game led to the lacing of socialism with pragmatism at all levels. More important still in producing such tendencies was the fact that British socialism – unlike most continental counterparts – had to make peace with a pre-existing context of strong and determinedly pragmatic trade unionism. One consequence of all this, as David Howell has noted of the ILP, was that the social side of local socialist activity became increasingly leisure-oriented and decreasingly part of a broader attempt to create socialist islands in capitalist society. One may even see such activities as prompted by the need to copy and to compete, with the facilities already offered by the older parties.

However, we should not exaggerate socialist pragmatism. Many socialists within the ILP, and socialist bodies to its left, undoubtedly saw the social side of their activities at least partly in ideological terms. Here, the comparison with the older parties becomes doubly interesting. Such socialists sought to provide a more than political environment partly because this flowed naturally from an ideology emphasising mutuality, and policies emphasising governmental care from cradle to grave; partly also because they wanted to insulate their members from the influence of the surrounding capitalist society.

The older parties' motivations were both similar and different – though they all pointed towards broad-ranging activity. Firstly, leading members sometimes seemed to see the clubs, and other social activities, as practical demonstrations of what their parties stood for, and of their attentiveness to working-class welfare. The *Salford Weekly News* illustrated the concern most clearly in arguing that the presence of so many local party leaders at one festivity was:

another proof that, while leading Conservatives simply pat

the backs of working men when they require them to serve their own party purposes, . . . Liberal leaders . . . take a truer, and deeper interest in everything that concerns their well-being.[95]

Liberals also liked to argue that they were the more serious party, pointing out that, 'they seldom found a Tory club promoting public lectures. . . . The hope of the Tory party lay in keeping the masses in ignorance.'[96] Not unnaturally, Conservatives disagreed, asserting that 'festive gatherings (like picnics) are essentially Tory . . . Liberals do not know how to enjoy themselves because they are always at war with the institutions of the country'.[97] Yet, though they disagreed about each other's contribution, both ventured beyond the political sphere in the hope that 'their politics would become a living reality, and an abiding blessing to the people'.[98]

Secondly, like the socialists, the old parties probably saw their activities as means of insulating their section of the working classes – not from the surrounding society, but from influences emanating from the other side of the political fence. They may also have been attempting to insulate them from influences coming from the unenfranchised residuum. One Conservative actually said as much right at the outset in 1867: 'The object of the [Salford] Constitutional Association was to prevent the lower classes combining with the rough class, and governing those above.'[99]

The third point leads naturally from the second. While some socialists used social activities partly to establish an environment wherein the virtues of the alternative society might be practised, the older parties used theirs to inculcate the values of the existing one. In their concern with political fitness, both in the narrow and in the wider sense, leading Conservatives and Liberals sought to ensure that the new proletarian entrants to the political system would not disrupt either that system or the society it controlled.

At this point, we can profitably return to political science, where we shall discover another way in which the term 'social integration' can be used. For most of this essay we have used it as a way of distinguishing a particular structural type of party.

The other usuage describes one of the functions that parties play within the broader social and political system. Political scientists have devoted some energy to analysing these in the later twentieth century. The functions so analysed include recruiting political leadership, controlling and co-ordinating government, and organising 'a chaotic public will': Sigmund Neumann's[100] description for activities like the generation of policy and electoral programmes, the presentation of electoral choice, and the organisation of elections. Finally, modern parties participate in activities that may collectively be termed socially integrative – at once attempting to gain satisfaction for the demands of their client groups (thus drawing them further into the system and preventing them from seeking their ends outside its channels), and persuading those groups to adjust their private interests to community needs.

Parties after 1867 were also clearly involved in all these functions.[101] They were agents for political recruitment (albeit mainly from a restricted socio-economic circle). In contrast at least to the twenty years before 1867, they were also organised, coherent and disciplined enough to give coherence to the will of a (still fairly restricted) public and to lend some co-ordination to government. Finally, they were involved in social integration.

However, in performing this last function, they begin to part company from their present-day counterparts. For, whatever their contributions, nationally and locally, to satisfying and reconciling group demands (and here, they clearly were important after 1867, particularly as government enactment became increasingly accepted as the main means to such ends), nineteeth-century local parties attempted social integration in other senses also. They sought to ensure that voters newly admitted to the constitution were equipped with political and social values, and with a life-style that would enable them to be digested by the existing political system with relatively little gastronomic disturbance. In modern terminology, local parties were attempting to be agents of political socialisation – and socialisation of an ambitious sort, stemming from their acute consciousness of being in near the beginning of some very important integrative processes. Furthermore, in attempting to

assist social integration as outlined here, they themselves
became very like 'parties of social integration' in our original
sense, and were prepared to impinge on much more than
political man.

7. British Foreign Policy, 1867–1900: Continuity and Conflict

PAUL HAYES

I

It has long been received wisdom that the national interest requires a foreign policy characterised by continuity. Indeed, the use of the term 'national interest' implies that it is both possible and desirable to establish an agreed framework for the conduct of foreign affairs which transcends personal and party disputes. Even politicians whose opinions on domestic issues have been controversial have frequently subscribed to this viewpoint. As Rosebery put it in 1890: 'I will never be party to dragging the foreign policy of this country into the arena of Party warfare.'[1] In fact he felt so strongly that in 1872 he noted in his journal 'the more the Secretary of State for Foreign Affairs is considered as a non-political officer, the better for the country.'[2] Many of his contemporaries shared these opinions, though perhaps few politicians felt them as strongly. In reality, however, foreign policy could not be treated in isolation from other aspects of government. The question of levels of expenditure was, for example, likely to lead to debate inside the government, between government and opposition, and, not infrequently, between Parliament and extra-parliamentary opinion.

The late Victorian years were full of debate about the ends and means of foreign policy. Strategic, financial and moral issues were hotly discussed – among them imperial expansion, the concert of Europe, free trade, the growth of nationalism and the independence of the dominions. Did this mean that

Rosebery's assertions were in principle meaningless or in practice ignored? Such a conclusion would be erroneous, for it is possible to identify certain basic characteristics common to the foreign policies of all governments of the period. They are easily listed: the preservation of peace, the protection of trade, the maintenance of the security of the British Isles, the avoidance whenever possible of peacetime alliances, the defence of freedom and the importance of economical management. Each foreign secretary approached problems in his own way. Governments held different opinions about the worth of one principle as measured against another. In general, however, policies differed more in terms of style and balance than on questions of principle.

Despite debate, there was a way of thinking about problems which was by late Victorian times deeply rooted in the body politic. It was widely assumed – and rarely contradicted – among the politically active classes in Britain that prosperity, security and moral worth were closely linked to the unique virtues and superiority of the British constitution. The conduct of foreign policy often seemed to provide opportunities to demonstrate these virtuous characteristics to a less fortunate world. These attitudes caused great offence among the statesmen of other nations. In 1887, Prince William of Prussia, referring to a visit he made to Britain in 1880, wrote: 'a foreigner was given condescendingly, if not pityingly, to understand that he lacked these advantages at home, sad to say, but that it would be best to follow England's example as quickly as possible.'[3] These self-congratulatory sentiments in Britain were common to all political groups, including the Radicals. Those who conducted foreign policy shared a common social background; unsurprisingly, therefore, they for the most part shared common values. The normal lines of party division in domestic affairs were thus less important or relevant when foreign affairs were under consideration.

However, such widespread consensus could always be threatened by a sudden change in circumstances, or, indeed, by conflict between different principles. Would it always be possible to protect trade without running the risk of war? Could the security of the British Isles be maintained in perpetuity without resorting to increased defence expenditure or to the protection of an alliance? In part consensus had been achieved because for much of the nineteenth century such questions arose only irregularly and occasionally to trouble governments. But as Victoria's reign drew to a close Britain's long-established and favourable economic and strategic position came under threat. Political debate about choices of action and about the desirability and consequences of increased expenditure inevitably sharpened. The acquisition of a large empire began to seem something of a mixed blessing once the economic and strategic dominance of Britain was no longer self-evident. Arguments arose concerning the economic value of the empire, the moral duties of an imperial power, and the extent to which British security in home waters was imperilled by the commitment of resources to far-flung territories or by the jealousy of other European powers newly and increasingly in competition for imperial territories and international trade.

If changing circumstances at the end of the century exacerbated the debate on foreign affairs it is nevertheless true that the whole period witnessed significant dissent from established policies. This was reflected in debates in Parliament; by 1864 the proportion of time devoted to foreign affairs had risen to 22 per cent.[4] It is scarcely to be imagined that debates involving Palmerston, Russell, Gladstone, Disraeli, Cobden and Bright had often concluded in agreement. But when so much of British policy was low-cost and passive and while it was generally agreed that Britain did not need elaborate armaments until a war had actually begun these divisions mattered more in theory than in practice. The character of public debate a generation later was much more intense because of the changes, internally and externally, in Britain's situation. By 1915 Bertrand Russell was arguing in different terms and shriller tone: ' "Continuity" represents no real need of national safety, but merely a closing up of the ranks among the governing classes against their common enemy, the people.'[5] Neither was it only from radical quarters that there was severe criticism of entrenched passivity in foreign affairs. During the Fashoda crisis of 1898 Chamberlain was reported to have remarked that 'Lord Salisbury's policy "peace at any price" cannot go on any longer and England has to show to the whole world that she can act.'[6] By the end of the century, then, foreign policy was a focus of debate and not consensus; it enjoyed little continuity as it was the victim of conflicting pressures and principles.

II

As has been indicated, certain *desiderata* in foreign policy were well-established in mid-Victorian Britain. What were important, however, were the methods and means to be used to reach these goals. Britain was fortunate in that her geographical situation enabled her policy-makers to adopt limited positions over many issues. This is plainly evident in the case of alliances. In Continental Europe it was almost impossible for a power of any significance to avoid an entangling association with another power. British opinion had long been that it was undesirable for Britain to behave in like fashion. This was the sense in which British policy was 'isolationist'. It did not mean that Britain could or should keep aloof from European affairs or that she should not enter into specific engagements when necessary. In fact the policy of limited liability actually required British diplomacy to be rather active: to monitor arrangements made between other powers, to try to balance between groupings when they came into existence, to support other powers when their interests and those of Britain were similar and, finally, when no alternative existed, to make a specific undertaking. In imperial matters many of the same considerations were also applicable.

Britain's objective was, of course, to protect her strategic and economic interests. She wished to avoid the domination of Continental Europe by any one power, as had occurred in Napoleonic times. Such domination would threaten British trade and if such a power were to become established within easy reach of the British Isles it might actually threaten invasion. Great attention was thus paid to political developments in France, Belgium and Holland and, as the century wore on, to the growth of German power. Britain also wished to protect her trade in the Mediterranean and the Levant; this helped explain her concern for the Ottoman Empire's survival in the face of Russian pressure on behalf of the Balkan nationalities and Russian interest in territorial acquisitions at the expense of the Turks. With a major commitment in India, Britain was nervous about Russian expansion into Central Asia and the Caucasus as well as St Petersburg's attempts to exercise influence on Afghanistan. For most of the century it was axiomatic that Anglo-Russian rivalry was a constant in international relations. There were also substantial Far Eastern interests in China, Malaya, Siam and Burma to be protected. South Africa was important both as a trading centre and, increasingly, as a producer as well as a staging post on the route to the Far East. Britain's trade with Latin America increased substantially after the Spanish colonies freed themselves. She had enormous possessions in Australia, Canada and New Zealand, and the United States was a major trading partner.

All of these interests existed in 1867 and they were added to in following decades. Although British naval supremacy and economic strength were potent factors in the preservation of this favourable situation, it is doubtful even then if they would have been sufficient to meet a number of serious challenges simultaneously. Britain was fortunate in that there was no serious threat to the security of Australia and New Zealand. Similarly, though there were points of dispute with the United States, there was no real threat from that quarter to Canada or to commercial domination of Latin America. These factors enabled British policy-makers to concentrate upon her more vulnerable areas of interest in Europe, the Middle East and the Indian subcontinent. Britain was also favoured by European political developments which prolonged British ascendancy. Russian weakness after the Crimean War, the problems of the Hapsburg monarchy, the economic and political collapse of Spain and Portugal, the struggles for German and Italian unification and, finally, the defeat of France in 1870 all worked against any challenge to British predominance. However, such a state of affairs could not last in perpetuity. The frustration of ambitions in Europe contributed to the pursuit of interests elsewhere. Russia and France were not content to be contained by Germany; Russia became more active in Asia, France in the Far East, the Levant and Africa. The successes of Germany and Italy did not lead them to abandon notions of a colonial and imperial future. A decade after France's defeat at Germany's hands the international situation was once again fluid; despite appearances Britain was not well equipped to meet new challenges.

The most important illustration of the problems facing traditional British foreign policy was provided by relations with the Ottoman Empire whose decay created difficulties because of its unwieldy size and the number of claimants to the inheritance. Britain was traditionally hostile to dismemberment of the empire for sound economic and strategic reasons. She wished to protect the security of the Levant, in which she had a great commercial stake, and to preserve her vulnerable line of communications via the Eastern Mediterranean to Arabia and India. Britain wanted to check Russian expansionism, to resist French claims to influence in North Africa and to minimise the disintegration of the empire in the Balkans into a multitude of principalities which could easily become involved in the machinations of great powers. At all costs a Russian presence in the Straits had to be avoided as this would ensure the defeat of British objectives.

This policy would in itself have been hard to sustain, involving the risk of conflict with France and Russia as well as of incurring resentment among the Balkan nationalities. The nature of Turkish government made it almost impossible. The Ottoman Empire was unwieldy, subject to internal feuding, corrupt and ruled by a succession of feeble incompetents and obstinate, if cunning, tyrants. These facts were well known and were acknowledged even by those who favoured the preservation of the Ottoman Empire. As Stratford Canning put it: 'the government is radically bad, and its members, who are all alive to its defects, have neither the wisdom nor the courage to reform it.'[7] British policy was based upon the notion of internal reform which would produce increased trade, better government, improved communications and a capacity to resist disintegration and external attack. This policy in fact encouraged the Turks in their intransigence so that, according to Hornby, 'within eighteen months of the treaty [of 1856] it was impossible to do anything with them.'[8] It was not long before domestic consensus concerning policy towards the Ottoman Empire vanished, though lack of agreement did not relieve British governments of the need to find a policy to meet the situation.

Conservative governments, being especially fearful of Russian designs, were more sympathetic to the Turks, whereas the Liberals were fiercely critical of Turkish behaviour, especially towards Christian minorities in Asia Minor and the nationalist movements in the Balkans. Both positions were inadequate. Conservative governments thus supported a capricious and incompetent administration in an area vital to British interests. The anxiety of the Liberals to effect meaningful reforms alienated the Porte without giving relief to the Sultan's oppressed subjects or securing diplomatic advantages for Britain. Until the early 1880s British policy oscillated uneasily between these inadequate and incompatible attitudes.

The collapse of the Crimean system and the defeat of the Ottoman Empire in the war of 1877–8 compelled adjustments to British policy. The danger of Russian ascendancy in the region seemed imminent. Although the Congress of Berlin looked like a traditional attempt to shore up the Turks it in fact marked the beginning of a new phase in policy. Britain did not abandon attempts to exclude Russia from Constantinople but shifted to a policy of increased direct involvement in the region. In 1878 Britain occupied Cyprus, thus effectively recognising that the Turks might shortly prove incapable of defending themselves. The occupation also meant that Britain was now taking part in the division of the crumbling empire, which was a sharp shift of emphasis from traditional conservative policy. The irony of arguing that British acquisitions would help preserve the Ottoman Empire whereas Russian gains would threaten its existence was doubtless not lost on Disraeli and Salisbury, though they were obviously not anxious to draw attention to their inconsistency. Once Britain, for reasons of *Realpolitik*, had decided to involve herself directly in the Levant on the basis of a permanent presence it was likely that any further crisis which challenged the existence of the Ottoman Empire – whether from internal or external sources – might be met by further British expansion into the area. If the façade of policy had not changed its internal structure certainly had. It is hardly surprising, then, that continued unrest in areas

nominally under Turkish control led to further European
involvement in the region. By the autumn of 1882 Britain was
in occupation of Egypt and France of Tunis. Britain was now
committed, though this was not fully realised in 1882, to defend
her Levantine interests from Cairo and Cyprus rather than
Constantinople. Furthermore, by occupying Egypt in 1882 she
incurred the enmity of France and confirmed the Turks in their
distrust – which had been growing ever since the cession of
Cyprus.

The occupation of Egypt was the most important single act
in British foreign policy in this period, having profound
consequences for relations with two major European powers.
Yet the political background to the despatch of Wolseley's force
in July 1882 was confused in the extreme. The purchase of the
Suez Canal shares in 1875, the establishment of the *Caisse de la
Dette Publique* in 1876, the financial and political bankruptcy of
Khedive Tewfiq and the revolt of Arabi produced a situation in
which even Gladstone's administration was obliged to pursue a
forward policy. French blunders and internal political disputes
resulted in her exclusion from control but not obstruction of
Egyptian affairs, a situation which was not remedied until the
signature of the Anglo-French Entente in April 1904. France's
economic interests in Egypt at the time of occupation were at
least as great as those of Britain and, in addition, French public
opinion held strongly to the view that ever since Napoleonic
times Egypt was properly a sphere in which France could exert
influence. The British presence was thus fiercely resented as a
humiliation equal to that of 1870–1. The fact that this
diplomatic reverse had not been intended by Britain made little
difference in France.

The history of British relations with other powers, but
especially France and Germany, in the next two decades
showed the fallibility of building policy upon *ad hoc* responses to
situations rather than upon clearly defined and specific
objectives. Britain blundered into Egypt because immediate
and temporary, though legitimate, fears about trade,
investment and security were given greater weight in a crisis
than long-term relations with other powers. This mistake was
to be repeated elsewhere. Policy-makers had not properly
adjusted to German domination of European politics.

Bismarck's supremacy was in fact detested by France, resented by Russia and viewed with suspicion by Britain. Yet powers sought in vain to escape from Bismarck's tight grip and only during the 1875 war scare did the other powers combine against Germany. This event had contributed to a closer relationship between France and Britain which could in turn have achieved major objectives: a better balance of political forces in Europe and a clearer resolution of problems in the Mediterranean. As Austria and Russia appeared tied to Germany it is arguable that the two western powers had no real choice but to work together.

The quarrel over Egypt destroyed any possibility of an Anglo-French understanding for 20 years. The effect was to increase German influence at a time when Russian resentment at Bismarck's behaviour in 1878 had imperilled his system. After 1882 Britain had to reckon with French and Russian obstruction in Egypt. German benevolence was not forthcoming without payment. As Chamberlain pointed out in 1898: 'we pay Blackmail to Germany to induce her not to interfere where she has no right of interference.'[9] Furthermore, British abandonment of the principle of the integrity of the Ottoman Empire paved the way for German ascendancy in Constantinople and the creation of a new threat to British security in the Middle East. British fears of Russian expansion into the Balkans, Persia and Afghanistan made good relations with St Petersburg impossible. As Milner observed: 'Everything . . . seemed bent upon going wrong at one and the same time. Alike in military matters, in diplomacy, and in politics, Great Britain was simply haunted by the Egyptian Question.'[10] Twenty years later Gorst welcomed the Anglo-French understanding on Egypt by arguing that: 'our occupation is no longer a bone of contention and an obstacle to the maintenance of friendly relations between ourselves and our neighbours across the Channel.'[11] In the meantime there were significant consequences for Britain.

Hostility between Britain and France over Egypt spilled into other areas, thus causing further strains. Rivalry gave an added impetus to imperial expansion and led to serious confrontation between the western powers in West Africa in early 1898 and at Fashoda in the autumn of the same year. Other powers were able to play upon this enmity; in various parts of the world Germany, Italy and Russia were the beneficiaries. Whenever Britain was negotiating with Germany over East Africa, South-West Africa, China, islands in the Pacific or the future of the Portuguese, Persian or Ottoman empires she had to bear in mind the need for German support in Egypt. The signature of the Franco-Russian treaty of 1894 was a further blow to Britain, though it held in the long term more serious consequences for Germany. The alliance of her two most formidable adversaries was viewed with gloom in Britain and it was several years before it became evident that the alliance would not work with great effect outside the European theatre. Even then, it placed a further constraint upon British policy in the Levant.

After 1882, then, Britain was faced with the task of preserving her interests all over the globe without allies of any consequence. Indeed, the range of British trading interests and the number of her territories meant that at any one time she was likely to have disputes to settle with several European nations. This difficult situation was made worse by two other important developments – the change in Britain's economic position and the acquisition of yet more territories – and it is to these that attention must now be given.

III

Until the 1870s Britain was obviously the most wealthy country in the world. She was still enormously prosperous in 1914, but the growth in wealth and its internal distribution had become more erratic. Agriculture and industry were subject to increased competition, so that, according to Read:

> Britain was no longer unchallenged economically. In 1840 she had controlled nearly one-third of the world's trade; by 1880 she controlled less than one-quarter. Depression was affecting British industry severely at intervals, while British agriculture was being submerged beneath an influx of cheap American corn. Some businessmen, economists and politicians began to ask if free trade still paid. Ought we, in

the face of economic nationalism elsewhere, to adopt policies of economic nationalism ourselves?[12]

The debate between free-traders, protectionists and tariff-reformers, which was to culminate in the tariff reform campaign launched by Chamberlain in 1903, had now begun in earnest.

Yet the pressures created by declining confidence in the international economic system were evident long before 1903. The foundation of the Fair Trade League in 1881 and the Imperial Federation League in 1884 were responses to growing awareness of economic problems and the need to take political action. Pressure groups and lobbying grew in the 1880s, a good example being the China Association, formed in 1889. Anglo-Chinese trade was unduly dependent on opium, which in 1878 had represented 38 per cent of British trade via the treaty ports. There were fears that once this trade declined, or was outlawed, the inability to compete with other European nations in supplying industrial goods to China would be all the more serious. After 1889 the China Association and its parliamentary allies pressed hard for increased activity by government to support trading interests. They urged a more sympathetic and interventionist attitude on the Foreign Office and the diplomats. As Pauncefote had noted in 1884:

other foreign Representatives do not keep within the limits observed by the British Minister, but actually negotiate Loans and Contracts for their nationals and bluster and machinate on their behalf and the complaint of the British community is that their efforts to compete are not supported.[13]

Such actions would have seemed unnecessary and undesirable to traders and diplomats only a decade earlier.

The protectionist policies of other nations made matters worse. By 1900 protectionism had become normal among most important trading nations except for Britain and the Netherlands. The United States had adopted a high tariff in 1861, regularly reinforced and reaching a peak with the McKinley Act of 1890. Although France was less consistently

or comprehensively protectionist than many nations, the
Cobden treaty lapsed in 1882 and by 1892 the Meline tariff
package was in place. Italy adopted tariffs on textiles and
ferrous metals in 1878 and extended these to agriculture and
machinery in 1887. In 1891 Vyshnegradsky made Russia the
most protectionist country in the world. Germany adopted
tariffs in 1879 and enlarged the system in 1888 and 1902.
Economic nationalism inevitably increased, and Britain
proved no exception to this trend. Even free-traders began to
question some aspects of their theories, doubting whether
universal free trade would automatically be advantageous to
Britain and, for the most part, abandoning the Cobdenite
notion that free trade would promote international peace.

The pressure for immediate action, together with
widespread questioning of the validity of traditional free trade
doctrines, naturally affected policy-making. Salisbury and his
political colleagues, Conservative, Unionist and Liberal, were,
however, reluctant to adopt any form of protectionism in the
1880s or 1890s. This reluctance was not derived solely from
conservatism or ignorance, but was the product of dislike for
the long-term implications for international relations of any
further expansion in economic nationalism. Furthermore, by
the end of the century the financial domination of London in
the world economy had become so great that there seemed
great risks attached to disturbing the *status quo*. Yet, at the same
time, the counter-argument could not be ignored. *Laissez-faire*
principles might be excellent, but, as Hobsbawm observed:

> The classic Manchester argument that an industry which
> could not produce more cheaply than any other on the world
> market ought to go out of business might bear the sacrifice of
> a few small occupations, or even of British agriculture, but
> hardly of a large chunk of Britain's basic industries and
> prospects.[14]

The conflict between different viewpoints was so strong that
policy-makers were often, as in South Africa, unable to
determine which course of action was correct. A mixture of
inaction and sporadic intervention in response to particularly
strong pressure was often the result.

The acquisition of new territories and enlarged responsibilities further complicated matters. In the last third of the nineteenth century Britain gained control, directly or indirectly, of Egypt, the Sudan, large areas in East, West, South and Central Africa, Malaya, North Borneo, Upper Burma, certain territories bordering on Afghanistan, Kuwait, Bahrain, Cyprus, the New Territories and a considerable number of islands in the Pacific. The costs of such expansion were significant because of the need to maintain civil and military establishments in these places. Expansion on this scale strained naval resources and produced serious diplomatic problems in relations with other European nations, the United States and even the Dominions. Strain was particularly evident in relations with France and Germany, not least because overseas possessions were usually, if not necessarily correctly, viewed both as economic assets and as symbols of strength and determination in a world of competitive powers. Social Darwinist thinking and language soon penetrated discussion of international affairs and invested apparently minor territorial or trade questions with undeserved significance. This dismal process was inadvertently assisted by the impossibility in many situations of distinguishing between strategic and economic interests. In some areas, for example the Levant and South Africa, it could be argued convincingly that strategic and economic factors reinforced each other. Elsewhere, however, minor trading interests were successful in depicting any threat as the first phase in the collapse of British power.

Among the older generation of politicians and diplomats there was thus stiff resistance to apparently limitless imperial expansion and to the demands for governmental support and intervention which such expansion seemed to encourage. Harcourt's diatribe of 1894 was not uncharacteristic: 'We have already got the lion's share; why should we insist upon taking the tiger's also? Not to say the jackal's.'[15] But there were plenty of robust imperialists. In 1897 Chamberlain argued forcefully for the retention of some areas of doubtful economic and no strategic value: 'We ought – even at the cost of war – to keep the hinterland for the Gold Coast, Lagos and the Niger territories.'[16] Demands of this kind had rarely been conceded in the past; by the end of the century they occurred with such frequency that they began to have an erosive effect upon supporters of non-intervention. Under the pressure of the Far Eastern crisis of 1898 even Salisbury was driven to tell the British minister in Peking that the government would support China 'against any Power which commits an act of aggression on China because China has granted to a British subject permission to make or support any railway or similar public work.'[17]

As well as pressures at home for a forward imperial policy, no matter what the consequence for relations with European powers, there were also the claims of the Dominions to be considered. The established political tradition of the devolution of power within Britain worked against a centralised foreign or defence policy, as the history of the Committee of Imperial Defence was later to show. Nevertheless, the largely self-governing territories of Australia, Canada and New Zealand were reluctant to take up the burden of defending themselves. Their leaders saw nothing inconsistent in demands for autonomy and a sizeable imperial garrison. Many citizens of the Dominions, especially in Canada, feared being dragged into war as a result of British policies elsewhere in the world. Yet they also demanded British action in support of their own territorial ambitions, as in the case of Australian interest in the New Hebrides in 1887, unflatteringly described thus by an exasperated Salisbury:

> They are the most unreasonable people I ever heard or dreamed of. They want us to incur all the bloodshed, the dangers and the stupendous cost of a war with France, of which almost the exclusive burden will fall upon us, for a group of islands which to us are as valueless as the South Pole, and to which they are only attached by a debating club sentiment.[18]

A succession of colonial conferences, in 1887, 1894 and 1897, did little to assuage the fears of those who considered colonial connections as not without risk and a great deal to encourage those like Chamberlain 'hurrying to prepare a British Empire to survive in a world of continental super-states'.[19]

The effects of imperialist clamour were seen most obviously

in South Africa and India. In these areas there were real strategic and economic interests at stake, so governments were compelled to pursue active policies even at the risk of conflict with European powers. The British position in South Africa was ill-defined in the days of Palmerston; wars with the Zulus in 1879 and the Boers in 1880–1 did nothing to clarify long-term problems. The establishment of Germany in South-West Africa in 1884 and fear lest the Portuguese control of Angola and Mozambique collapse added an unwelcome international dimension to existing difficulties. The growth of Afrikaner intransigence and the development of the imperial-commercial ambitions of Rhodes provided two more explosive ingredients. In October 1899 the Boer War began. It was argued by Chamberlain that: 'What is now at stake is the position of Great Britain . . . and with it the estimate formed of our power and influence in our Colonies and throughout the world.'[20] British action was denounced by the other European powers and at one point there were fears of a Continental League. This did not materialise, but the strain put upon British resources – naval, military and diplomatic – by the long war played a key role in the abandonment of old policies after 1900.

In the case of India pressures were even stronger. Russia was seen as the threat to the jewel of British imperial possessions; her expansion southwards encouraged the formation of a school of apocalyptic strategists. In their view the only way to preserve India was by the pre-emptive occupation of adjoining territories, in Tibet, Afghanistan and Persia. If this strategy proved impossible then a huge army should be maintained in an India insulated by an array of neutralised buffer-states. The emotion generated by the Penjdeh incident in 1885 showed how powerful was the combination of men on the spot in India backed by a strong lobby at home. Although foreign secretaries were naturally reluctant to confront Russia they had to take into account the strength of public opinion on Indian issues. Furthermore a succession of viceroys – Dufferin (1884–8), Lansdowne (1888–94), Elgin (1894–9) and Curzon (1899–1905) favoured aggressive policies. As Salisbury wearily observed when Curzon wished to seize southern Persia: 'Curzon always wants me to talk to Russia as if I had five hundred thousand men at my back, and I do not.'[21]

Britain thus had to reckon with the hostility of Russia in the Levant, the Middle East, Central Asia and the Far East. France was an enemy in Egypt and a colonial rival in parts of Africa and Asia. Germany not only threatened to dominate Continental Europe but was by the mid-1880s established in Tanganyika, South-West Africa and the Ottoman Empire, all strategically important areas for Britain. The comfortable situation of Britain in the 1860s looked very different by 1885 when Queen Victoria reviewed the efforts of Gladstone's ministry of 1880–5 as follows: 'Look at our relations abroad! No one trusts or relies on us.'[22] Fifteen years later Curzon told Selborne: 'I never spend five minutes in inquiring if we are unpopular. The answer is written in red ink on the map of the globe.'[23] Britain had too many claims on her resources in 1867, declining economic power and the growth of imperial ambitions among other nations had left her hugely overextended by 1900.

Successive foreign secretaries were not unaware of the disparity between commitments and resources and of the gulf between what was expected and what was possible. While some were more realistic – or pessimistic – than others, all were prisoners of public hubris. Their preferred methods, then, of meeting challenges were cautious and piecemeal in character. They were usually reluctant to embrace nationalistic or aggressive policies and were wise to take this attitude. Perhaps the Continental League might have sprung to life if Hamilton had listened to Curzon: 'If only it [the Foreign Office] would now and then roar, or even show its claws! But it is so very deferential and polite to all the other lions and to many who are not even leopards.'[24] Foreign secretaries were grateful that poor relations between France and Germany precluded an anti-British association, except on rare occasions as in 1884, but they were anxious about the danger to peace of such antipathy and they prudently did nothing to exacerbate the situation. Indeed, both Rosebery and Salisbury rejected arguments that Britain could solve her problems by joining Germany and her partners in an alliance. Salisbury's resistance to some strong pressure stemmed not from complacency but because he knew that 'neither we nor the Germans are competent to make the suggested promises.'[25] Bertie, the assistant under-secretary, outlined the long-term dangers of such an alliance:

> we shall never be on decent terms with France our neighbour in Europe and in many parts of the world, or with Russia whose frontiers are coterminous with ours or nearly so over a large portion of Asia.[26]

It was logical, therefore, to adopt a policy of trying to improve relations with France, Germany and even Russia. Wherever possible, colonial disputes were to be settled by compromise rather than confrontation. There were some successes for this policy in the Pacific, the Far East and in Africa in the 1890s, though Britain preferred to make concessions to weaker powers, Italy and Belgium, with whom a quarrel seemed unlikely. Many interests could not, of course, be protected in such a fashion, especially in the Mediterranean. In this region British policy was severely constrained not only by French hostility but also by fears of imminent Turkish collapse. In 1887 Britain concluded the Mediterranean Agreements with Italy and Austria, the purpose of which was to maintain the *status quo*. The extent to which Britain was bound by these agreements was not entirely clear, and therefore not wholly satisfactory, but at least an attempt had been made to try to avoid an instability which could only endanger British interests. In the 1890s these arrangements looked less suitable; they were disliked by the Liberal ministry of 1892–5, and by 1897 continued unrest in the Ottoman Empire had made support for the Turks extremely unpopular in Britain. This was less serious in strategic (though not moral) terms than a decade earlier because, as Salisbury admitted, 'the idea that the Turkish Empire is on the verge of dissolution has been dissipated'.[27]

In effect, then, policy-makers tried to minimise risks and commitments – a policy which was all the more significant at a time of territorial expansion. Any issue which might disrupt an already strained situation had to be avoided. For example, it was clear by the 1890s that Britain would not confront the United States; having made that assumption naval resources were redeployed elsewhere. Similarly, Britain sought to avoid conflict between the alliance systems in Europe, not just because of the interruption to trade that would ensue, but because it would probably require Britain to face an unpalatable decision concerning the treaties of 1839 and 1867 guaranteeing, respectively, Belgium and Luxembourg. This policy of limitation was a calculated response to the fact that Britain was struggling to preserve political and economic influence obtained during a period of virtual monopoly of power. The character of political debate, and the fact that so many political figures adopted attitudes which were a strange mixture of pessimism and overconfidence, fairly consistently argued against honest public admission of the fact that Britain was not an entirely free agent in international affairs.

The long-established policy of frugality in public expenditure encouraged those who wished to resist courses of action requiring heavy spending. Even if circumstances were changing, governments remained Cobdenite on this issue. If expenditure rose beyond revenue then a painful choice had to be made between increased borrowing and increased taxation. This argument was used to sustain the tradition of non-intervention or, at worst, limited liability. Hicks Beach was arguing as late as 1899: 'Nothing but increased taxation will turn people's thoughts to some regard for economy and aid us in resisting the wild demands for expansion and expenditure everywhere.'[28] Increasingly, however, popular opinion favoured active policies and disregarded the problem of cost, especially if it involved naval expenditure. In this the general public was not altogether out of step with the policy makers for, as Gooch has observed: 'the navy had a commercial as well as a prophylactic value, and expenditure on it was the more acceptable in that it would protect the trade as well as the persons of the inhabitants of the United Kingdom.'[29]

The policy of maintaining a strong navy was thus favoured both by those who were cautious and those who were bold. A large navy would ensure an adequate home defence as well as being able to protect trade routes and many newly-acquired territories. It would be expensive but less expensive than a large army. Naval expenditure was also, rightly or wrongly, seen even then by those of a radical persuasion as essentially defensive in character; until the close of the century there was surprisingly little challenge to this thesis even among Britain's main competitors. At the end of the 1860s naval estimates ran at about £10m a year and remained fairly steady for the next 20 years. But by 1901 naval estimates had risen to £30m, mainly as a result of the Naval Defence Act of 1889, which had established the principle of building to a two-power standard. This Act represented the triumph of the 'Blue Water' school of strategists, whose central idea was that as long as the navy remained in command of the seas it would be possible for Britain to remain aloof from European affairs for much of the time. This interpretation was not accepted by those who realised that European affairs were too important and too finely balanced for Britain to adopt an essentially negative policy, but as they too wished to protect home waters they accepted naval expansion as the least unpalatable solution to their problems. However, they were aware that perhaps too much was expected of the navy and that it might not always be possible, either politically or economically, to build to a two-power standard. The Franco-Russian alliance of 1894 and the German Navy Laws of 1898 and 1900 demonstrated (to those willing to see) that a strong navy was not the only diplomatic card required by Britain.

The Boer War confirmed the younger generation of politicians, Balfour, Hamilton and Selborne, in their belief that the navy could not meet all dangers simultaneously and that therefore a new diplomatic initiative was necessary. No other course was plausible and thus Britain embarked upon the negotiations which led to the Anglo-Japanese alliance of January 1902, the first peacetime alliance Britain had accepted for many years. The treaty confirmed that Britain could no longer sustain her burdens alone even though Lansdowne asserted that: 'It has been concluded purely as a measure of precaution, to be invoked, should occasion arise, in the defence of important British interests.'[30]

IV

In retrospect it may seem puzzling that British policy took so long to adjust to diminished resources and augmented burdens, particularly when there were obvious dangers. In part the explanation lies in the fact that policy-makers realised potential enemies would find it difficult to combine against Britain. Recognition of this fact meant that cautious, conservative, limited and piecemeal strategies seemed to remain viable even in rapidly changing circumstances. They were not pursued out of ignorance or stupidity. The conservatism of policy can also be attributed, however, in no small measure to the Foreign Office itself and to those who ran it.

At the very highest level, that of foreign secretary, the continuity so disliked by radical critics was unchallenged. From 6 July 1866 to 11 December 1905 the post was held only by peers, mainly of venerable creation. The most dominant figure was Salisbury, who discharged the duties of foreign secretary for nearly 14 years of the period 1878–1900. His influence was particularly pervasive because for the most of his years of office he was also prime minister. He held strong opinions and was acknowledged to be expert in the field of foreign affairs. While he subscribed to the notion of democratic control in politics when it suited him, many of his attitudes were based upon a paternalist and oligarchic view of society, as was clear when he wrote in 1867 of the duty of every Englishman: 'to lend their best endeavours to secure the success, or to neutralise the evil, of the principles to which they have been forced to succumb.'[31] Yet throughout his career as a statesman Salisbury was willing to fall back on the rather specious argument that the parliamentary constitution of Britain rendered any certain alliance with her impossible. While he was not alone in advocating this theory it was, according to Howard, 'especially characteristic of Salisbury'.[32] In fact the five peers (Derby, Granville, Salisbury, Rosebery and Lansdowne) who dominated foreign policy in this period held many attitudes in common. Their view of participation in public life as a responsibility, and as an obligation derived from their social position, helped sustain continuity against occasional wild swings in public opinion. Changes of government were less likely to have a serious effect upon the formation of foreign policy while the two parties were dominated by patrician figures at the Foreign Office.

Continuity was also sustained by the personnel and

machinery of the Foreign Office. From 1854 to 1906 there were only five permanent under-secretaries: Edmund Hammond (1854–73), Charles Tenterden (1873–82), Julian Pauncefote (1882–9), Philip Currie (1889–94) and Thomas Sanderson (1894–1906). All were in due course elevated to the peerage; all exerted a substantial influence on their political masters. Yet, as Steiner has observed:

> there were no 'grey eminences' at the Foreign Office . . . since the days of Lord Hammond, those close to the foreign secretary had a voice in his deliberations . . . but they worked within the context of their department and a parliamentary Government.[33]

Salisbury's relationships with Currie and Sanderson were particularly close; after Salisbury's retirement Sanderson remained the most influential of those advising caution at a time when the balance of opinion favoured, in Grenville's phrase, 'partial-commitment'.[34] The permanent officials, then, very largely subscribed to the opinions and attitudes of the foreign secretaries and in some cases, such as Tenterden in 1876, were ready to press their opinions upon reluctant members of the Cabinet.[35]

The influence of permanent officials sprang from three different sources. In general they were, at every level of the service, well-informed, efficient and dedicated; they commanded respect for their professionalism. Secondly, the permanent under-secretaries knew how important it was to be able to work with different political masters. Permanent officials had their likes and dislikes; Derby irritated Hammond and Tenterden as well as many diplomats, just as politicians had their own preferences among civil servants. Yet this did not lead to substantial difficulties which might have affected policy-making. Finally, the permanent officials were drawn from roughly the same sections of society as the politicians. They thus shared many social, political, cultural, educational and religious perspectives. This common background was a significant element in preserving continuity. The five permanent under-secretaries in this period were all either members of, or connected by marriage to, aristocratic families.

No politician, therefore, was likely to treat their views as the product of an inferior education or a different class.

These characteristics were reinforced by the system of recruitment. It was slow to change – and even slower in the Diplomatic Service which was belatedly merged with the Foreign Office staff in 1919 – despite pressure after 1850 for more open methods of recruitment. Reforms were instituted in 1857, and in 1871 a full system of competitive examination was introduced for entry into the Foreign Office. From 1892 this examination was also taken by aspirants to the Diplomatic Service. In fact the social composition of the services hardly altered because the qualifications demanded effectively excluded all candidates whose families were not prosperous. Vansittart's account of his preparations in 1903 is revealing: 'Entrance into the Foreign Service then required a high standard in four languages besides English. . . . We needed moreover a detailed knowledge of modern history and of a grand new subject, geography.'[36] Such qualifications were not easily obtained. Even Vansittart, who had been educated at Eton from 1893 to 1899, at a cost of £300 a year, was compelled to spend time abroad in order to secure the fluency required.

The shared background of politicians and officials produced mixed effects. It promoted harmony among the higher echelons of policy-makers and it encouraged consistent application of widely held beliefs. However, shared perceptions could easily lead to an increased risk of inertia. Once the supremacy of Britain was challenged the lack of a substantial tradition of argument and debate among policy-makers repeatedly worked to British disadvantage. The paucity of area specialists able to provide different arguments based upon knowledge of local conditions impeded the evolution of new policies. The rapidly changing international situation, together with a huge territorial expansion, generated a large volume of extra work. Whereas previously ministers had enjoyed 'the time and privacy necessary to conduct their affairs according to the conventions of the "old diplomacy"',[37] the new situation was quite different. The number of despatches handled by the Foreign Office grew from 51,000 to 111,000 in 1905. In 1861 the professional staff numbered 37, but had risen only to 52 by 1914.[38] An increase in staff was urgently needed, in particular among specialists. The failure to fuse the services until 1919 reduced the impact on policy-making of those with experience in different parts of the world at a time when such expertise was badly needed. Lack of specialists made policy more vulnerable to the activities of pressure groups whose arguments proved difficult to rebut.

The system of education, recruitment and promotion thus encouraged conformity. Dissent from established views carried risks. As Vansittart lamented: ' "Better agree with 'em", said a young cynic, whom I remembered when in later years dissents became imperative.'[39] Although British governmental and bureaucratic structures and practices made it difficult to adjust policy this was not a uniquely British problem. Dilatory and ultra-traditional attitudes were common in Berlin, Paris, Vienna and St Petersburg. But in the British case this conservatism mattered more because it had long been assumed that the dimensions of policy were largely unchanging and that adjustments would be essentially minor and *ad hoc* in type. Salisbury himself admitted that:

> The commonest error in politics is sticking to the carcasses of dead policies. When a mast falls overboard, you do not try to save a rope here and a spar there, in memory of their former utility; you cut away the hamper altogether. And it should be the same with a policy. But it is not so. We cling to the shred of an old policy after it has been torn to pieces; and to the shadow of the shred after the rag itself had been torn away.[40]

This was the adverse aspect of that continuity of policy which in so many ways had served so well for so long. In foreign as well as in domestic affairs the comfortable conservatism of mid-Victorian Britain gave way by the end of the century to an era of dissent, debate, controversy, conflict and, ultimately, the revision of assumptions. The world had changed and Britain had to change with it.

8. Late Victorian Women

PAT THANE

THE late Victorian woman is fixed in our minds in a series of striking images: the ladylike 'angel in the house', the overworked skivvy, the desperate prostitute, the sexually passive wife, the 'sweated' worker, the dependent housewife. They are all images of passivity, of woman as victim. Underlying the historiography, indeed, is an assumption of *increasing* passivity, of dependence, enforced withdrawal from the public sphere, diminished engagement with politics, work or with male-dominated public lives compared with some past time. There is an acknowledged counter-current of assertiveness, from the 'new woman' demanding the vote and other advances for women, but as a minority middle-class protest against an inexorable, impersonal drive to subordination. This passive image conflicts with all that we know of the strong sense of social responsibility, purpose and commitment to hard work with which Victorians of all classes and both sexes were socialised. It also conflicts with the evidence of resilient, determined activism of women at all social levels and in a variety of spheres. What, then, was the reality behind the stereotypes with which 'the Victorians' are so uniquely beset?

I

If one set of events, more than any in history has transformed women's lives it must be the long-run fall in the birth rate and the spread of modern habits and techniques of contraception which began in this period and has continued at variable rates to the present. The birth rate in England and Wales was 35.2 per 1000 in 1870, 29.1 in 1899. The illegitimacy rate was stable and low. The fertility decline was fastest among higher social classes, but common to and simultaneous among all classes. Between the 1850s and 1880s completed family size fell by 33 per cent for families headed by professionals and higher administrators and by 21, 20 and 15 per cent respectively for those of skilled, semi-skilled and unskilled workers. There were variations within these broad groups, both occupational and regional. The decline was only 15 per cent among agricultural workers. It was slowest (10 per cent) among miners. However, the birth rate was exceptionally low among Staffordshire miners. Many of these were married to pottery workers, among whom the ingestion of lead in the course of their work was known to inhibit fertility and also to induce abortions.

The fall in the birth rate appears to have been primarily due to the spread of the practice of limiting births within marriage and to a fall in the size of family generally regarded as desirable. There were no significant changes in the numbers of women marrying, and though the age of women at marriage was rising slightly, it was insufficient to account for the fertility decline. The difficult question is why the practice of quite drastic family limitation became apparently *permanently* embedded in our culture (and in that of most other economically developed countries) at this time? Modern contraceptive techniques became theoretically more widely available as a by-product of the growth of the rubber and chemical industries, but in practice they were difficult to acquire or even obtain information about in Britain. Most couples used methods known for centuries – the 'safe period' or *coitus interruptus*. So why at this time did they start to use them more systematically? J. A. Banks argued that the change began in the upper-middle class, for whom it was the answer to the rise in costs of maintaining a suitable standard of living. However, the evidence that such costs *were* rising is tenuous and although the fall in fertility was fastest among the higher social classes, as we have seen, it was simultaneous and significant in *all* social classes. Changes among the working class are likely indeed to have been more important, though less investigated, because they formed a decided majority of the population.

The explanation must be embedded, in no simple way, in the complex changes in experiences and expectations associated with urbanisation and rising living and educational standards. Expectations about the number of births required in order to achieve a specific family size must also have been influenced by the simultaneous falling trend in the infant mortality rate, masked though this was by the killer effects of urbanisation. Falling infant mortality was both a cause and a consequence of important changes in women's lives. To some (so far unquantified) degree it was a product of improvements in public health provision; hence mortality levels varied locally according to the enthusiasm with which legislation was implemented. Also important was the fall in fertility itself. As women gave birth to fewer babies and ceased child-bearing at younger ages the survival chances of both infants and mothers were enhanced. One thing that infant mortality cannot be shown to relate to, despite much contemporary assertion, was the mother's involvement in paid work. Improvements in living standards leading to the improved health of mothers must also have been an important contributor, though this is also under-researched.

This is the period in which the 'modern' mortality pattern, in which females have a greater life expectancy than males in all age groups, began decisively and permanently (at least to the present in Britain) to replace the pattern of excess female mortality characteristic of poor rural societies. In the 1870s mortality began to decline for both sexes. By 1880 it was clear that women were benefiting slightly more from this trend: death rates fell by 5 per cent for males of all ages but by nearly 10 per cent for females of all ages; females could expect, at birth, to live 3.27 years longer than the average male. These statistics disguise complex age, time, regional and class variations, most of them underexplored, but it seems clear that the reduction in female mortality was not associated with the changing experience of childbirth, since it also affected females below child-bearing age; the major reason appears to have been a decline in tuberculosis which was the greatest single killer of males and females throughout the nineteenth century and the incidence of which fell fastest among females.[1]

Again the cause of this historically striking change has been sought in middle-class experience (in, for example, the decline in the practice of tight corseting) despite the considerable numerical superiority of the working class; hence, perhaps, the lack of success of the enterprise. It is possible, though unproven, that middle-class females did, in fact, experience improved conditions in this period; in view of the evidence of the harsh treatment and underfeeding of some of them as girls in the mid-nineteenth century, there was clearly room for improvement. Improvement, however, is more probable among some at least of the working class due to the general rise in living standards. It is possible that some working-class women may have benefited disproportionately. There was a general tendency when times were hard for females to receive a smaller proportion of household resources, especially of food (usually allocated by the women themselves) than males. In better times females had less need to go short. It is also possible that when females worked for wages they could claim a higher proportion of household resources. But this is speculative, and mortality rates are not necessarily precise indicators of states of health. There are indications that females continued to experience higher rates of malnutrition than males. Though they outlived men they did not necessarily experience better health. Men were more likely to die of sudden acute illnesses, while women lived on, but in poor health, suffering chronic but not fatal conditions, such as anaemia resulting from poor nutrition. Many working-class women can never have been in good health, dragging on their lives with limited access to treatment or opportunity for rest and recovery even from childbirth, due to domestic pressures. As Clementina Black put it: 'The horrible boast, "I never missed but one week's wash with any of my babies" . . . tells its own tale.'[2]

Whatever the precise overall picture, the period saw changes of dramatic importance concerning female health. Above all, more women felt, and were, able to control not only the number of their pregnancies and the size of their families but could feel, as a result, a potential for control over their lives that was historically unprecedented.

II

But not all women married and not all who married had

children. There was a surplus of females over males which increased steadily from 1871 to 1911. This was partly due to the changing mortality patterns already described and also to the higher emigration rates of males. Both non-marriage and childlessness appear to have been more prevalent among the middle classes, middle-class males demonstrating a high and unexplained propensity for bachelorhood until around the First World War. Contrary to another myth, however, marriage was not the preserve of the youthful woman; they were not 'on the shelf' by their later twenties. Throughout the period more than 5 per cent of single women married at all ages between 20 and 39 and more than 2 per cent at all ages between 18 and 44.[3] It is possible, however, that more middle-class women *chose* 'spinsterhood' in this period in preference to the considerable constraints of marriage and family, in probably the first historical period that provided occupational and domestic space for small numbers of them outside the family or the convent. The women's college, boarding school, nurses' home, settlement house or shared 'digs' were a haven for a small but significant number of women.[4] As Shaw perceived, 'nobody has yet done justice to the modern, clever Englishwoman's loathing of the very word Home'.[5]

Neither did all marriges survive. Divorce was infrequent, but increasing. There were some 150 divorces per year in the 1860s, following the 1857 Matrimonial Causes Act, a surprisingly high proportion of them (perhaps approaching 50 per cent) among working- or lower-middle-class people. An unexpected windfall, or patient saving, could give even a relatively poor woman her chance of ending an unhappy marriage. The annual average number of divorces was 582 between 1890 and 1900. Informal separation followed by co-habitation undoubtedly occurred, especially in sections of the working class though probably on a small and diminishing scale. The legal mechanisms for ending a marriage were somewhat eased, though it remained more difficult for a wife than for a husband to obtain a divorce. Only in 1891 did case-law establish that a husband could not physically force his wife to live in his home. Thereafter she could, in principle, take legal action against him for use of force. In 1878 judicial separation became possible, a cheap though less final alternative to divorce for poor wives, chiefly important for enabling them to sue an absent husband for maintenance through the magistrates court, though not for ensuring the payment was made by husbands who had vanished or simply earned too little – poverty having often precipitated the breakdown of the marriage. This legislation was one outcome of the powerful campaign against 'wife-battering' conducted in the 1860s and 1870s, most actively by Frances Power Cobbe. It gave magistrates power to grant separation orders and maintenance to a wife whose husband was convicted of aggravated assault against her, plus the custody of children under 10. A series of statutes strengthened these powers. From 1897 about 8000 separation orders per year were being granted. From 1883 a 'guilty' divorced wife also could petition for maintenance. The social opprobrium attaching even to an 'innocent' divorced woman in respectable circles (though not to a separated wife in the working class, the figures suggest) may have remained a considerable deterrent to ending a marriage. We know, however, very little about the extent of such attitudes or of how they may have varied according to social position or the circumstances of the divorce; there is reason to believe that attitudes were more varied and flexible than is often assumed. All but the very rich woman might, however, experience equally serious problems of financial survival especially if they had never been in the paid labour market. From 1870 all wives were allowed by law, for the first time, to retain any property or earnings acquired after marriage rather than, as before, losing them to their husbands and from 1882 they could retain any property possessed at the time of marriage, thus extending to all women with property a right which the better-off had previously been able to acquire through establishing a trust in equity. Even after 1882 it is likely that relatively few women had sufficient income or property on which to live comfortably alone or with children after divorce. The courts, however, were increasingly disposed to make adequate settlements and, once more, we know almost nothing of the actual practice of property settlement and the division of control over the woman's income within marriage. The reality was almost certainly more variable than the strict legal position.

A divorced mother also risked the loss of her children. From 1839 an 'innocent' mother might legally be granted care and custody of children under 7. This was extended to 16 in 1873 and from 1886 the welfare of the child rather than the 'guilt' or otherwise of the parents was supposed to determine custody. It could still be extremely difficult for a woman to prove to a court the unfitness of a comfortably-off father to bring up his heirs and, if she succeeded, to support them on her own. In 1879, Annie Besant, known as a radical and freethinker and three years previously prosecuted, unsuccessfully, for publishing an outdated text on birth control, lost custody of her daughter to her estranged, and exceedingly strange, clergyman husband. Yet, increasingly, less notorious women were being awarded custody and adequate maintenance after divorce. Gradually, it seems, in complex ways still incompletely explored, divorce court judges were moving towards a conception of marrige as a contract embodying reciprocal rights and obligations between husband and wife, which both were expected to observe, rather than as a relationship of patriarchal domination and dependence. In uneven ways, case law was reflecting contradictory and as yet barely understood social changes. Nevertheless divorce was still not an easy path for a woman to take and in the circumstances it is surprising that so many had the courage and determination to end their marriages.

Many of these changes had at least as much to do with the late Victorian movement for reform and rationalisation of the judicial system as with any desire to liberate women from degrading constraints. Some, though by no means all, active female supporters of women's rights were indeed equivocal about liberalisation of the divorce laws (and also encouragement of contraception) on the grounds that in late Victorian conditions this would go further to liberate philandering males than respectable females. However, from the late 1880s there was an unprecedented level of public discussion and criticism of marriage and the family from all corners, including fiction (as in such plays as Shaw's *The Philanderer*), pamphlets and the press. When, in 1888, the *Daily Telegraph* asked its readers' opinion of the marriage laws it received 27,000 letters in a month, expressing all points of view.[6]

The growing challenge to the conventions of marriage among the middle classes appears to have coincided with a peak of enthusiasm for formal marriage and associated religious ritual among the working class. Older irregular customs of co-habitation and separation were disappearing except in remote rural areas; illegitimacy rates were exceptionally low. The changes in both sections of society had much to do with the fact that marriage was itself changing. Among the working class, as we shall see, *both* men and women were dependent for a reasonable standard of living upon a stable partnership. The argument that formal marriage was promoted by working-class women as a source of security, as expanding capitalism forced them into increasing dependency, does not, among other things, account for the enthusiasm of working-class *men* for stable partnerships.[7] Their lives were considerably eased by the support of a practical woman. Furthermore, for all classes but especially for the longer living middle classes, falling mortality meant that marriage was becoming a commitment of unprecedented length. Up to this time death was the major cause of marriage break-up among relatively young adults, statistically comparable with divorce today. Women were more likely than men to be widowed and were less likely to remarry. In 1901 one woman in eight was a widow. Falling mortality meant that a stressful marriage might have to be endured for longer, a fact which in itself might induce reconsideration. High male death rates meant that the female-headed one-parent family was as frequent then as now and as often a cause of poverty. For the comfortably-off woman widowhood could be an enviable condition giving her a legal and actual independence, for example over the control of her own property, even in certain circumstances the local vote, denied to married women; but for poorer women rapid remarriage could be the only route to security.

III

But whatever the realities and the hazards, marriage and motherhood was the expected female goal. It was urged upon them with fervour at least as great, though with somewhat different emphasis, than earlier in the century, buttressed by a variety of theoretical justifications from the natural and social sciences and from theology. An important sense in which the late Victorian period differs from its predecessors is in the pervasive awareness of a heightened sense of international rivalry – economic, military and imperial. One outcome was an intensified sense of nationhood and an associated concern with the quality and quantity of the population of each nation; economic and military success were assumed to be associated with national superiority in both numbers and in fitness. It was a blend which could, and in some places did, open the door to more or less virulent forms of racism. More generally it encouraged governments and elite groups to seek means to discourage too drastic a decline in the birth rate, to reduce infant mortality and to improve the physical quality of surviving children. The origins of these concerns lay not in the Boer War, where they are often located, but in the rivalries of the two preceding decades, of which the Boer War was itself a product, though the war certainly enhanced such pressures in Britain.

One outcome was the demand for more and better motherhood, especially among the lower classes, to promote the raising of healthier national stock. Earlier in the century good mothering was proposed as woman's contribution to stability *within* a rapidly changing British society – a stable home was expected to produce secure, responsible citizens. Later, its additional role was to help secure Britain's *international* position. In a similar fashion 'surplus' unmarried women were being urged, in these years, to migrate to the empire. There they would find men to marry, with whom they could maintain both the size of the white British population in the colonies and, equally important, perpetuate the hegemony of British values, while civilising the men through their womanly inspiration. As one advocate put it:

What can be more ennobling, more healthy or more truly womanly than the doing of domestic work as our ancestresses did it? . . . and how new countries benefit by the presence of more women of culture and high principle none can realize who have not seen for themselves. They maintain the chivalry of men, raise the tone of their less favoured sisters and uphold the standards of morality and good manners as only women can do.[8]

A better fate, it was urged, than wasting their lives in embittered feminism born of frustration at their inability to achieve fulfilment as women.

Back at home, local authorities established 'hygienic milk depots' (the first in St Helens in 1899) to provide sterile milk to promote the survival of infants. In the 1890s a number of local authorities appointed lady health visitors and district nurses to advise not always welcoming mothers on childcare practices. Elementary schools played increasing (though not overwhelming) attention both to physical exercise, to enable girls, like boys, to grow up to perform their expected roles in maximum fitness, and to teaching domestic skills and infant care.

Hence there was an enhanced public emphasis upon motherhood and the importance of stable family life at a time when more women than before were challenging women's expected role and the family faced an unprecedented level of criticism.

IV

Central to this debate, necessarily, was the question of relationships between men and women. The beliefs that 'the Victorian family' was more or less universally patriarchal, and that 'the Victorians' believed a woman to be sexually dormant until her passions were aroused by a man in the lawful marriage bed, whereafter, contradictorily, she contemplated sex with, at best, resignation, may well be instances of historians mistaking minority prescriptive literature for authentic experience. Against the slender evidence that this was reality can be placed equally slender evidence of contented and sharing partnerships, of female desires recognisable to the modern observer and sexual fulfilment for women.[9] Passionlessness certainly does not for example, surprising as it might seem, characterise the diaries of Beatrice Webb in this period. It is

also possible, in a secret area where nothing can be certain, that
more people grew up in sexual ignorance in this urbanised
society than before. Belief in the desirability of a reticence
about sexuality which promoted ignorance was not confined to
the God-fearing middle classes. Anxious mothers in
overcrowded working-class homes worked hard to ensure that
children of the opposite sex slept, washed and dressed
separately. Maternal pregnancies, however frequent, were
rarely discussed or, apparently, noticed by children in such
households. The need to separate the children in small homes
often forced the parents also to sleep apart.[10]

Amid such uncertainty it would be foolish to offer confident
explanations of the widespread use of prostitutes by men of all
classes. This too came under challenge in this period, though
not without difficulty. Shaw's *Mrs Warren's Profession* (1892)
was banned for eight years, perhaps because it was not only
fierce but funny, and unmistakably clear in its message. Shaw
shared the perception of a more singleminded campaigner,
Josephine Butler, that what led many women into prostitution
was not female depravity or male lust but an economy which
did not provide for many women any other stable means of
earning a living. It is clear that there was not a strict divide
between depraved prostitutes and respectable women, but that
need drove many otherwise respectable women into it at some
point in their lives. Legislative attempts to control prostitution
were not, however, derived from concern about female poverty
or designed to prevent it, but from fear of an epidemic of VD.
The contentious Contagious Diseases Acts of 1864, 1868 and
1869 which resulted were designed to police female prostitutes
rather than their male clients. They enabled police in naval and
barrack towns (where VD was especially visible to service
doctors) to enforce the medical inspection of women suspected
of prostitution. This legislation understandably angered
women, and many men, the more so in view of the opportunities it offered for police harassment of women. It
drove many women, following Josephine Butler, to the
courageous task of speaking publicly, often to hostile
audiences, on such a delicate issue. It was a challenge of
unprecedented force to an unusually explicit official expression
of the age-old double standard.

An important theme of the long but eventually successful (in 1886) campaign for the repeal of the Contagious Diseases Acts was to counter the belief that innate male sexual needs made the supply of prostitutes essential. Rather, argued Josephine Butler and her supporters, males could and should practise chastity, monogamy and respect for the other sex. They should, in fact, accept the moral lead of women and adopt the values conventionally ascribed to the idealised woman; take *seriously* the rhetoric about woman's moral superiority and her role as man's guide towards a more spiritual existence. An important characteristic of many of the women who sought to promote women's causes in this period was their acceptance of such essential elements of the ideology of separate spheres and their determined reinterpretation of it as a basis from which to promote the notion of female *superiority*.

Such values need not, and in Josephine Butler's case did not, lead to a repressive attitude to sexuality in general. Some of her supporters, however, moved on to the 'social purity' campaigns of the 1880s and 1890s which have given the Victorians their most enduring stereotype. Butler was involved in their first, and partially commendable, success, the Criminal Law Amendment Act, 1885. This, following W. T. Stead's campaign against child prostitution, raised the age of consent for females to 16. By tightening the law against brothels it also drove more women onto the more violent environment of the streets; and it introduced new penalties against male homosexual behaviour, for the first time penalising private as well as public actions (this was the law under which Oscar Wilde was prosecuted ten years later). Certainly in this period the law intruded more vigorously than before into private lives in a concern to confine sexual behaviour within 'normal' bounds which went beyond its previous concern with *public* decency.[11]

The 'social purity' vigilantistes sought to enforce this more intrusive law, but there is no reason to believe that they were any more representative of widely held beliefs than were the other minority who explicitly challenged convention. They were, however, probably closer than the self-conscious sexual radicals to a dominant, though not necessarily puritanical, respectability. Undoubtedly a certain sober, ordered, respectability in all spheres of life was more predominant in later than in earlier Victorian society. Among leading supporters of women's rights married respectability or single celibacy were the rule in contrast to the racier style of Mary Wollstonecraft and her generation. The passionate, lasting, friendships between so many prominent women have often a rather touching innocence about them, though they could also go deeper and be profoundly emotionally disturbing, unsupervised by a legal system which made no comment upon lesbianism.[12] Certainly few women activists – even so radical a 'new woman' as Olive Schreiner – demanded sexual freedom for women; liberation from sexual exploitation by men appeared more urgent in a society in which few women could in fact lead independent lives.

V

Many women, of course, had no choice but to try to do so, and often also to support others. Exactly how many women were active in the paid labour market, and at what, is by no means simple to establish. The censuses substantially under-recorded part-time and seasonal work, in which many, especially married, women were engaged. They also under-recorded the work of women who worked alongside their husbands in shops, small businesses or farms. Neither are they wholly reliable guides to full-time paid employment, even in factories. Historians routinely comment on the inadequacy of the census in this respect – then proceed to rely upon it due to its accessability and the absence of clear alternatives. This procedure will not do, especially if we are seeking national aggregates and trends. The census is an immensely valuable source, but only if used with close attention to what was actually being recorded and it is important to distinguish between what it can and cannot tell us.[13] It can, for example, probably give an accurate enough guide to the numbers of full-time female school teachers, married and unmarried, since such an occupational group were likely to record themselves and to be recorded accurately. It was, as we shall see, a poor guide to the much larger category of domestic servants. An accurate national statistical picture of Victorian female paid labour may be one of the important sets of historical data that we shall, in reality, never possess; though local, including business, records may enable us to build up a reasonably accurate picture for specific firms, occupations or districts.

There is no reason to doubt, however, that the largest single female paid occupation was domestic service. There *is* serious reason to doubt certain widely held assumptions relating to it, in particular that the British employed significantly more servants in this period than their European neighbours, and that the numbers of servants were falling substantially by the end of the century. In the 1871 census the number of paid domestics in Britain may have been inflated by as much as one-third, due to the enumerators' practice of categorising as 'housekeeper' or 'servant working at home' women living at home, such as daughters in middle-class families who were unlikely to have been paid for their labour, or to have performed domestic service for payment in any other household. The registrar-general's office was aware of this problem and sought, census by census, to make a more careful distinction between paid and unpaid labour. Hence what has appeared as a late-century decline in the servant population may be, rather, the census achieving greater precision. This suggests that there is also little substance in another well-established assumption: that servants were primarily an item of conspicuous consumption, an indicator of middle-class status, of whom households bought as many as they could afford. It is increasingly evident that servant-keeping was determined at least as much by need as by status: relatively wealthy households containing a sufficient number of fit grown females required them least (though they might have employed non-resident daily or other 'help'). Relatively poor artisan households containing children or other dependents and no adult female other than the mother could, and did, employ workhouse girls for little more than their board.

Most servants were the sole general servant in a not very wealthy household, hence the harshness of their working lives. It was certainly an unpopular occupation from which women escaped at the first opportunity to any acceptable alternative, especially if they were town dwellers. Unmarried women of rural origin were most likely to become servants, probably because they lacked the skills or the contacts which might give them access to alternative urban occupations.[14] Lack of freedom and companionship or petty mistreatment by employers in the immensely variable environments in which servants worked could drive them to leave even for relatively worse paid jobs. And many women hated the subservience; 'I couldn't bow and scrape'[15] was one reason for leaving. Hannah Mitchell, a country girl, left her first post in service, aged 16, in 1887 to earn an inadequate 8s. a week in a dressmaking shop because it gave her more control over her own life, the opportunity to make friends and her Sundays free for reading – a change which she never regretted.[16]

VI

This shift in our perspective on the role of servants has to be complemented by a shift in our image of women who were not in the paid workforce. The stereotype of the functionless 'angel in the house', in so far as it is derived at all from life rather than from satire can be based on, at most, a narrow stratum of the upper and upper-middle class. Even at this level the management of a complex household, amid the dirt and pollution of a late Victorian town or city, with minimal assistance from domestic technology, was no trivial task. The better-off gained from technological change: easier access to gas and electricity, improved water supplies, cooking, heating and lighting facilities, commercial laundries, more accessible ready-made clothing and household linen. But such changes were at least as likely to raise the standard required of household management as to reduce its demands. The poorer housewife's task of managing much scarcer resources was obviously still more exacting and often combined with paid work, perhaps in someone else's household. Below the level of the very comfortably-off household which can be reconstructed from Mrs Beeton's *Book of Household Management* (1861) (at most around 10 per cent of the middle class) females at home worked as hard as women and men outside the home, though

how hard, in what environment and with what assistance
varied with income level and the stage of the family life cycle.[17]

Given the centrality of purposeful work to Victorian
socialisation this should not be surprising. Similarly, many of
the middle class who were too wealthy to be consumed by
household tasks, or with time to spare from the domestic
environment with which they may otherwise have been
content, or for various reasons without family responsibilities,
felt a powerful drive to use their time purposefully for the good
of others and an equally strong sense of frustration and
desperation when they could find no such role. Since paid
employment was, for most of them, neither available nor
socially acceptable, voluntary action – philanthropy, or the
active promotion of 'causes' – provided the main alternative.
This form of activity also was not so easy, lightly undertaken or
trivial as it is sometimes portrayed, and it should not be seen as
primarily a means to affirm social status. Though unpaid,
women often saw it as a long-term commitment, akin to a
profession in the seriousness with which it was undertaken and
in the skills required and acquired. It was estimated that in
1893 around 500,000 women worked 'continuously and semi-
professionally' in voluntary activities. Many others were more
marginally involved. To work, often unwelcome, in the slums of
a late Victorian city required courage and resilience, as did
speaking on a public platform, for women brought up to be
reticent. It was often religious conviction which gave them the
required strength. Far from being *less* visible in the public
sphere than earlier in the century, many *more* women were
visible, as effective and dedicated activists promoting every
imaginable cause, from womens' trade unionism to temperance
and sabbatarianism.

In so doing they acquired organisational and political skills
and knowledge about the workings of government,
administration, the law, education and the social services,
which they wielded formidably. Many of them acquired the
conviction that only when women had the vote could they hope
to achieve their other aims. Women at all social levels
participated in an unusually rich associational life, both formal
and informal. The large numbers who were members of
organisations undermine the notion of female isolation in the

home: 200,000 belonged to the Mothers' Union which was as dedicated to better conditions for mothers as to upholding Christianity; 50,000 belonged to the Women's Liberal Federation; 12,000 to the Women's Co-operative Guild; thousands more to such organisations as the powerful Women's Temperance Association. These organisations are important in themselves, for the effective way in which women lobbied at local and national level, and for the confidence and mutual support they gave to the women who built strong networks within and among these organisations.

Sometimes comfortably-off women gained in experience and confidence through activities directed at an abstract and misguided conception of the lives and needs of poorer women, which were not always appropriate or helpful; but it is by no means the case that they were invariably or mainly 'lady bountifuls' blind to the 'real' needs of the working class.[18]

VII

Increasing numbers of women, however, either wanted or were forced by financial exigencies to seek an independent paid career. Where it was not financially necessary family opposition could be formidable and often successful. Even in the 1870s and 1880s Mary Kingsley (niece of Charles and Henry) was prevented by her parents not only from working but from acquiring an education above a basic level. Like other women in all classes she became a secret autodidact, but she never escaped from the psychic ill-effects of this frustration, the kind of experience which led too many women to crisis and breakdown in this period.[19]

However, a significant proportion of middle-class households were well enough off for everyday comfort, but could not afford to keep their daughters in idleness, perhaps indefinitely if they did not marry. This material reality encouraged many middle-class men to support improved secondary education for girls, as a path towards a respectable career, probably in teaching.[20] Fewer of them showed enthusiasm for female higher education, which threatened to tempt women to compete in the masculine professions. This period saw the unprecedented expansion of serious education for females at private secondary, teacher-training and university levels, but the latter developed least and with least funding (as the limited endowments and austere environments of the Oxford and Cambridge women's colleges suggest).

Teaching in these same private schools and colleges was the predominant career of women educated in such institutions. Alternative careers suited to women from the substantial middle class were opening up only slowly: they could be lady factory inspectors from 1894; hospital matrons; in the early 1870s the medical register was open to women, though there were only 212 female doctors by 1901. An adventurous few became journalists, 6400 were actresses, 3700 artists, 22,600 musicians. Less exotically, many more went into the newly developing, routine, but respectable jobs as telephonists, clerks and typists, generally vastly underusing their abilities.

This latter development, and also the expansion of nursing and of the genteel department stores and of state education after 1870 provided most for women in the layers of respectability below the comfortably-off middle class. They rarely had the choice but to work, at least until marriage, and were encouraged, indeed expected, by their families to do so. The technological innovations which transformed the Dickensian counting-house into the modern office offered a new range of skilled, if subordinate, jobs to women. The telephone, telegraphy, the typewriter, dictating and adding machines, new methods of filing and retrieving data were operated mainly by women. They appropriated or were assigned such work where it was new, without a male tradition, and where it could be routinised and clearly separated from a career ladder. Above all, they gained from its expansion during a period in which the supply of suitably educated women with limited alternative prospects greatly outstripped that of suitably qualified males. Though recruited for their supposedly docile qualities and low expectations, over time a number of women used their growing experience and skills to bargain individually for higher pay, status and independence, often with their feet in a seller's market for competent women. Without benefit of unions, women made the most of their skills and scarcity value. The Civil Service was not for long able to forbid its typists to leave

the building at lunchtime. Women did not make dramatic
gains but they were real; some by these means could achieve a
modest degree of upward social mobility, through their own
efforts.[21] Real, too, were those gains due to the increased
respectability of nursing and the expansion of state education.
With a curious lack of public discussion elementary education
was extended to girls on the same terms as boys at the very time
that middle-class girls were fighting for similar privileges. The
parliamentary debates centred on the need to educate boys
especially for their roles as voters and workers. An unforeseen
outcome was to provide not only education, but teaching jobs
for clever working- and lower-middle-class girls. The life of the
village school teacher could be lonely, but the urban female
teacher, especially in London, enjoyed an unusual degree of
independence and access to leisure and cultural activities.
Many of them refused to give this up on marriage and even after
childbirth, though teaching was no easier to combine with
Victorian household management than any other occupation.
Economic necessity was plainly not normally the main
motivation. Personal fulfilment combined with the desire to
continue to be able to afford some of the cultural pleasures and
comforts accessible to the single teacher over-rode the
imperatives of Victorian domestic ideology without, it appears,
great social opprobrium.[22]

VIII

Many working-class women also worked after, as before,
marriage, but less often, it can be assumed, from choice. How
many, as we have seen, is uncertain, as are the precise reasons.
It is reasonable to assume that very many worked due to
material necessity, because husbands were dead, disappeared,
un/or underemployed, disabled or low-paid. But definitions of
'necessity', above the level of starvation, were variable and
patterns of married women's work were also influenced by the
local economy, local custom, the family life cycle, domestic
routine, by the husband's attitudes and occupation and by the
individual responses and experiences of women. Some clearly
chose to work. As one woman told Clementina Black: 'A

shilling of your own is worth two that *he* gives you.' Black convincingly described the process whereby, for some women, working which began as necessity became over time both habit and a source of comfort, companionship and independence even when the husband's earnings improved. And some women might continue to work in order to save, to educate the children, to get a better house or for some similar goal.[23] In the potteries, a major employer of women, married women who did not contribute to the family income were regarded as 'lazy' and 'the figure of the totally dependent woman is not easily discovered'. The rhythm of work, with frequent breaks in production, the tradition of self-imposed work routines and the fact of workers living close to the potbank eased the integration of domestic and paid labour, as did a certain local acceptance of role-sharing between the sexes.[24]

In the Leicester hosiery industry it was taken for granted that married women would work.[25] In Preston, a town with exceptionally stable work opportunities for women in weaving, in 1881 the wives of relatively well-paid skilled and supervisory workers worked in significant numbers though it cannot have been necessary to keep their families from starvation. Indeed the wives of worse-paid, irregularly employed men in Preston were *less* likely to be recorded in the census as being in full-time work. They may have engaged in the low-paid, casual labour which was least likely to appear in the census.[26]

For many, probably most, married women the pattern of their work lives was most influenced by the age of their children. Indeed the norm was the reverse of that of today, women being more likely to work when children were young and demands upon the family resources greatest, giving up, often with relief, when children were old enough to earn; though they sometimes had to return to the labour market at a later age when the children left home. Faced with the grimness of the double burden in late Victorian conditions women often saw giving up paid work, rather than entry to it, as liberation.

The acquisition of additional household resources through paid work was indeed for very many women an extension of the role of household manager and inseparable from it; their paid and unpaid work roles were complementary rather than opposed alternatives. It appeared to contemporaries that by the end of the century fewer married women were in paid work, but the precise extent and distribution of this decline is unclear. It is certainly arguable that in households that could acquire sufficient to meet their immediate needs from other sources, unless the wife was in the rare situation of being able to earn substantially, it made more sense for her to stay at home. She might add more to the family standard of living through careful household management than from low earnings. Her skill in extracting maximum value from the household resources – her role as 'chancellor of the domestic exchequer' – was a vital determinant of its standard of living and of its outward respectability and status. Her skill with a needle, at shrewd shopping and nutritious cooking could in fact, and not merely in middle-class fantasy, make an essential difference to the living standard and style of a household where every fraction of a penny counted; not to mention her skill at using the pawnshop to stretch resources further. Where space was available, earning could be combined with household management by taking in lodgers, cooking food for sale, or small shopkeeping. Wives took justifiable pride in their skills. Housewifery was a *job* and very many women saw it as such. A related point, which should not be underestimated, is that the enthusiasm with which so many women gave up work on marriage arose from exhilaration at the prospect of being for the first time free of the control of either parents or employer and in possession of their own lives and homes. Control by the husband was not necessarily or initially comparable. Unfortunately for many women the exhilaration was short-lived, as Hannah Mitchell's experience of exchanging paid for increasingly gruelling unpaid work again illustrates.[27]

In practice a very high proportion of working-class households depended upon earnings from the wife at some point in the life cycle. In such circumstances it seems inappropriate to characterise the wife's relationship to her husband, as is conventionally done, as one of dependency, indeed of growing dependency as the onward march of capitalism penned her up increasingly in the home. The reality of working-class lives, in which very few even among higher status working men experienced complete security at work, due to seasonality, periodic depression, disputes or other hazards, and rarely had adequate protection against unemployment, accident or sickness, bred a conscious and valued *interdependence* between the different skills and contributions of husband and wife within the household. Hence the enthusiasm of men for marriage, mentioned earlier. Stereotypes of the dependent working-class woman assume a stability of male working life which was rarely the case.

Furthermore there is little sign that wives who engaged in paid labour outside the home necessarily thereby acquired greater independence or status within the community, while many women clearly did derive a sense of self-worth from their household skills; and some were propelled by their determination to defend and extend the family living standards into political campaigns on housing, education and similar issues. Women who were not engaged in paid work did not necessarily retreat wholly into the private sphere. The relationship between 'public' and 'private' in the lives of married women was more complex than is suggested by the frequent identification of absence of paid employment with a wholly 'private' existence.

There is no need to romanticise the interdependence of husband and wife and it did not necessarily imply any degree of equality between male and female; it arose from material necessity and could co-exist with a variety of types of relationship within marriage. Dependence perhaps more accurately characterised the status of middle-class wives in this period, and it was in this milieu that criticism of marriage was strongest.

The paid manual work available to married and unmarried women outside the home (their own or someone else's) of course varied regionally and over time, due to changes in technology, in management practices, in consumer demand and in government intervention. Technological change in the direction of increased automation of work processes might be accompanied by the replacement of male with cheaper female labour, but examples of this are not frequent. It was not necessarily in an employer's interest to replace male with female labour in such circumstances if, for example, this might lead to higher labour turnover due to the tendency of women to leave on marriage, or to conflict with male workers and their unions. The move towards automated processes and the 'de-skilling' of the labour force was in any case less rapid and commonplace in this period than is often assumed. In more complex ways new skills were replacing old. Certainly overall 'de-skilling' is not the most helpful framework within which to analyse female or male factory employment in this period.

There were circumstances not associated with technological change in which employers might seize opportunities to replace male with female labour as a means of cutting costs or of creating a supposedly more docile labour force. For example they could use an unsuccessful male strike to this effect, as in the Edinburgh printing industry in 1872. Thereafter there was an unusually high proportion of females in the Edinburgh printing industry. But this did not occur in other printing centres.[28] Opportunities for the substitution of male with female labour did not readily present themselves. Whether they did so, or whether employers were disposed to take advantage of them, was highly contingent upon the nature of the occupation, the condition of the labour market and of industrial relations within the industry, among other things.

Consumer demand accompanied by technological change boosted the garment industry, an increasing employer of women. Government factory legislation may have helped to determine the highly exploitative character of much of this classic 'sweated' industry, one of the scandals of the period. Increased regulation of factories provided some incentive for the use of domestic outworkers and the spread of small, unregulated workshops. But this was only possible because the new technology which facilitated the growth of the industry (above all the sewing machine) was cheaply available to the small entrepreneur who faced strong temptation to drive his workers hard, and because the workshops were a useful buffer between the large factory and a seasonally fluctuating market.[29]

The influences upon employment patterns were complex. The historiography appears to present a clear picture of female manual work, in which there was strict demarcation between occupations defined as male and female, however arbitrary its origins, and changes in definition were rare, slow and painful. In general, women's work is said to have been of lower status and less skilled than men's, and paid at around one-half of the rates. This is the conventional picture. More striking, on closer inspection, is the *variety* of levels of skill and pay at which women worked. The largest source of full-time paid employment for women, after domestic service, was in the textile industry. Within cotton textiles alone, the tasks performed by women, the proportion of them working and their pay levels varied not only between spinning and weaving, the two main division of the trade, but between different towns specialising in either branch. Local variations in earnings appear to have been even greater in the Yorkshire wool textile industry.

In the cotton-weaving towns of Blackburn, Burnley and Preston, where both men and women worked on the looms and women could earn a good and regular wage, married women were highly likely to work, though most did so in Preston which had poorer work opportunities for males than the other towns. Women weavers in Preston earned more than in Wigan, where they also predominated in the weaving workforce but where men had good work opportunities in the mines. In wool-weaving Bradford, where women weavers predominated, they earned less than in the mixed weaving community of Huddersfield. In the cotton-spinning towns of Bolton and Rochdale and in wool manufacture generally married women were less likely to work in textiles though most unmarried women in these towns would spend some time in the mill.[30]

In general women could earn more in cotton-weaving than in any other branch of textiles and were a majority of all weavers, though weaving supervisors (overlookers) were invariably promoted from among the male minority. Male and female weavers were usually on the same piece rates though males generally took home higher pay each week (*c.* 29s. compared with 25s. for females). The reasons are complicated. Men were likely to operate more looms than women (four or six) and to be engaged in heavier weaving, which earned more. This might come about due to their greater strength or because male overlookers put more profitable work the way of men. Men also tended to work longer hours, due partly to legislative restrictions upon female hours. But also, male weavers were likely to be older (up to 55 or beyond) than female, most of whom were under 25. Weaving was a skilled job, since looms were not automatic and needed familiarity and constant attention to ensure smooth production. Longer serving workers, male or female, became more skilled, more productive and practised at repairing their machines, hence avoiding loss of time and money waiting for the overlooker to do the job. Such realities account for a great deal of the disparities between aggregate male and female wages. In general men did better. But not always due to discrimination. Some female weavers earned more than some males in the same occupation and many of them earned more than men in other occupations, for example agricultural labourers.[31]

In another important source of female employment, the potteries, women's jobs were largely lower paid, less skilled and involved less exercise of authority or control than did men's. The employers used women as cheap labour during the trading crises of the 1880s and 1890s. Yet women worked in every department and throughout the main skill divisions of the potteries. Women's skill at decorating had long been highly valued and better paid than a high proportion of male work in the industry. As in weaving, a comparison of aggregate male and female earnings puts men well ahead but such comparisons obscure variations in female earnings and, again, the fact that females were generally markedly younger than males. When these variables are allowed for, the disparity between male and female experience is much less stark. Most manufacturing sectors contained gender-segregated hierarchies of skill and pay which offered men the most favourable prospects, but they were *hierarchies* rather than gender-determined *strata*; in all sectors some women earned more than some men.

Comparison of male and female earnings is, in fact, more complicated than is sometimes apparent. *Any* statements about earnings for this period should be treated with caution since the available data are, at best, patchy. This is partly because actual earnings can be difficult to establish. Many workers were paid on piece rates, with results which varied among individuals and from week to week, but in some occupations (e.g. in the potteries) there were complicated group rates; and the systems of bonuses and fines could crucially affect take-home pay. And, when comparing male and female pay, it is not easy to compare like with like since they rarely performed precisely comparable tasks. Where they did so, women did not *always* come off worst. In printing, the slowness of the more complex tasks undertaken by highly skilled men (one-off layouts or printing a foreign language) could bring them lower earnings than less experienced women on more routine typesetting jobs.

Women's earning prospects were not good, but neither were those of many men and little purpose is served by making them appear worse than they were. What is important is to establish what those earnings were and how they were constructed. Even in domestic service, which is generally regarded as a seriously low-paid occupation, an estimate of the earnings of living-in domestics adjusted to include the value of board and lodgings shows general servants actually to have had real earnings of around the industrial average (£25–£30 a year for the period of the 1870s, 1880s and 1890s) and the skilled elite of cooks to be earning the good wage of £35–£40 a year.[32] Not that this made domestic service any the more attractive; and lower-paid work was not always relentlessly grim. The account of Hannah Mitchell, an astute and highly political observer, testifies to the supportive and enjoyable atmosphere of the low-paid dressmaking workshops to which she escaped from service.

In general women's opportunities on the labour market were inferior to those of men but precisely how inferior and for what reasons is a more difficult question than is often apparent. To gain a fuller picture we need to know more about their mode of access to jobs. Dependent as this so often was upon contacts, in the near universal absence of a formal labour market, it could depend upon their relationships to local networks. In this respect as in others the worlds in and outside the workplace were not distinct but interdependent. In Preston it appears that a male network controlled female workers' careers, as male overlookers recruited through male friends and neighbours. In the potteries female contacts were the key to women getting and keeping jobs.

In rare cases high levels of female employment could buy a level of independence similar to that of men. Dundee in 1901 was unique in having more women in paid employment (in the jute and other textile industries) than men. Unmarried women set up households together – and more women than men were convicted of drunkenness. More typically, unmarried girls lived at home, handing all their wages to their mothers. Or if they worked away from home, they lived in lodgings with little enough surplus to be able to eat, still less to drink to excess. Hannah Mitchell escaped starvation in her first job only when her landlady noticed she could not afford an evening meal and saved her a portion of the daily family dinner, probably not an uncommon form of support of young working people. But such young female workers also found time to enjoy themselves and certainly appreciated their independence. Comparable with the middle-class girls who sought independence, there was also a generation of ambitious but frustrated working girls produced in the 1890s, anxious to leave home for freedom and education. They were reacting against their mothers' hopeless drudgery, female autodidacts seeking education in libraries or university extension courses, and friends and activities in the ILP or in bicycling clubs.

Limited male work opportunities and wages clearly played a part in determining whether women worked and to some extent in what conditions. Women are often portrayed as victims both of employers and of male trade unionists, pawns in the class struggle, as employers sought to use them as cheap and docile replacements for male labour and unions strove to resist by excluding women from the workforce. An important part of this strategy is said to have been the demand for a 'family wage', sufficient to enable men to support their families without help from female earnings.

So far as it has been researched (and the empirical data are, so far, very slight) this is the truth of the core of a much more complex story. There is very little evidence of men using family obligations as an explicit basis of wage negotiations, though public statements about the desirability of a 'family wage' (e.g. by male weavers) were commonplace; and the supposed absence of family obligations was used by employers to justify keeping female clerical pay low and to defend the lower wages of female than of male teachers, in this occupation in which, unusually, men and women did identical work on fixed pay scales. The family wage was clearly an aspiration which many men, and women, shared, though few can have thought it immediately attainable.

Henry Broadhurst's statement to the 1877 conference of the TUC is frequently quoted as typical of the attitudes of male trade unionists:

> they had the future of their country and children to consider and it was their duty as men and husbands to use their utmost efforts to bring about a condition of things where their wives should be in their proper sphere at home, seeing after their house and family, instead of being dragged into the competition for livelihood against the great and strong men of the world.

Read in the context in which it was delivered, in one of a series of debates on factory legislation, in which the Women's Trade Union League challenged legislative controls on the hours and type of work available to women (they argued that women workers would be better protected by the appointment of female factory inspectors), it is clear that the women had explicit male support, and that the virulent tone of Broadhurst's frequently reiterated antagonism was *untypical*. Year after year he failed to get majority support for his opposition to female factory inspectors and the women found outspoken male defendants.[33]

Trade union attitudes seem to have been variable and contingent upon personal and trade circumstances. Many trade unionists had good reason to want to relieve their wives from the double burden, while being more ambivalent about the effects of exclusion upon their unmarried daughters. And they all fought at least as hard to exclude other *male* workers from their trades. Furthermore union membership was not large enough, neither was its power sufficient to bear much of the weight of responsibility for female subordination at work. Unions were, indeed, strongest in trades which employed few women. Certainly unions in trades which included women could have striven harder on their behalf. The textile unions especially (women predominated in the Cotton Weavers' Union) overlooked the problem of women without male support. Again, there were local and individual variations in attitude, but in so far as it is possible to generalise about the unions with the limited data available Zeitlin's comment on the printers is probably widely applicable:

> Women were to be excluded as a consequence of the general logic of craftmen's attempt to restrict entry to the trade and to maintain their wages and working conditions rather than because of sexual antipathy as such, though the male compositors were quite prepared to sanction sexual discrimination to further their larger aims.
>
> ('Craft Regulation', p. 161)

The ability of the unions of this period, struggling for survival, to enhance the position of *any* subordinate group, as distinct from protecting existing privilege, was extremely limited. More important than trade union patriarchalism in determining the position of women in the labour market were the decisions of management, wider labour market conditions, changing technology and local customs and relationships.

IX

All of this placed most women in a position of subordination, which some accepted, but which allowed to others some space for independence, manoeuvre and control. Certainly not all of them accepted subordination passively. Women's inactivity in trade unions is generally stressed and attributed to innate female passivity, lack of commitment to the job, male opposition to their membership, lack of time due to domestic commitments and of money to pay dues. Yet female trade union membership rates were not lower than those among men in comparable occupations, were high in Britain compared with most other countries and indeed followed a similar pattern of growth to male membership. It can reasonably be asked whether the reasons why the great majority of women were not in trade unions were different from the reasons why the great majority of male workers were not. There were about 10,600 female trade unionists in 1876, 117,888 in 1896 (102,847 in cotton textile unions), when women were 7.8 per cent of all trade unionists. The rapidity with which female membership increased at certain times (e.g. the increase in the potteries from 2000 to 23,000 between 1914 and 1918) casts doubt on most general explanations of female reluctance to unionise.

Levels of activism are necessarily hard to measure. Women were certainly active in major strikes. The well-known action at Bryant and May in 1888 was only temporarily successful in improving conditions and did not lead to the formation of a permanent union (it was very weak in the 1890s and died after an unsuccessful strike in 1902). In the following year there were strikes of female blanket-weavers in Yorkshire, cigar-makers in Nottingham, cotton and jute workers in Dundee, and mill girls in Kilmarnock. Women (not necessarily unionised) initiated the long and unsuccessful Manningham mills strike in Bradford in 1892 which led to the formation of the ILP. Evidence for a later period suggests that women's involvement in strikes can be in *excess* of their numerical involvement in industry.[34]

But strikes are an extreme and infrequent form of protest. Women, like men, appear to have responded to unfavourable working conditions in a variety of ways. Despite their reputation for docility 'it was rare for a working class child to grow up cowed and spiritless. If and when the need arose authority . . . would be challenged.' Women resisted and evaded authority by negotiating and complaining, individually or collectively, by being awkward and by changing jobs,[35] as Hannah Mitchell did, until at the time of her marriage in 1895 (when she gave up paid work) she was earning 25s. per week at dressmaking.

Some women did not join the union because their menfolk forbade it (apparently a custom of weavers' overlookers in Preston); others were ordered to join by fathers or mothers; others found unions irrelevant to their needs. Some who joined, because they were expected or pressured to do so, never thought of turning to it for help over shopfloor problems, which perhaps also applied to many men. An important difference, however, between the male and female trade union movements was that the organisations formed to promote female unionism

(The Women's Trade Union League, founded 1874; the Women's Trade Union Association, founded 1889; later the Women's Industrial Council) and some of their unions were led by middle-class women (such as Mary Macarthur, an organiser for the WTUL) without experience of manual work. This did not necessarily meant that they misunderstood working women's needs, but there are strong signs of divergent perspectives between them, in particular in the tendency of the women's leaders to give higher priority to their roles as women than as workers. They did not always understand or encourage female solidarity with male workers' grievances. In 1910, for example, female compositors in Edinburgh struck alongside the men for higher pay for all, despite feminist pressure to use the opportunity to see the men defeated and more women admitted to the trade by refusing to join the strike. In the 1900s Mary Macarthur differed from the ex-mill girl Julia Varley (an officer of the wool textile workers' union in 1895 and a member of Bradford trades council at the age of 14; later the first female officer of the Workers' Union) over whether women should be organised separately from or together with men. Varley's use of the latter strategy in the Workers' Union was the more successful.

The women leaders tended also to reinforce the general belief in the incapacity or disinclination of women to unionise, indeed to be more likely than women workers themselves to define them as victims. Partly for this reason, leaders of the Women's Industrial Council, such as Clementina Black, became in the 1880s increasingly disillusioned with trade unionism as the chief route to improvement of the conditions of working women and looked increasingly to state action, for example through the implementation of a minimum wage. The WIC became a highly effective political pressure group mainly responsible for the implementation of Trade Boards in 1909.

The WIC also, more realistically, recognised that the working and domestic lives of women could not be separated. They generally thought it preferable that wives and mothers should not work and hence that male wages should rise to enable men to support their families. They recognised, however, that many women would be without male support at some stage of their lives and that good motherhood and work were in no sense incompatible, even though undesirable in the circumstances of the time.[36]

x

Working women also protested through political channels about social and economic conditions. It is commonly asserted that women became *less* active in popular protest as it became increasingly institutionalised in the course of the nineteenth century: that male-dominated political parties allowed them less space than the relatively unstructured movements of the early part of the century. Lack of systematic evidence makes comparison difficult, but the number of prominent women in the various branches of labour politics is striking. The number of female Fabians has often been noted and women played a prominent role in the ILP from its foundation. Such women as Annie Besant, Eleanor Marx, Margaret and Rachel MacMillan, Julia Varley (also the editor of *Clarion*) were the famous figures in a movement which at least in some localities, such as Clydeside, depended rather crucially upon the mobilisation of women's networks.[37] This was partly because the political labour movement, especially the ILP, in its early days derived much of its strength from organisation around local and social issues (housing, education, the Poor Law) in which women had a strong interest and which were an extension of their role as defenders of family living standards. The Women's Co-operative Guild (founded in 1883, with 4000–5000 members in 1891–2 and 12,800 in 1899–1900) did much to encourage the organisation of women around these issues, including their standing for local authority elections.

The contacts of working-class women within the community were of more than purely local and personal value; they could be mobilised for national and political purposes, and not only by the labour movement: in Preston, from 1906, the Conservative Primrose League built up a membership among women in working-class neighbourhoods which Labour could not match.

The mobilisation of women around important issues of local

government has been underestimated partly because we tend to forget that women had the vote at the local long before the national level. This is understandable in view of the complexity of the relevant legislation. Local issues were defined as lying within the female, caring, sphere. Women householders (i.e. ratepayers) had been eligible to vote in elections for Poor Law Guardians since 1834, but no woman tested their right to run for office until 1875 when Martha Merrington was successful in South Kensington. By 1885 there were 50 female guardians. The reduction of the rating qualification for candidates to £5, in 1892, increased the numbers eligible to stand and by 1899 there were 1975 female guardians. From 1870 women could vote and stand for school boards, as around 200 did by 1900. Women were prominent in protests about the abolition of school boards in 1902.

An Act which slipped quietly through Parliament in 1869 (two years after women were refused the national vote) enabled female householders to vote for municipal and (after their creation in 1888) county councils, but until 1907 they might not stand for either.[38] When in 1879 the Manchester Suffrage Society organised, in a working-class district, a meeting of women possessing the right to vote in local elections they were amazed by the number of women who packed the meeting hall on three separate occasions.[39]

We know, however, very little about the political involvement of women at all social levels and their roles in holding party organisations together. The number who surface in accounts of the ILP, the 50,000 women in the Women's Liberal Federation, the 5000 in the Women's Liberal and Unionist Association in 1891 and the perhaps 700,000 female members of the Primrose League in 1901 suggest that it was considerable.

Out of contacts formed through local politics and through philanthropy and single-cause campaigns, the campaign for the National Suffrage developed. It grew steadily, if without public drama or hope of immediate success, throughout the period, including among working women, through the activities of the local suffrage societies such as those of the North: 23,359 women cotton workers signed a suffrage petition in 1901.[40]

208   LATER VICTORIAN BRITAIN 1867–1900

Opposition was also strong among men and women and many active women judged it wiser to pursue single attainable issues rather than to pursue the vote. Feminist as she was, Emily Davies withdrew her support from the suffrage campaign lest it endanger her foundation, Girton College. The views of women who campaigned to promote the interests of women were in no sense homogeneous though the variety of their interests, ideas and perceptions has been underexplored. The most prominent of them were divided by generation: those born before 1830, and active in this period (such as Florence Nightingale, Frances Power Cobbe, Barbara Bodichon) were generally from wealthy and often radical backgrounds. They boldly, sometimes flamboyantly, laid the foundations and provided the inspiration for the generation born in the 1840s and 1850s. These (such as Emily Davies) cautiously, but very determinedly, built and protected new institutions which nurtured another generation, born in the 1870s and 1880s, which went on, boldly again, to demand political and social changes.

All three generations, however, avoided confrontation with men whenever possible, but proceeded by colonising and building bases in new or empty spaces, such as school boards or the nursing profession and then moving outwards. Very few feminists argued publicly that women were equal with men though some, such as Emily Davies, certainly believed it. The earlier ideas of Mary Wollstonecraft were lost, silent or transformed, as many women indeed came to believe that women had different and superior qualities from those of men, which deserved nurture, or thought it tactical wisdom to say so. They presented themselves as an influential source of the respectability and social responsibility which their contemporaries valued so highly and which they indeed did much to promote.[41] In a changing and changed society the meanings of 'equality', 'equal rights' or 'equal opportunities' for females with males were far from clear and likely to differ for different groups and individuals. The variety of women's beliefs and aspirations was a source of strength rather than of weakness, for never in history had male predominance been challenged simultaneously on so many fronts.

9. The General and the Bishops: Alternative Responses to Dechristianisation

STUART MEWS

'COLOUR, soup, soap and hope' is how a historian in the 1970s summed up the response of that quintessentially late Victorian creation, the Salvation Army, to the plight of the so-called 'submerged tenth' in late-nineteenth-century England.[1] Richard Shannon's words convey very well the attitude of a generation which largely accepts and appreciates the Salvation Army's social work but treats with mild amusement and some disdain its anachronistic 'blood and fire' theology, bands and bonnets. A hundred years ago, this genial consensus did not exist and the Salvation Army was either welcomed for being in the frontline against dechristianisation and working-class assertiveness, or criticised for itself posing, or at least comprising part of, a social and religious threat. Attitudes to the Army, in other words, have not moved in a single, straight line of development from hostility to acceptance; from its earliest days reactions have been mixed and have indeed moved with considerable speed through a variety of changes in the public and ecclesiastical mind. Within an astonishingly short space of time, the Army could be, on the one hand, praised, patronised, and even courted by other religious leaders, and almost overnight, castigated like a precursor of the Moonies for brainwashing teenagers, keeping them beyond their parent's reach, expropriating their money, and marrying them off at the earliest legal age, to other sect members. In short, the development of the Salvation Army, especially in the 1880s, and social and ecclesiastical reactions to it, has much to reveal about what the notions of responsibility and respectability meant in a religious context in late Victorian Britain. 'The Salvation Army', Kitson Clark has suggested, 'is perhaps the most significant and notable product of this exciting period'.[2]

In the second half of the nineteenth century, the leaders of all the churches had many grounds for concern. They shared the difficulty of knowing how to respond to the challenges of an estranged working class, a more secular intellectual climate, and the competition of the new opportunities for leisure and recreation. Within the religious culture, Anglicans felt themselves on the defensive against the aggressive claims of Nonconformists and the refined attractions of Rome, which not only threatened from without but also, in Anglo-Catholic ritualists, seemed to have a fifth column within. But the Anglican ability to respond to this situation was weakened by an archaic system of organisation and finance, and undermined by internal divisions. Tremendous efforts had been made with the support of the new Ecclesiastical Commission to set up new dioceses and extend the parish system to urban England through the erection of over 3500 new churches between 1836 and 1875.[3] Yet despite such evidence of vigour many churchmen felt apprehensive about the future, especially after the Reform Act of 1867 which immensely increased the political muscle of middle-class dissent.

William Connor Magee, Bishop of Peterborough and briefly in 1891, Archbishop of York, was by his own admission 'a Celtic Cassandra' who by 1876 was convinced that the church's 'bankruptcy is far nearer at hand than country parsons and Erastian archbishops dream'.[4] 'We are, I suppose, as usual *drifting* and getting nearer and nearer to our Niagara', he wrote a month later, adding that with Archbishop Tait at the helm, 'the crew mutinying and the deck cargo of antiquated abuses shifting perilously . . . the good ship Church of England, lies becalmed off Disestablishment point.'[5] By 1880, three clergymen who rejected the Public Worship Regulation Act had been put in prison for acts of defiance which brought Parliament into contempt and cast doubt on the judgement of the bishops.[6] Then, in the same year, came a general election which put into power a Liberal Party which had in many constituencies followed the lead of Joseph Chamberlain in calling for disestablishment, while the victory of the atheist Charles Bradlaugh in Northampton sent shivers down Anglican spines. It was not just Bradlaugh's triumph in one of the towns in his diocese which alarmed Bishop Magee, but the fact that he was supported by the leading Dissenters and was allowed during his campaign to speak from a chapel pulpit: 'This is really *horrible*, and shows what Nonconformity has become under political influences.'[7] And three months later, he could lament:

> Poor dear clergy! what a time this is for them between Burials Bill, Deceased Wife's Sisters, damaged hay crops, defaulting tenants! I do not wonder than they are hairsore all over and ready for anything desperate against Dissenters and bishops.[8]

This assessment of the Anglican clergy waiting apprehensively for radical action against their church, feeling the pinch as the value of tithe fell in the agricultural depression, and manifesting little confidence in their spiritual leaders, who had betrayed them by surrendering the churchyards for Nonconformist funeral services, goes some way to explaining the intense fury which many of them felt, especially in the villages and small towns of southern England when militant dissent in the form of the Salvation Army displayed itself in a singularly provocative but at the same time intensely vulnerable form.[9]

William Booth was a former pawnbroker's apprentice from Nottingham who, after a standard Methodist conversion and brief ministerial career in Methodist circuits at Spalding and Gateshead, refused to toe the connectional line and set up his own Christian Mission in East London in 1865. As such it was part of a patchwork of revivalist bodies which appeared in the mid-Victorian period, influenced by American evangelists such as Charles Finney and James Caughey. The exponents of this 'new evangelicalism' have been described as 'lay in spirit, urban in concern, disaffected from the ministry, indifferent to denominational frontiers'. William Booth had heard Caughey preach in 1846, and during his Gateshead ministry in 1859 both he and perhaps even more, his wife Catherine, fell under the spell of the American holiness preacher, Phoebe Palmer.[10] It was an Independent minister's denunciation of women preachers which first drove Catherine Booth to write a tract in her sister's defence. Subsequently she herself preached in chapel and proved to be a highly effective orator. It was to be a feature of the Salvation Army, that women were to have the same opportunities as men.[11] Both of the Booths had clearly absorbed much from visiting Americans, in particular beliefs about the possibility of 'entire sanctification' which were a matter of much debate in evangelical circles, especially after the visit of yet another American, Robert Pearsall Smith, to the Brighton Holiness Convention of 1875. The Booths evidently belonged to a network which included many middle-class sympathisers, which transcended denominational boundaries, and which was willing to provide the financial backing for the grand design of a Salvation Army which he inaugurated in 1878. The choice of name and the use of military ranks and metaphors belongs to a Christian militarist tradition which emerged from the Crimean War, and was seen to be appropriate in an age of romantic imperialism, in which service in the Rifle Volunteers was comparatively common.[12] The Salvation Army used 'all the elements of applied romanticism', noted Kitson Clark, 'the rhetoric, the melodrama, the music, the evocative ritual symbolism but in this case not the ritual of mediaevalism but of war'.[13] It is not a sufficient explanation of the Army, to attribute it, as K. S. Inglis does, to 'the creation of dissatisfied Methodists'.[14] Many of the significant personalities of the Army such as George Railton and Elijah Cadman, had like the Booths turned away from Methodism, but their dissatisfaction was in part because of the playing down by Methodist officialdom of American holiness teaching, as well as a sense of frustration that the gospel which they believed could save the world was being stifled by confinement to the chapels. Booth and his young followers believed in attacking sin wherever it made itself most manifest: the public houses, the fairs, the streets. They believed that the immense social chasms in British society could not be bridged by well-meaning gentlemen visiting the poor, but that those at the bottom of society would respond only to a message from those of their own class. Most of all, they knew that an army can only succeed if its officers obey orders. They abandoned the democratic conference, inherited from Methodism, and centralised all power in the absolute rule of the general.

In its new guise, Booth's organisation expanded rapidly. Starting with less than 5000 members in June 1877, the Army claimed 100,000 by 1900.[15] Its fastest growth was in its early years. In 1882 Booth reported that his army had 320 corps which were led by 760 full-time officers.[16] But in the religious censuses, taken in several towns in the late 1880s, some surprise was expressed that the Army had not reached higher totals. Hensley Henson has remarked that religious statistics 'express aspiration rather than achievement' and recalled checking on Salvation Army converts when he was vicar of Barking in 1888. His local corps published the number of new converts every week, leading him to conclude that if they were permanent, 'the whole parish must be in a much more godly state than I supposed'. His enquiries led him to conclude that the Army was not reaching the very bottom of the social strata but recruited from lapsed chapel-goers.[17] This impression is confirmed by Ward's survey of 500 officers of 1884. Almost half were women, most of whom had either been in domestic service or employed in the clothing industry. Some of the men had been colliers, navvies and labourers, but many were regular wage-earners in skilled manual or lower clerical jobs.[18]

In the early 1880s, the Salvation Army gave an impression of fabulous success. Its officers were pushing forward on all fronts, new corps were multiplying – it was providential for the Army that the craze for ice skating was declining as rapidly as ten-pin bowling nearly a century later, and a large number of ice rinks could be acquired cheaply and turned into very impressive but unecclesiastical-looking headquarters.[19] Best of all, the Army was paid the supreme compliment of opposition. Its methods of drawing attention to itself invited ribaldry and rough horseplay from slightly tipsy patrons of alternative sources of refreshment. People out to enjoy themselves at fairs or race meetings could derive amusement from barracking and knocking-about a group of pious cold-sober Salvationists.

Sometimes the attitude of the Anglican clergy was significant. At Ipswich, the rural dean, the evangelical Samuel Garratt, wrote to the mayor asking that police protection might be given 'from the rowdyism of the mob',[20] but at Basingstoke the clergy appeared to give encouragement to the opposition.[21] Sometimes, it was the Army which seemed to be looking for trouble. At Chester, they deliberately chose to march into the Irish quarter, despite police requests to keep out. The Irish matched the flags and bugles of the Army by turning out in force, 'armed with cudgels and stones and carrying flags of various kinds'. Not surprisingly, a pitched battle was fought in which Mrs 'Captain' Falconbridge, who was dubbed on Army posters 'the Zulu Queen', was struck in the face by a stone. Later that day, about 1000 Irish marched to the Salvationist headquarters in the converted ice rink to storm the building. On this occasion, the police acted decisively and stopped the ringleaders.[22] The Army believes that 1882 was the year of most acute physical conflict; 56 buildings were attacked and partly wrecked, 669 Salvationists including over 250 women were assaulted.[23]

Relations between the Army and the other denominations varied. Somewhat surprisingly, the Wesleyan conference tried to make amends, and perhaps discover the secret of his success, by inviting the General to address it in 1880. The first episcopal reaction came in an uninformed denunciation from the Bishop of Carlisle. Catherine Booth, always the Army's best apologist, travelled to Carlisle and neatly turned the tables by presenting their methods as the best defence against revolution: 'the day is coming when these masses will require to be dealt with. Will it not be better to face them with the Gospel than the sword?'[24]

Dealing with the unchurched masses and beating back the pretensions of militant Dissent were constant preoccupations of the bishops, who were quicker than the clergy to grasp that the Army could provide the key to both problems. In fact, it was *The Nonconformist and Independent* which spotted that in the unofficial surveys of church and chapel attendances taken in 1881, 'the "Army" largely swells the total as against the Established Church'. With the 72,387 who attended Army meetings counted as Nonconformists the Church was outnumbered, but if they were subtracted from the

Nonconformists total and added to that of the Church, the situation was reversed.[25]

In December 1881, the Nottingham corps of the Army was invited to attend St Mary's, the ancient parish church. The opening hymn, 'How sweet the name of Jesus sounds' was sung to the tune 'Auld Lang Syne'. Early in January 1882, the Army joined the congregation of All Saints church for a procession through Newcastle-upon-Tyne. Similar joint ventures took place in front of St John's, Bethnal Green, where the vicar was described as 'a thorough Hallelujah man'. According to the curate of St Michael's, Coventry, C. R. Shaw Stewart, many hoped that 'the Holy Spirit would descend with power and baptize the church with fire' when 400 Salvationists accepted an invitation to attend service on Whit Monday, 1882. In his sermon on that occasion, the Rev. E. Gill described himself as 'a clergyman of the Church of England and a chaplain of the Salvation Army'.[26] The kind of language used on that occasion suggests that the clergy concerned were thoroughly soaked in Brighton and Keswick convention holiness teaching.

Attending church was one thing – for the Army it was valuable recognition by the establishment of their role – but pens as well as eyebrows were raised when they took communion. Early in 1882, the Archbishop of York, William Thomson, permitted the sacrament to be given to 400 Salvationists in St Paul's, York. This indiscriminate admission of unconfirmed men and women sparked off furious protests, especially from high-church clergy. Archbishop Thomson was a low-church evangelical who was at the time locked in bitter conflict with the Anglo-Catholic ritualist G. C. Ommaney, vicar of St Matthew's, Sheffield. In June of that same year, the archbishop ensured that no money would be made available for a curate for the parish. He could be expected to want co-operation with a religious movement which seemed to have demonstrated that it *was* possible to reach the very lowest social classes without resort to illegal ritual.[27] According to Bramwell Booth, the general's son, the archbishop wrote to his father early in 1882, requesting the opening of conversations about co-operation between the Army and the Church of England.[28]

Thomson was not the only bishop who found good reason to welcome the Army in 1882. E. W. Benson, Bishop of Truro, said in March that the voice of the Army was the voice of the masses against secularism.[29] Booth, not Bradlaugh, provided the authentic articulation of their true feelings. Moreover, noted Bishop Benson, the Army was not antagonistic to the churches because he understood that their practice was to request their converts to return to their former places of worship. A week later, the most representative newspaper of the church, the *Guardian*, devoted a leading article to the theme of 'undoing the evils which the expulsion of Wesley produced', which it suggested might be accomplished by reaching an accommodation with General Booth. 'If at present Ritualists and Evangelicals can shake hands and be thankful that they are not rival sects', it was argued, 'surely it would not be difficult for both parties to extend the same good fellowship to General Booth.' Leaving the accuracy of this cosy view of the relations between the parties in the church on one side, and the suggestion recently made by Professor Kent that the Victorian Church of England provided an umbrella for what were in fact different sects in all but name, the leader is an important pointer to one strand in official Anglican thinking which sought a remedy for the mistakes of the past, and a preservative against the unpleasant possibilities of the present. The leader urged action 'in view of such an opportunity, and the distant sound of disestablishment'.[30]

The bishops had higher hopes of the Army than the clergy had. 'We in the West Riding see nothing new', claimed one unenthusiastic clergyman, adding that he did not see how the Army differed from 'the Primitive Methodists or Ranters or Glory Bands or Hallelujah societies, or Trotteries.' He claimed that most of its popular support was poached from Methodism, but that it was promoting as much evil as it was removing. He accused the Army of encouraging 'a shameful familiarity between the sexes; disobedience to parents on the part of children who forsake their proper school for the sense of excitement; midnight returns home of young girls (to the exasperation of their parents).' Worried parents had appealed to this West Yorkshire clergyman to use his influence to stop their children going to what he called the Army's 'fanatical meetings'.[31] In early 1882 these charges of enticing young people, undermining parental authority, and removing the conventional restraints between the sexes were to be heard, but at this stage appeared to be exaggerations. Even less credence was given to the warnings of those like the vicar of Gateshead Fell that the appeal of the Army was ephemeral. He had lent his mission room to the Army in 1879. After being initially crowded 'by types you meet in Beerhouses', it was now half-empty.[32]

These cautionary tales from east of the Pennines did not find corroborative evidence in the experience of J. A. Atkinson, the rural dean of Ardwick, Manchester. He was confronted by a desperate situation. He reminded his colleagues on 9 May that their bishop, the clear-sighted James Fraser, had already foreseen that the parochial system had broken down. Atkinson maintained that if the church was serious about faith in the cities, it needed a body of mission-clergy and lay evangelists to work on Salvation Army lines. He had heard complaints about profanity and vulgarity but he had also heard Catherine Booth and she impressed by the 'charm of her manner', her 'power of riveting attention', and 'the soundness of her teaching'. Would the Church learn from the Army? 'I have no faith in anything being done', he lamented. It was, he said, always the old familiar story: 'always shocked at displays of zeal – always intolerance of innovation'.[33]

On the same day, 9 May 1882, that Atkinson was uttering his jeremiad, Canon George Wilkinson rose in the Lower House of the Convocation of Canterbury and obtained support for a request to the bishops to enquire into the teaching and techniques of the Salvation Army and explore the possibilities of co-operation. The bishops discussed the request on 12 May 1882. Bishop Browne of Winchester had investigated the Army when the rioting had taken place at Basingstoke, some of the worst scenes of civil disorder. He had found that while its methods were extravagant, its doctrine was sound. Especially impressive for the bishop was the fact that 'they not only induced men to live lives of sobriety, but they had such influence over people that they had also induced them to give up smoking', though he did not know 'whether they were wise in so doing'.[34] When attacked, the Army did not retaliate, and was not antagonistic to the church. The Bishop of Llandaff used the occasion to criticise the changes in worship which had taken place in the Church of England. He contended that now their services were 'very much too elaborate and too artificial for the minds of uneducated people, who want their feelings excited as well as their minds to be instructed'. Suspecting that 'the aesthetic tendency' which had recently been growing in the church was a barrier rather than a bridge, 'he did not think that uneducated people cared or took pleasure in anthems or elaborate music' though they did seem to like congregational singing. Moreover, the bishop did reject utterly the view that 'without the use of vestments they could never hope to teach the people the spiritual meaning of the Lord's Supper'. The 'great thing was to bring the doctrines of the Gospel home to the hearts of the people'.[35] Bishop Benson noted in his diary that the speeches of the bishops were 'very kindly'. He believed that it had been the laity not the clergy who had excluded Wesley but in the case of General Booth, 'I am sure the Bishops are in earnest'.[36]

'The Salvation Army have powerful friends', remarked the *Spectator* on 20 May. It remarked on the 'decided friendliness' of the bishops' debate and the sympathy shown in the House of Lords a few days later when Lord Fortescue drew attention to the ill-treatment of the Army's members, especially at the hands of the Hampshire justices. Even the Archbishop of Canterbury, A. C. Tait, had risen in support, declaring that the leaders of the movement were 'persons of irreproachable character, and desirous of checking the extravagance of their followers'. The sight of the Salvation Army basking in the warm embrace of the bishops and the barons set alarm bells ringing for the editor of the *Spectator*: '"General" Booth must congratulate himself on all his support, but if he does not take care . . . his army will be invested with Respectability, and then what will become of his influence over the Roughs? It ought not to be Respectable for at least five years yet, if it is to do much work.'[37]

For William Booth, upper-class sympathy was not a pinnacle on which to rest, but a plateau from which to launch an even more ambitious assault on the enemy. Encouraged by George Railton, his most capable and uncompromising officer, he was convinced that this was the right psychological moment to mount a spectacular venture which would tap establishment support (with the social recognition which that would bring) and demonstrate the Army's total determination to beat back Satan and wrest his kingdom from him.

The Eagle Tavern and adjacent Grecian theatre and dance halls were in City Road, East London. They were said to have become 'a notorious amusement centre' in which 'all manner of devilry went on', though the report of an Anglican observer, J. W. Horsley, chaplain of Clerkenwell prison, was more tentative:

> I think the badness of the Grecian has been chiefly found in its audiences and the drinking encouraged all over the place. Just about there is a great colony of burglars and other varieties of finger-smiths.[38]

Here was the stage from which Macdermott in 1877 had given the word 'jingoism' to the English language. Here was the public house immortalised in the cockney song 'Pop goes the weasel':

> Up and down the City Road,
> In and out of the Eagle.

It was George Railton who had the imagination to see that these sleazy premises could become the Army's cathedral in East London. He was opposed by the general's son, Bramwell Booth, who foresaw many legal and financial complications. When his father made up his mind to go ahead, Bramwell advised him to enlist the support of fifty or sixty sympathetic public figures: men such as Lord Kinnaird, Samual Morley, Wilfrid Lawson. 'Mind my proposed meeting of swells goes upon the plea not of S.A. acquiring this', Bramwell advised his father, 'but of S.A. shutting up this wicked place.'[39] It was in response to a plea on these latter grounds that Archbishop Tait wrote a public letter of support and sent a nominal contribution of £5. To the intense annoyance of the archbishop, and even greater annoyance of his son-in-law (and eventual successor) Randall T. Davidson, the Army published just the concluding part of the letter, which taken in isolation appeared to give blanket approval, and omitted the first part which was hedged about with caveats about the 'extreme difficulty' of co-operation between the Church and the Army. The impression created, that the Archbishop of Canterbury was a contributor to Salvation Army funds and a supporter of its work, puzzled some clergy and church people.[40] It particularly enraged the elderly godfather of mid-century Anglican evangelicalism, Lord Shaftesbury.

Shaftesbury had given a dusty answer when invited to join the Salvation Army in 1881 by Admiral Fishbourne, the eccentric freelance evangelical. His private response indicated a preference for a religious movement 'headed and expanded by Mrs Booth', whom he admired, rather than her husband. He disliked what had emerged under the general because he could not find any Scriptural basis for it and he feared that its methods might discredit Christianity. Moreover Shaftesbury felt that the Army was treading on the toes of hundreds of city missions where diligent lay workers were quietly, gradually and unostentatiously taking the gospel to the poor. The day after Archbishop Tait's letter, as doctored by Booth, appeared in the press, Shaftesbury let fly for the first time in public.[41]

The Bishop of Truro had been surprised by the aversion of Anglican evangelicals to the Army. 'Of course', the Bishop of Peterborough had suggested, there was 'no body so odious to one as poor relations.'[42] So Booth snared his *Eagle* but from that moment onwards, there were many Anglican vultures ready to swoop.

So far, criticisms of the Army had come mainly from the parochial clergy while the bishops had in general maintained a sympathetic, if somewhat patronising attitude. Shaftesbury's onslaught burst the dam, and encouraged others in high places to distance themselves from the general episcopal approval. The week after Shaftesbury's attack, a leading Church dignitary, F. W. Farrar, announced from the pulpit of Westminster Abbey that he considered the Army to have been 'abundantly eulogized by Bishops and dignitaries' and denounced 'the fantastic vanity of usurped military titles'. He was disgusted and repelled by religious services advertised as 'Great Exhibition of Hallelujah Lasses', and questioned the need to begin what was supposed to be divine worship by a parade of Salvationists dressed in Indian costumes riding on an

THE GENERAL AND THE BISHOPS

elephant. The Army's phraseology, he complained, was grotesque and irreverent, while Christian experience was not deepened by shrieking, laughing, dancing, handkerchief waving, clapping of hands, or by 'nocturnal orgies of religious excitement'.

> Unless those who now belong to it get sick of its pantomime, and give up their places to others who have not yet learned that Christianity is inward, and not a beating of big drums, it cannot possibly end in making those who join it true Christians.

The *Guardian*, *Record* and *Spectator* devoted considerable space to Farrar's sermon and agreed with him that having made its impact, the Army should now be channelling its converts into the churches. The *Guardian* now saw the banners, bands and processions as a form of 'Ritualism' 'of a rather vulgar type'. Moreover, there was much evidence now, that the Army, despite assurances to the contrary, was forming itself into a sect.[43] Nearly 50 years later, Bramwell Booth recalled that Canon Farrar had 'denounced the Army in perhaps the most unqualified terms ever employed against us by any minister of Christ. He effectively blotted us out of recognized society.'[44] In fact even more damaging allegations were soon to be found in the evangelical *Record* from the poisoned pen of Dean Close, and in a long article in *The Churchman* by John F. Kitto.[45]

Changes in ecclesiastical opinion did not, however, cancel the resolution of convocation. The bishops had appointed Benson of Truro, Lightfoot of Durham, B. F. Westcott of Cambridge, Canon G. H. Wilkinson, and Randall Davidson, the archbishop's chaplain, to carry out its investigation into the Army. On 9 June 1882, Bishop Benson had a long talk with General Booth. The general insisted that the distinctive feature of Army organisation was 'the restoration of discipline to the church':

> Every single person in office comes & goes, continues or 'farewells' on the next Sunday, marries or puts marriage off, on my order absolutely. We mean to move exactly as the 'Killing Army' does and we shall succeed. If a man hesitates

to obey, he goes. With us there is but one rule 'Everything must be given up for GOD'.

One social consequence was an insistence on asceticism which took the form of the prohibition of alcohol and tobacco. The reason they had not succeeded in mining areas, said the general, was because 'They won't give up the pipe'. Officers had orders never to speak ill of the Church: 'Neither do we set up sacraments against your sacraments.' At that stage, Booth was unable to say whether marching a corps to church for the sacraments was practicable. 'You can have no idea of the roughness and coarseness of our people', he said, 'with them controversy would be awful.' Yet Booth insisted that some understanding between them was desirable. He claimed that when clergymen had asked to join his Army, 'we bid them stay where they are'. And as evidence of the way in which the Army was helping the Church, he cited the case of the wife of the vicar of Limehouse: 'Mrs Charlesworth finds her Bible Classes much increased by our work.'[46]

Ten days later, Benson talked with Randall Davidson about a conversation the latter had had with Bramwell Booth about Holy Communion: 'They do not have it in Congress Hall but if any student wished to celebrate it' in their corps no objection would be made. Communion, he was told, 'was celebrated in many places'. 'This indeed makes a difference', noted Benson.[47] Two days later, Benson and Davidson went to Congress Hall in Clapton. About 150 men and women students were led in prayer by Bramwell Booth: 'all wore a very devout expression, eyes mainly closed'. Then the pace of the meeting quickened: hands began to clap, shouts of 'Amen' arose, and one cadet jumped. 'It was pathetic', the bishop recorded, 'to hear them sing with infinite repetition "when he leads me I will follow, I will follow all the way" to a pretty tune.' Meanwhile the cadets on their knees were swinging backwards and forwards all the time 'like Dervishes'. Benson talked to two of Booth's sons: 'the elder's eyes were beautiful'. According to Bramwell Booth, the possessor of the beautiful eyes, after the meeting, Benson took both his hands and exclaimed, 'O my dear brother, the Holy Spirit is with you!'[48]

In Bramwell Booth's recollections of these conversations,

Randall Davidson stuck out as the hardliner who was determined to wrest authority from the general.[49] Meanwhile the committee was sifting letters and reports from all over the country. Benson remarked to Davidson that the Army's work 'is more favourably reported from the north than from the south'.[50] It had been agreed that Benson would prepare a first draft which would be presented to the committee. But in the next fortnight, Benson made slow progress. Circumstances had changed even on his own Cornish doorstep: 'I am afraid the Salvation Army is working nothing here but confusion', he wrote to Westcott, 'and the *Report* seems a hopeless task. They made me draft it – and I *can't* so far.'[51] Providence, however, was at hand. Two days later, Gladstone offered Benson the primacy in succession to Tait, and gave him a respectable excuse for never finishing the report on the Salvation Army.

When the Upper House of Convocation reconvened in April 1883, the committee was discharged, but more serious damage was done to the Army's reputation when the bishops of Oxford and Gloucester took the opportunity to allege that immoral behaviour leading to unwanted pregnancies had occurred as a result of late-night Army meetings. The Booths were incensed by these charges. A detailed survey was conducted, which vindicated the Army. The bishops eventually retracted, but not until months later, by which time other sensations had blackened the Army's copybook in Anglican eyes.[52]

Thirty years later, when Harold Begbie was writing his life of William Booth, he wrote to Randall Davidson, by then Archbishop of Canterbury, asking him to reflect on the general's attitude in the conversations: 'whether it was an honest anxiety to co-operate with the Church, or a shuffling effort to preserve the friendship of the Church without its jurisdiction?' Begbie realised that Holy Communion was a real difficulty for the Army, but maintained that to the end of his life Booth 'was occasionally haunted' by the question. The failure to observe the sacraments was part of the insistence that they were an evangelistic movement, not a settled sect or denomination. In this decision, Begbie was convinced that Bramwell Booth had been the dominant influence but that his father 'rather wistfully looked towards the idea of the Eucharist'. Davidson made no comment on this interpretation, but substantially agreed with Begbie's account of the talks.[53]

Sensing a change of mood in the church's leadership, the more sensible clergy now had to restrain them in their worst fears about the Army. In July 1882, the Dean of Wells noticed that in the Army headquarters at Bristol 'a young female baptized a child and afterwards churched the woman'.[54] Frances Power Cobbe, who had been associated with Lord Shaftesbury in the anti-vivisection campaign, reported that city missionaries claimed that in the London public houses, 'the Salvation Army now forms the topic of interminable laughter and jests, amid which the most sacred names and the deepest human feelings and hopes come in for their share of ridicule'.[55]

Bishop Lightfoot, one of the members of the ill-fated committee, devoted part of his Primary Charge to the Durham clergy to it in December 1882. He insisted that the Army still had valuable lessons to teach, and that its successes could not be denied. From what he had seen: 'I should certainly place it higher than it is placed by others whose larger experience I respect, or than that the extravagances of its own organ would suggest.' He accepted that a 'certain amount of sensationalism may be pardoned. But the exaltation of sensationalism into a system is perilous in the extreme.' The time had come, he argued, for the sensational elements to give way 'to calm and patient methods of instruction'. But sensationalism, far from being phased out, seemed to be being stepped up:

> the most solemn events of Biblical history are travestied and the Saviour's name is profaned in parodies of common songs. Awe and reverence are the soul of the religious life. He therefore who degrades the chief objects of religion strikes however unintentionally at the very root of religion.

Another feature of Army practice which Lightfoot found objectionable was 'the encouragement given to children six or eight or ten years old to advertise publicly their own conversion and as publicly to proclaim the non-conversion of their parents'. As one who had encouraged his clergy to develop friendly relations with the Army, he confessed that 'I can see that such sympathy and co-operation is becoming daily more difficult'.[56]

The final straw for many of the remaining Anglican sympathisers of the Army came when reports of bizarre events in France and Switzerland reached Britain. The general had sent his daughter Catherine to hold meetings in Paris in 1881.[57] She was reinforced by the arrival of Arthur Clibborn, whom she subsequently married, taking the surname Booth-Clibborn. She was also assisted by a few young Englishwomen, the youngest of whom was Maud Charlesworth, aged 17. Her father, Samuel Charlesworth, had been vicar of Limehouse when Booth had started his Christian Mission there, and her mother was the lady already mentioned by Booth in his talks with Benson as an example of the good relations between Church and Army. However, in a letter to Archbishop Benson, Charlesworth recalled that after his wife's death in 1881, his schoolgirl daughter, then aged 15, had been 'secretly drawn into the organisation':

She was soon instigated to desert me and her home and the Church of her youth, at 18 she was induced to give herself up to the Army, or rather to its pseudo-General for life, involving the relinquishment of her property, to the Army funds, and at 21, 3 days after her majority, she was dragged into a shameful marriage to one of Mr Booth's sons, a man eight years her senior.

The whole system, he concluded, was a vulgar imitation of the Jesuit order, demanding total obedience.[58]

That letter was written seven years after the case of Maud Charlesworth had first attracted public attention. A lengthy report had appeared in *The Times* in February 1883 in which Miss Charlesworth appeared as an adventurous, self-composed young woman who easily ran rings round the magistrate in the Swiss court.[59] By contrast, her father came over as a rather pathetic figure. Even the Anglican paper, the *Guardian*, had to admit that in the correspondence provoked by news of the court case, 'Mr Booth is a far more skilful controversialist than Mr Charlesworth'. Indeed the paper had little sympathy for him. He had, after all, allowed his daughter to go to Paris at 17 where she was sent out with other English girls in front of the Paris Bourse and Opera House to attract purchasers for the French equivalent of the *War Cry* 'by their pretty looks and remarkable uniforms':

> If he allowed his daughter to remain one day in Paris after he had heard of the exposure . . . in the public streets, he ought not to have been surprised at anything that has happened since.

The *Guardian* concluded: 'Is this picture of a girl of 17, disregarding her father's wishes and ostentatiously brushing aside all ordinary sentiments of feminine and youthful modesty' likely to commend the Army to unbiased observers? Was it 'a becoming thing that English girls should be sent out into the streets of Paris "in full Salvation Army uniform" to sell newspapers to promiscuous crowds, who – they are Mr Booth's own words quoted by Mr Charlesworth – "have all their eye-glasses up" to gaze at them?'[60]

The *Spectator*, which six months before had praised the Army and warned it against the dangers of 'Respectability' now took a severe view of the case. It recognised that Miss Charlesworth 'was too attractive and too useful a convert to be lightly let go', but warned that parents who did not want their children to become Salvationists should keep them away from its meetings. That was particularly true for daughters:

> The part which the Army assigns to women has extraordinary attractions for these times. They can be in every way rivals of men, they can take an absolutely equal part in the establishment and building-up of the new organisation.

By comparison, the ordinary routine of home appeared intolerably dull. Where in Clapham could Mr Charlesworth hope to offer his daughter a career which offered the same responsibilities, opportunities and sheer excitement?[61]

Speaking in the Regent's Hall, Oxford Street, on 1 March 1883, Mrs Catherine Booth felt that *The Times*' correspondent in Geneva had vindicated the Army against what she claimed were the misrepresentations of Charlesworth. She deplored the circumstances which had thrust her own daughter before the public as much as Mr Charlesworth. She would, she said, leave God and time to answer his charges. God and time, she continued, had done a great deal for the Army in its 17 years' existence. The slanders and misrepresentations of recent months had, however, had their effect on the Army's funds, and she appealed for a good collection.[62]

On this occasion, however, God and time did not come to the rescue. The Salvation Army never recaptured that moment of enthusiastic mobilisation which enabled it to make such spectacular progress in 1881 and 1882. As the spiritual tide ebbed, General Booth and his followers perceived the need to rescue bodies as well as souls. In 1885 Bramwell Booth joined W. T. Stead in the campaign to outlaw child prostitution.[63] Five years later came the *Darkest England* scheme which in the public mind switched the emphasis from the gospel circus to night shelters, soup kitchens and farm colonies. The Salvation Army then became the 'established sect', tolerated by society, which it has remained to this day.[64]

Anglicans had better reason for thinking that God and time were on their side. Their Church, whose bishops had first wooed and then spurned the Salvation Army as part of a strategy to avoid disestablishment, counter the attacks of Nonconformists and secularists, and draw the teeth of working-class hostility, amazingly survived intact. The passage of the Burials Act of 1880 turned out to be the end of an era in which (in the towns at least) Free Church grievances had been largely removed.[65] Moreover by following Gladstone on the Irish home rule question in 1886, the Nonconformists separated themselves from the one politician, Joseph Chamberlain, who might have had the will and strength to carry through disestablishment.

Atheism as a fixed intellectual position never advanced much beyond an intellectual minority. Opinion polls have continued to show conclusively that though there is massive indifference in Britain to all religious institutions, there is little overt hostility; the overwhelming majority of the population claim to be Christian believers who wish to retain religious teaching in schools.[66] These attitudes are quite possibly part of the residue of that 'important qualitative change' in working-class religion which historians have noticed in the second half of the nineteenth century. This change links working-class religion with a concept of 'respectability' which found supreme expression in temperance, a cause taken up with enthusiasm by the Baptists, Primitive Methodists – and especially, the Salvation Army.[67] It may be that though the Salvation Army in 1882 offended upper- and middle-class Anglican concepts of respectability and responsibility which laid particular stress on the unity of the family, it continued to contribute to the concept and practice of a separate working-class variant of respectability and personal responsibility which has since been forever linked, however vaguely, with religion.

10. The Irish Problem

ALAN O'DAY

In 1867 Ireland was in turmoil. The Irish Republican Brotherhood, popularly known as Fenians, staged a potentially explosive armed rebellion. According to the proclamation which declared an abortive Irish Republic the revolt was justified because the rights and liberties of the people had been trampled on by an alien aristocracy which had confiscated the land and sucked wealth out of the country.[1] As successive British governments had not ended injustice in Ireland, no honourable alternative remained but this resort to revolution. Only a few men in Ireland responded to the Fenian call to arms but it was evident that there was more widespread sympathy for the rebellion. British military superiority swiftly suppressed this insurrection but the event sent a shock wave through the political elite and initiated an era when Irish reform was a top priority with British ministries.

Irish disaffection was not a sudden revelation in 1867. It had been discussed and various remedies put forward since the passing of the Act of Union in 1800. Politics in the 1820s had been dominated by the Catholic question – those of the 1840s by several strands of Ireland's wants. No decade was minus an instalment of the Irish problem in one or another guise. Neither did British governments fail to appreciate the fundamental importance of appeasing the expectations of the majority of that country's people. For instance, even 'Orange Peel' in the 1840s spent much of his time formulating Irish reforms. The Fenian revolt, however, highlighted the failure of past remedies and concentrated attention on how Ireland could be conciliated. That concern was manifested in January 1868 by Lord Stanley, a member of the existing Conservative Cabinet, when he said:

we have, indeed, in that country a strange and perplexing problem to solve. I suppose there never was a time when Englishmen of all parties and all classes were more anxious to give all reasonable satisfaction to Irish demands, and even as far as can be done without national injury, to humour the feelings and prejudices of the Irish people.[2]

At the close of the century politicians were still engaged in attempting to give satisfaction to Irish demands and humour the feelings and prejudices of the country's people. In 1898, for example, Arthur Balfour, though opposing a Dublin parliament, was anxious to grant responsible local government to Ireland and to give the Catholics the university they had long sought for 'from the point of view of the Union, the refusal to pass a measure would be a plain admission that on some subjects, at least, a Unionist Parliament could not legislate for Ireland'.[3]

Between 1867 and 1900 much changed in Ireland and in Anglo-Irish relations but it still remained true, as one recent commentator has put it, that 'with the exception of Southern Ireland, Britain, unlike France, has always been able to accommodate subordinate identities such as those of the Scots or Welsh'.[4] Anglophobia was as pronounced at the end of Victoria's reign as it had been in 1867. The *Annual Register* for 1899 observed of the local councils created under the Act of the previous year, 'only too often the new bodies made occasions for political demonstrations and the display of disloyal sentiments'.[5] It went on to note:

> a very bitter anti-British feeling was exhibited, as the South African war approached, by several of the district councils and municipal corporations. These bodies, not content with passing resolutions altogether outside the sphere of their duties, occasionally spent their time in framing manifestations of disloyalty.

Despite some popular enthusiasm for the old queen on her only visit to Ireland in 1900 about half of the municipal corporation absented themselves from the presentation of an Address.[6] In an obvious sense, then, the mission which Gladstone had declared for himself, as one to pacify Ireland, had not succeeded.

British failure in Ireland has been the subject of an extensive and ever-expanding literature. Explanations have revolved around three major inter-related hypotheses: that British attempts to deal with Irish grievances were too limited and unduly delayed; that the good which reform might have achieved was undermined by repressive or coercive law and order legislation; and that leaders and public simply did not comprehend the fundamental character of the quest for self-government. The torrent of specialist studies of the last three decades has added sophistication to analysis of the Irish problem without, it seems, challenging the essence of the long accepted and appealing consensus on why Britain failed in Ireland. Mansergh and Lyons, both historians of Irish Protestant origin, have vigorously argued that orthodox position. They have placed particular stress on the undying aspiration of the Irish to secure full self-government and on the essentially political dimension of the problem. The first, in his critique of Marx, has observed that he neglected 'to allow for the dominantly political character of the Irish Question'.[7] He also asserts:

the failure of English statesmen to resolve the Irish Question at a date earlier than 1921, and then only after violence, was due to continuing inability to understand the Irish political outlook, to some confusion of mind as to the distinction between good government and national government, and by the refusal of the electorate to decide finally in favour of one particular policy.

And, for him, the unfortunate aspect proved to be that 'a new order in Ireland was *inevitable*. English statesmen did nothing to facilitate its emergence.' In attempting to check the flowing tide 'they prolonged the travail and the birthpangs of a new state'. Similarly, in his *Ireland Since the Famine*, Lyons insists:

the Irish did not change the question between the Famine and the war of independence any more than they had changed it between the Union and the Famine. The 'national demand', as it used to be called, remained in essence what Wolfe Tone had declared it to be as long ago as 1791, 'to break the connection with England, the never-failing source of all our political evils'.[8]

He has maintained that though men differed on precise goals and tactics 'they were emphatic that the first step towards real independence was to recover for Irishmen the right to control their own affairs'.

The orthodox view espoused by Mansergh, Lyons and others has been comforting in two vital respects: it has enabled historians to treat Ireland as an interesting but unique case and, despite its obvious centrality to politics at the time, to downgrade the problem as a key issue in late Victorian development. Hence the Irish problem is often viewed as something which diverted attention from pressing and in the longer term more crucial questions. To use the analogy of the age, Ireland blocked the rails. Joseph Chamberlain complained, 'thirty millions of people must go without much-needed legislation because three millions are disloyal'.[9] But the accepted orthodoxy deserves closer examination for it is by no means so obvious that Ireland was unusual, other than in being exceptionally adept at articulating discontent, or that it was so simply and purely a political problem arising out of a conflict of nationalities or a supposed clash of cultures as suggested in Lyons's final book, *Culture and Anarchy in Ireland, 1890–1939*. There is, of course, some truth in this view but contemporary evidence and opinion reveals a more complex pattern which makes the British failure of wider proportions, including aspects of social and economic history, and less simple to explain than by reference to political development alone.

At a certain level the Irish problem is fairly easily defined. In essence the majority of the island's people did not believe that being part of a United Kingdom rendered sufficient political, economic or psychological value to accept the Union as a permanent feature. In origin that feeling was an inheritance from the past but it also arose from an appreciation that the Catholic majority was not treated as equal either in the wider British state or in Ireland. The reason for Catholic reticence was apparent. In the 1860s Catholics enjoyed little respect or responsibility. Life was characterised by what sociologists term a cultural division of labour. Throughout the period Catholics composed about three-quarters of the population but at its outset commanded relatively little political, economic or social power. Bias against Catholics then was underlined by the existence of the Church of Ireland's established status as the state religion when its adherents numbered merely the small but dominant Anglican community. Aggregate religious statistics mask significant geographical imbalances. Most of the Protesant minority resided in a series of pockets mainly located in the east of the country. In 8 of the 32 counties Catholics exceeded 95 per cent of the population and in others in the south and west their distribution approached these proportions.[10] Outside the Protestant enclaves, Ireland, in effect, was a Catholic country.

Formally, Catholics bore only a tiny number of legal disabilities either in Ireland or Britain. They possessed the franchise in Ireland on a completely equal basis though until 1885 the property qualification for the ballot was more restrictive in the sister island than in England and Wales. Informally, though, Catholics found substantial hurdles limiting access into official life. Few gained entry to the upper echelons of the Irish Administration, judiciary or Royal Irish Constabulary at any point in the Victorian age. Within the civil service and police Catholics were numerous but concentrated in lower grades often in posts wholly lacking in responsibility. Local administration revealed a similar tale. It was notorious that even in overwhelmingly Catholic counties most appointive dignitaries – lord lieutenants, deputy lord lieutenants, sheriffs and JPs – were Protestants. Also, such vital local organs as grand juries and boards of poor law guardians which exercised wide authority were firmly under Protestant control at the beginning of the period. Catholics' intrusions into public life centred on municipal councils and parliamentary representation. In 1866 they numbered 43 of Dublin's 60 member corporation.[11] By 1874 Catholics were only narrowly in a minority among Ireland's MPs and were always in a majority after 1880.[12] However, unlike grand juries and Poor Law unions, municipal councils had limited functions and Catholics in the House of Commons inevitably were swallowed up in a sea of Protestant MPs. Ireland in the 1860s may be characterised as being governed by Britain in wider affairs and by a Protestant ascendancy at home.

Economic life similarly revealed Catholics to be at an immense disadvantage. They provided labour with Protestants tending to own the land and capital. Modern research has established that Catholics had been making advances in the economic sphere since 1800 but by the 1860s they still laboured rather than owned. Though numerous in commerce they were most notable as small shopkeepers and especially as publicans in Dublin and other towns. Industry and large shops typically were owned by Protestants. Many Catholics were clerks and commercial travellers but few held more responsible or respectable posts. Over 60 per cent of lawyers, physicians, surgeons, dentists, engineers and other professional men were Protestants and they monopolised the most favoured situations.[13] Nationalists were known to groan that the commerce of the country was in 'alien' hands. But Ireland was an agrarian society and what mattered most was access to and control over land. Catholics had acquired land in recent decades but still owned little more than 10 per cent of acreage – much of that being poor quality as well. In the census report of 1871 it was noted that the quantity of property 'in Protestant Episcopal ownership exceeds so largely the surface under all other proprietorship, as to constitute the land proprietary of the country Episcopalian Protestant by emphasis'.[14] At the other end of the scale, over 80 per cent of tenants and labourers were Catholics. In many sections of the south and west there were virtually no Protestant labourers or small tenants. Catholic feeling of being an under-class was underlined by a deep-rooted belief that the land was really theirs – an emotion common to most agrarian communities even when a religious or nationality element was absent. Additionally, tenants suffered by an absence of defined security, fears of arbitrary rent increases and over the potential loss of the value of their own improvements when they vacated a holding. Recent research has demonstrated that tenant security was greater than had been believed but there is no doubt that those who worked the land worried constantly about their position. Insecurity was a vital ingredient in rural Ireland and a key factor in generating disaffection with the Union since most Catholics felt themselves to have no binding stake in its existence.

The Catholics of Ireland had ample scope for discontent. As outsiders, they bore similarities to Nonconformists, the working classes, women and certain other groups with the vital distinction of being geographically concentrated and conscious of a historic self-identity. The majority in Ireland differed within itself over precise goals but because of the cultural division of labour found a high level of agreement that demands were formulated most appropriately in ethnic terms rather than in those of social class. For British leaders the question was one of how to satisfy the majority, or as the general who commanded the army in Ireland in 1867 put it, of adopting 'those remedial measures, the mottoes of which, I hope, will be policy, justice, and above all, a moderation, which will ensure equal rights to adverse parties, without giving either a triumph.'[15]

Between the 1860s and 1900 successive governments of both political complexions made a sustained effort to adhere to the general's dictum. Catholics made steady and significant advances throughout the period over the range of Irish life. The Church, particularly, was able to enhance its status. Disestablishment of the Church of Ireland in 1869 ended the glaring inequity which gave special legal recognition to the faith of the minority. Catholic prelates, even on the eve of disestablishment, found their position elevated in numerous informal and official ways, sometimes seeming to replace leaders of the Church of Ireland in the eyes of Dublin Castle. Legislation under Conservative governments in the 1870s and 1880s gave the Catholic bishops improved access to charitable endowments and increased influence over education. By the turn of the century the hierarchy had secured nearly complete control over the education provision for their flock, excepting only the creation of the much desired state-endowed Catholic university. Arthur Balfour, for one, was anxious to give satisfaction to the bishops on this claim. Catholic advances were of such proportions that, as a recent writer has observed, 'by the year 1900 the Irish Church was no longer a minor, tolerated, though respected sect in the United Kingdom, but was at the centre of a worldwide sphere of influence and prestige'.[16] 'As far as Catholic affairs were concerned', the same author has noted, 'Maynooth was the centre of the English-speaking world.' Catholicism moved forward in the late Victorian age in three respects: within Ireland vis-à-vis other sects; within the whole of the United Kingdom; and over the extent of the English-speaking lands particularly those regions belonging to the British empire. Britain's place in the universe had direct implications for the Catholic Church in Ireland.

Catholics in public life became more numerous and achieved additional prominence. Many posts in the Irish Administration proved to be elusive but Catholics came to fill the bulk of intermediate grades. Their progression was uneven but was aided by improved educational opportunities and a willingness on the part of political chiefs at Dublin Castle to place them in responsible positions. At the beginning of his viceroyalty in 1882 Lord Spencer, though he 'disliked introducing religion into questions of qualification for offices of importance', nevertheless recognised, 'it is impossible, however, if we are to carry with us public opinion of the majority of the Irish, to ignore this'.[17] He and his successors made zealous efforts to recruit Catholics. Later in 1882 he explained to a prominent Liberal that, when making a key appointment, 'had an equally efficient Irishman been available I should have preferred him'.[18] Public appointments were a matter of importance in Ireland for as Lord Randolph Churchill reminded the Tory viceroy in mid-1885, 'in Ireland as in France', "chacun veut être quelque chose de par le roi". The number of places are limited, the good places are few.'[19] Equally, the political masters at Dublin Castle came to eschew elevating people who would prove offensive to the Catholic community. As early as May 1883 the Irish chief secretary argued against a certain appointment to the bench as it would prove unpopular.[20] Catholics remained under-represented in local administration at the century's end but things were changing in this area also. Between 1892 and 1895, John Morley, the chief secretary, recollected giving 554 of the 637 JPships to Catholics and reducing the predominance of Protestants in local administration from three or four to one to approximately two to one.[21] His function was less to hold the ring as between Protestant and Catholic than between contesting nationalist factions. As he reported to Lord Rosebery, 'if I please Dillon, I displease Healy, and vice versa. I cut the knot by pleasing myself.'[22]

In some local institutions Catholics rapidly established an ascendancy. By the mid-1880s they controlled the parliamentary seats, municipal councils and Poor Law guardianships in districts where they formed majorities. Abolition of the grand juries' powers, except over certain criminal matters, and the creation of responsible elective local government under the Act of 1898 transferred effective power to representatives of the Catholic community. That legislation was proceeded with by a Conservative regime in the teeth of the sometimes bitter resentment of its own allies. In Ulster it was decried as 'a notable instance in which the Government have deserted their supporters, going out of their way to please a faction that never will be pleased with anything short of political independence, and for that purpose plunging into a revolutionary measure.'[23] The effect of responsible local government was to legitimise the control of majorities. In the south and west the minority remained potent but the basis of its influence was altered. Sufficient wealth remained in Protestant hands there which when combined with their access to sources of influence plus the backstop of the Westminster Parliament ensured the minority's rights would be safeguarded. However, in much of Ulster the Catholic minority had little useful protection. No matter how the transition is viewed, by 1900 it could no longer be held that the Catholic portions of Ireland were crushed under a Protestant jackboot. In fact, it could be argued that then the country had self-government of a kind which largely fitted the peculiar circumstances of the island.

Catholics made impressive strides in economic life as well. The expansion of shopkeeping and a widening of the professions enabled more of them to make a mark. But it was in control over and ownership of land where the change was most profound. A long string of legislative enactments ensured tenants of security of tenure, regulated rents, decreased fear of eviction, guaranteed compensation for self-made improvements and provided state financial backing for land purchase. These acts were the fruit of both Liberal and Conservative regimes. An even more extensive Purchase Act was passed in 1903, which, though it did not settle the land question completely, succeeded in lessening the main agrarian grievances. By 1905, according to Raymond Crotty, almost all agricultural land in Ireland was either subject to judicial rents or in the ownership of former tenants.[24] Parliamentary legislation, the same writer has contended, probably reduced gross Irish rentals to £7.5m from a notional £30m which might have been achieved had landlords been willing and able to let on competitive terms. Landlord control over the supply and management of land was broken. The landed class, though, retained its wealth. Not they but landless labourers were the real losers and purchase legislation tended to confirm their status as marginal men in Irish society. By 1900 it would no longer be true to say that Ireland had a cultural division of labour.

Not all Catholic grievances and aspirations had been satisfied but the rate of change was genuinely impressive. Some of it had little directly to do with political policy – British demand for Irish foodstuffs and the spread of railways, for example, were only casually linked to politics. Yet it is also evident that legislation was the critical factor in accelerating and altering relationships in late Victorian Ireland. Between 1868 and 1900 every ministry undertook significant Irish reforms. Only the Tory government of 1874–80 was able to avoid the white heat of the Irish problem and even that regime passed two pieces of important education legislation. Westminster politicians and Parliament stood at the nexus of Anglo-Irish affairs. From the 1860s at least the idea of a *laissez-faire* or minimalist state was being eroded and nowhere more so than in Ireland.

British priority given to Irish demands is particularly impressive when it is borne in mind that Parliament had to shuffle competing demands; anti-catholicism, anti-hibernianism could amass large popular followings; and the Home Rule Bill of 1886 polarised opinion and left Conservatives with little to gain from taking up Ireland's claims. Successful legislation required a favourable public opinion, government sponsorship, readiness of an Official Opposition not to obstruct indefinitely, concurrence of the House of Lords and the assent of the sovereign. Legislating was a complex affair. Moreover, parliamentary sessions were of limited duration with large numbers of issues presenting themselves for treatment. Ireland always had to jostle for time with other pressing claims. In the later 1870s, when Ireland did not receive much parliamentary attention, Parnell complained of this neglect but acknowledged that his country fared better than Scotland.[25] During the later Victorian years, Ireland was accorded more time than any other single issue received, including the claims of the British working classes, the empire, or the well-ventilated grievances of Nonconformists. In addition, interest in Ireland was sustained in the face of a not insignificant populist hostility to Catholics which showed itself in numerous riots and violent demonstrations. In view of this feeling the political preoccupation with Ireland is remarkable. Also, Gladstone's proposed grant of home rule in 1886 unleashed the greatest political controversy of the age. His efforts were of no avail in convincing either the House of Commons or the nation of the necessity of a Dublin Parliament with extensive powers over domestic Irish matters. Even his own party remained relatively united only because it was generally supposed that his plan must fail. Gladstone's enduring legacy was to polarise political life, leaving Conservatives with little apparent advantage in continuing to legislate for Ireland. Yet that is precisely what they did even at the risk of alienating their own supporters.

During the 1890s Conservative governments attempted to deal with the particular problems of the impoverished west through the Congested Districts Board, made provision for financial grants for local purposes, established the Department of Agriculture and Technical Instruction, passed further land purchase measures, encouraged Sir Horace Plunkett and the Co-operative Movement and implemented elective local government. The ideal of what they hoped to achieve was equality within Ireland and the fuller integration of that country into a true United Kingdom. Gerald Balfour, when defending the Local Government Bill, put the reformist view when he stated:

if you establish minority representation, you can do so only by admitting that there is a minority that requires special

240   LATER VICTORIAN BRITAIN 1867–1900

protection, and I am anxious as far as possible to obliterate and do away with all class distinctions. I wish no longer to keep up, so far as local government is concerned, anything that emphasized the distinction between landlords and tenants, between large and small cesspayers. My own belief is that if you succeed by a system of minority representation in getting a larger proportion of landed gentry on these councils you would do so with the accompanying disadvantages that those who by this means secure seats on the councils will not have the influence on the councils that they would otherwise possess.[26]

Despite a long-standing fear of democracy and Irish nationalism, Conservatives, like Liberals, were prepared to replace the garrison with representatives of the people.

Additionally, much of the general legislation of the period was applicable to Ireland. One example, the Reform and Redistribution Acts of 1884–5, illustrates the point. With these Acts Ireland's franchise qualifications and election procedures were harmonised for the first time under the Union with those of Britain. The legislation, in fact, slightly favoured Ireland, leaving it with more MPs than population warranted and within the country presenting the Catholic areas with an advantage over the Protestant north-east.[27] Gladstone, supported by the future leader of the Liberal Unionists, Lord Hartington, specifically declined to consider fancy franchises to aid the minority.

If Ireland experienced disappointment at Westminster, or found concessions granted in a grudging tone, the reality remains that the sister island reaped a rich harvest. Often the first attempt to meet Irish claims was insufficient, as in the case of the land, but politicians were prepared, when necessary, to enact further measures. That was precisely the same process which took place in purely English questions. Stress upon the intensity of change is essential to constructing an understanding of why Catholic loyalism in Ireland was as tenuous at the conclusion of the Victorian age as it had been in 1867. While the hypothesis that Britain paid inadequate attention to Ireland is not to be cast aside completely, its value as an explanation for Irish disloyalty is limited. Indeed, it was

frustrating for British leaders, who had done so much, to
achieve so little in the way of reconciling the majority of
Ireland's people.

Did pacification fail because of coercion? A myth concerning
the deleterious effect of coercion has grown up in the historical
literature. It might even be supposed that policing in Ireland
was harsh, even vicious, if some of the historical literature is
accepted. What is true is that incidents of shootings, assaults,
destruction of property and animals and intimidation ran at
unacceptably high levels, particularly when compared with the
peaceful state of Britain. Ireland was a turbulent community in
much the way English cities had been earlier in the century. To
combat disorder Ireland was subjected to heavier policing than
England. In the battle against outrage the Irish Administration
secured through Parliament suspension of certain common law
procedures. Nationalist propagandists painted a portrait of a
country governed by draconian laws. In reality, a police state
reign of terror did not exist. Infringements of individual's
liberties were exceptional.

Coercion is the broad term for a suspension or modification
of ordinary or common law rights. At any single moment the
deviation from regular procedures included some or all of
things such as denial of *Habeas Corpus*, enlarged powers of
search and detention, arrest on suspicion, widened definition of
seditious writing and speech, authority to limit or suppress
public assembly when it might give rise to disturbance,
restriction of firearms, the impanelling of special juries or trial
by judges sitting alone, and similar matters. Ireland, though,
remained a community governed by defined laws. Citizens
were not tortured, murdered or apt simply to disappear.
Representatives of the state were accountable. People in
Ireland had access to lawyers and the courts. Moreover, as one
writer has noted recently, the intense legalism of the Irish
Administration, reinforced by the hesitancy of its own law
advisers and the supervisory function of Parliament, put a
heavy restraint on the application of unnecessary force.[28]

In the mid-1880s the debate on coercion sometimes seemed
to revolve around the Maamtrasna incident. The culprits in a
particularly brutal murder were about to be hanged when it
was alleged that one of them was innocent. Appeals failed to

spare the man, Patrick Joyce, from his dreaded appointment on the scaffold. His fate became the centrepiece in the controversy over the administration of justice under Lord Spencer's viceroyalty. Were nationalist invective taken literally, it would be supposed that communication and co-operation with Spencer and his colleages would be all but impossible. However, Irish words were fiercer than their intent. During this same period Parnell urgently sought accommodation with the Liberals. Also, much of the personal animus directed at Spencer exaggerated true feelings. In early 1886 Justin McCarthy recorded his pleasure at seeing the Red Earl again after a lapse of several years when the two men met by chance.[29] With Liberal adoption of home rule the remains of poor Joyce were allowed at last to rest in peace and Spencer became a much praised ally rather than an ogre. Victims of Tory coercion soon filled the void. After a panic police shooting at Mitchelstown, Co. Tipperary, in September 1887 the legend of 'Bloody Balfour' was in the making. Yet Parnell, and later John Redmond were not inhibited from reaching understandings with Conservatives. What the Irish people most resented about coercion was that its financial burden was levied on them. Coercion as a cause of friction cannot be dismissed out of hand but its actual impact on Anglo-Irish relations must be kept in perspective. If coercion did little to better feeling, there is also no sufficient evidence that it proved a fatal impairment.

Inevitably, then, it is necessary to return to the generally held hypothesis that Catholic loyalism failed to materialise on a grand scale because the British statesmen and public did not grasp the full motive force of the self-governing aspiration of Ireland's people. That view, it will be recalled, was identified earlier with the writings of Mansergh and Lyons. There are two substantial grounds for suspicion of this appealing analysis. The first has been demonstrated above, in the discussion of British leaders' very evident commitment to introduce Irish reforms. Moreover, key politicians in both parties understood the nature of the Irish claim. They had every reason for such comprehension for nationalist speakers reminded them constantly while the English press and opinion journals were full of Ireland throughout the area. Most importantly, one party had actually proposed twice, in 1886 and 1893, to

establish a Dublin Parliament and the other introduced
wide-sweeping local government. By 1900 there was, in fact,
every reason to suppose both that further reform and even full
home government were just over the horizon. Such
considerations ought to have been sufficient to spark an overt
display of Catholic loyalism. Indeed, one of the main Tory
arguments against home rule was the absence of Irish loyalty.
In 1891 Salisbury made this very point when he said:

> the revelation of the experience of the last five years is that
> we know the Irish cause to be what it is. The English people
> know the seamy character of Irish heroism, and they know
> that the character of the men to whom they are asked to hand
> over their friends and brothers in Ulster is such as to cover
> with disgrace any nation who for any cause made such
> tremendous sacrifices and exertions.[30]

Conservative responses remained similar in 1914. Catholics,
especially their spokesmen, had an incentive to prove
Conservatives wrong and show an exaggerated public
patriotism. Unwillingness to engage in such demonstrations no
doubt faithfully reflected a public opinion which would have
found that sort of display abhorrent. Presumably, Catholic
reticence resulted from feelings so deep that even home rule was
placed at risk.

Also, the Lyons/Mansergh view assumes that the Irish
people were exceptionally politicised. Contemporary evidence
does not point in that direction. Though the Fenians claimed a
considerable membership, few joined in the rising in 1867. The
movement's nominal numbers were inflated by young men
seeking fraternal association, recreational outlets, and a
measure of release from constraints imposed by priests and
their elders.[31] In the 1870s the home rule movement never
succeeded in creating a strong network of local organisations.
In the mid-1870s there were complaints about the emphasis
given to home rule at the expense of the land question and
references to 'our apathetic people' on the self-government
demand.[32] It was generally conceded that the task of educating
the Irish people to the idea of home rule was enormous. A little
later at the height of the land war (1879–81) it was noted:

very few in Mayo, and hardly anybody at all in Connemara, seem to take any account of Home Rule, or of any other rule except that of the Land League. The possibility of a parliament on College-green affects the people of the West far less than the remotest chance of securing some share of the land.[33]

Throughout the 1880s the land and other social issues were usually regarded as more pressing than self-government. Even in 1885 and 1886 Parnell's emphasis on home rule was tentative and short-lived.[34] Though he declared for a single plank, self-government, as the theme of the nationalist election campaign in autumn 1885, his plea was little adhered to and Irish speakers continued to stress the central role of the land question. By 1895 Archbishop Thomas Croke, an ardent nationalist himself, noted: 'the country is notorious and, indeed, shamefully apathetic. There is no desire for Home Rule.'[35] Many other observers were dubious about Irish concern for the self-government claim. At the close of the period William O'Brien, who had tired of the home rule focus of the parliamentarians, established the United Irish League, in part, to press social and economic issues.[36] Those movements which enlisted support throughout the later Victorian era were economic rather than purely political. The land problem, in this respect, replaced the religious questions of an earlier period as the central motif of nationalism.

While it is unquestionably the case that nationalist leaders and the movement laid stress on home or self-government throughout the period and undoubtedly wished for it in the long run, this emphasis was the consequence of a complex Irish political framework. Self-rule was the one, indeed almost the sole, issue which when not too carefully defined could command the assent of virtually the whole Catholic population. In contrast, other leading demands such as religion, education and economic questions aroused disputes over priority and about the best means of meeting each claim. The Hierarchy was divided within itself over the education question. Similarly, land demands revealed sharp splits between graziers and tillage agriculturalists, between regions, and between tenants and labourers. Land purchase exposed a vast chasm in the Catholic community. Some welcomed it, as Parnell always did from his entry into politics, as the best means to root the people in the soil while others, like Michael Davitt and John Dillon, mistrusted and resisted purchase. The tensions within the nationalist movement were evident during 1885 and 1886 when only one issue, home rule, could pull the disparate factions together. Thus, emphasis on self-government somewhat overstresses Irish concern for the question. That, at least, enables a reconciliation of the apparent focus on self-government in the face of acknowledged public apathy about the quest.

Had the Irish people been exceptionally politicised, it may be supposed that they would have provided generous finance for the national movement. They were remarkably stingy in practice. By 1875 the Home Rule League's never very expansive functions had to be pruned when contributions remained below expectations.[37] By 1878 the movement found itself in desperate financial condition. The testimonial for the nationalist leader, Isaac Butt, was a miserable disappointment. Evidently, the Irish in Britain were no readier to subscribe to the allied organisation on the mainland. The Home Rule Confederation of Great Britain lived from hand to mouth with its nominal membership inflated by holding meetings in public houses frequented by Irishmen. If Parnell's movement fared better its good fortune proved ephemeral with the coffers kept healthy by Irish-American rather than domestic contributions. After 1890 Yankee dollars dwindled. During the second half of the 1890s the situation approached breaking point and the reunification of the warring political factions was seen as the only possible means of financial salvation through renewed Irish-American support.

Interest in political activity can be placed in a wider and revealing frame. Fewer people took part in politics than in religious life. Contemporaries regularly noted the piety of the people. There seems to have been no shortage of cash had the Irish wished to put some of it towards political purposes. Bank deposits swelled, much money went into land acquisition, and the rapid increase in provincial shops indicated that funds were available. The Church was the beneficiary of immense gifts and engaged in massive ecclesiastical building.[38] Catholics in

Ireland were generous in support of religious, not political, pleas. In Britain the Irish contributions also went to non-political purposes. Even Irish-American contributions for political causes were modest when placed alongside support for family emigration, religious institutions in Ireland, and remittances for the home farm.

Britain's Irish community is a useful control group for assessing the failure of Catholic loyalism to emerge. This sizeable group by and large was absorbed into the host community within two or three generations while retaining its adherence to catholicism. Nationalist activism was kept alive by the continuing stream of new immigrants. By 1900 the Irish in Britain manifested the same characteristics of loyalty as others. Many would serve in the Boer War with distinction. There were by the turn of the century countless instances of Catholics rising to high station in Britain and the empire. It seems that it was not the fact of being of Irish Catholic origin but being a Catholic in Ireland which shaped attitudes towards the British connection. But even in Ireland itself Catholics expressed no wholesale rejection of English ideology or institutions. They merely wished to exercise more direct control over their own destiny.

Irish disenchantment with the Union obviously had political and nationalist dimensions but these expose only a part of the picture. Irish dissatisfaction also had an economic ingredient and that sharpened the edge of political discontent. Ireland and her people were wealthier in 1900 than they had been in 1867 but the way that improvement was gained left them feeling little gratitude towards Britain. The continued pattern of emigration exemplified the economic problem.

Prior to the famine in the 1840s there was already a substantial flow of people from Ireland. Between the end of the Napoleonic war and the mid-1840s more than a million souls deserted the country.[39] That trend was accelerated by the disaster of the 1840s. Between then and the mid-1850s approximately 2½ million people left Ireland and a further 4 million had departed by 1914. There were peaks in the emigration cycle but it was a virtually continuous process. Of the several motivations for emigration, the economic was clearly the decisive factor. And it should be remembered that though most of Europe experienced a heavy outflow of people at this time, the number of Irish emigrants as a proportion of total population exceeded all other individual cases. Emigration was not a completely negative force. In economic theory it had the two-fold effect of relieving population pressure at home and enabling those who left to enjoy an improved standard of living abroad. Most of those who remained in Ireland were able, in fact, to enhance personal economic prospects as a consequence of a diminished population. However, a recent commentator has noted that the effect of emigration was seldom to remove enough of the surplus people to raise wages significantly or cure underemployment. Families in Ireland came to depend on emigration as a solution for excess population and for the remittances their children or kin sent back. Remittances as a way of life became more prominent during the long late Victorian slump in demand for Irish harvesters for it was no longer possible for male heads of households to ensure the survival of the home farm by seasonal labour in Britain as they had earlier done. Indeed, the Irish increasingly found themselves locked into a cycle of spawning large families for emigration and the concomitant remittances.

Emigration was a way of life for the ordinary people of rural Ireland – especially for the agricultural labourers, younger sons and also for those daughters with little prospect of finding husbands with land. Despite obvious attractions, it was bitterly resented by priests, politicians and the families caught up in the emigration treadmill. For ecclesiastics the flow of people presented a threat to the faith and morals of their flock. They rarely passed up an opportunity to condemn emigration and the nationalist press of the period frequently featured articles about the misfortunes of some of those who settled in American or British cities. This propaganda was ineffective in the face of remittances, encouraging letters home and an absence of economic opportunity in Ireland. Like churchmen, Irish politicians were swift to decry emigration and to blame Britain for its necessity. Indeed, they argued that home rule was the only cure to the country's economic plight – the sole means to create an Ireland sufficiently prosperous to put a halt to emigration. Nationalists insisted that the Union and British rule had destroyed Ireland's industries. Emigration was elevated as the symbol of British failure and, therefore, took on a political as well as an economic coloration.

British policy had no riposte to the emigration crisis – in fact, it probably exacerbated the flow. Existing distinctions between those who held land and the labourers, for instance, were reinforced by the Land Act of 1881. Land purchase legislation carried the process a step further. Medium and large size farmers turned British legislation to advantage but the poorer members of the rural community were less fortunate. Thus, labourers, cottiers, younger sons and many daughters had few attractive options to emigration. British legislation was aimed at adjusting rural relationships and contained little to make Irish agriculture prosperous. Adherence to the so-called natural market forces and free trade meant that marginal regions, including many sections of Ireland but also other parts of Britain, were abandoned to their fate. Moreover, to make matters worse, British responses to emigration were ambivalent. Though it was sometimes cited as a solution to Ireland's economic ills, scant public funds were allotted to assist emigrants. Britain received blame without the corresponding gratitude of emigrants or their families. Perhaps most importantly in view of Catholic suspicion of Protestant intentions, Britain was left open to a charge that emigration was encouraged in order to depopulate a Catholic province. It was an allegation repeated with great regularity in Irish society.

Emigration was only the tip of an iceberg. Britain had no clear device for aiding the Irish economy or replacing the role of private capital by state finance when the first was not readily available. Ireland, outside Ulster, suffered from a shortage of non-agricultural employment. Dublin's economic decay in the period highlighted the problem. The Royal Commission on the Housing of the Working Classes in 1885 visited the Irish capital and noted the prevalence of miserable slums – a condition intensified by the fragmented nature of the political jurisdiction. Furthermore, Ireland experienced an adverse balance of payments for most of the period which, in the absence of a capital inflow, impeded economic development.[40] That imbalance resulted from overtaxation and a fall in the

value of agricultural output. By the mid-1870s home rule MPs
were regularly protesting against the taxation burden. During
the 1880s they routinely demanded that more government
contracts and expenditure be made in Ireland. Only in 1896
was the imbalance recognised. By then it was estimated that
the deficit was £2,750,000 per annum and had amounted to
£100,000,000 over the previous 30 years.[41] Only in the 1890s
did British governments begin to seek ways of injecting cash
back into sections of the Irish economy. Earlier, when
Chamberlain had suggested this approach he had horrified his
orthodox Liberal colleagues.[42] But even in the 1890s there was
still a tendency to exploit Irish sources of revenue rather than
pump British funds into the country.

Thus, despite rising standards of living and other evidences
of improvement, the economic roots of Catholic loyalty were
still weak. Too few people felt they owed this improvement
directly to Britain or to the Union. The new landowning
peasants found themselves subject to substantial mortgages
but faced an unstable price structure and uncertain prospects
for their produce. Prosperity had been achieved but at a heavy
social cost. Insecurity remained at the core of Irish life. British
leaders were responsive to Ireland's political demands but less
willing to intervene in the political economy of the country.
They were prepared to trust the Irish people politically up to a
point but loth to ensure the sort of economic conditions which
would make institutional reforms a success. That failure of
perception had little to do with Ireland but was contingent on
other wider considerations. What was never lost sight of was
the reality that the concessions granted to Ireland today could
not be denied to the rest of Britain in the longer term. This
realisation was part and parcel of how and when leaders acted
on Irish grievances. If the Irish problem was something more
than a simple collection of economic insecurities, it was also
greater than a mere political question. Even the admission of
the Irish majority to the veil of respect and responsibility in a
political sense did not, in the end, implant the Union on the
hearts of the people.

11. Did the Late Victorian Economy Fail?

KEITH BURGESS

I

Improvements in machine tools and in methods of executing work, although they exert the most powerful claim on the attention of mechanical engineers, do not and must not wholly engross it. To the makers of steam engines and machinery of all kinds, it is rapidly becoming a matter almost of life and death to be in a position to deal on favourable terms with the originators and projectors of strikes, but the public at large do not care quite so much for these things. If a steam engine can be had – other things being equal – more cheaply from France or Prussia than it can be had in England, the purchaser will go to Prussia or France for it. Therefore the English engine builder must put himself in a position to supply the demand more cheaply and better than his continental rivals; and, as we have stated, his only hope of doing this at present lies in dispensing as far as possible with manual labour.

(*The Economist*, 15 March 1873, 12)

THE view expressed in this quotation has a familiar ring for students of Britain's recent economic history. Yet its timing in 1873 coincided with one of the most dynamic periods of growth for the British economy. Much ink has been spilt seeking to identify the 'climacteric' of the Victorian economy, that is the turning point from comparatively rapid rates of expansion to years of slower growth and relative decline. Put more directly, to what extent and when did the Victorian economy begin to fail? Or, to use the metaphor of one historian, how far did the

changes (and non-changes) of the late Victorian era bear
witness to a *cordon sanitaire* encircling the forces of economic
development – technology, industry and commerce – which
led to a decline of the 'industrial spirit'?[1]

In the first place, it is important to appreciate that notions
like the 'industrial spirit' presuppose a unilinear and often
teleological view of the process of capitalist industrialisation.
The latter is assumed to be a never-ending and ever-
accelerating spiral of technological change, initiated by way of
competition amongst risk-taking entrepreneurs, and sustained
by multiplier effects reverberating through increasingly
integrated spheres of economic activity. Yet this model tends to
ignore the barriers capitalist development itself erects against
perpetually accelerating technological and organisational
change, especially in the temporally specific context of a
national economy, irrespective of the direction of global trends.
Thus it is proposed to focus in this chapter upon the emergence
of these barriers to economic development in the specific
context of late Victorian Britain.

The task of understanding the late Victorian economy must
begin with a grasp of the different theoretical perspectives
adopted in the literature. Economic development was
understood by Victorians themselves in terms of the
assumptions of classical economic theory, which had its origins
in the writings of Smith and Ricardo, but which was developed
subsequently in the general equilibrium model of Alfred
Marshall, and continues to influence the interpretations of
more recent neo-classical economic historians. This approach
is implied in the quotation above, where it is assumed that
'demand' and 'supply' are equilibrated by price and other
'market' signals, and which has been refined in the work of the
'revisionist' school of cliometric economic history to exonerate
from 'failure' the late Victorian economy, in general, and in
particular, the late Victorian entrepreneur.

The problems with such an approach are manifold. Firstly, it
is clear that the sets of historical statistics available have been
insufficiently analysed in terms of the sophisticated techniques
used to draw conclusions from them. Thus the focus of
econometricians upon long runs of commercial and industrial
statistics, in order to chart trends in output, costs, profits and

productivity, requires that they study forms of economic activity which have not only been in existence for some time, but which have been considered to be sufficiently important to justify compilation in the first place.[2] With respect to the late Victorian economy, this approach is inappropriate for the study of the development (or non-development) during this period of economic activities associated with the 'Second Industrial Revolution' based upon electricals, the internal combustion engine and synthetic chemicals.

Secondly, neo-classical econometrics has considered the measures of productivity, cost and profit in isolation from the wider historical context. Thus the same set of productivity, cost or profit figures can be made to yield markedly different 'measures' of economic performance, depending on how these are related to the long-term development of product, capital and labour markets. It has been noted, for example, that British shipyards in 1904 achieved a productivity per man of 12.5 tons, compared with 6.8 tons in the USA and 3.3 tons in Germany, despite having less advanced technology.[3] What explains the British superiority, however, lay outside the isolated measures of output, cost and productivity, but was rooted in Britain's long dominance of world trade and abundance of artisanal skills, which more than compensated for technological obsolescence. Given changes in these wider variables, the productivity superiority of British shipyards was to be fatally undermined during the twentieth century.

Thirdly, the neo-classical approach assumes as unproblematic that there exists a constant supply of individual initiative or elan, fully informed about the state of the market, and equally willing and able to act rationally according to its signals. The doubts cast about the validity of this assumption by recent historical and other empirical research have led to the growth of the 'entrepreneurial school' of British economic history.[4] Yet although it owes its intellectual pedigree to the seminal writings of Schumpeter, it has generally ignored the temporal context of his work and the extent to which he qualified the role of the *individual* entrepreneur as the prime mover of economic development.[5] Effective entrepreneurship in the Schumpeterian sense of doing things differently – or getting things done – requires that a firm, an industry or an economy be *organised* to provide the entrepreneur with the information appropriate to a new stage of economic development; and this depends, in turn, on the availability of at least potentially entrepreneurial *structures* capable of overcoming market constraints or imperfections. This emphasis points to the significance of the wider institutional and social contexts for economic development, which are seen as increasingly central to an understanding of the late Victorian economy, especially in the light of Britain's long-term economic decline during this century.[6] The directive to employers urged by *The Economist* in 1873 to dispense as much as possible with manual labour, in response to the growth of foreign competition, was more a manifestation of the problem, as perceived by contemporaries, rather than a solution to it.[7]

II

The arguments for and against the failure of the late Victorian economy depend crucially, of course, on the statistical evidence available and how this has been interpreted, bearing in mind the already noted limitations of long statistical runs. The task of proving failure is ultimately a measure of relativities, that is, did the late Victorian economy fail relative to earlier periods; or did it fail relative to the performance of other countries; or, was there failure on both these measures? In answer to the first of these questions, the most recent literature has revised the established view of rapid acceleration of growth in Britain during the late eighteenth century, to be followed by a subsequent slowdown in growth.[8] Instead, the rate of growth of national income per capita shows a steady acceleration from 0.27 per cent per annum in 1770 to 0.33 per cent by 1815, and then rising to 0.86 per cent in 1841 at the beginning of the Victorian period (Harley, 1982). By 1840, according to Crafts, income per capita in Britain stood at $567 in terms of 1970 $US, but it is only after 1870 that the availability of data makes international comparison possible.[9] During the period 1840–70, the rate of growth of national income per capita was about

59 per cent, equivalent to an annual rate of growth of 1.56 per cent. Thus it would appear that Britain's national income accelerated steadily during the first half of the nineteenth century, culminating in the widely observed prosperity of the 1850s and 1860s. After 1870, however, the growth rate fell markedly, rising by 25 per cent per capita between 1870 and 1890, and by only 15 per cent between 1890 and 1910. According to the measure of the late Victorian economy's performance in relation to earlier periods, therefore, the record of the post-1870 era was indeed one of relative failure.

It is also possible to assess the performance of the Victorian economy relative to other countries for the period after 1870. In this respect, it is clear that per capita incomes remained higher in Britain than in the rest of Europe for the duration of the Victorian period, despite the post-1870 slowdown of the rate of growth, although this advantage was narrowing slightly in comparison with the more advanced European countries. Thus in 1870 Britain enjoyed a 25 per cent superiority in per capita income over Belgium which had the highest per capita income in continental Europe.[10] By 1890, this advantage had narrowed to 21 per cent, and by 1910 it was reduced again to 17 per cent. In contrast to the late Victorian economy's performance in relation to earlier periods, the measure of Britain's prosperity in comparison with the rest of Europe can scarcely be assessed in terms of failure. Britain also continued to compare favourably with other European countries according to other criteria of development such as birth and death rates. Significantly, however, the two development criteria where Britain *did* compare unfavourably with the European norm were school enrolment and investment as a percentage of national expenditure.[11] As many contemporaries in late Victorian society were clearly aware, Britain remained undoubtedly prosperous in comparison with most of Europe, but there were nagging doubts about whether enough was being done to secure this prosperity for the future. After 1890, at least, it would appear that Britain's wealth began to increase more slowly than in any other major European country.

Changes in national income represent aggregates of data, thus their explanatory value is limited. This is why there has been so much debate in recent years over the significance of capital accumulation, labour productivity and, above all, total factor productivity, for the growth of the British economy since the nineteenth century. Because of the specificity of the data, however, it is not possible to pursue these debates into the pre-1850 period, and the most ambitious work has been concerned primarily with twentieth-century developments.[12] In this connection, therefore, the performance of the late Victorian economy has been analysed more in terms of international comparison, rather than in terms of earlier periods of British economic history, although questions must remain about the comparability of the statistical series since national differences in accountancy principles and methodologies are rarely discussed.[13]

Capital accumulation has traditionally been regarded as the key to economic growth, although it has been assigned less of a leading role more recently as concern has centred upon total factor productivity. As recorded in the statistical series, the concept of fixed capital includes a wide range of investments from residential houses to machine tools, which are not necessarily of equal importance to the performance of a national economy. For the entire period 1856–1913, Britain's capital stock was growing on trend by 2 per cent per annum, but the highest rates of growth for the Victorian era of 2.5 and 2.4 per cent per annum were recorded during the business cycles of 1860–5 and 1873–82 respectively, while a growth rate of only 1.6 per cent was achieved during the business cycle of 1882–9, and the recovery to 1.8 per cent per annum during the cycle of 1889–99 was based substantially on a boom in residential house-building.[14] The phasing of capital accumulation in 'long swings' of economic activity, on the other hand, shows a more marked downward trend after 1882. Although the extent of this was relatively modest, its timing was ominous in the light of developments in other advanced economies. As early as 1870, the European norm of investment as a percentage of national expenditure was already double the British figure, and this gap had widened even further by 1890.[15] This disparity could now no longer be justified on the grounds that other countries were still 'catching up' with Britain, but was indicative of the latter's tentative involvement in the so-called 'Second Industrial Revolution'.

An analysis of labour productivity is complicated by the remarkably low rate of growth of 0.5 per cent per annum recorded during the relatively short business cycle of 1856–60, which has yet to be explained.[16] Thereafter, labour productivity rose to a peak of 1.6 per cent per annum during the business cycle of 1865–73, and then fell gently to 1.1 per cent during the cycle of 1889–99. The phasing of labour productivity in 'long swings' shows a less dramatic decline after 1882 than is the case for capital accumulation. This accords with contemporary evidence of the 1880s and 1890s that there was a widespread intensification of labour, using existing methods of production, rather than a shift to new methods of production.[17] The late Victorian economy's record for labour productivity is thus not one of clear-cut failure, although the outcome led on balance to a probable deterioration in working conditions and an upsurge in industrial strife, especially during the 1890s.

An understanding of changes in total factor productivity is marred by disagreements over the assumptions upon which it should be based, which have yet to be resolved.[18] Yet all the recent calculations point to lower rates of growth for the post-1870 period than previously thought, especially during the 1890s.[19] This is despite the fact that total factor *input*, defined as the weighted average of the rates of growth of employment and fixed capital, expanded at a virtually constant rate throughout the late Victorian period.[20] It would appear that neither lack of capital nor shortages of labour acted as a brake upon economic development during this period. Rather, it would seem that Britain's early start as an industrial nation locked the Victorian economy into a unique trajectory of economic development that proved impossible to alter after 1870, in the absence of any fundamental transformation of state-economy structures and relations.

This survey of the statistical evidence concludes with a consideration of late Victorian failure in terms of the living standards and quality of life of the British people. This aspect of Britain's economic history has proved to be a veritable minefield of controversy, although the fiercest dissension has been confined to the years prior to 1850. Previous discussion of trends in national income shows a marked downturn in growth rates after 1870, although Britain remained the most prosperous of European countries in terms of national income. Since Britain was the world's most urbanised and industrialised country by the 1880s, with an estimated 75 per cent of its population dependent exclusively on wages, the trend of wages is clearly crucial to an understanding of changes in living standards. There is no doubt that real incomes benefited from the fall in prices brought about by the 'Great Depression' of 1873–96, although its impact should not be exaggerated, and recent calculations underline its uneven impact upon different sectors of the economy.[21]

It is important to appreciate, moreover, that the surviving wages data are not representative of all British wage-earners since they are based upon trade union returns that are biased against the majority of unorganised and generally lower paid workers. In addition, the wages data are calculated on the basis of nominal rates of pay and do not take into account the effects of unemployment, overtime or short-time working. Thus one of the most recent cliometric studies of the Victorian standard of living extrapolates earnings and real wages from aggregated daily and weekly rates, up to a 52-week year, and the resulting index of real earnings for all workers is as follows (1901 = 100):[22]

1851 –   54.5
1861 –   45.9
1871 –   56.0
1881 –   68.8
1891 –   87.8
1901 – 100.0

There was clearly no late Victorian failure of living standards on the basis of this measure.

This positivist resolution of the issue of the British standard of living has, however, been criticised for the first half of the nineteenth century,[23] and similar criticism could be made of it for the late Victorian period as well. Firstly, it purports to construct a national index based upon the random survival of wage data that cannot measure objectively a national human reality. In the building industry, for example, the trend of wage rates confirms the accuracy of the above index. Yet this is derived from trade union-negotiated rates in an industry where, as late as the 1890s, less than 20 per cent of even skilled tradesmen were trade union members, while one of the few guides to the actual *earnings* of building workers is a contemporary record made of two Gateshead bricklayers during the 1880s and 1890s.[24] Thus during the decade 1882–91, the weekly working hours of one of them varied from an average of almost 31 hours in 1885 to more than 49 hours in 1889, and there was a similar variation in earnings, ranging from an average of 33s.1½d. weekly during the first six months of 1891 to an average of 20s.7¼d. weekly in 1885. Thus it would seem that the national wage indices that have been devised can only stand the explanatory burden placed upon them if it can be shown that rhythms of work had become more regular by the late Victorian era, in comparison with previous periods. Not only has this not been decisively proved, but in the case of London – the largest single centre of economic activity in Britain during this period – there is some evidence pointing in the opposite direction.[25]

This raises the question of the regional unevenness of the Victorian economy, which undermines the utility of notional national averages. Again, there is little evidence to suggest that this had diminished by the 1880s and 1890s, and if sources other than wage rates are considered, the ameliorist interpretation of living standards during the second half of the nineteenth century looks increasingly vulnerable.[26] In fact, what is noteworthy is how the 'data' produced by positivist historians often fail to sustain the arguments based upon them. It has been argued, for example, that there was an 'unambiguous, pronounced, and pervasive' egalitarian trend in Britain's income distribution from the 1860s to 1914.[27] Yet what the figures presented show is that between 1867 and 1880 both the top 10 per cent and the top 5 per cent increased their income shares, while the share going to the 40–90 per cent group actually fell. There was some redistribution of income from the 40–90 per cent group to the bottom 40 per cent, but this was not at the expense of the top 10 per cent. After 1880, any levelling of inequality took the form of a 0.2 per cent gain for the bottom 40 per cent and a 0.6 per cent gain for the 40–90 per cent group on the 1867 distribution. Focusing upon the period 1881–1901, thus avoiding the complications of the Edwardian period, the same author's estimate of *intra*-occupational earnings distribution shows that earnings inequality increased among manual workers during these years.[28]

The phrase 'poverty amidst plenty', with finely nuanced gradations in between, most aptly captures the 'condition of England' in the late Victorian period. Even generally acknowledged improvements like the reduction in the working week to 54 hours during the 1870s was of real benefit only to male workers organised in effective trade unions, since factory legislation regulating the hours of unorganised women and juveniles could be violated with impunity by employers; a shorter working week often had to be traded off against augmented workloads; and important areas of employment like domestic service were not covered by factory legislation. Finally, the benefits of falling wholesale food prices during the 1870s and 1880s were not always reflected in retail outlets, particularly in the poorer districts of the large cities, while adulteration and malnutrition persisted.[29] If the case for the failure of the late Victorian economy remains not proven, in so far as this applies to the standard of living of the majority of Britons, there is now considerable doubt about the extent of improvement in relation to earlier periods.

III

It would seem, therefore, that an assessment of the extent and timing of the failure of the late Victorian economy requires an explanation capable of identifying the significant links between institutions, economic structures and measures of performance, and how these evolved to shape the context for economic activity in the late nineteenth century. In this respect, one of the most powerful contexts for economic activity has been set by the institutions and practices of nation states. Britain's early start as an industrial nation, together with the spontaneously unplanned character of its 'Industrial

Revolution', has conventionally tended to understate the importance of decisive links between state and economy forged in the pre-industrial period but which have continued to affect the course of British economic development during the nineteenth and twentieth centuries.

To begin with, it should be made clear what is meant by the state. The state is something more than merely 'government'. It is a continuum of administrative, legal, bureaucratic and coercive systems that attempts not only to establish acceptable relationships between civil society and public authority, but also to establish acceptable relationships *within* civil society, including economic relations. Thus well before the onset of industrialisation in Britain, there had developed a well-established set of state–economy relations, arising from the necessity of financing the military power required to protect the state from its enemies, both at home and abroad. During the Napoleonic Wars, for example, tax revenue in Britain was rising in real terms twice as fast as national income, and the share of taxes in the national income rose from 15 to 24 per cent, while general levels of taxation in Britain were almost three times the French level.[30] What made such levels of taxation tolerable was that the British state had been remarkably successful in forming alliances with specific social classes who were prepared to accept them in return for the protection state power provided. At the same time, the huge cumulative national debt of about £800m at the end of the Napoleonic Wars was funded by generally the same social classes, who benefited in interest payments to the tune of more than 50 per cent of total public expenditure.

This process of alliance-making between the state and specific social classes was not, of course, unique to Britain, but it had a national specificity that was unique, reflecting Britain's commercial dominance prior to industrialisation. In so far as state–economy relations are concerned, this dominance depended, firstly, on the production of stable money forms (via the Bank of England); and secondly, it required conditions that encouraged the maximisation of continuous exchange opportunities. Both were needed for the international trading role played by the institutions of the City of London, and which had, in turn, been so essential in meeting the British state's financial requirements. This alliance between the state and the City of London, mediated by the Bank of England and the Treasury, determined economic policy-making throughout the nineteenth and twentieth centuries. The twin bases of this policy were to be the gold standard, or later more precisely, the gold-sterling standard, providing a stable money form for the City's international trading operations; and, secondly, free trade, which maximised continuous exchange opportunities. Thus Huskisson, the president of the Board of Trade, conceived the measures leading to freer trade during the 1820s with the aim of making Britain the Venice of the nineteenth century rather than the 'Workshop of the World'.[31]

This policy orientation of the British state established the long-term trajectory of Britain's economic development that did have a 'climacteric' in the late Victorian period. The historic precedent of Venetian decline was echoed in the widely acknowledged slowdown in Britain's rate of economic growth, which emphasised the dangers of having based wealth and power on insecure and uncontrollable mercantile activities. The Baring financial crisis of 1890 highlighted the vulnerability of the City as the centre of international trade, and underlined the burden of unpredictable rises in interest rates falling upon domestic producers when there was a flight of capital from London.[32] Chambers of Commerce representing manufacturing districts complained bitterly about the effects of rising tariffs abroad and called for 'fair' trade rather than free trade.[33] The gold-sterling standard also came under attack. In 1886, for example, a motion was carried by Glasgow Chamber of Commerce declaring as 'evil' the displacement of silver money over large areas of the world, and demands for bimetallism persisted into the 1890s.[34] Yet these criticisms failed to present a coherent alternative to orthodox financial policy.

Thus the priorities of this commercial capitalism meant that by the late Victorian period the course of British economic development was fixed in its basic structure by a highly centralised financial system, under the control of the Bank of England, whose interests were international, fiscal and narrowly monetary, and where the stabilisation of sterling had priority over the domestic producer. Continuity in economic policy should not be interpreted, however, to mean that the British state did not take on new responsibilities during the nineteenth century, and public expenditure grew fifteen times in real terms for the century as a whole. By the late Victorian period, successive waves of administrative expansion and reform had sought to ameliorate, with some effect, the social costs of industrialisation and urbanisation with legislation dealing with poverty, public health and public order. The Victorian state was clearly not a 'weak' state. Yet what this transformation marked was the growth of a 'regulation' but not of a 'development' state. In this respect, the contrast with late-nineteenth-century Germany is instructive. There, a strong and interventionist state had enabled Germany's heavy industries increasingly to escape the domination of free market forces, making possible long-term research and investment, and enterprise-based welfarism that made state-led 'regulation' less necessary.[35] In late Victorian Britain, in comparison, the historical process of alliance-making between state and society had produced a polity fixed in a commerical frame that subordinated production to exchange and distribution.

While it is easy to make such judgements with the benefit of hindsight, what is often overlooked is the extent to which contemporaries at the time were aware of the more rapid economic progress being made by 'poorer' countries. As the president of Glasgow's Chamber of Commerce wryly observed in 1898:

When trying to enquire further into the causes of the growth of foreign competition, I come to the conclusion that it is the unavoidable consequence of great national wealth that much time and energy is devoted to the administration of this wealth. A whole army of accountants, lawyers and brokers is constantly at work in Great Britain, to mould business, trades, and ventures of every kind and description, into shapes more profitable and convenient to the parties interested. Construction and reconstruction, splitting of stock, creation of preferred, deferred, and ordinary stock can, however, scarcely lay claim to be an occupation 'productive' in the true sense of the word. Meanwhile, the poorer nations devote their whole energy to fresh business, and inasmuch as the value of capital in this country has decreased and that of labour increased, the more recent manufacturing country will make more progress than the former.[36]

The institutions and practices of the state constituted probably the single most important context for British economic development in the late Victorian period. Thus from the 1850s, one of the major economic developments made possible by government legislation was the growth of limited liability companies, which promised to enlarge significantly the capital base for economic activity through the sale of shares on the stock market. Despite being a relatively capital-abundant economy, however, the late Victorian capital market remained a highly fragmented system. This reflected, in part, the historic orientation of the City of London towards overseas issues, but it was reinforced further by circumstances surrounding the launching of the early limited liability companies. The first of these was the lax regulation of the public disclosure of the affairs of the companies, which gave their directors 'virtually unchallengeable and unchecked possession' of their assets.[37] A related problem was the backwardness of British accountancy practice that was slow to emerge from the mercantile world of the double-entry system and adapt to the needs of large-scale enterprise.[38] Finally, the British banking system withdrew from *active* risk-sharing with borrowing firms, in contrast to German practice, at the very time that limited liability became an accepted form of business organisation.[39]

The outcome led to an emphasis on short-term 'construction, reconstruction, and splitting of stock', with the aim of making a quick profit. This emphasis upon short-term financial manipulation also encouraged company promoters and directors to maximise shareholder wealth in order to bid up stock prices further, and this was a vastly remunerative activity during the boom of the 1890s.[40] The cost of this strategy for long-term development, however, was such that it raised expectations of 'acceptable' returns, with the result that investment in projects yielding 'substandard' returns, or having lengthy time horizons, was discouraged. In particular, limited companies were compelled to retain a substantial part of their resources in the form of liquid reserves in order to satisfy the dividend expectations of shareholders, in the event that the latter could not be met out of current profits.[41] Most British limited liability companies did not have much long-term lending support from the banks, relying instead upon equity capital, which meant that they had a less highly geared capital structure than was the case, say, in Germany. In consequence, their *real* capital costs were higher and they could not grow as fast at equivalent operating margins.

Again, it is important to appreciate the timing of these constraints when industrialisation was entering a new stage of development, demanding not only much larger capital outlays but also much longer gestation periods. Technological and organisational changes incur direct as well as indirect costs, which in late Victorian Britain were either objectively high or at least perceived to be high. Among the direct costs, the most significant would include the outlays on new plant and equipment, the cost of retraining the work force, and other direct costs of implementation like the changeover from steam to electric power. Moreover, any firm would have to weigh the costs and benefits of change in relation to both existing and expected states of competition, and these would have to be judged in relation to the potential costs arising from the premature retirement of fixed capital not yet fully amortised, which were unlikely to be calculated realistically on the basis of technically deficient accountancy practices. Among the indirect costs, the most important would include managerial inexperience with new techniques or new forms of authority, labour resistance to methods not understood or regarded as otherwise 'degrading', and a host of unforeseen externality effects that may not have entered the initial calculation. Above all, firms would be naturally reluctant to implement innovations that would increase their output beyond a level that the market could absorb.

Such questions were central to many of the issues that concerned observers of late Victorian Britain. Consider, for example, the question of education and training. It can be argued that the education service provided by the expansion of the Victorian 'regulation' state was based upon the priority of habituating the mass of the population to the needs of industrialism, as these were perceived in Britain during the first half of the nineteenth century. A modicum of literacy and numeracy was leavened by a hefty incalculation of morality aimed at the acquisition of 'industrious habits', where religion played a prominent role. There was little acceptance of either the American model, which conceived of education as a means to individual social mobility, or the Prussian tradition, which assigned a major role for education in the service of the state. Thus the Report of the Newcastle Commission in 1861 had claimed that it was neither possible nor 'desirable' to keep children at school after the years of 10 or 11.[42]

Attitudes began to change somewhat during the second half of the nineteenth century, but the extension of educational provision, especially in secondary schools and in technical and higher education, was painfully slow. Thus in 1870 Britain's school enrolment was less than one-third of the European norm, and compared even more unfavourably with countries like Germany.[43] This gap began to narrow late in the nineteenth century but it would appear that Britain continued to neglect education as an investment in human capital. An emphasis upon on-the-job learning and the cult of the 'practical man' continued to predominate, and even if this kind of learning outside formal education is taken into account, the overall rate at which Britain's population was improving its skills during the late Victorian era was inadequate for the needs of the new phase of industrialisation, and which has been judged a 'failure' by an otherwise optimistic historian of the period.[44] Moreover, this failure was even more marked in the spheres of technical and business training.[45]

It has been argued, however, that Britain did not want more graduate engineers, for example, on the grounds that product specialisation and limited output runs depended more upon artisan skills acquired by apprenticeship.[46] Yet this view was not universal, even in the more traditional sectors of engineering, and it was scarcely true at all for rapidly developing industries such as chemicals.[47] As one chemical employer declared at the turn of the century:

There is no doubt that the Educational System as regards Chemistry is infinitely superior in Germany to what it is here. . . . There is more public spirit in Germany than there is in England. If a man here is educated as a Chemist they talk of a Chemist, and they would consider him a man in a Druggist's shop. . . . A Chemist in Germany holds a Scientific Degree which is greatly respected.[48]

Other firms complained about the difficulty of obtaining suitable supervisors, managers and commercial travellers, which was again blamed on poor education.[49] While there is no automatic correlation between levels of educational provision and economic performance, it would seem that late Victorian Britain did neglect education as a form of investment in human capital, and this reinforced rigidities elsewhere in the economy.

What is meant by 'rigidities', in this context, can be illustrated with reference to the problem that, above all, so greatly agitated contemporaries, namely, rising tariffs abroad and the threat of increasing competition from tariff-protected rivals, particularly Germany. While free trade was regarded as essential to the successful operations of the City of London, the attitude of British industry to this issue was much more equivocal. As a representative of Sheffield's cutlery trades complained:

There are merchants in the City of London who used to buy goods for the colonies and for foreign countries in England 10 years ago, but they now go and buy in Germany goods apparently equal and at a much less price, and the orders are to buy German goods and not to buy English goods, and so they beat us.[50]

This is a graphic instance of how Britain's mercantile dominance came into conflict with the interests of industry during the late Victorian period. The outcome was that industries which had flourished in response to overseas demand were now crowded out of many of the most rapidly growing markets abroad, and including the British market itself, with the result that future innovation and investment were discouraged. The trajectory of the late Victorian economy was thus fixed by the stock of factor endowments based upon Britain's early start as an industrial nation, while the terms of comparative advantage enjoyed by Germany, the USA and even France were centred much more on 'new' and technologically more sophisticated industries.[51] Representatives of the latter in Britain were at pains to make clear that there was a 'virtuous spiral' of certainty and continuity of demand, made possible by tariff protection, which led to larger and more continuous runs of production, and which, in turn, afforded better trained labour, increased efficiency, and lower costs.[52] Ultimately, the failure of the late Victorian economy implied here was essentially a political one in that productive industry remained highly heterogeneous and fragmented, in contrast to the relative homogeneity of the City of London, which prevented it from implementing an alternative to free trade orthodoxy.[53]

The heterogeneity and fragmentation of industry in late Victorian Britain is underlined by the persistence of family control of firms, despite the advent of limited liability and the growth of large-scale companies at the turn of the century. The latter generally came about as a result of mergers of existing firms, with the aim of stabilising competition and prices, rather than achieving genuine economies of scale as part of a broader strategy to overcome market constraints.[54] They were also concentrated in the relatively low-technology sectors of consumer foods and chemicals, which had limited export potential, and the majority of the largest non-financial enterprises were railway companies. At the same time, the degree of interlocking between the City of London financial institutions and the more dynamic sectors of manufacturing industry was relatively weak, with less than one-fifth of firms interlocked by the 13 London clearing banks being manufacturers.[55] In 1900, less than 6 per cent of the paid-up capital of securities quoted on the London Stock Exchange was in the industrial, commercial or mining sector, while the vast majority were either government bonds or railway shares.[56] The late Victorian capital market and its institutions were thus unsuited to the task of raising the much larger capitals and satisfying the much longer time horizons associated with the economic developments of the future.

Finally, the pattern of regional specialisation that had evolved in Britain since the early nineteenth century began to exhibit 'rigidities' of its own by the late Victorian period, which did not augur well for the future. By the 1880s and 1890s, London and the Home Counties had reasserted their predominance in the economy as a whole, following the phase of economic advance associated with the 'Industrial Revolution' in northern Britain. In fact, it has been argued that London and the Home Counties had become virtually a single, highly integrated 'economy within an economy', linked to the growth of service industries and related consumer and internally orientated manufacturing trades, outside the City of London itself.[57] In contrast, the rest of the British economy was much more directly dependent upon exports to overseas product markets, and was much more vulnerable, therefore, to its relative loss of international competitiveness at the end of the nineteenth century. While regional specialisation has been a feature generally of economic development, this had evolved to a unique degree in Britain by the late Victorian era, when the new high-technology, consumer-orientated industries of the future, such as the electrical engineering industry, had become heavily concentrated in the metropolitan area.[58] The extent of 'failure' of the late Victorian economy was thus not regionally uniform. Firms that remained rooted to their bases in provincial Britain, and having an external orientation abroad, were already failing during these years.[59] In short, it would appear that the regional structure of the late Victorian economy meant that the costs and benefits of ongoing as well as future economic development were to be very unevenly shared.

To conclude this survey, attention is refocused upon the quotation with which it began. The extent and timing of the failure of the late Victorian economy is clearly a rather more complex problem than *The Economist* was prepared to concede in 1873. An appreciation of one manifestation of a problem is not the same as a proper understanding of its causes. The historian should be similarly wary of mono-causal approaches and explanations. Economic development takes place in the context of spatially and temporally defined realities, rather than according to abstract theories or ideological imperatives, although the latter clearly influence our understanding of the former. Ultimately, a judgement on the failure or success of the late Victorian economy depends upon the assumptions and concerns of the observer, especially the scope that is allowed for human agency in its capacity to shape economic development. The achievement of the Victorian economy was considerable, but much more could have been achieved, and a less problematic legacy passed on to the future, if human agency had not been so constrained by established orthodoxies.

12. Science and the Anglo-German Antagonism

PETER ALTER

WHEN a festive Britain indulged in celebrating Queen Victoria's diamond jubilee in 1897 her vast empire had long become the envy of other powers and her political system was widely regarded, particularly in Europe, as a model for parliamentary democracy. But beneath the dazzling display of might and glory, of pageantry and military strength on the occasion of the jubilee there was uncertainty and deep anxiety, and behind the ostentatious self-assertion of an imperial nation there was a feeling of political and economic vulnerability. As the sun went down on the Victorian age, to many contemporary observers Britain's political influence and modernity, so much admired abroad, stood in striking contrast to her obvious deficiencies and her backwardness in other fields, which raised doubts about her future international standing and security.

The organisation and achievements of British science, to single out but one much-discussed example, were in particular described by informed observers as being highly inadequate and by no means up to the standards of the time. In the winter of 1900, at the height of the Boer War, the London mathematician Karl Pearson asked in a public lecture which attracted a great deal of attention whether 'our supply of trained brains is sufficient, or, at any rate, whether it is available in the right place at the right moment'.[1] Four years later Sir William Huggins, president of the Royal Society, referred to the 'scientific deadness of the nation'.[2] And in 1905 Richard B. Haldane, later to become war secretary in Campbell-Bannerman's Liberal Cabinet, said: 'We live in a country where science is not so much appreciated as it should be. Our people like to see cash over the counter, and they do not like to wait for deferred payment.'[3] A number of factors have been cited since the 1870s as evidence for these and similar assessments: unlike comparable Western European countries and the United States, Britain had few universities and institutes of technology; the statistics for Britain showed a relatively low number of students at universities in comparison especially with the political rival Germany; British industry as yet possessed practically no large research laboratories of the type already well established in Germany and the United States. In the birthplace of the Industrial Revolution, moreover, there were only few research institutions outside the universities, of the sort which had been created in considerable numbers in Germany since the foundation of the nation-state in 1871.

From the early nineteenth century onwards, the British scientific community[4] had repeatedly discussed the conspicuous discrepancy between the degree of modernity of Britain's political system on the one hand, and the alleged backwardness of its scientific system on the other. David Brewster, Charles Babbage, Lyon Playfair, John Tyndall, T. H. Huxley, Norman Lockyer – all of them shared the view that the social and political climate in Britain was not conducive to higher education, scholarship and scientific research. However, their insistence that the relationship between government, with its financial resources, and science had to be thoroughly redefined did not evoke a wide response from either leading politicians or the public. Throughout the whole of the Victorian age, the dialogue which the scientists hoped for between the government and the scientific community about the basic conditions necessary for modern research never took place. The many attempts made by British scientists to influence political decision-making processes in favour of science, and to mobilise the government and its resources in the interests of science failed almost without exception. In historical retrospect, it is therefore possible only to speak of a very limited debate about the financial, organisational and institutional needs of science in Victorian Britain. Moreover, it was a debate from which as a rule one of the two partners persistently withdrew, and for this reason it was restricted essentially to the small but growing circle of the scientific community. Agitation by numerous scientists, largely in the forums provided by the professional journals, learned societies and scientific conferences, produced an image of a passive state which did practically nothing to improve the institutional and financial conditions of science in Britain, indeed, abandoned it almost totally to an attitude of liberal *laissez-faire*. Subsequently, this impression was also accepted, largely without question, by many modern historians of science. The sociologists of science, Hilary and Steven Rose, for example, write that for science in Victorian Britain self-help was the 'order of the day'.[5] And the historian Gerard L'E. Turner has emphasised that in Queen Victoria's England and even later it was perfectly normal for scientists to finance their own research.[6] The widespread notion of the British government's *laissez-faire* attitude towards science is also supported by D. S. L. Cardwell's useful survey of the development of scientific organisations and institutions in England between 1800 and 1914.[7] He confirms the view that as late as the second half of the nineteenth century there was no systematic promotion of science based on long-term planning by the government in London.

This raises the question of why the scientific community's hitherto largely internal debate about a more efficient and generous fostering of science in Britain had become a public issue in a totally unprecedented way towards the end of the Victorian age. Why was it that the co-existence of political modernity and partial underdevelopment in certain areas such as science and science organisation in Britain, which had so frequently been pointed out by spokesmen from the scientific community, was rather suddenly perceived as a problem by the wider community? What moved some politicians, such as Haldane, Lord Rosebery and Arthur J. Balfour, or in more general terms, what caused the government to intervene, apparently very suddenly, in the debate about the organisation and financing of science in Britain, and to revise its traditional attitude, or at least what had been regarded as its traditional attitude? According to historians of the subject, the period from about 1897 to 1918 – that is, the two decades between the diamond jubilee and the end of the First World War – mark 'the origins of the organisation of scientific research as we now understand it'.[8] From this historiographical premise follows the question of what repercussions the remarkable change in attitude which had taken place since the late Victorian era had on the social status of science and the scientific professions in Britain.

The questions are of interest not least because in comparison with earlier periods, the nineteenth century was, generally speaking, exceptionally rich in important scientific and technological innovations which clearly showed that science and technology had become keys to future economic progress. But contrary to the expectations of many British scientists, this did not lead to a more general acceptance of the legitimacy of scientific activity and its claim for generous financial backing. In Britain even prominent scientists remained under constant pressure to justify in detail demands for financial and organisational support from the government throughout the Victorian and Edwardian ages. A famous example is the speech made by Sir Norman Lockyer, as president of the British Association for the Advancement of Science, at the Association's annual meeting in Southport in 1903. The connection forcefully made in this speech between politics, the fostering of science and the Darwinian principle of the survival of the fittest, guaranteed it an unusual amount of publicity. The arguments put forward in Lockyer's presidential address can be regarded as typical for the position taken by many members of the scientific community at that time. The title of the speech, 'The Influence of Brain-Power on History', was a direct allusion to a seminal work by the American naval historian Alfred Thayer Mahan, *The Influence of Sea Power upon History*, published in 1890. It is probably not enough to see only the general maritime enthusiasm of the age at work in this reference to sea power. Rather, it expressed the idea that in an age when competing industrial countries were energetically expanding overseas, military power, and industrial and technological power were all of equal importance and indispensable for maintaining claims to great power status. Political power, in Europe and overseas, could no longer be upheld by military power alone, be it a strong army or a large fleet. Lockyer eventually pushed his equation of 'sea-power' and 'brain-power' so far as to demand equal expenditure on both, thus arriving at rather astronomical figures for education and science.[9]

In his speech at Southport, which came close to a biting reckoning up with the policy of successive British governments since the early Victorian years, Norman Lockyer deplored the financial and idealistic neglect of science generally to be observed in Britain and the alleged far-reaching economic consequences of this fateful neglect. For him, fostering science was equivalent to an act of national self-assertion. Thus it had very much in common with armament. In a sweeping condemnation of past failings Lockyer summed up:

> We have lacked the strengthening of the national life produced by fostering the scientific spirit among all classes, and along all lines of the nation's activity; many of the responsible authorities know little and care less about science; we have not learned that it is the duty of a State to organise its forces as carefully for peace as for war; that universities and other teaching centres are as important as battleships or big battalions; are, in fact, essential parts of a modern State's machinery, and, as such, to be equally aided and as efficiently organised to secure its future well-being.[10]

In comparison with these tasks and the necessity of making technological and scientific discoveries available to commerce and industry, the debate about free trade and tariff reform which was just beginning to gain momentum under Joseph Chamberlain's moving influence was, in Lockyer's view, of secondary importance for the future of the British economy. Statesmen and politicians, he suggested, would most certainly have 'to pay more regard to education and science, as empire-builders and empire-guarders, than they have paid in the past'. The organisation of the entire range of a state's resources was, according to him, all the more necessary as 'every scientific advance is now, and will in the future be more and more, applied to war'. Lockyer continued rather emphatically: 'It is no longer a question of an armed force with scientific corps; it is a question of an armed force scientific from top to bottom.'[11]

Lockyer's well-publicised speech not only provides a striking example of the British scientific community's traditional complaints about inadequate support for science, in particular by the government, which had resulted in Britain becoming a country 'peripheral' to the 'centres of learning' such as Germany or the United States in the late nineteenth and early twentieth centuries.[12] Lockyer's passionate speech also testifies to the growing self-assurance of scientists since the late Victorian era, particularly in the context of the social, political and economic uncertainties Britain faced in the years before the First World War.[13] During this period, when the empire had reached the height of its position in the world, complaints were more frequent than ever before about 'the neglect of science by the British nation in the past',[14] about 'this national weakness', that is, 'the general want of appreciation of research here',[15] and about the lack of a 'scientific spirit among our administrators and teachers'.[16] There was almost complete unanimity in the scientific community about the validity of these basic points which were brought up more urgently than ever before in the ongoing discussion about the role of science in British society. In this context, from the closing years of the nineteenth century onwards, criticism of the treatment of science in Britain increasingly used the German system of science organisation and science promotion as a standard against which to judge the British system. The recourse to Germany was not a particularly new one, but now it became almost an obsession. Undoubtedly, the image spread by representatives of the British scientific community about the conditions under which scientific research took place in Germany was often highly idealised, with the obvious political purpose of pointing out the negative aspects of Britain's scientific organisation all the more strongly. Any reference to Germany, moreover, was a most suitable means to attract wide public attention because of that country's ambitious colonial and naval aspirations which heightened political tensions in Europe. The 'Anglo-German Antagonism', primarily a problem of Britain's external relations, thus became an emotive issue to be cleverly used in British domestic policy.

Contemporary claims that late Victorian Britain was rather backward in the field of scientific research and the organisation of science, and that Germany (and the United States) had gained a lead in modernisation cannot easily be proved empirically. From today's point of view, however, it is open to debate whether, and to what extent, British science had actually fallen behind that of comparable industrial countries in the late nineteenth century. The criteria on which contemporary observers based their often fairly impressionistic judgements cannot always be clearly discerned. Although there are no definitive answers to these problems, the fact remains that British scientists were oriented towards conditions for science in Germany from the second half of the nineteenth century onwards. The reputation and influence of the German – or Prussian – organisation of science and of German scientists are revealed not least by the circumstance that, until 1914, a visit to Germany for study purposes or for obtaining a PhD was almost obligatory for British scientists. According to Cardwell 'virtually every professor of chemistry in a British university before 1914 held a German doctorate'.[17] And in a few cases German institutions of scientific research were indeed closely studied, though ultimately not copied, before similar institutions were launched in Britain. The National Physical Laboratory at Teddington, founded in 1900, and later the Imperial College of Science and Technology in South Kensington, established in 1907 after long years of planning, are perhaps the best-known examples.[18]

The German organisation of science, with its heavy dependency on state aid and state intervention, was widely regarded in Victorian Britain as a model worth studying, because it was said that: (i) Germany had developed an efficient, secularised and, in social terms, largely open tertiary sector in its educational system; above all, the equal emphasis placed on research and teaching in Germany was frequently pointed to; (ii) science in Germany enjoyed generous financial support from the government; (iii) there was a fruitful exchange of ideas and experience between science and industry; and (iv) the German organisation of science was distinguished by a large range of research institutions, not only within the framework of the universities and the newly established institutes of technology (*Technische Hochschulen*). Towards the end of the nineteenth century, more and more research institutions were founded outside the universities, and they undoubtedly enlarged the already impressive provisions for scientific work in this country.

An international comparative perspective, always closely intertwined with the element of social Darwinism, had unmistakably gained in significance in the British scientific community's arguments for more financial support for science in the closing years of the century. In comparison with conditions at home, the German organisation of science was regarded by the overwhelming majority of the British scientific community as entirely admirable – and as menacing at the same time. But in government circles, understandably enough, their constant references to Germany often provoked opposition and irritation. Looking back to the time before 1914 the geologist Sir Archibald Geikie wrote:

> The example of that country [Germany] was often cited here, and contrasted with the unsympathetic attitude and stingy support of our authorities, much to the surprise and annoyance of the permanent officials of the Treasury, who rather seemed to think that their grants to science were remarkably liberal. I remember an occasion when I had to go to the Treasury about a matter connected with the Geological Survey. The official on whom I called was one of the heads of the Department. . . . He began the interview by saying that he would be glad to hear me, but begged that the example of Germany might not be mentioned.[19]

How general and uncritical the scientists' views and representations of German conditions often were can be easily gauged from the response which the most significant innovation in science organisation in Germany before the Great War evoked in Britain. In spite of its pioneering new conception, the Kaiser-Wilhelm Society created little interest in Britain when it was founded in 1911. There was certainly no question of expert information being made available about this new institution for the advancement of science. The most comprehensive reports about its foundation appeared in *Nature*. It not only printed long extracts from the speeches held at the inaugural meeting in Berlin, but also commented in broad outline on the aims and organisational structure of the new society. Its close connection with industry, anchored in the society's constitution, was particularly stressed. In a journal like *Nature*, which was fervently committed to the interests of the scientific community, the description of this German innovation could not fail to lead to a moralising conclusion. With reference to the fostering of research, the article points out that it is instructive 'to note the difference between their [the Germans' method and ours'. The Kaiser-Wilhelm Society was to serve only the progress of science, without consideration of how scientific results could be put to use in practical terms, because according to this argument: 'Our neighbours have learned the lesson that science, like virtue, brings its own reward.' The editorial in *Nature* finished on an idealistic note, it is

> wonderful how deeply the spirit of trust in science has penetrated the whole German nation. . . . This spirit, which permeates the German people, from the Emperor on his throne to the representatives of the peasants, causes admiration; would that it could inspire imitation![20]

The fact that this type of statement, in part at least an exaggeration of the situation in Germany, attracted more attention in Britain in the years preceding the war than ever before, is certainly connected with the feeling of crisis which had permeated the politically aware public especially since the Boer War. This colonial war in South Africa with its heavy losses had revealed organisation and logistic weaknesses in the British army, and technical faults in its armaments.[21] It generated an increasingly agitated public discussion, in which slogans such as 'national efficiency' and 'social reform' figured prominently.[22] The debate, in conjunction with several other factors, revealed a far-reaching uncertainty in British society,[23] signs of which had already been visible in the last years of the nineteenth century. These factors included social tension, which was vented in long strikes, often conducted with an extraordinary toughness; the political rivalry with Wilhelmine Germany which was expanding economically and pursuing its own colonial ambitions; and the mounting competition for industrial products in world markets. The impression that late Victorian Britain had fallen behind comparable countries, notably Germany, in scientific and technical achievements as well as in economic efficiency also contributed to a general loss in confidence (see Table 12.1). Seen in this light, the reality of

TABLE 12.1   Percentage share of world manufacturing production

Year(s)	UK	Germany	USA
1870	31.8	13.2	23.3
1881–5	26.6	13.9	28.6
1896–1900	19.5	16.6	30.1
1913	14.0	15.7	35.8

Source: League of Nations, Industrialization and World Trade (New York, 1945), p. 13.

the late Victorian and Edwardian ages in Britain was hardly captured by the cliché of a country at the pinnacle of its glorious imperial position, which, understandably enough, belonged to a nostalgic view of the past after the Great War. The ideology of national efficiency, however, which increasingly gained currency at that time in Britain, produced a climate receptive to the demands of the scientific community. At the beginning of the new century, the mass circulation Daily Mail wrote a pessimistic commentary about Britain's declining role in the world economy. It concluded with the words: 'If the position which this country is slowly losing is to be regained, there can be no doubt that England must improve her education and more richly endow research.'[24]

The realisation that in comparison to other countries, and to Germany in particular, Britain was stagnating economically and scientifically was one of the most significant among the factors which made apparent the latent doubts and feeling of uncertainty in British society since the late nineteenth century. Even long before Queen Victoria's diamond jubilee there was no lack of contemporary evidence illustrating an awareness that Britain's economic position was declining, that its manufacturing industry was losing its competitiveness and that the Germans and Americans, benefiting from their heavy investment in technical and scientific education, were in a much better position to exploit the opportunities that science was offering to industry. In 1896 Ernest E. Williams began his famous pamphlet *Made in Germany* with the words: 'The Industrial Supremacy of Great Britain has been long an axiomatic commonplace; and it is fast turning into a myth. . . . The industrial glory of England is departing, and England does not know it.'[25] In the context of the controversy over tariff reform, which had been triggered primarily by growing competition from German and American trade, the Treasury pointed in the summer of 1903 to Britain's lack of new research-intensive industries. A memorandum for the Cabinet on the state of the aniline dye industry in Germany and Britain, perhaps *the* growth industry of the day, described the relative decline of the organic chemicals industry in Britain as 'humiliating'. It pointed to similar developments in the field of medical and scientific instruments, the production of which was also in danger from innovating German firms[26] (see Table 12.2). The government and the upper ranks of the civil service were now perceiving more clearly the problems which had arisen in the development of British industry and science since the second half of the nineteenth century.

TABLE 12.2   British imports of scientific and optical instruments in 1913

From	£
Germany	362,891
United States	182,293
France	108,040
Belgium	28,939
Switzerland	19,872

Source: Nature, 94 (1914–15), 523.

Economic historians today give different and partly contradictory reasons for Britain's relative economic decline and the loss of the leading position of her industry in the four or five decades prior to the First World War. The continuing discussion of this rather tricky problem has been treated in detail elsewhere.[27] The explanations given range from the 'early start theory' – that Britain's relative economic decline since the later Victorian age was rooted in the industrial lead which it had achieved at great cost, and maintained for a long time – to the very general theory of the failure of the British entrepreneurs who, dazzled by their earlier successes and caught up in conservative attitudes, had, by the turn of the century, lost most of their readiness to take risks: they were prone to complacency. Derek H. Aldcroft, for example, has put forward the view that the slowdown in Britain's economic growth since the last quarter of the nineteenth century can largely be explained by the 'failure of the British entrepreneur to respond to the challenge of changed conditions' – a proposition which has been refuted convincingly by D. C. Coleman and others.[28]

Taking into consideration the extensive literature on the subject, it seems that a generally acceptable explanation for the specific course of British economic history since the late nineteenth century cannot yet be given. But one thing has emerged clearly from the discussion so far: historians should be sceptical of any interpretation which, in the final analysis, attempts to reduce the explanation to a single cause. Any adequate diagnosis of Britain's relative economic decline must take into account a combination of different factors, some based on empirical facts, others of a more speculative nature. One of these factors, also emphasised by economic historians, is the well-known assertion made by the British scientific community in the late nineteenth and early twentieth centuries that Britain's 'industrial retardation', if compared with Germany, resulted from a long-standing neglect of scientific research, an unsatisfactory application of the results of research to industry (see, for example, Table 12.3), and an inadequate system of scientific and technical education. According to the British scientific community's spokesmen, the permanent cure for this condition was perfectly obvious and a matter of some urgency. Firstly, the institutional and financial conditions for science needed to be greatly improved by the government which would have to promote and guide science to a much greater extent than it had in the past. Secondly, the cure also involved permanently raising the status of scientists in Britain, reforming university courses, expanding career opportunities (particularly in the civil service) and improving pay for scientists. Only then would Britain have a fair chance to compete successfully with Germany which, in the idealising

TABLE 12.3   Number of patents granted for synthetic dyes in Britain, 1876–1910

	To German individuals and companies	To British individuals and companies
1876–80	47	13
1881–5	113	15
1886–90	201	39
1891–5	386	29
1896–1900	427	52
1901–5	447	38
1906–10	561	30

Source: Ed. 24/1579, Feb. 1915 (PRO).

view of the British scientific community, had benefited so enormously from the work of its scientists and its well-endowed research institutions.

The British scientists clearly saw that the realisation of their catalogue of demands would be tantamount to a comprehensive 'nationalisation' of science and its organisation along German lines, in a form hitherto unknown in Britain. They also perceived the potential danger to science and its independence of outside influence and control. Shortly before the turn of the century the historian W. E. H. Lecky, who generally favoured a generous allocation of public money to science and the arts, listed the well-worn arguments against more state support for science. His verdict seemed to amount to a flat rejection of a model of science promotion as it was practised in Germany. 'There is a weakening of private enterprise and philanthropy', Lecky wrote,

> a lowered sense of individual responsibility; diminished love of freedom; the creation of an increasing army of officials . . .; the formation of a state of society in which vast multitudes depend for their subsistence on the bounty of the State.[29]

This was, of course, an exaggerated, though not uncommon vision. Only a few years later, the Cambridge physiologist and MP for the University of London, Sir Michael Foster, categorically opposed the idea of the scientist as a civil servant.

In an essay entitled 'The State and Scientific Research' he wrote of the 'paid scientific servant of the State, who for hire is working out the answer'. A scientist in this position would not be permitted, in Foster's view, to deviate from the prescribed aim of research for a specific purpose. The freedom necessary for scientific work would be restricted in an unacceptable manner. Foster therefore glorified the 'independent man of science', the 'private worker in any inquiry', because only he could work in the 'spirit of perfect freedom', independently determining the objectives of his work and the problems to be solved. Experience had shown that 'absolute freedom to follow wherever Nature leads is the one thing needful to make an inquiry a truly fruitful one'. Foster's verbose plea for the 'independent inquirer' who could be 'reckless in his research'[30] was, however, far removed from reality in its orientation towards a world which, even in Britain, was rapidly disappearing. It therefore evoked little response. But it reveals how strongly the ideal of the scientist of independent means who pursued his research almost as a hobby still affected even the scientific community at a time when it no longer corresponded to the real social situation of the majority of scientists in Britain.

What conclusions did the British government draw from the vigorous debate about the organisation and promotion of science which, due to specific circumstances, had found a much wider forum since the closing years of the century for practically the first time in Britain? A detailed description, especially of the establishment of numerous scientific institutions, universities and institutes of technology which were founded with state support after about 1890 cannot be given here.[31] All these new initiatives pointed to the fact that the attitude of the government towards science had at last begun to undergo a change. In retrospect, it can be considered accepted that the 'climate' for the fostering of science in the nineteenth century, and later, was generally more favourable in Germany than in Britain. In Germany, for reasons which cannot be discussed here,[32] the state's interest in promoting science had been unusually strong since the beginning of the century, while in Britain, until the eve of the Great War, scientists complained that the state's attitude towards science was too strongly determined by the liberal principle of *laissez-faire*. It had thereby contributed greatly to the decline of science in this country. But at the end of the Victorian age the government seemed to have learnt a lesson.

It is, of course, almost unnecessary to point out that the scientists' agitation for a reform of Britain's organisation and funding of science was not free of distortion, exaggeration and polemic. A thorough examination of the relationship between state and science in Britain since the second half of the nineteenth century shows that it was much more differentiated than suggested by the representatives of British science, who were tireless in referring to conditions in Germany. At the latest, since Oliver MacDonagh's article 'The Nineteenth-Century Revolution in Government'[33] and the ensuing debate about the role of the state in Victorian Britain, it has become clear that the relationship between state and science cannot be reduced to the simplified alternative of private enterprise or public enterprise. This black and white picture, which sees the state only as fulfilling the famous role of nightwatchman, misrepresents historical reality. Even in liberal Victorian Britain *laissez-faire* did not mean that the state refused on principle and under all circumstances to intervene in social and economic matters. In practice, the principle meant basically only that the liberal state left certain economic and social tasks primarily to private initiative. This position should not be equated with a lack of interest on the part of the government in the problems to be solved. It by no means excluded state intervention when, as a result of constantly changing circumstances and conditions, excessive demands were made of private initiatives.

Thus a characteristic mixture of *laissez-faire* and state intervention was also typical for the relationship between state and science in nineteenth-century Britain.[34] However, a certain emphasis can be detected in the government's attitude towards science in that, if asked, it preferred to support projects with some practical application rather than pure research, the usefulness of which for the state, for administration and for the community as a whole was less directly obvious. A change in this respect developed only gradually since the end of the century. In 1902 the Conservative prime minister Arthur J.

Balfour, replying to a question in the House of Commons, openly admitted that 'the amount of Government money given to experiments in the country is not very large'.[35] Late in 1904 the president of the Royal Society interpreted the growing number of scientific projects the government was contracting out to the society as a sign of 'the fuller recognition by the government and the public of the need for scientific advice and direction in connection with many matters of national concern'.[36] A government report with an introduction by the president of the Board of Education, Walter Runciman, referred in 1910 to a 'marked and growing public interest in University Education during recent years'.[37] And in 1907 King Edward VII wrote in his capacity as chancellor of the University of Wales: 'We must look ahead and endeavour to be ready to meet all the requirements of scientific and intellectual progress. The imperative necessity for higher education and research is becoming more and more recognised.'[38]

But in spite of these observations, there can be no question of a government science policy based on long-term planning between, say, 1890 and 1914. Neglecting the scientific community's advice to follow the German example in this respect, the state's support for science continued on the same sort of *ad hoc* basis. But it must be pointed out that, at the same time, the institutional and financial conditions of science improved markedly as a result of closer co-operation between state and science in Britain. Since the beginning of the twentieth century, the government had been much more willing to be associated with private initiatives, and to support them financially, than it had been in the preceding decades. As the British government was readier to take up suggestions which came 'from outside', it gradually went beyond its classic areas of activity and expanded into spheres in which it had hitherto given precedence to private initiatives, organisations and financing. At the end of 1917 *Nature* wrote that the state in Britain had never concerned itself with questions relating to scientific research.

They were subjects to be left to private enterprise and individual effort. But the circumstances of the time have changed much in our time-honoured and traditional view of the mutual relations of the individual and the State. Public opinion, under the hustling influence of the moment, now compels the State to accept responsibilities and exercise initiative to an extent hitherto undreamt of.[39]

That is a telling verdict at a time when Britain and Germany were mobilising all their resources in order to emerge victorious from a terrible war.

Was this change in public opinion and in the attitude of the state towards science, to which *Nature* referred, associated with an improvement in the social standing and employment prospects of scientists? The British scientific community had continued to point out that, well into the late Victorian era, 'researcher' or 'scientist' was not, generally speaking, a profession which could, unlike in Germany, support anyone in Britain. The idea that a scientist could receive a fixed salary – indeed, one drawn from public funds – for his research activities was not current in late Victorian or Edwardian England. Career prospects were correspondingly limited for scientists. In the nineteenth century British scientists who did not have ample access to private means faced the difficult task of assessing what chance there was of earning a living by science. Basically, there were only three courses open to the young scientist in Britain: (i) he could try to get a position in a school or university college, with all the teaching duties this involved; (ii) he could become a scientific consultant, thereby keeping in close touch with research in his field; (iii) he could attempt to get one of the few scientific positions in industry or the civil service.

Under the circumstances chemists and engineers had the best chances of finding appropriate employment. Nevertheless, at the beginning of the twentieth century, the president of the Chemical Society still spoke of the 'poor outlook for chemical research as a career'.[40] Employment prospects for biologists, physicists and astronomers were even worse because of the extremely restricted job market in these fields, and their limited applicability to industrial production processes. It has been estimated that at the end of the Victorian era there were about 300 positions for scientists at British universities. In addition, there were approximately 250 positions in the civil service, and between 180 and 230 in industry.[41] In contrast, at almost the same time, that is in 1897, a total of 4000 chemists were allegedly employed in Germany. The prospering German chemical industry alone was said to have employed 3000 chemists.[42] Since the early 1870s British scientists had repeatedly drawn attention to the increasingly scientific nature of industrial production abroad (the German chemical industry providing a model case), while at the same time pointing to the omissions of British industry. In 1902 Sir William Huggins, president of the Royal Society, summed it up:

> The supreme value of research in pure science for the success and progress of the national industries of a country can no longer be regarded as a question open to debate, since this principle has not only been accepted in theory, but put in practice on a large scale . . . in a neighbouring country, with the most complete success.[43]

British industries had been establishing their own laboratories in significant numbers only since about 1890, much later than their German competitors. *Nature* was, therefore, able to write:

> There is little doubt that the value of employing numerous chemists in chemical works is becoming more and more appreciated in this country. The supply of well-trained chemical workers which is available for the coming struggle will be the most important factor in its decision.[44]

But all the available figures suggest that the number of positions for scientists in British industry had not kept up with the increase in the number of trained scientists and engineers. Particularly from 1895 onwards, the number of scientists in Britain seems suddenly to have leapt ahead, while the number of positions available more or less stagnated by comparison. Around 1900 it was estimated that there were 2000 scientists in Britain, half of whom were school teachers. By 1914 the number of scientists had increased to 7000.[45] The expansion of university colleges, combined with the late development of new science-related industries in Britain resulted in an imbalance between supply and demand which persisted for some time. The mounting supply of scientists was presumably also one of the main reasons why payment for scientific work did not improve significantly. There was little change in the low status of scientists which compared so unfavourably with that of their German colleagues. In 1907 the president of the Chemical Society publicly expressed his surprise that

> so many men of ability can be found willing to take service in these newer institutions [the university colleges], the more especially as, apart from the absurdly inadequate remuneration often given to the chiefs of the chemical departments, the payment of the subordinate members of the staff is generally on a scale which is nothing short of a scandal to the wealthiest of European nations.

He found it almost incredible that 'the average scale of remuneration should not exceed the wages earned by an artisan, and is often below that standard'. In this way, 'the best brains of the nation' would be kept away from science.[46]

One conclusion to be drawn, therefore, is that in the nineteenth and early twentieth centuries, science was not a particularly attractive career in Britain. On the contrary, minimal social recognition, limited job opportunities and a low income meant that British students at this time opted for professions which had nothing to do with science. While in Germany a scientific career could be a path to social advancement, this was seldom the case in Victorian and Edwardian Britain. The country's imperial position, 'the success of Britain as an imperial power in the nineteenth century',[47] continued to shape the attitudes of the elites in society and politics. In spite of all the efforts of the scientific community the innovative power of science was not valued highly in Britain well into the twentieth century. Since the closing years of the Victorian age, initiatives from military men, industrialists and scientists, persistently conjuring up the example of a dynamic and successful Germany, were necessary before the government undertook more general administrative responsibility for guiding and promoting science, and making considerable amounts of public money available for improving the institutional conditions of science. The importance of the asserted connection between a country's industrial and technological efficiency on the one hand and its organisation and funding of science on the other was impressed on politicians only when alleged weaknesses and inadequacies of British science became the subject of public discussion. The belief spread in late Victorian Britain that the scientific and economic decline of the country must be reversed. This happened, to a considerable degree, as a result of increasing trade competition from other industrial countries, particularly Germany and the United States.

In other words, the British government seems to have become more closely involved in science patronage since the late nineteenth century not because of a real concern for the issue *per se*, but primarily because of public, economic and military pressures. The scientific community's persistence in demanding reorganisation and better promotion of science in Britain had made little impression in the past. But the emergence of powerful competitors in the world markets for industrial goods since the 1870s, the growing political rivalry with a challenging Germany and, finally, the traumatic experience of the Boer War brought about a change. Victorian Britain's liberal political system – 'modern' in comparison with that of other countries at the same time – had obviously revealed certain weaknesses when it came to developing ways of encouraging scientific research in the industrial age. The political system of Bismarckian and Wilhelmine Germany, comparatively less liberal and less democratic than Britain's, had proved to be much more successful in this respect. The British system, however, once again proved its ability to reform, though somewhat reluctantly and only when put under pressure. Since the closing years of the Victorian age, the organisational and administrative framework for the extraordinary achievements of British scientists from the 1920s onwards was laid. This should be considered as a notable legacy of the age, bequeathed to a very large extent by the Anglo-German antagonism, which is often underestimated.

Bibliographical Notes

The place of publication of books is London, except where otherwise stated or for the publications of learned societies.

2. THE RISE OF THE PROFESSIONS

The best short introduction to the subject remains W. J. Reader, *Professional Men. The Rise of the Professional Classes in Nineteenth-Century England* (1966), while for detailed information on each occupation there is still considerable value in A. M. Carr-Saunders and P. A. Wilson, *The Professions* (1933). A provocative sketch of the implications of professionalisation (with particular reference to employment) is provided by Frank Musgrove, 'Middle-Class Education and Employment in the Nineteenth Century', *Economic History Review*, xii (1959), but see H. J. Perkin's critical note in ibid., xiv (1961). Some of the textbooks contain an instructive précis of professional development, notably G. Kitson Clark, *The Making of Victorian England* (1962) and Perkin's *The Origins of Modern English Society* (1969). G. Stedman Jones, *Outcast London. A Study in the Relationship between Classes in Victorian Society* (1976) develops *inter alia* the concept of an 'urban gentry'. There is a wealth of sociological material on the professions. Most useful for historians are the path-breaking work by Geoffrey Millerson, *The Qualifying Associations. A Study in Professionalization* (1964); Margali S. Larson, *The Rise of Professionalism. A Sociological Analysis* (Berkeley and Los Angeles, 1977); Dietrich Rueschemeyer, *Power and the Division of Labour* (1986), which focuses on the key concept of power relations; and two important short surveys, Eliot Freidson, 'The Theory of Professions: State of the Art', in Robert Dingwall and Philip Lewis (eds), *The Sociology of the Professions. Lawyers, Doctors and Others* (1983), and Daniel Duman, 'The Creation and Diffusion of a Professional Ideology in Nineteenth Century England', *Sociological Review*, xxvii (1979). See also note references in the chapter. Reading on the individual occupations is patchy. There is a great deal on the medical profession, for example, but very little on the clergy or the engineers. Notable recent contributions offering a wider perspective include Avner Offer, *Property and Politics 1870–1914. Landownership, Law, Ideology and Urban Development in England* (Cambridge, 1981); Terry Johnson, 'The State and the Professions: Peculiarities of the British', in Anthony Giddens and Gavin Mackenzie (eds), *Social Class and the Division of Labour. Essays in honour of Ilya Neustadt* (Cambridge, 1982), which draws attention to the relationship between professions and the state and the relevance for both of imperial expansion; and Jeffrey L. Berlant, *Profession and Monopoly. A Study of Medicine in the United States and Great Britain* (Berkeley and Los Angeles, 1975). For the broader consequences of professionalisation and, in particular, the relationship between education, the professions and the economy, see the thought-provoking Martin J. Wiener, *English Culture and the Decline of the Industrial Spirit, 1850–1980* (Cambridge, 1981), noting the reservations of Donald Coleman and Christine Macleod, 'Attitudes to New Techniques: British Businessmen, 1800–1950', *Economic History Review*, xxxix (1986); T. W. Heyck, *The Transformation of Intellectual Life in Victorian England* (1982); and Bernard Elbaum and William Lazonick (eds), *The Decline of the British Economy* (Oxford, 1986).

3. URBAN BRITAIN

The best introduction is the general survey by P. J. Waller, *Town, City and Nation: England, 1850–1914* (Oxford, 1983, paperback edn) which is a comprehensive and elegant account of the varieties of towns. A similarly stylish evocation of the metropolis may be found in D. J. Olsen, *The Growth of Victorian London* (1976: paperback edn Harmondsworth, 1979). The earliest scholarly account of the building process was H. J. Dyos, *Victorian Suburb: A Study of the Growth of Camberwell* (Leicester, 1961; paperback edn 1973) which has now acquired the status of a classic. The best of subsequent studies of the role of landowners in the building of towns and suburbs is D. Cannadine, *Lords and Landlords: The Aristocracy and the Towns, 1774–1967* (Leicester, 1980). Attention has subsequently turned from the construction of the houses to their ownership and management, and to the impact of taxation upon profitability. Three complementary books have covered these areas: M. J. Daunton, *House and Home in the Victorian City: Working-Class Housing, 1850–1914* (1983); D. Englander, *Landlord and Tenant in Urban Britain, 1838–1918* (Oxford, 1983); and A. Offer, *Property and Politics, 1870–1914: Landownership, Law, Ideology and Urban Development in England* (Cambridge, 1981). The development of planning is covered by the British section of A. Sutcliffe, *Towards the Planned City: Germany, Britain, the United States and France, 1780–1914* (Oxford, 1981 paperback edn). The politics of London government are explained in K. Young and P. L. Garside, *Metropolitan London: Politics and Urban Change, 1837–1981* (1982). The development of approaches to urban government in provincial cities is analysed in depth for Birmingham and Leeds in E. P. Hennock, *Fit and Proper Persons: Ideal and Reality in Nineteenth-Century Urban Government* (1973). The work of historical geographers is explained, and subjected to criticism, in R. Dennis, *English Industrial Cities of the Nineteenth Century: A Social Geography* (Cambridge, 1984).

4. JOSEPH CHAMBERLAIN: A REASSESSMENT

Chamberlain's own extensive correspondence forms part of the Chamberlain Papers at Birmingham University library. His innumerable speeches were printed in the local or national press and *Hansard*. Many of the more important ones were included in *Mr Chamberlain's Speeches*, edited by C. W. Boyd, in two volumes (1914). Chamberlain's own partisan but invaluable account, *A Political Memoir 1880–1892*, has been edited by C. H. D. Howard (1953). The earliest biography, *The Rt. Hon. Joseph Chamberlain*, by N. Murrell Marris (1900), contains some insights overlooked by his later biographers. It was soon followed by *The Life of the Rt. Hon. Joseph Chamberlain*, by Louis Creswicke (n.d.), which contains many quotes from his speeches and some useful material relating to the tariff reform controversy. The standard biography, *The Life of Joseph Chamberlain*, six volumes (1932–69) was begun by J. L. Garvin and completed by J. Amery. It provides the fullest account of his career and contains much of his correspondence, but it pays less attention to his speeches and articles. Garvin and Amery presented Chamberlain as more decisive, clear-cut and independent than he really was. They oversimplified his views on imperialism and tariff reform and rather neglected his preoccupation with Unionism. P. Fraser, *Joseph Chamberlain: Radicalism and Empire 1868–1914* (1966) is a disappointing study which misleadingly stereotypes Chamberlain as a middle-class professional politician. D. H. Elletson, *The Chamberlains* (1966) is an interesting but slender exercise in family history. H. Browne, *Joseph Chamberlain: Radical and Imperialist* (1974) is a short and rather superficial account with documents for use by students. D. Judd in *Radical Joe* (1976) argues that Chamberlain retained his radical outlook in later life. J. Enoch Powell, *Joseph Chamberlain* (1977) tells us more about the author than the subject. R. Jay, *Joseph Chamberlain: A Political Study* (Oxford, 1981) is a concise but detailed and elegantly written account. The concluding essay is a useful and stimulating overview. However, Jay fails to place Chamberlain in the broader political context of his era. M. Balfour, *Britain and Joseph Chamberlain* (1985) provides more background than foreground but fails to convince at either level.

Many books deal with one or other aspect of Chamberlain's career. Only a few of these, however, provide recent and original analysis which supplements the biographical studies. B. Semmel, *Imperialism and Social Reform: English Social-Imperial Thought 1895–1914* (1960) falsely depicts Chamberlain as a Birmingham industrialist trying to arrest British economic decline by tariff reform. C. V. Kubicek, *The Administration of Imperialism: Joseph Chamberlain at the Colonial Office* (Duke, 1969) keeps to its title. M. Hurst, *Joseph Chamberlain and Liberal Reunion: The Round Table Conference of 1887* (1967) is also self-explanatory. A. Sykes, *Tariff Reform in British Politics 1903–1913* (Oxford, 1979) is the best modern study on this subject, but it says little about the evolution of Chamberlain's views on this topic before 1903.

Some of the more interesting insights into Chamberlain's career can be found in periodical articles. C. H. D. Howard reassessed the radical phase in 'Joseph Chamberlain and the Unauthorized Programme', *English Historical Review*, LXV (1950) and 'Joseph Chamberlain, Parnell and the Irish Central Board scheme 1884–5', *Irish Historical Studies*, VIII (1953). M. C. Hurst looked at Birmingham in 'Joseph Chamberlain, the Conservatives and the Succession to John Bright 1886–89', *Historical Journal*, VII (1964) and in 'Joseph Chamberlain and West Midland Politics 1886–95', *Dugdale Society Occasional Papers*, 15 (1962). P. Fraser, 'The Liberal Unionist Alliance: Chamberlain, Hartington and the Conservatives 1886–1904, *English Historical Review*, LXXVII (1962) deals with an important aspect of Chamberlain's later career. S. H. Zebel, 'Joseph Chamberlain and the Genesis of Tariff Reform', *Journal of British Studies*, VII (1967) notes, but does not develop, Canada's role. R. Quinault, 'John Bright and Joseph

Chamberlain, *Historical Journal*, xxviii (1985) examines a neglected relationship.

5. ELECTORAL REFORMS AND THEIR OUTCOME IN THE UNITED KINGDOM

K. Theodore Hoppen, 'The Franchise and Electoral Politics in England and Ireland 1832–1885', *History*, lxx (1985) is a valuable discussion of the detailed nature of the franchise and its political implications. B. M. Walker, 'The Irish Electorate, 1868–1915', *Irish Historical Studies* xvii (1972–3) provides much statistical information on both the Irish and the British electorate. D. C. Moore, *The Politics of Deference* (Hassocks, Sussex, 1976) discusses the local context of electioneering in England and the connection between the break-down of the old system and the Second Reform Act.

Other perspectives on that Act include F. B. Smith, *The Making of the Second Reform Bill* (Cambridge, 1966) – probably the standard account – and Maurice Cowling, *1867, Disraeli, Gladstone and Revolution* (Cambridge, 1967). The best guides to the Third Reform Act are M. E. J. Chadwick, 'The Role of Redistribution in the Making of the Third Reform Act', *Historical Journal*, xix (1976) and P. Marsh, *The Discipline of Popular Government. Lord Salisbury's Domestic Statecraft 1881–1902* (Hassocks, 1978); see also A. Jones, *The Politics of Reform 1884* (Cambridge, 1972). The story is continued by Neal Blewett, 'The Franchise of the United Kingdom 1885–1918', *Past and Present*, xxxii (1965) and M. Pugh, *Electoral Reform in War and Peace 1906–18* (1978), while H. C. G. Matthew, R. I. McKibbin and J. A. Kay argue in 'The Franchise Factor and the Rise of the Labour Party', *English Historical Review*, xvi (1976) that the fact that the franchise fell well short of adult male suffrage was an insurmountable barrier to real Labour progress before 1918. In 'British Local Government Reform: the Nineteenth Century and After', *English Historical Review*, xlii (1977), J. P. D. Dunbabin discusses the politics of making local government elective (with special reference to the 1880s and 1890s).

Bruce L. Kinzer writes on *The Ballot Question in Nineteenth-Century Politics* (New York, 1982), M. Pinto-Duschinsky on *British Political Finance 1830–1980* (Washington, DC, 1981). H. J. Hanham surveys *Elections and Party Management. Politics in the time of Disraeli and Gladstone* (1959), Henry Pelling *The Social Geography of British Elections 1885–1910* (1967), while M. Kinnear, *The British Voter. An Atlas and Survey since 1885* (1981), P. F. Clarke, 'Electoral Sociology of Modern Britain', *History*, lvii (1972), J. P. D. Dunbabin, 'British Elections in the Nineteenth and Twentieth Centuries, a Regional Approach', *English Historical Review*, xcv (1980), and K. D. Wald, *Crosses on the Ballot* (Princeton, 1983) offer psephological comment (sometimes controversial).

Corinne C. Weston, 'Salisbury and the House of Lords, 1868–1895', *Historical Journal*, xxv (1982) charts the rise of the Conservative doctrine of electoral mandates. P. C. Griffiths, 'The Caucus and the Liberal Party in 1886', *History*, lxi (1976), B. McGill, 'Francis Schnadhorst and Liberal Party Organization', *Journal of Modern History*, xxxiv (1962) and F. H. Herrick, 'The Origins of the National Liberal Federation', ibid., xvii (1945) bear on the development of party organisation, as do the books by Hanham and Marsh cited above and also M. Pugh, *The Making of Modern British Politics* (Oxford, 1982) and A. R. Ball, *British Political Parties. The emergence of a modern party system* (1981). C. Cook and B. Keith, *British Historical Facts 1830–1900* (1975) is a valuable work of reference.

6. PARTIES, MEMBERS AND VOTERS AFTER 1867

There is no published work precisely on these themes. For an analysis of twentieth-century political parties in the light of the concepts utilised here, see S. Neumann, *Modern Political Parties* (Chicago, 1967). The activities of nineteenth-century parties in the light of more general concepts in political science are analysed by John Garrard, *The Functions of Nineteenth Century Political Parties* (Occasional Papers in Politics and Contemporary History, University of Salford, 1986). A brief, general, and more conventionally historical survey of party operations in the wake of the 1867 Reform Act can be found in Paul Adelman's *Gladstone, Disraeli and Later Victorian Politics* (1970). There is a somewhat more detailed survey of the same theme, utilising much recent research on the subject, by Martin Pugh in *The Making of Modern British Politics 1867–1939* (Oxford, 1982) Chapters 1–3. For a hostile, but very readable, analysis of the effects of franchise extension upon the party machines, written from the standpoint of a European liberal, see M. Ostrogorski, *Democracy and the Organization of Modern Political Parties* (1902, republished in New York, 1970) vol. I. The influence of the factory on late Victorian urban electoral politics is sensitively analysed by Patrick Joyce in *Work, Society and Politics: The Culture of the Factory in Later Victorian England* (Brighton, 1980) especially Chapters 6–8, though it is uncertain how far his analysis extends beyond the towns of industrial Lancashire. The character and impact of Labour and socialist politics is capably examined in a general way by James Hinton, *Labour and Socialism: A History of the British Labour Movement 1867–74* (Brighton, 1983). For an already classic analysis of the ILP, set within the context of the existing political framework, see David Howell, *British Workers and the ILP 1886–1906* (Manchester, 1983). Finally, for an examination of the way in which many of these developments were anticipated in the years before 1867, see John Vincent, *The Formation of the British Liberal Party 1857–1868* (Aylesbury, 1972).

7. BRITISH FOREIGN POLICY, 1867–1900

There exists a vast array of excellent work on British foreign policy in the nineteenth-century. K. Bourne, *The Foreign Policy of Victorian England, 1830–1902* (Oxford, 1970) is a key source of documents. A. J. P. Taylor, *The Trouble Makers: Dissent over Foreign Policy, 1792–1939* (1957) provides not only important information but also interesting opinions. Other aspects are covered in C. J. Bartlett, *Britain Pre-eminent. Studies in British World Influence in the Nineteenth Century* (1969), P. M. Kennedy, *The Realities behind Diplomacy: Background Influences on British External Policy. 1865–1980* (1981), K. Robbins, *The Eclipse of a Great Power: Modern Britain, 1870–1975* (1983), C. D. H. Howard,

Splendid Isolation (1967) and *Britain and the Casus Belli, 1822–1902* (1974), J. A. S. Grenville, *Lord Salisbury and Foreign Policy: The Close of the Nineteenth Century* (1964), and G. Martel, *Imperial Diplomacy. Rosebery and the Failure of Foreign Policy* (1986).

A considerable number of traditional biographies are far from useless. Among these the most noteworthy are: J. L. Garvin and J. Amery, *Life of Joseph Chamberlain* (1932–69), A. G. Gardiner, *Life of Sir William Harcourt* (1932), Lady Gwendolen Cecil, *Life of Robert, Marquis of Salisbury* (1921–32) and Lord Fitzmaurice, *The Life of Lord Granville* (1905). Important among more modern studies of the statesmen of the period are: R. R. James, *Rosebery* (1963), H. C. G. Matthew, *The Liberal Imperialists* (Oxford, 1973), R. Blake, *Disraeli* (1966) and T. H. O'Brien, *Milner* (1979). There is also useful information in a number of memoirs, particularly Sir Edmund Hornby, *An Autobiography* (1928), Viscount Knutsford, *In Black and White* (1926), Lord Vansittart, *The Mist Procession* (1958), Lord Hardinge, *Old Diplomacy* (1947) and V. Chirol, *Fifty Years in a Changing World* (1927).

The Foreign Office itself is admirably treated in Z. S. Steiner, *The Foreign Office and Foreign Policy, 1898–1914* (1969) which deals not only with the period referred to in the title but also gives a full background to the earlier operations of the FO. The activities of pressure groups are less well-documented, but an important exception is N. A. Pelcovits, *Old China Hands and the Foreign Office* (New York, 1948). Imperial questions are examined in R. Robinson and J. Gallagher, *Africa and the Victorians* (1967), M. Beloff, *Imperial Sunset: Britain's Liberal Empire, 1897–1921* (1969) and C. C. Eldridge, *Victorian Imperialism* (1978). The vexed question of Anglo-German relations is thoroughly examined by P. M. Kennedy in *The Rise of the Anglo-German Antagonism, 1860–1914* (1980) and 'Idealists and Realists: British views of Germany, 1864–1939', *Transactions of the Royal Historical Society* (1975) and R. J. Sontag, *Germany and England: Background of Conflict, 1848–1894* (New York, 1938). Naval questions were also important and can be examined in K. Bourne and D. C. Watt, *Studies in International History* (1967) and P. M. Kennedy, *The Rise and Fall of British Naval Mastery* (1976).

Finally, the problems confronting the major states at the close of the nineteenth century are well treated in W. L. Langer, *The Diplomacy of Imperialism, 1891–1902* (New York, 1950), G. W. Monger, *The End of Isolation* (1964), F. R. Bridge and R. Bullen, *The Great Powers and the European States System, 1815–1914* (1980) and two books by G. F. Kennan: *The Decline of Bismarck's European Order* (Princeton, 1979) and *The Fateful Alliance* (Manchester, 1984).

8. LATE VICTORIAN WOMEN

Jane Lewis, *Women in England 1870–1950* (Sussex, 1984) is a good general survey. Martha Vicinus, *Independent Women. Work and Community for Single Women 1850–1920* (1985) is of immense value not only in its treatment of its immediate subject matter but for its perspective discussion of ideologies of and about women and for studies of education, nursing, philanthrophy and other women's activities.

On specific topics referred to in the chapter: on demography: J. A. Banks *Victorian Values. Secularism and the Size of Families* (1981); D. E. Baines, 'The Labour Supply and the Labour Market 1860–1914', in R. C. Floud and D. N. McCloskey, *The Economic History of Britain since 1700*, vol. 2, *1860 to the 1970s* (Cambridge, 1981); on motherhood: Jane Lewis, *The Politics of Motherhood* (1980). On working women's lives: Jill Liddington and Jill Norris, *One Hand Tied Behind Us. The Rise of the Womens Suffrage Movement* (1978) is good on women's home and working lives in Lancashire and many of their observations are of wider interest. Elizabeth Roberts, *A Woman's Place. An Oral History of Working Class Women 1890–1940* (Oxford, 1984) also draws its material from Lancashire but her rich material and her interpretation have wider relevance. Melanie Tebbutt, *Making Ends Meet. Pawnbroking and Working Class Credit* (Leicester, 1983) is again Lancashire-based, but also sheds much light, from a slightly unexpected angle, upon the wife's role as domestic manager. Pat Thane, 'Women and the Poor Law in Victorian and Edwardian England', *History Workshop*, 6 (Autumn 1978) discusses the reasons for poverty among women and its treatment. F. K. Prochaska, *Women and Philanthropy in 19th Century England* (Oxford, 1980) is a good and subtle study of an important subject which is illuminating about the lives and motivations of middle-class women as well as about their 'causes'. Patricia Branca, *Silent Sisterhood* (1975) puts a strong case for the hard-working middle class housewife. Jeffrey Weeks, *Sex, Politics and Society* (1981) discusses sexuality, marriage and divorce. Two volumes edited by Martha Vicinus, *Suffer and Be Still* and *A Widening Sphere* (both 2nd edn paperback, 1980) contain a variety of important essays. Elaine Showalter, *A Literature of Their Own. British Women Novelists from Brontë to Lessing* (Princeton University Press, 1977; paperback edn 1982) is good on women novelists in relation to their time, a topic neglected in this chapter.

Of contemporary material: *The Diary of Beatrice Webb*, vols 1 and 2 (1973); Hannah Mitchell, *The Hard Way Up* (1977) and almost any of George Bernard Shaw's plays of the period are highly accessible.

9. THE GENERAL AND THE BISHOPS

On Victorian religion, the standard work is Owen Chadwick, *The Victorian Church*, 2 vols (1966–70). It is a masterly survey which is generally 'optimistic' about the place of the Christian churches in national life. It needs to be supplemented for the 1870s and 1880s by P. T. Marsh, *The Victorian Church in Decline* (1969) which comes to more pessimistic conclusions about Tait's tenure of the primacy. For a view of late Victorian religion which sets it in a wider context, see A. D. Gilbert, *Religion and Society in Industrial England* (1976). The background to, and battles over, the Public Worship Regulation Act are explored in James Bentley, *Ritualism and Politics in Victorian Britain* (Oxford, 1977), but for a more general survey see Edward Norman, *Anti-Catholicism in Victorian England* (1968). Norman has also written a well-documented but controversial study, *Church and Society in England 1770–1970* (Oxford, 1976). On revivalism, a stimulating and critical account has been provided by John

Kent in *Holding the Fort* (1978), while the secularist challenge has been discussed by Susan Budd, *Varieties of Unbelief* (1977). A blow-by-blow account of Bradlaugh's attempt to sit in Parliament without having to take the Oath using religious forms, which as a Freethinker he could not accept, is provided by W. L. Arnstein, *The Bradlaugh Case* (Oxford, 1965).

Three outstanding studies of specific areas which have more than local significance are: Hugh McLeod, *Class and Religion in the Late Victorian City* (1974) which covers London; Stephen Yeo, *Religion and Voluntary Organisations in Crisis* (1976) on Reading; and Jeffrey Cox, *The English Churches in a Secular Society: Lambeth 1870–1930* (Oxford, 1982).

The pioneer work on the attempts of the churches to combat working-class indifference is K. S. Inglis, *Churches and the Working Classes in Victorian England* (1963). For a discriminating survey which assesses the main points of controversy, Hugh McLeod provides a reliable guide in *Religion and the Working Class in Nineteenth Century Britain* (1984).

There is no serious academic book on the Salvation Army, but Roland Robertson has provided a substantial sociological study, 'The Salvation Army: The Persistence of Sectarianism' in Bryan R. Wilson (ed.) *Patterns of Sectarianism* (1967). Two important articles by Victor Bailey set the Army in the late Victorian social context: 'Salvation Army Riots, the "Skeleton Army" and Legal Authority in the Provincial Town', A. P. Donajgrodzki (ed.) *Social Control in Nineteenth Century Britain* (1977) and ' "In Darkest England and the Way Out" ', The Salvation Army, Social Reform and the Labour Movement, 1885–1910', *International Review of Social History* (1984). Asa Briggs has dealt with 'The Salvation Army in Sussex, 1883–1892' in M. J. Kitch (ed.) *Studies in Sussex Church History* (1981).

10. THE IRISH PROBLEM

Although there is no general survey confined to the period, F. S. L. Lyons, *Ireland Since the Famine* (revised edn, 1973); Nicholas Mansergh, *The Irish Question, 1840–1921* (3rd edn, 1975); and Joseph Lee, *The Modernisation of Irish Society, 1848–1918* (Dublin, 1973), are dated but remain useful. Other books covering general themes are D. G. Boyce, *Nationalism in Ireland* (1981); Tom Garvin, *The Evolution of Irish Nationalist Politics* (Dublin, 1981); and Charles Townshend, *Political Violence in Ireland* (Oxford, 1983).

A substantial array of specialist studies cover a range of issues. Some of the ablest work first published in academic journals can be found in Alan O'Day (ed.) *Reactions to Irish Nationalism, 1865–1914* (1987). Political violence is considered in Townshend (above); Leon Ó Broin, *Revolutionary Underground* (Dublin, 1976); R. V. Comerford, *Fenianism in Context* (Dublin, 1985); and certain articles in Yonah Alexander and Alan O'Day (eds) *Terrorism in Ireland* (1984); and, *Ireland's Terrorist Dilemma* (The Hague, 1986). T. W. Moody, *Davitt and the Irish Revolution, 1846–82* (Oxford, 1981) contains further useful information in an otherwise over-long account. Politics and the Irish Parliamentary Party form the material for David Thornley, *Isaac Butt and Home Rule* (1964); C. C. O'Brien, *Parnell and his Party, 1880–90* (Oxford, 1957);

F. S. L. Lyons, *The Irish Parliamentary Party, 1890–1910* (1951); and Alan O'Day, *The English Face of Irish Nationalism* (Dublin, 1977). T. K. Hoppen, *Elections, Politics, and Society in Ireland 1832–1885* (Oxford, 1984) examines the Irish local context. The British aspect can be approached through a large number of books and biographies. Home rule is treated in A. B. Cooke and J. R. Vincent, *The Governing Passion* (Hassocks, 1974); Grenfell Morton, *Home Rule and the Irish Question* (1980); and recently in Alan O'Day, *Parnell and the First Home Rule Episode* (Dublin, 1986) and James Loughlin, *Gladstone, Home Rule and the Ulster Question, 1882–93* (Dublin, 1986). There are a number of important studies of the land question which have been neatly summarised in pamphlets: W. E. Vaughan, *Landlords and Tenants in Ireland* (Dublin, 1985) which is also an original contribution; and Michael J. Winstanley, *Ireland and the Land Question, 1800–1922* (1984). Additional insights can be gained from another pamphlet, David Fitzpatrick, *Irish Emigration, 1801–1921* (Dublin, 1984), a stimulating and original piece. Religion is considered in E. R. Norman, *The Catholic Church and Ireland in the Age of Rebellion* (1965); James O'Shea, *Priests, Politics and Society in Post-Famine Ireland* (Dublin, 1984); Mark Tierney, *Croke of Cashel* (Dublin, 1976); and Emmet Larkin, *The Roman Catholic Church and the Creation of the Modern Irish State, 1878–1886* (Dublin, 1975); *The Roman Catholic Church and the Plan of Campaign, 1886–88* (Cork, 1978); and *The Roman Catholic Church and the Fall of Parnell, 1888–91* (Liverpool, 1980). Desmond Keenan, *The Catholic Church in Nineteenth-Century Ireland* (Dublin, 1983) is an interesting account from a sociological perspective. Unionism is studied in several volumes, especially Patrick Buckland, *Irish Unionism*, vols I and II (Dublin 1972/73); Peter Gibbon, *The Origins of Ulster Unionism* (Manchester, 1975); David W. Miller, *Queen's Rebels* (Dublin, 1978); and A. T. Q. Stewart, *The Narrow Ground* (1977). For the Irish overseas, see Roger Swift and Sheridan Gilley (eds) *The Irish in the Victorian City* (1985); Oliver MacDonagh and W. F. Mandle (eds) *Ireland and Irish-Australia* (1986); Lynn Lees, *Exiles of Erin* (Manchester, 1979); and T. N. Brown, *Irish-American Nationalism, 1870–90* (Boston and Philadelphia, 1966). Dublin's history can now be traced through Joseph V. O'Brien, *Dirty Old Dublin* (Berkeley and Los Angeles, 1982), and Mary Daly, *Dublin, Depossessed Capital* (Cork, 1984). Another important question is taken up in Elizabeth Malcolm, *Ireland Sober, Ireland Free* (Dublin, 1986).

Biographies of Irish figures are not numerous but F. S. L. Lyons, *John Dillon* (1968), and *Charles Stewart Parnell* (1977) are lengthy; Paul Bew, *C. S. Parnell* (Dublin, 1981) is valuable; Joseph V. O'Brien, *William O'Brien and the Course of Irish Politics* (Berkeley and Los Angeles, 1976) and L. W. Brady, *T. P. O'Connor and Liverpool Politics* (1983) are serviceable.

11. DID THE LATE VICTORIAN ECONOMY FAIL?

The literature on the Victorian economy has been not surprisingly voluminous, and discussion here will be confined to recent work, having its focus upon the extent and timing of 'failure' in the late Victorian period. An accessible and usefully referenced introductory survey is François Crouzet,

The Victorian Economy (1982), and Chapter 12 deals specifically with the late Victorian 'climacteric'. The revisionist cliometric school of thought on the Victorian economy was initiated by D. N. McCloskey in 'Did Victorian Britain Fail?', *Economic History Review*, 2nd series, XXIII (1970), no. 3, which has been comprehensively assessed most recently in N. F. R. Crafts, *British Economic Growth during the Industrial Revolution* (Oxford, 1985). The highly quantitative character of this approach contrasts with the neo-Weberian 'culturalist' view of Martin J. Wiener's *English Culture and the Decline of the Industrial Spirit 1850–1980* (Cambridge, 1981), which is provocative if not altogether convincing.

Important critiques of the assumptions and methodology of the cliomectricians are to be found in Stephen Nicholas, 'Total Factor Productivity Growth and the Revision of Post-1870 British Economic History', *Economic History Review*, 2nd series, XXXV (1982), no. 1; and in Robert R. Locke, *The End of the Practical Man: Entrepreneurship and Higher Education in Germany, France and Great Britain, 1880–1940* (Greenwich, Connecticut, 1984). The problems of this approach are also highlighted in a recent debate between Mark Thomas, 'Accounting for Growth, 1870–1940: Stephen Nicholas and Total Factor Productivity', and Stephen Nicholas, 'British Economic Performance and Total Factor Productivity Growth, 1870–1940', *Economic History Review*, 2nd series, XXXVIII (1985), no. 4.

Alternatively, the recent emergence of the 'entrepreneurial school' of British economic history is surveyed in P. L. Payne, *British Entrepreneurship in the Nineteenth Century* (1974), although this school's intellectual ancestor was careful to stress the constraints acting upon individual entrepreneurship, especially in his later work – see, for example, Joseph A. Schumpeter, *Capitalism, Socialism and Democracy* (1943). The significance of the wider institutional and social contexts for economic development is also emphasised in Bernard Elbaum and William Lazonick (eds) *The Decline of the British Economy* (Oxford, 1986), which has its starting point in the late Victorian era.

A valuable statistical context for understanding the late nineteenth century, in relation to earlier periods, is contained in C. Knick Harley, 'British Industrialisation Before 1841: Evidence of Slower Growth During the Industrial Revolution', *Journal of Economic History*, XLII (1982), no. 2; and this is also discussed in Crafts, cited above. This task is similarly undertaken for later periods in R. C. O. Matthews, C. H. Feinstein and J. C. Odling-Smee, *British Economic Growth 1856–1973* (Oxford, 1982), although of more particular value is C. H. Feinstein, R. C. O. Matthews and J. C. Odling-Smee, 'The Timing of the Climacteric and its Sectoral Incidence in the UK, 1873–1913', in C. P. Kindleberger and G. di Tella (eds) *Economics in the Long View* (1982), vol. 2, while Locke, cited above, has serious reservations about the explanatory value of long statistical runs.

The latter apply especially to the cliometric approach to Victorian living standards offered by Jeffrey G. Williamson's *Did British Capitalism Breed Inquality?* (1985), which should be read together with the same author's 'Earnings Inequality in Nineteenth-Century Britain', *Journal of Economic History*, XL (1980), no. 3; and R. S. Neale, 'The Poverty of Positivism: from

Standard of Living to Quality of Life, 1780–1850', in the same author's *Writing Marxist History. British Society, Economy and Culture since 1700* (Oxford, 1985). Other work that questions the ameliorist interpretation of living standards during the second half of the nineteenth century include: D. J. Oddy, 'Working-Class Diets in Late Nineteenth-Century Britain', *Economic History Review*, 2nd series, XXIII (1970), no. 2; Keith Burgess, *The Origins of British Industrial Relations. The Nineteenth Century Experience* (1975); Eric Hopkins, 'Small Town Aristocrats of Labour and their Standard of Living, 1840–1914', *Economic History Review*, 2nd series, XXVIII (1975), no. 2; A. A. Hall, 'Wages, Earnings and Real Earnings in Teeside: A Re-Assessment of the Ameliorist Interpretation of Living Standards in Britain, 1870–1914', *International Review of Social History*, XXVI (1981), Pt. 2; Elizabeth Roberts, 'Working-Class Standards of Living in Three Lancashire Towns, 1890–1914', *International Review of Social History*, XXVII (1982), Pt. 1; and James A. Schmiechen, *Sweated Industries and Sweated Labour. The London Clothing Trades, 1860–1914* (1984).

The context established by state–economy relations for the late Victorian economy is provided in Peter Mathias, 'Taxation and Industrialisation in Britain, 1700–1870', in the same author's *The Transformation of England* (1979), and more ambitious in scope is Geoffrey Ingham's *Capitalism Divided? The City and Industry in British Social Development* (1984), which is a persuasive study of the background influences on the making of British economy policy; while there is much to be learned, in this respect, from the more specifically focused analysis by Marcello de Cecco, *Money and Empire. The International Gold Standard, 1890–1914* (1974). Finally, a thought-provoking context for international comparison is set out in David Blackbourn and Geoff Eley, *The Peculiarities of German History. Bourgeois Society and Politics in Nineteenth-Century Germany* (1984), which also has numerous references to Victorian Britain.

An assessment of the economic environment of late Victorian Britain is provided by Barry J. Eichengreen, 'The Proximate Determinants and Domestic Investment in Victorian Britain', *Journal of Economic History*, XLII (1982), no. 1; William P. Kennedy, 'Notes on Economic Efficiency in Historical Perspective: the Case of Britain, 1870–1914', *Research in Economic History*, 9(1984); and by R. C. Michie, 'The London Stock Exchange and the British Securities Market, 1850–1914', *Economic History Review*, 2nd series, XXXVIII (1985), no. 1. Aspects of education and training, which have been given prominence recently, are treated in Paul L. Robertson, 'Employers and Engineering Education in Britain and the United States, 1890–1914', *Business History*, XXIII (1981), no. 1; Locke, cited above; and Williamson (1985); while the political fragmentation of the British business community is analysed suggestively in John Turner (ed.) *Businessmen and Politics. Studies of Business Activity in British Politics 1900–1945* (1984), which has relevance for the late Victorian period although it deals mainly with the twentieth century.

The extent of the emergence of the large-scale company in late Victorian Britain is the subject of P. L. Payne's pioneering article, 'The Emergence of the Large-scale Company in Great Britain, 1870–1914', *Economic History Review*, 2nd series, XX (1967), no. 3; and has been systematically pursued for later periods in John Scott and Catherine Griff, *Directors of Industry. The British*

Corporate Network 1904–1976 (1984), while an˙ authoritative international comparison is provided by Alfred A. Chandler's 'The Growth of the Transnational Firm in the United States and the United Kingdom: A Comparative Analysis', *Economic History Review*, 2nd series, xxxii (1980), no. 3. Finally, the importance of regional variations is highlighted in C. H. Lee's 'Regional Growth and Structural Change in Victorian Britain', *Economic History Review*, 2nd series, xxxiv (1981), no. 3, and interesting case-studies are contained in M. W. Kirby, *Men of Business and Politics. The Rise and Fall of the Quaker Pease Dynasty of North-East England 1700–1943* (1984); and in Schmiechen, cited above.

12. SCIENCE AND THE ANGLO-AMERICAN ANTAGONISM

The literature on Anglo-German relations between about 1850 and 1914 is extensive, but scattered and of varying quality. The most valuable and comprehensive recent work is undoubtedly P. M. Kennedy, *The Rise of the Anglo-German Antagonism 1860–1914* (1980). For the domestic background in Britain and her foreign policy, E. J. Feuchtwanger, *Democracy and Empire. Britain 1865–1914* (1985) provides a useful survey. It should be complemented by D. Read, *England 1868–1914. The Age of Urban Democracy* (1979) who puts much emphasis on the social history of the period and offers a wealth of statistical material. The notable essays in A. O'Day (ed.) *The Edwardian Age: Conflict and Stability 1900–1914* (1979) focus on some key problems in the years before the War. G. Jones, *Social Darwinism and English Thought: The Interaction between Biological and Social Thought* (Brighton, 1980) should also be consulted. On some aspects of the intellectual climate of the time see the relevant chapters in M. J. Wiener, *English Culture and the Decline of the Industrial Spirit, 1850–1980* (Cambridge, 1981).

The history of higher education and the promotion of science in Britain still needs further exploration. Very informative is G. W. Roderick and M. D. Stephens, *Education and Industry in the Nineteenth Century: The English Disease?* (1978). G. C. Allen, *The British Disease* (1976) discusses educational deficiencies and the consequences of inadequate scientific research in Britain. D. S. L. Cardwell's *The Organisation of Science in England*, 2nd edn (1972) is a pioneering work which covers the period from about 1800 to 1914. Though sometimes sketchy and outdated in parts, it has not yet been replaced by a modern survey, but M. Sanderson's stimulating study on *The Universities and British Industry 1850–1970* (1972) provides a very good analysis of the relationship between the universities and industry. The funding of science in the late Victorian age is ably investigated by R. M. MacLeod, 'Resources of Science in Victorian England: The Endowment of Science Movement, 1868–1900', in P. Mathias (ed.) *Science and Society, 1600–1900* (Cambridge, 1972), pp. 111–66. The patronage of science in Victorian and Edwardian Britain and the changing role of the state is the theme of P. Alter, *The Reluctant Patron: Science and the State in Britain 1850–1920* (Leamington Spa, 1987). Richard Haldane's remarkable commitment to the interests of scholarship and science can be gleaned from E. Ashby and M. Anderson, *Portrait of*

Haldane at Work on Education (1974). R. R. Locke, *The End of the Practical Man: Entrepreneurship and Higher Education in Germany, France and Great Britain, 1880–1940* (Greenwich, Conn., 1984) offers a valuable comparative perspective.

In addition to the studies cited in the notes, solid information about the organisation of science in Germany, the German academic community and its influence in Britain is given by C. E. McClelland, *State, Society, and University in Germany 1700–1914* (Cambridge, 1980), F. K. Ringer, *The Decline of the German Mandarins. The German Academic Community, 1890–1933* (Cambridge, Mass., 1969), and G. Haines, *Essays on German Influence upon English Education and Science, 1850–1919* (Hamden, Conn., 1969). All three books have aroused much interest in Germany.

Notes and References

2. THE RISE OF THE PROFESSIONS   *T. R. Gourvish*

1. J. C. Stamp, *British Incomes and Property* (1922 edn) pp. 448–9. Stamp gave estimates of 306,700–319,500 and 833,000–867,700, and for those earning over £160 p.a. 267,700–280,400 (1860–1) and 727,000–761,700 (1894–5).

2. Harold Perkin, *The Origins of Modern English Society 1780–1880* (1969) pp. 252–5, and for a critique see for example Daniel Duman, 'The Creation and Diffusion of a Professional Ideology in Nineteenth Century England', *Sociological Review*, xxvii (Feb. 1979) 113–14, 132–3. On the term 'urban gentry' see G. Kitson Clark, *The Making of Victorian England* (1962) p. 252ff. and G. Stedman Jones, *Outcast London. A Study in the Relationship between Classes in Victorian Society* (Penguin edn, 1976) p. 268.

3. The literature is enormous. See, for example, Talcott Parsons, 'The Professions and Social Structure', *Social Forces*, xvii (1939) 457–67, and 'Professions', in D. Sills (ed.) *International Encyclopaedia of the Social Sciences*, xii (New York, 1968) pp. 536–47; Geoffrey Millerson, *The Qualifying Associations. A Study in Professionalization* (1964); Howard S. Becker, 'The Nature of a Profession', in his *Sociological Work. Method and Substance* (Penguin edn 1971) pp. 87–103; Eliot Freidson, 'Professionalisation and the Organisation of Middle-Class Labour in Post-industrial Society', in Paul Halmos (ed.) *Professionalisation and Social Change* (Keele, 1973) pp. 47–59, and 'The Theory of Professions: State of the Art', in Robert Dingwall and Philip Lewis (eds) *The Sociology of the Professions. Lawyers, Doctors and Others* (1983); Terence J. Johnson, *Professions and Power* (1972), and 'The Professions in the Class Structure', in Richard Scase (ed.) *Industrial Society: Class, Cleavage and Control* (1977) pp. 93–110; Margali S. Larson, *The Rise of Professionalism. A Sociological Analysis* (Berkeley and Los Angeles, 1977); Dietrich Rueschemeyer, *Power and the Division of Labour* (1986).

4. S. E. D. Shortt, 'Physicians, Science, and Status: Issues in the Professionalization of Anglo-American Medicine in the Nineteenth Century', *Medical History*, xxvii (Jan. 1983) 51.

5. Such a remark must inevitably be an over-simplification: note, for example, that Millerson's own approach to a definition was cautious. See Millerson, *Qualifying Associations*, pp. 1–13, Freidson, 'Theory of Professions', 21–6, and Rueschemeyer, *Power*, pp. 118–20.

6. 'Remarks on the Industrial Statistics of 1861', loc., *inter alia*, in *Return on Poor Rates and Pauperism*, July 1864, Parliamentary Paper (PP) 1986, li.

7. Freidson, 'Theory of Professions', 23.

8. Cf. Robert Dingwall, 'Introduction', in Dingwall and Lewis, *Sociology of the Professions*, pp. 5–8, and Rueschemeyer, *Power*, pp. 104–12.

9. Census of England & Wales, Scotland, and Ireland, 1861, PP 1863, LIII, 1864, LI, 1863, LX; England & Wales, 1901 (contains UK summary), PP 1904, CVIII. Quite apart from the problem of equating 1861 data with those for later years, there are difficulties in incorporating Irish data, which were assembled on a different basis in 1861. The percentages of professionals in the occupied population should also be taken to be very approximate. Cf. B. R. Mitchell and P. Deane, *Abstract of British Historical Statistics* (Cambridge, 1962) p. 60, which used the 1911 classification as the basis of comparison and produced figures of professionals in Great Britain as follows: 1861 305,000 (2.9 per cent of occupied population); 1901 674,000 (4.1 per cent).

10. Census of England & Wales, General Report, 1901, p. 91, PP 1904, CVIII; General Report, 1911, p. 103, PP 1917–18, XXXV.

11. See Census Reports, and note also Edward Higgs, 'Counting Heads and Jobs: Science as an Occupation in the Victorian Census', *History of Science*, XXIII (December 1985) 335–49. Other useful commentaries are W. A. Armstrong, 'The use of information about occupation', in E. A. Wrigley (ed.) *Nineteenth-century society. Essays in the use of quantitative methods for the study of social data* (Cambridge, 1972) p. 191ff, and Richard Lawton (ed.) *The Census and Social Structure. An Interpretative Guide to Nineteenth Century Censuses for England and Wales* (1978) chapters by Joyce Bellamy and J. A. Banks, pp. 185ff.

12. F. Musgrove, 'Middle-Class Education and Employment in the Nineteenth Century', *Economic History Review*, 2nd series, XII (1959) 99–111.

13. N. David Richards, 'Dentistry in Great Britain. Some Sociologic [sic] Perspectives', *Milbank Memorial Fund Quarterly/Health and Society*, XLIX (July 1971) 135–9.

14. Michael Sanderson, *From Irving to Olivier. A Social History of the Acting Profession in England 1880–1983* (1984) pp. 12–23.

15. Musgrove, 'Middle-Class Education', 105–6, and cf. H. J. Perkin, 'Middle-Class Education and Employment in the Nineteenth Century: A Critical Note', *Economic History Review*, 2nd series, XIV (1961) 122–30.

16. UK data for professional occupations and subordinate services, including nurses.

17. For a list of qualifying and non-qualifying associations in England and Wales see Millerson, *Qualifying Associations*, pp. 246–58.

18. A. H. Manchester, *A Modern Legal History of England and Wales 1750–1950* (1980) p. 50. See also Brian Abel-Smith and Robert Stevens, *Lawyers and the Courts. A Sociological Study of the English Legal System 1750–1965* (1967), Harry Kirk, *Portrait of a Profession. A History of the Solicitors' Profession, 1100 to the Present Day* (1976), and Avner Offer, *Property and Politics 1870–1914. Landownership, Law, Ideology and Urban Development in England* (Cambridge, 1981).

19. See, *inter alia*, W. J. Reader, *Professional Men* (1966) pp. 41, 50–3; S. W. F. Holloway, 'The Apothecaries' Act of 1815: A Reinterpretation', *Medical History*, X (July 1966); Noel and José Parry, *The Rise of the Medical Profession* (1976); M. Jeanne Peterson, *The Medical Profession in Mid-Victorian London* (Berkeley and Los Angeles, 1978); and Ivan Waddington, *The Medical Profession in the Industrial Revolution* (Dublin, 1984).

20. 21 and 22 Vic. c.90. See also Peterson, *Medical Profession*, pp. 24–8, Parry, *Medical Profession*, pp. 112–17, 126–31.

21. Beatrice Webb's notes, Webb Mss. on 'Professional Organisation', Misc. 248, vol. 5, British Library of Political and Economic Science, London; Jeffrey L. Berlant, *Profession and Monopoly. A Study of Medicine in the United States and Great Britain* (Berkeley and Los Angeles, 1975) pp. 153–67; Terry Johnson, 'The state and the professions: peculiarities of the British', in Anthony Giddens and Gavin Mackenzie (eds) *Social Class and the Division of Labour. Essays in honour of Ilya Neustadt* (Cambridge, 1982) pp. 196–200.

22. The British Dental Association (1880), Matrons' Aid Society [later the Midwives' Institute] (1880), British Nurses' Association (1887), and Incorporated Society of Trained Masseuses (1894). The Dentists' Act, 1878, failed to secure effective registration (not rectified until 1921), while the midwives, who had lost status to the emerging GPs, secured registration by an Act of 1902, but were subordinated to the General Medical Council and the local authorities. Nurses did not obtain registration until 1919. See Richards, 'Dentistry', 138–42; Jean Donnison, *Midwives and Medical Men. A History of Inter-Professional Rivalries and Women's Rights* (1977) pp. 99ff.

23. Parry, *Medical Profession*, p. 134.

24. Shortt, 'Physicians, Science, and Status', 62, 67–8.

25. See, *inter alia*, Waddington, *Medical Profession*, pp. 176–205; Steven J. Novak, 'Professionalism and Bureaucracy: English Doctors and the Victorian Public Health Administration', *Journal of Social History*, VI (Summer 1973) 440–62; M. Jeanne Peterson, 'Gentlemen and Medical Men: The Problem of Professional Recruitment', *Bulletin of the History of Medicine*, LVIII (Winter 1984) 457–73; and Christopher Lawrence, 'Incommunicable Knowledge: Science, Technology and the Clinical Art in Britain 1850–1914', *Journal of Contemporary History*, XX (Oct. 1985) 503–20.

26. Alan D. Gilbert, *Religion and Society in Industrial England. Church, Chapel and Social Change 1740–1914* (1976) p. 132.

27. Henry Jones, *An Entrance Guide to Professions and Business* (1898) p. 25.

28. Reader, *Professional Men*, pp. 127–45; Michael Sanderson, *The Universities in the Nineteenth Century* (1975) pp. 79–80, 142–6.

29. T. W. Bamford, *Rise of the Public Schools. A Study of Boys' Boarding Schools in England and Wales from 1837 to the Present* (1976) pp. 17–18; J. R. de S. Honey, 'Tom Brown's Universe: The Nature and Limits of the Victorian Public Schools Community', in Brian Simon and Ian Bradley (eds) *The Victorian Public School* (Dublin, 1975) pp. 19–33; Brian Simon, *Education and the Labour Movement 1870–1920* (1965) p. 113.

30. Sheldon Rothblatt, *The Revolution of the Dons: Cambridge and Society in Victorian England* (1968) pp. 84–5, 189–90, 242–3; A. J. Engel, *From Clergyman to Don. The Rise of the Academic Profession in Nineteenth-Century Oxford* (Oxford, 1983) pp. 5–10, 158–67, 280, 292.

31. Reader, *Professional Men*, p. 115; Asher Tropp, *The Schoolteachers. The Growth of the Teaching Profession in England and Wales from 1800 to the present day* (1957) pp. 125–6, 130, 135, 151, 155–9.

32. Reader, *Professional Men*, p. 163; T. R. Gourvish, 'The Railways and

the Development of Managerial Enterprise in Britain, 1850–1939', in Kesaji Kobayashi and Hidemasa Morikawa (eds) *Development of Management Enterprise* (Tokyo, 1986) pp. 188–9, and T. R. Gourvish, 'Professionalisation and Railway Management', unpublished paper, summarised in *Social History Society Newsletter*, III (Spring 1978).

33. R. A. Buchanan, 'Institutional Proliferation in the British Engineering Profession, 1847–1914', *Economic History Review*, 2nd series, XXXVIII (Feb. 1985) 43–4. The figures quoted include dual membership. They differ from those cited by Buchanan in an earlier article, 'Gentlemen Engineers: The Making of A Profession', *Victorian Studies*, XXVI (Summer 1983) 416.

34. Buchanan, 'Institutional Proliferation', 43, and see Robert R. Locke, *The End of the Practical Man. Entrepreneurship and Higher Education in Germany, France and Great Britain, 1880–1940* (Greenwich, Conn. and London, 1984) pp. 30, 48–9.

35. Cf. Reader, *Professional Men*, p. 161; Nicholas A. H. Stacey, *English Accountancy. A Study in Social and Economic History, 1800–1954* (1954) p. 13.

36. Edgar Jones, *Accountancy and the British Economy 1840–1980. The Evolution of Ernst & Whinney* (1981) p. 61.

37. Beatrice Webb, paper on Accountants, Webb Mss. Misc. 248, vol. 20, BLPES; Millerson, *Qualifying Associations*, pp. 51–2, 68–70, 74, 163; Jones, *Accountancy*, pp. 29–32, 66–73; John R. Edwards, 'The Origins and Evolution of the Double Account System: An Example of Accounting Innovation', *Abacus*, XXI (Mar. 1985) 19–43.

38. Millerson, *Qualifying Associations*, p. 83; F. M. L. Thompson) *Chartered Surveyors. The Growth of a Profession* (1968) pp. 14–15, 108, 131.

39. The Institute of British Architects, 1834 (RIBA from 1866); Pharmaceutical Society, 1841; Royal College of Veterinary Surgeons, 1844; Society of Professional Musicians, 1882 (Incorporated Society of Musicians from 1892); Amalgamated Musicians' Union, 1893; National Association of Journalists, 1883 (Institute of Journalists from 1890); The Society of Authors, 1884. See, *inter alia*, A. M. Carr-Saunders and P. A. Wilson, *The Professions* (1933) pp. 125–41, 176–94, 265–70 [and also for other occupations]; Victor Bonham-Carter, *Authors by Profession*, I (1978) pp. 119–20; Cyril Ehrlich, *The Music Profession in Britain since the Eighteenth Century. A Social History* (Oxford, 1985) pp. 126–33, 146–8; Barrington Kaye, *The Development of the Architectural Profession in Britain. A Sociological Study* (1960) pp. 79–82, 88–104.

40. Larson, *Rise of Professionalism*, p. 91.

41. D. C. Coleman, 'Gentlemen and Players', *Economic History Review*, 2nd series, XXVI (Feb. 1973) 96–101.

42. Keith Burgess, 'Did the Late Victorian Economy Fail?', Chapter 11, this volume.

43. Martin J. Wiener, *English Culture and the Decline of the Industrial Spirit, 1850–1980* (Cambridge, 1981) pp. 14–16. See also P. Warwick, 'Did Britain Change? An Inquiry into the Causes of National Decline', *Journal of Contemporary History*, XX (Jan. 1985) 99ff.

44. Donald Coleman and Christine Macleod, 'Attitudes to New Techniques: British Businessmen, 1800–1950', *Economic History Review*, 2nd series, XXXIX (Nov. 1986) 599–600.

45. Bernard Elbaum and William Lazonick (eds), *The Decline of the British Economy* (Oxford, 1986).

46. T. W. Heyck, *The Transformation of Intellectual Life in Victorian England* (1982) pp. 155–87, 226–7.

47. T. H. S. Escott, *England: its People, Polity and Pursuits* (Oxford, 1885) p. 332, cited in Reader, *Professional Men*, p. 151.

3. URBAN BRITAIN   M. J. Daunton

1. J. Saville, *Rural Depopulation in England and Wales, 1851–1951* (1957) pp. 53–9.

2. P. Geddes, *Cities in Evolution: An Introduction to the Town Planning Movement and to the Study of Civics* (1915) pp. 34–45; A. Weber, *The Growth of Cities in the Nineteenth Century* (New York, 1899) pp. 47, 59.

3. G. Stedman Jones, *Outcast London: A Study in the Relationship between Classes in Victorian Society* (Oxford, 1971) Chapter 6.

4. J. Brown, 'Charles Booth and the Labour Colonies', *Economic History Review*, 2nd series XXI (1968); A. Marshall, 'The Housing of the London Poor: 1. Where to House Them', *Contemporary Review*, XLV (1884) 224–31.

5. A. Sutcliffe, 'In Search of the Urban Variable: Britain in the Later Nineteenth Century', in D. Fraser and A. Sutcliffe (eds) *The Pursuit of Urban History* (1983) pp. 234–63.

6. On the changes in approach to social problems, see E. P. Hennock, 'Poverty and Social Theory in England: the Experience of the 1880s', *Social History*, 1 (1976).

7. D. Bythell, *The Sweated Trades: Outwork in Nineteenth-Century Britain* (1978); F. B. Smith, *The People's Health, 1830–1910* (1979).

8. W. Isard, 'A Neglected Cycle: The Transport-Building Cycle', *Review of Economics and Statistics*, 24 (1942).

9. J. P. McKay, *Tramways and Trolleys: The Rise of Urban Mass Transport in Europe* (Princeton, 1976); S. B. Warner, *Streetcar Suburbs: The Process of Growth in Boston, 1870–1900* (Cambridge, Mass., 1962); D. Ward, 'A Comparative Historical Geography of Streetcar Suburbs in Boston, Massachusetts and Leeds, England, 1850–1920', *Annals of the Association of American Geographers*, 54 (1964) pp. 477–89; A. O. Ochojna, 'Lines of Class Distinction: An Economic and Social History of the British Tramcar, with Special Reference to Edinburgh and Glasgow', unpublished PhD thesis, University of Edinburgh, 1974; T. C. Barker and R. M. Robbins, *A History of London Transport: Passenger Travel and the Development of the Metropolis, vol. I, The Nineteenth Century* (1963) and *Vol. II, The Twentieth Century to 1970* (1974); G. C. Dickinson and C. J. Longley, 'The Coming of Cheap Transport: A Study of Tramway Fares on Municipal Systems in British Provincial Towns, 1900–14', *Transport History*, VI (1973).

10. M. Falkus, 'The Development of Municipal Trading in the Nineteenth Century', *Business History*, 19 (1977) 135.

11. A. Briggs, *Victorian Cities* (1963), Chapter 5; D. Matthews, 'Laissez-

Faire and the London Gas Industry in the Nineteenth Century: Another Look', *Economic History Review*, 2nd series, xxxix (1986).

12. M. J. Daunton, *House and Home in the Victorian City: Working-Class Housing 1850–1914* (1983) Chapter 10.

13. B. Benjamin, 'The Urban Background to Public Health Changes in England and Wales, 1900–50', *Population Studies*, 17 (1963–4) 225–48; E. Lampard, 'The Urbanizing World', in H. J. Dyos and M. Wolff (eds) *The Victorian City: Images and Realities*, vol. I (1973) pp. 20–1.

14. A. Offer, *Property and Politics, 1870–1914: Landownership, Law, Ideology and Urban Development in England* (Cambridge, 1981) Part IV.

15. Falkus, 'Development of Municipal Trading', 134.

16. E. P. Hennock, *Fit and Proper Persons: Ideal and Reality in Nineteenth-Century Urban Government* (1973) and 'Finance and Politics in Urban Local Government in England, 1835–1900', *Historical Journal*, vi (1963) 212–25.

17. M. J. Daunton, *Coal Metropolis: Cardiff, 1870–1914* (Leicester, 1977) pp. 172–3.

18. E. Bristow, 'The Liberty and Property Defence League and Individualism', *Historical Journal*, 18 (1965) 761–89; Offer, *Property and Politics*, Part III.

19. Daunton, *Coal Metropolis*, Chapter 9.

20. Offer, *Property and Politics*, Chapter 18; D. Englander, *Landlord and Tenant in Urban Britain, 1838–1918* (Oxford, 1983) Chapter 6.

21. Offer, *Property and Politics*, Chapters 13, 14, 23; Daunton, *House and Home*, Chapter 9.

22. D. A. Reeder, 'The Politics of Urban Leaseholds in Late Victorian England', *International Review of Social History*, vi (1961); Offer, *Property and Politics*, Chapters 12, 22, 23; J. S. Nettlefold, *A Housing Policy* (Birmingham, 1905).

23. D. Fraser, *Power and Authority in the Victorian City* (Oxford, 1979) Chapter 6.

24. D. Owen, *The Government of Victorian London, 1855–89: The Metropolitan Board of Works, the Vestries and the City Corporation* (Cambridge, Mass. and London, 1982); K. Young and P. Garside, *Metropolitan London: Politics and Urban Change, 1837–1981* (1982) Chapters 1–5.

25. See, for example, the comments of H. J. Gans, *People and Plans: Essays on Urban Problems and Solutions* (abridged edn, Harmondsworth, 1972) Chapter 1.

26. M. J. Daunton, 'Public Place and Private Space: The Victorian City and the Working-Class Household', in Fraser and Sutcliffe (eds), *Pursuit of Urban History*, pp. 212–33.

27. Briggs, *Victorian Cities*, pp. 227–9; C. M. Allan, 'The Genesis of British Urban Redevelopment with Special Reference to Glasgow', *Economic History Review*, 2nd series, xviii (1965); Stedman Jones, *Outcast London*, Part II; A. S. Wohl, *The Eternal Slum: Housing and Social Policy in Victorian London* (1977); J. N. Tarn, *Five Per Cent Philanthropy: An Account of Housing in Urban Areas between 1840 and 1914* (1973); J. A. Yelling, *Slums and Slum Clearance in Victorian London* (1986).

28. Sutcliffe, *Planned City*, pp. 72–87; S. M. Gaskell, *Building Control:*

National Legislation and the Introduction of Local Bye-Laws in Victorian England (1983); R. Harper, *Victorian Building Regulations: Summary Tables of the Principal English Building Acts and Model Bye-Laws, 1840–1914* (1985).

29. A. Sutcliffe, *Towards the Planned City: Germany, Britain, the United States and France, 1780–1914* (Oxford, 1981) Chapter 3; W. Ashworth, *The Genesis of Modern British Town Planning: A Study in Economic and Social History of the Nineteenth and Twentieth Centuries* (1954) Chapter 7.

30. M. W. Beresford, 'The Back-to-Back House in Leeds, 1787–1937', in S. D. Chapman (ed.) *The History of Working-Class Housing: A Symposium* (Newton Abbot, 1971) pp. 114–21; F. D. Case, 'Hidden Social Agendas and Housing Standards: The New York Tenement House Code of 1901', *Housing and Society*, VIII (1981) 3–17.

31. G. Stedman Jones, 'Working-Class Culture and Working-Class Politics in England, 1870–1900', *Journal of Social History*, VII (1973–4); S. Burman (ed.) *Fit Work for Women* (1979); H. W. Singer, 'An Index of Urban Land Rents and House Rents in England and Wales, 1845–1913', *Econometrica*, IX (1941) 230; B. R. Mitchell and P. Deane, *Abstract of British Historical Statistics* (Cambridge, 1962) pp. 472–3; Census of Scotland, 1911, vol. ii, table XLVIII; R. Giffen, *The Progress of the Working Classes in the Last Half Century* (1884) p. 13.

32. Census of England and Wales, 1911, vol. VIII, Tenements in Administrative Counties and Urban and Rural Districts, tables 3 and 4; PP 1908 CVII, Report of an Enquiry by the Board of Trade into Working-Class Rents, Housing and Retail Prices.

33. Report of an Enquiry . . . into Working-Class Rents; F. Worsdall, *The Tenement: A Way of Life: A Social, Historical and Architectural Study of Housing in Glasgow* (Edinburgh, 1979); N. J. Morgan and M. J. Daunton, 'Landlords in Glasgow: A Study of 1900', *Business History*, XXV (1983).

34. R. G. Rodger, 'The Law and Urban Change: Some Nineteenth-Century Scottish Evidence', *Urban History Yearbook 1979*; 'The Invisible Hand: Market Forces, Housing and the Urban Form in Victorian Cities', in Fraser and Sutcliffe (eds) *The Pursuit of Urban History*; 'The Evolution of Scottish Town Planning', in G. Gordon and B. Dicks (eds) *Scottish Urban History* (Aberdeen, 1983).

35. R. G. Rodger, 'The Victorian Building Industry and the Housing of the Scottish Working Class', in M. Doughty (ed.) *Building the Industrial City* (Leicester, 1986), p. 178; J. Parry Lewis, *Building Cycles and Britain's Growth* (1965).

36. B. Thomas, *Migration and Economic Growth* (Cambridge, 1954); Daunton, *House and Home*, pp. 161–3; S. B. Saul, 'House Building in England, 1890–1914', *Economic History Review*, 2nd series, xv (1962–3); H. J. Dyos, 'The Speculative Builders and Developers of Victorian London', *Victorian Studies*, XI (1967); R. G. Rodger, 'Scottish Urban Housebuilding, 1870–1914', PhD thesis, University of Edinburgh, 1975.

37. Daunton, *House and Home*, pp. 162–3.

38. Morgan and Daunton, 'Landlords in Glasgow', pp. 274–81; Englander, *Landlord and Tenant*, Chapter 8.

39. Englander, *Landlord and Tenant*, Chapters 6 and 7.

40. R. Dennis, *English Industrial Cities of the Nineteenth Century: A Social Geography* (Cambridge, 1984).
41. H. J. Dyos, *Victorian Suburb: A Study of the Growth of Camberwell* (Leicester, 1961); D. J. Olsen, *Town Planning in London: The Eighteenth and Nineteenth Centuries* (New Haven, 1964); D. J. Olsen, 'House upon House: Estate Development in London and Sheffield', in H. J. Dyos and M. Wolff (eds) *The Victorian City: Images and Realities* (1973) pp. 333–57; D. Cannadine, 'Urban Development in England and America in the Nineteenth Century: Some Comparisons and Contrasts', *Economic History Review*, 2nd series, XXXIII (1980) 309–25; D. Cannadine, *Lords and Landlords: The Aristocracy and the Towns, 1774–1967* (Leicester, 1980).
42. A. Sutcliffe, 'Introduction', in Sutcliffe (ed.), *Multi-Storey Living: The British Working-Class Experience* (1974); L. Davidoff, *The Best Circles: Society, Etiquette and The Season* (1973) pp. 73–5; R. Sennett, *Families Against the City: Middle-Class Homes of Industrial Chicago, 1872–90* (Cambridge, Mass., 1970).
43. A. Adburgham, *Shops and Shopping, 1800–1914* (1964); R. Thorne, 'Places of Refreshment', in A. King (ed.), *Buildings and Society* (1980) and paper on offices presented to Urban History Group Colloquium, 1984.
44. Briggs, *Victorian Cities*, brings out the variation between towns; J. Walton, *The English Seaside Resort: A Social History, 1750–1914* (Leicester, 1983).

4. JOSEPH CHAMBERLAIN: A REASSESSMENT   *Roland Quinault*

1. Birmingham University Library, Chamberlain papers, JC 5/16/55: J. Chamberlain to J. Collings, 30 June 1876.
2. Winston S. Churchill, 'Joseph Chamberlain', in *Great Contemporaries* (1947) p. 54.
3. J. L. Garvin and J. Amery, *The Life of Joseph Chamberlain*, 6 vols (1932–69) vol. I, p. vii.
4. Richard Jay, *Joseph Chamberlain, a political study* (Oxford, 1981) p. 340.
5. Michael Balfour, *Britain and Joseph Chamberlain* (1985) p. xiii.
6. R. E. Quinault 'John Bright and Joseph Chamberlain', *Historical Journal*, XXVIII, 3 (1985) 632–46.
7. Garvin and Amery, *Life*, II, p. 602.
8. *The Times*, 20 Jan. 1904.
9. Jay, *Joseph Chamberlain*, p. 330.
10. Garvin and Amery, *Life*, II, pp. 369, 498–500.
11. Chamberlain papers, JC 5/54/141: J. Chamberlain to J. Morley, 24 Dec. 1976.
12. *The Times*, 22 Sept. 1885.
13. N. Murrell Marris, *The Rt. Hon. Joseph Chamberlain* (1900) p. 420; Keith Feiling, *The Life of Neville Chamberlain* (1946) p. 33.
14. A. G. Gardiner, *The Life of Sir William Harcourt*, 2 vols (1923) vol. I, p. 495.
15. Asa Briggs and Conrad Gill, *History of Birmingham*, 2 vols (Oxford, 1952) vol. II, p. 2.

16. Jay, *Joseph Chamberlain*, pp. 25–8; Balfour, *Britain and Chamberlain*, pp. 78–80.
17. Chamberlain papers, JC 5/16/54: J. Chamberlain to J. Collings 6 June 1876.
18. P. J. Waller, *Town, City and Nation England 1850–1914* (Oxford, 1983) p. 304.
19. Joseph Chamberlain, 'The Labour Question', *The Nineteenth Century*, CLXXXIX (Nov. 1892) 703.
20. Garvin and Amery, *Life*, I, p. 214.
21. *The Times*, 4 July 1914 (citing the *Birmingham Daily Mail*).
22. *The Times*, 15, 20 Oct. 1885.
23. Garvin and Amery, *Life*, I, p. 214.
24. *The Times*, 15 Jan. 1885.
25. G. W. E. Russell, *Portraits of the Seventies* (1916) p. 168.
26. Joseph Chamberlain, *A Political Memoir 1880–92*, ed. C. H. D. Howard (1953) p. 253.
27. *The Times*, 6 Oct. 1904.
28. *Parliamentary Debates*, 3rd series, 1886, CCCVI, 681.
29. Chamberlain papers, JC 5/39/22: J. Chamberlain to W. Harris, 18 June 1885.
30. Garvin and Amery, *Life*, I, pp. 96–8, 118, 122.
31. Chamberlain papers, JC 5/8/25: J. Chamberlain to J. Bunce, 16 Feb. 1877; JC 5/54/182: J. Chamberlain to J. Morley, 3 Oct. 1877.
32. Garvin and Amery, *Life*, II, p. 426; J. Chamberlain to Hartington, 21 Jan. 1889.
33. Ibid., I, pp. 246–7: J. Chamberlain to J. Collings, 18 Feb. 1878.
34. For this concept see Michael Hurst, *Joseph Chamberlain and West Midland politics 1886–95* (Dugdale Society Occasional Papers no. 15, Oxford, 1962).
35. Churchill, 'Joseph Chamberlain', p. 52.
36. *The Times*, 10 July 1906.
37. *Parliamentary Debates*, 1886, CCCVI, 694–8.
38. Chamberlain, *Political Memoir*, pp. 248–60.
39. *The Times*, 13 Oct. 1887; Louis Creswicke, *The Life of the Rt. Hon. Joseph Chamberlain*, 4 vols (n.d.) vol. II, p. 150.
40. *The Times*, 7, 12 Nov. 1895.
41. Ibid., 26 Mar., 10 June 1896. Garvin and Amery, *Life*, V, pp. 214–15.
42. *The Times*, 28 Mar. 1901.
43. Gerald Friesen, *The Canadian Prairies: A History* (Toronto, 1984) pp. 276, 327.
44. Carman Miller, *The Canadian Career of the Fourth Earl of Minto: The Education of a Viceroy* (Waterloo, Ontario, 1980) pp. 125–6, 195–6.
45. *The Times*, 16 May 1903.
46. Garvin and Amery, *Life*, VI, p. 966: J. Chamberlain to Denison, 3 Oct. 1911.
47. Ibid., VI, p. 440: J. Chamberlain to H. Chaplin, 12 Sept. 1903.
48. Ibid., pp. 169–70: J. Chamberlain to Denison, 6 April 1903.
49. *The Times*, 9 July 1904.
50. Sir Henry Lucy, *The Diary of a Journalist* (1920) p. 314.

51. Jay, *Joseph Chamberlain*, p. 338.
52. Lucy, *Diary*, p. 312.
53. Rt. Hon. Sir Richard Temple Bt, MP, *Letters & Character Sketches from the House of Commons* (1912) pp. 147–8.
54. Henry W. Lucy, *A Diary of the Salisbury Parliament 1886–92* (1892) p. 403.
55. Feiling, *Neville Chamberlain*, p. 205.
56. Churchill, 'Joseph Chamberlain', p. 43.

5.   ELECTORAL REFORMS AND THEIR OUTCOME   *J. P. D. Dunbabin*

(Fuller references are to be found in the original, and longer, version of this paper, in Italian, in P. Pombeni (ed.) *La Trasformazione politica nell'Europa liberale 1870–90*, Bologna, Mulino, 1986.)

1. The Cave (of Adullam), or Adullamites, were a group of Liberal MPs who had successfully resisted the 1866 Russell/Gladstone Reform Bill in clandestine co-operation with Disraeli. Most were on the right of the party, and many had personal as well as political grounds for discontent.

2. The English county electorate, after the 1867 Act, totalled about 730,000.

3. There were loop-holes, like Coronation gifts to children, and candidates were expected to contribute liberally to local charities; to some extent, too, questionable practices were displaced from local to central fund-raising.

4. The first constituency to go would have been loyalist Trinity College, Dublin. And an Irish reduction would necessitate a corresponding Welsh one, with knock-on effects for small counties elsewhere.

5. Whereby each elector had as many votes as there were seats to be contested and could distribute them as between candidates in any proportions he pleased.

6. Royden Harrison argues (*Before the Socialists*, Chapter IV) that in 1868 there was definite potential for independent working-class political action, and that the alignment behind the Liberals of such labour and Reform League leaders as Howell and Cremer was due not only to reluctance to split the vote and let in Tories, but also to their personal and political need for Liberal money. Still, as Trygve Tholfsen observes, 'the deal . . . would not have worked had not the vast majority of the artisan class been very favourably disposed to the Liberal party' – 'The Transition to Democracy in Victorian England', *International Review of Social History*, VI (1961) 248; but see also Tholfsen's more nuanced book, *Working Class Radicalism in Mid-Victorian England* (1976).

7. The Scottish Highlands are sometimes said to have seen a more immediate response to franchise extension. In 1885 the newly enfranchised crofters inflicted striking electoral defeats on pro-landlord official Liberals, and 1886 saw land legislation. However, this did not concede the crofters' principal demand (the expansion of their holdings). Indeed Gladstone gave no more than he had originally intended before the elections; neither were the

1892–5 Liberal governments very forthcoming. It was only in the longer run that Scottish Liberal attitudes to the land question were transformed.

8. In Ulster farmers were not swept by such overwhelming community pressures, but did feel more strongly over tenant right than their English counterparts; and the secret ballot facilitated the political expression of these views (to the Liberals' benefit).

9. K. Theodore Hoppen, *Elections, Politics and Society in Ireland 1832–1885* (Oxford, 1984) esp. pp. 32–3, 276–7; D. C. Savage, 'The Origins of the Ulster Unionist Party, 1885–6', *Irish Historical Studies*, xii (1960–1).

10. On one computation: 1865 Lib. majority, 62, 1868 106; 1874 Cons. majority 52, 1880 Lib. 176; 1885 Libs. 334, Nationalists 86, Cons. 250; 1886 Unionist majority 120, 1892 Lib. 40, 1895 Unionist 152.

11. Party votes (defined, rather toughly, as ones in which 90% of one party faced 90% of the other) represented: in 1836 23% of all Commons divisions: in 1850 16%, 1860 6%, 1871 35%, 1881 47%, 1894 76%, 1899 69%.

12. This *had* a mandate, but not (as was now claimed to be necessary) a British one.

13. Conservative net gains (1880 on 1868) represented 18 of the total 65 seats in London, Kent, Middlesex, Surrey and Sussex.

14. It is often claimed that the Third Reform Act's reduction (to 27) in the number of two-member constituencies made it harder to preserve Liberal unity by running a Whig and a Radical as a balanced ticket. This must be doubtful; but, where two-member constituencies survived, a Liberal and a Labour candidate were quite often run together in the early twentieth century. Also the 1885 redistribution is supposed to have encouraged class politics by separating suburbs from city centres; working-class city centre seats (especially in East London) could prove erratic; they provided possible openings for 'labour' candidates, but Labour did not really monopolise them until after 1918. The other type of single-class constituency was that dominated by coal-miners; these often returned working-class MPs, but of a generally Liberal persuasion.

15. He refused the hoped-for £12,400. So the Liberal Central Association probably supported only 21 Labour candidates; a further 19 stood either independently or in opposition to official Liberals.

6. PARTIES, MEMBERS AND VOTERS AFTER 1867　　*John Garrard*

1. This is a revised version of an article originally appearing in the *Historical Journal*, xx, i (1977).

2. S. Neumann, *Modern Political Parties* (Chicago, 1967) p. 405.

3. The terminology of 'mass parties' is largely that of M. Duverger in *Political Parties* (1964).

4. D. A. Chalmers, *The Social Democratic Party of Germany* (New Haven, 1967) p. 405.

5. See Duverger, *Political Parties*, Book 1, Chapter 2, esp. pp. 116–32.

6. See John Vincent, *The Formation of the British Liberal Party 1857–68*

LATER VICTORIAN BRITAIN 1867–1900

(Aylesbury, 1972); also D. Walsh in forthcoming MSc thesis, University of Salford.

7. See Patrick Joyce, *Work, Society and Politics: The Culture of the Factory in Later Victorian England* (Brighton, 1980) Chapter 8.

8. Chairman Ordsall Constitutional Club, *Salford Weekly Chronicle* (hereafter *SWC*) 18 Mar. 1871, p. 3.

9. *SWC*, 6 Aug. 1870, p. 3.

10. See M. Ostrogorski, *Democracy and the Organization of Political Parties* (1902, republished New York, 1970) vol. I, pp. 165f.

11. Trinity Ward Liberal Association, *Salford Weekly News* (hereafter *SWN*) 13 Apr. 1884, p. 3.

12. Mr Slater, St Phillips District Liberal Association, *SWN*, 23 Jan. 1869, p. 3.

13. Annual Report, *Salford Reporter* (hereafter *SR*) 27 Feb. 1905, p. 5.

14. Report, Womens' Liberal Association, *SR*, 25 Apr. 1891, p. 6.

15. W. T. Charley, MP for Salford, at second Annual Soiree of Pendleton Conservatives, *SWC*, 4 Feb. 1871, p. 4.

16. Rev. John Hyde to Broughton Liberal Association, *SWN*, 17 Feb. 1872, p. 3.

17. *SWN*, 7 Nov. 1874, p. 3.

18. Report of Pendleton Constitutional Association, *SWC*, 7 Aug. 1869, p. 4.

19. *SWN*, 17 Feb. 1872, p. 3.

20. *SWN*, 23 Jan. 1869, p. 3.

21. *SR*, 3 Mar. 1888, p. 5.

22. *SWN*, 17 Mar. 1879, p. 3.

23. *SWC*, 2 Aug. 1873, p. 2.

24. *Stockport Advertiser*, 25 June 1875, p. 5.

25. *SWN*, 30 Aug. 1879, p. 3 and 6 Sept. 1879, p. 3.

26. *SR*, 1 Sept. 1900, p. 7.

27. *Rochdale Observer*, 26 Dec. 1868, p. 5.

28. *Rochdale Observer*, 18 Mar. 1871, p. 5.

29. *Rochdale Observer*, 25 May 1878, p. 6. See also *Rochdale Times*, 5 July 1873, p. 6.

30. Quoted *Bolton Chronicle*, 3 Feb. 1872, p. 2; see also *Bolton Chronicle*, 23 Dec. 1873, p. 7. and 16 Apr. 1870, p. 7.

31. Robert Leake to Trinity and Greengate Liberals, *SWN*, 22 Jan. 1870, p. 3.

32. President of Salford Liberal Association, *SWN*, 28 Jan. 1871, p. 3.

33. *SWN*, 19 June 1869, p. 2.

34. George Binns to Blackfriars Conservatives, *SWC*, 2 Oct. 1869, p. 3.

35. Chairman Salford Liberals, *SWN*, 10 Aug. 1878, p. 3.

36. Verdict on St. Thomas' Ward Liberals, *SR*, 13 June 1891, p. 8.

37. At opening of St Stephens' Liberal Club, *SWN*, 18 Apr. 1874, p. 3.

38. Letter *SWN*, 25 Feb. 1871, p. 2.

39. C. E. Cawley, MP for Salford, to Crescent Conservatives, *SWC*, 30 Apr. 1870, p. 3.

40. William Hough to South Salford Liberal Association, *SWN*, 23 Mar. 1878, p. 3.
41. For this culture see Joyce, *Work, Society and Politics*.
42. See John Garrard, *Leadership and Power in Victorian Industrial Towns 1830–1880* (Manchester, 1983) Chapters 2 and 3.
43. See Joyce, *Work, Society and Politics*; Garrard, *Leadership and Power*.
44. *Bury Times*, 30 Jan. 1869 p. 7.
45. See Robert Blake, *Disraeli* (1966), Chapter XXI; Asa Briggs, *Victorian People* (Harmondsworth, 1965) esp. pp. 240–71; Maurice Cowling, *Disraeli, Gladstone and Revolution* (Cambridge, 1967) for example pp. 23, 29, 34, 48, 50–67; Gertrude Hummelfarb, *Victorian Minds* (1968) esp: Chapter XIII; F. B. Smith, *The Making of the Second Reform Bill* (Cambridge, 1966) pp. 1–14.
46. N. McCord, 'Some Difficulties of Parliamentary Reform', *Historical Journal*, x (1967) 376–90.
47. Alderman McKerrow, opening Crescent Liberal Club, *SWN*, 16 May 1874, p. 3.
48. G. H. Ormerod to Rawtenstall Constitutional Association, *Bury Times*, 30 Jan. 1869, p. 7.
49. Annual Report, St Stephens' Liberal Club, *SWN*, 11 Mar. 1876, p. 4.
50. Annual Report, *SWN*, 28 Jan. 1871, p. 3.
51. *SWC*, 3 July 1869, p. 3.
52. At inaugural tea meeting, St Matthias Constitutional Association, *SWC*, 27 Jan. 1872, p. 2.
53. To Cutgate Liberal Club, *Rochdale Observer*, 29 Nov. 1873, p. 8.
54. *SWN*, 17 Mar. 1879, p. 3.
55. *SWN*, 27 Feb. 1875, p. 3.
56. *SWN*, 22 Jan. 1876, p. 4.
57. Annual Report of Liberal Council, *SWN*, 17 Feb. 1872, p. 3.
58. *Bolton Chronicle*, 16 Apr. 1870, p. 7.
59. *Bolton Chronicle*, 23 Dec. 1871, p. 7.
60. *SWN*, 11 Mar. 1876, p. 3.
61. AGM, *SWN*, 19 Nov. 1881, p. 3.
62. Arthur Arnold to Crescent Liberal Club, *SWN*, 20 Dec. 1879, p. 3.
63. Henry Lee to Crescent Liberal Club, *SWN*, 23 Jan. 1875, p. 3.
64. *SWN*, 15 Apr. 1882, p. 3.
65. Councillor Hewitt, *SR*, 20 Apr. 1889, p. 5.
66. For an alternative, Marxist interpretation of what such 'dilutions' of the message, whether political or religious, signified, see Stephen Yeo, *Religion and Voluntary Organizations in Crisis* (1976).
67. G. Southern to Pendleton Liberals, *SWN*, 29 Jan. 1870, p. 3.
68. Joseph Snape to Broughton Constitutional Club, *SWC*, 22 Mar. 1879, p. 3.
69. Mr Osborne, *Rochdale Observer*, 9 Dec. 1871, p. 7.
70. To Pendleton Liberal Club, *SWN*, 17 Nov. 1877, p. 4.
71. To Crescent Liberal Club, *SWN*, 16 May 1874, p. 3.
72. *SWN*, 17 Mar. 1879, p. 3.
73. Annual Report, *Rochdale Observer*, 15 Nov. 1873, p. 7.

74. *Rochdale Observer*, 29 Nov. 1873, p. 8.
75. *SWC*, 2 Jan. 1875, p. 3.
76. *SWC*, 19 Feb. 1870, p. 3.
77. C. E. Cawley to St Matthias Constitutional Club, *SWC*, 27 Jan. 1872, p. 2.
78. To Broughton Constitutional Club, *SWC*, 12 Nov. 1870, p. 3.
79. To St Phillips Constitutional Association Annual Soiree, *SWC*, 23 Apr. 1870, p. 3.
80. To Crescent Constitutional Association, *SWC*, 30 Apr. 1870, p. 3.
81. J. L. Barrett, *SWC*, 30 Jan. 1875, p. 2.
82. George Binns to Blackfriars Conservatives, *SWC*, 2 Oct. 1869, p. 3.
83. Letter W. H. Bailey, *Manchester Examiner*, 15 Dec. 1881, p. 3.
84. J. Wigley to St Stephens Liberal Club, *SWN*, 11 Mar. 1876, p. 3.
85. William Hough to Greengate Liberal Club, *SWN*, 17 Mar. 1879, p. 3.
86. Councillor William Mather to Crescent Liberal Club, *SWN*, 16 May 1874, p. 3.
87. I am indebted for this suggestion to David Walsh. For fuller development, see his forthcoming MSc thesis, University of Salford, 1986.
88. See Vincent, *British Liberal Party*, see also Garrard, *Leadership and Power*. Also worth noting here are James Epstein's arguments about the character of Nottinghamshire Chartism in James Epstein and Dorothy Thompson (eds) *The Chartist Experience, Studies in Working Class Radicalism and Culture 1830–1860* (1982) pp. 221–68.
89. *Blackburn Standard*, 27 Nov. 1839, p. 4.
90. I am indebted for this suggestion to Dr Alan O'Day.
91. See K. Inglis, *Churches and the Working Classes in Victorian England* (1963) Chapter 3; Hugh McLeod, *Class and Religion in the Late Victorian City* (1974) pp. 72f.
92. See Brian Harrison, *Drink and the Victorians* (1971) esp. Chapters 5 and 6.
93. J. Nuttall, *SR*, 16 Nov. 1901, p. 8.
94. See David Howell, *British Workers and the ILP 1888–1906* (Manchester, 1983); James Hinton, *Labour and Socialism: A History of the British Labour Movement 1867–1974* (Brighton, 1983); for SDF, see Howell, op. cit. and Paul Thompson, *Socialists, Liberals, Labour and the Struggle for London* (1967).
95. *SWN*, 5 Aug. 1871, p. 3.
96. W. McKerrow, *SWC*, 27 Feb. 1875, p. 2.
97. W. T. Charley MP at Annual Picnic, *SWC*, 2 Aug. 1873, p. 2.
98. W. Holland; arguing that the party should 'endeavour . . . to better the lot of the people amongst whom they lived', *SR*, 1 Feb. 1890, p. 5.
99. Mr Snape, proposing formation of Salford Constitutional Association, *SWN*, 7 Feb. 1867, p. 3.
100. Neumann, *Modern Political Parties*, p. 397.
101. See J. A. Garrard, *The Functions of Nineteenth Century Political Parties* (Salford, Occasional Papers in Politics and Contemporary History, 1986).

7. BRITISH FOREIGN POLICY, 1867–1900   *Paul Hayes*

1. *Hansard's Parliamentary Debates*, Third Series, vol. 346, col. 1284, 10 July 1890.
2. G. Martel, *Imperial Diplomacy. Rosebery and the Failure of Foreign Policy* (1986) p. 31.
3. E. T. S. Dugdale (ed.) *German Diplomatic Documents, 1871–1914*, vol. I (1928) p. 246.
4. A. J. P. Taylor, *The Trouble Makers* (1969) p. 58.
5. B. Russell, *The Policy of the Entente, 1904–14: a reply to Professor Gilbert Murray* (1915) p. 70.
6. J. L. Garvin, *Life of Joseph Chamberlain*, vol. 3 (1934) p. 232.
7. S. Lane-Poole, *Lord Stratford de Redcliffe* (1890) p. 19.
8. Sir Edmund Hornby, *An Autobiography* (1928) p. 81.
9. Garvin, *Life of Joseph Chamberlain*, vol. 3, p. 315.
10. Viscount Milner, *England in Egypt* (1920) p. 74.
11. Ibid., p. 405.
12. D. Read, *Cobden and Bright: A Victorian Political Partnership* (1967) p. 241.
13. N. A. Pelcovits, *Old China Hands and the Foreign Office* (1948) p. 131.
14. E. J. Hobsbawm, *Industry and Empire* (1968) p. 206.
15. A. G. Gardiner, *Life of Sir William Harcourt*, vol. 2 (1923) p. 326.
16. Garvin, *Life of Joseph Chamberlain*, vol. 3, p. 211.
17. G. P. Gooch and H. Temperley (eds) *British Documents on the Origins of the War, 1898–1914*, vol. 1 (1927) p. 36.
18. Viscount Knutsford, *In Black and White* (1926) p. 217.
19. R. Robinson and J. Gallagher, *Africa and the Victorians* (1967) p. 404.
20. P. M. Hayes, *Modern British Foreign Policy: The Twentieth Century, 1880–1939* (1978) p. 83.
21. Earl of Midleton, *Records and Reactions, 1856–1939* (1939) p. 193.
22. A. Ponsonby, *Henry Ponsoby, his Life from his Letters* (1942) p. 232.
23. Earl of Ronaldshay, *Life of Lord Curzon*, vol. 1 (1928) p. 254.
24. Ibid., pp. 252–3.
25. Gooch and Temperley, *British Documents*, vol. 2 (1927) p. 68.
26. Ibid., p. 76.
27. Hayes, *Modern British Foreign Policy*, p. 70.
28. Lady Hicks Beach, *Life of Sir Michael Hicks Beach*, vol. 2 (1932) p. 91.
29. J. Gooch, *The Plans of War* (1974) p. 11.
30. Gooch and Temperley, *British Documents*, vol. 2, p. 114.
31. M. Pinto-Duschinsky, *The Political Thought of Lord Salisbury* (1967) p. 152.
32. C. D. H. Howard, *Splendid Isolation* (1967) p. 77.
33. Z. S. Steiner, *The Foreign Office and Foreign Policy, 1898–1914* (1969) p. 212.
34. J. A. S. Grenville, *Lord Salisbury and Foreign Policy: The Close of the Nineteenth Century* (1964) p. 3.
35. Steiner, *The Foreign Office*, p. 7.
36. Lord Vansittart, *The Mist Procession* (1958) pp. 39–40.

37. Steiner, *The Foreign Office*, p. 2.
38. Ibid., p. 4.
39. Vansittart, *Mist Procession* p. 45.
40. Lady Gwendolen Cecil, *Life of Robert, Marquis of Salisbury*, vol. 2 (1921) p. 145.

8.   LATE VICTORIAN WOMEN   *Pat Thane*

1. Sheila Ryan Johansson, 'Sex and Death in Victorian England: an examination of Age and Sex-Specific Death Rates 1840–1910', in M. Vicinus (ed.) *A Widening Sphere, Changing Roles of Victorian Women* (Bloomington, Indiana, 1977; paperback edn, 1983) pp. 163–81.
2. Clementina Black (ed.) *Married Women's Work*. 2nd edn (1983, paperback edn) p. 10.
3. Michael Anderson, 'The Social Position of Spinsters in Mid-Victorian Britain', *Journal of Family History* (Winter 1984) 392.
4. Ruth Freeman and P. Klaus, 'Blessed or not? The New Spinster in England and the United States in the late Nineteenth and early Twentieth Centuries', *Journal of Family History* (Winter 1984); Martha Vicinus, *Independent Women. Work and Community for Single Women 1850–1920* (Chicago, 1985; paperback edn, 1985).
5. Bernard Shaw, *Plays Unpleasant* (Harmondsworth, 1983) 'Preface', p. 19.
6. Margaret D. Stetz, 'Turning Points: Mona Caird', *Turn of the Century Woman*, II, no. 2 (Winter 1985). I owe with gratitude many of my comments on divorce to the current research of Dr James Hammerton of La Trobe University.
7. John R. Gillis, *For Better, For Worse. British Marriages 1600 to the Present* (Oxford and New York, 1985).
8. A. James Hammerton, *Emigrant Gentlewomen* (1979) p. 162.
9. F. Barry Smith, 'Sexuality in Britain, 1800–1900: Some suggested revisions', in Vicinus, *Widening Sphere*, pp. 182–98.
10. Elizabeth Roberts, *A Woman's Place. An Oral History of Working Class Women 1890–1940* (Oxford and New York, 1984).
11. J. Weekes, *Sex, Politics and Society. The Regulation of Sexuality Since 1800* (1981); J. Walkowitz, *Prostitution and Victorian Society* (Cambridge and New York, 1980; paperback edn).
12. Vicinus, *Independent Women*, pp. 289–90.
13. Anderson, 'The Social Position of Spinsters', 380–7.
14. E. Higgs, 'Domestic Servants and Households in Victorian England', *Social History*, 8, 2 (May 1983) 201–10; E. Higgs, 'Domestic Service and Household Production', in Angela V. John (ed.) *Unequal Opportunities. Women's Employment in England 1800–1918* (Oxford, 1986, hardback and paperback edn) pp. 125–50.
15. Belinda Westover, '"To Fill the Kids' Tummies". The Life and Work of Colchester Tailoresses, 1880–1918', in L. Davidoff and B. Westover (eds)

Our Work, Our Lives, Our Words. Women's History and Women's Work (1986, hardback and paperback edn) p. 64.

16. Hannah Mitchell, *The Hard Way Up* (1977) pp. 68–9.

17. On middle-class women in the home, see Patricia Branca, *Silent Sisterhood* (1975); on upper-class women, Leanore Davidoff, *The Best Circles. Society, Etiquette and the Season* (1973).

18. F. K. Prochaska, *Women and Philanthropy in Nineteenth Century England* (Oxford, 1980).

19. C. Stevenson, 'Female Anger and African Politics: The Case of Two Victorian "Lady Travellers"', *Turn of the Century Woman*, II, no. 1 (Summer 1985); Elaine Showalter, 'Victorian Women and Insanity', *Victorian Studies*, 23, 2 (Winter 1980).

20. Sheila Fletcher, *Feminists and Beaurocrats. A Study in the Development of Girls' Education in the Nineteenth Century* (Cambridge, 1980); Joan N. Burstyn, *Victorian Education and the Ideal of Womanhood* (1980); Vicinus, *Independent Women*, pp. 121–210.

21. Meta Zimmeck, 'Jobs for the Girls: The Expansion of Clerical Work for Women, 1850–1914', in John (ed.) *Unequal Opportunities*, pp. 153–78. Kay Sanderson, 'A Pension to Look Forward To . . .?: Women Civil Servants in London, 1925–1939', in Davidoff and Westover, *Our Work . . .*, pp. 145, 160.

22. Dina M. Copelman, '"A New Comradeship between Men and Women": Family, Marriage and London's Women Teachers, 1870–1914', in Jane Lewis (ed.) *Labour and Love. Women's Experience of Home and Family 1850–1940* (Oxford, 1985; hardback and paperback edn).

23. Black, *Married Women's Work*, p. 4.

24. This and all other references to the potteries are from R. Whipp, 'Potbank and Union: A Study of Work and Trade Unionism in the Pottery Industry 1900–1925', University of Warwick PhD thesis, 1983.

25. N. G. Osterud, 'Gender Divisions and the Organization of Work in the Leicester Hosiery Industry', in John (ed.) *Unequal Opportunities*, pp. 45–70.

26. This and all subsequent references to Preston are from M. A. Savage, 'The Social Basis of Working Class Politics: the Labour Movement in Preston 1890–1940', University of Lancaster PhD thesis, 1984.

27. Roberts, *A Woman's Place*, pp. 135–8; Melanie Tebbutt, *Making Ends Meet. Pawnbroking and Working Class Credit* (Leicester, 1983); Jill Liddington and Jill Norris, *One Hand Tied Behind Us. The Rise of the Women's Suffrage Movement* (paperback edn, 1978) pp. 32–6; Sanderson, 'Pension to Look Forward to . . .?', pp. 156–7.

28. This and all other references to printing are from J. H. Zeitlin, 'Craft Regulation and the Division of Labour: Engineers and Compositors in Britain, 1890–1914', University of Warwick PhD thesis, 1981; Mary Freifeld, 'Technological Change and the "self-acting" Mule: a Study of Skill and the Sexual Division of Labour', *Social History*, 11, 2 (October 1986).

29. James Schmiechen, *Sweated Industries and Sweated Labour* (1984); Jenny Morris, 'The Characteristics of Sweating: the Late Nineteenth Century London and Leeds Tailoring Trade' in John (ed.) *Unequal Opportunities*, pp. 95–119.

30. Savage, 'Social Basis of Working Class Politics'; Liddington and

Norris, *One Hand Tied Behind Us*; J. Bornat, 'Lost Leaders: Women, Trade Unionism and the Case of the General Union of Textile Workers, 1875–1914', in John (ed.) *Unequal Opportunities*, pp. 207–34.

31. Liddington and Norris, *One Hand Tied Behind Us*, p. 112.

32. Higgs, 'Domestic Service', pp. 138–9.

33. Broadhurst's statement is quoted by, among others, Barbara Drake, *Women in Trade Unions* (first pub. 1920, 2nd edn 1984, paperback edn) p. 16; Bornat, 'Lost Leaders', p. 209; Jane Lewis (ed.) *Labour and Love*, p. 103; B. Taylor, *Eve and the New Jerusalem* (1983 paperback edn) p. 274; W. Seccombe, 'Patriarchy Stabilized: the Construction of the Male Breadwinner Wage Norm in 19th Century Britain', in *Social History*, 11, 1 (Jan. 1986) p. 55 (who dates it in 1875); *Reports* of the Annual Conference of the TUC: 1877, pp. 17–18; 1879, pp. 29–30; 1880, pp. 28–30.

34. Steve Tolliday, 'Militancy and Organization: Women Workers and Trade Unions in the Motor Trade in the 1930s', *Oral History*, 11, 2 (Autumn 1983); Liddington and Norris, *One Hand Tied Behind Us*, p. 42; L. J. Satre, 'After the Match Girl's Strike: Bryant & May in the 1890s', *Victorian Studies*, 26 (Autumn 1982).

35. Roberts, *A Woman's Place*, pp. 46–50; Zimmeck, 'Jobs for the Girls', pp. 165–7.

36. Bornat, 'Lost Leaders', pp. 207–34; D. Thom, 'The Bundle of Sticks: Women, Trade Unionists and Collective Organization before 1918', in John (ed.) *Unequal Opportunities*, pp. 261–89; E. Mappen, 'Strategists for change: Social Feminist Approaches to the Problem of Women's Work', in ibid., pp. 235–60.

37. J. Melling, *Rent Strikes. Peoples' Struggle for Housing in West Scotland, 1890–1916* (Edinburgh, 1983).

38. D. Rubinstein, *Before the Suffragettes. Women's Emancipation in the 1890s* (Brighton, 1986) p. 150.

39. Liddington and Norris, *One Hand Tied Behind Us*, p. 72.

40. Ibid., p. 149.

41. Vicinus, *Independent Women*, pp. 10–45.

9. THE GENERAL AND THE BISHOPS   *Stuart Mews*

1. Richard Shannon, *The Crisis of Imperialism 1865–1915* (1974; paperback edn Frogmore, 1976) p. 210.

2. G. Kitson Clark, *The Making of Victorian England* (1962; paperback edn, 1965) p. 189.

3. Alan D. Gilbert, *Religion and Society in Industrial England, 1740–1914* (1976) p. 130.

4. W. C. Magee to J. C. MacDonnell, 1 Feb. 1876, J. C. MacDonnell, *Life and Correspondence of William Connor Magee*, vol. II (1896) p. 35.

5. Ibid., 26 Apr. 1876, p. 35.

6. James Bentley, *Ritualism and Politics in Victorian England* (Oxford, 1978) pp. 108ff.

7. W. C. Magee to J. C. MacDonnell, 2 Apr. 1880, MacDonnell, *Life and Correspondence*, p. 128.

8. Ibid., 16 July 1880, p. 138. On 1 Dec. 1881, Magee referred to 'the explosive condition of the Church at this moment', p. 167.

9. Victor Bailey, 'Salvation Army Riots, the "Skeleton Army" and Legal Authority in the Provincial Town', A. P. Donajgrodzki (ed.) *Social Control in Nineteenth Century Britain* (1977) pp. 231–53.

10. John Kent, *Holding the Fort* (1978) pp. 101ff, 325ff.

11. Olive Anderson, 'Women Preachers in Mid-Victorian Britain', *Historical Journal*, XII (1969) 480ff.

12. Olive Anderson, 'The Growth of Christian Militarism in Mid-Victorian Britain', *English Historical Review*, 86 (1971); Hugh Cunningham, 'Jingoism in 1877–8', *Victorian Studies*, 14 (1971).

13. Kitson Clark, *Making of Victorian England*, p. 189.

14. K. S. Inglis, *Churches and the Working Classes in Victorian England* (1963) p. 176.

15. Gilbert, *Religion and Society*, p. 42f.

16. William Booth, 'What is the Salvation Army?', *Contemporary Review*, XLII (1882) 175.

17. H. Hensley Henson, *Bishoprick Papers* (Oxford, 1946) pp. 188ff.

18. C. Ward, 'The Social Sources of the Salvation Army, 1865–90', M.Phil. thesis, University of London, 1970, Chapter 5.

19. At Hull, Colchester, Oldham and Chester, ice rinks were bought by the Army. The Colchester rink was bought by the Army for £2410 though it had cost over £7000 to build, excluding the cost of the site: *Guardian*, 5 Apr. 1882.

20. Samuel Garratt to Mayor, 1 Dec. 1881, Evelyn R. Garratt, *Life and Personal Recollections of Samuel Garratt* (1908) p. 85.

21. *War Cry*, 25 May 1882.

22. *Guardian*, 29 Mar. 1882.

23. Carvosse Gauntlett, 'The Army and the Churches', *The Warrior* (1941/2) pp. 179ff.

24. F. de L. Booth-Tucker, *Life of Catherine Booth*, vol. 2 (1892) p. 233.

25. Roland Robertson, 'The Salvation Army: The Persistence of Sectarianism', in Bryan R. Wilson (ed.) *Patterns of Sectarianism* (1967) pp. 91ff.

26. Gauntlett, 'The Army and the Churches', p. 180; *War Cry*, 8 June 1882.

27. *Church Times*, 10 Mar. 1882: H. Kirk-Smith, *William Thomson, Archbishop of York* (1958) pp. 32, 44.

28. W. Bramwell Booth, *Echoes and Memories* (1925) p. 59.

29. *Guardian*, 22 Mar. 1882.

30. Ibid., 29 Mar. 1882; Kent, *Holding the Fort*, p. 304.

31. *Guardian*, 5 Apr. 1882.

32. Ibid., 12 Apr. 1882.

33. James A. Atkinson, *The Salvation Army and the Church* (Manchester and London, 1882) pp. 9, 10, 13.

34. *Chronicle and Convocation* 1882, pp. 219ff.

35. Ibid., pp. 224ff.

36. Trinity College, Cambridge: E. W. Benson Ms: Diary 12 May 1882.

37. *Spectator*, 20 May 1882, p. 647.
38. Lambeth Palace Library: Tait Ms 285/38 J. W. Horsley to A. C. Tait, 5 July 1882.
39. W. Bramwell Booth to William Booth, 1882, quoted in Catherine Bramwell Booth, *Bramwell Booth* (1933) p. 175.
40. *The Times*, 24 June 1882; R. T. Davidson and W. Benham, *Life of Archibald Campbell Tait, Archbishop of Canterbury*, vol. II (1891) pp. 511ff.
41. E. Hodder, *Life and Work of the Seventh Earl of Shaftesbury*, vol. III (1886) pp. 433ff, G. B. A. M. Finlayson, *The Seventh Earl of Shaftesbury* (1981) p. 582.
42. Benson Ms: Diary 17 June 1882.
43. *Guardian*, 5 July 1882, *Spectator*, 15 July 1882.
44. Bramwell Booth, *Echoes and Memories*, p. 196.
45. *Record*, 7, 14 July 1882.
46. Benson Ms: Diary 9 June 1882.
47. Ibid., 19 June 1882.
48. Ibid., 21 June 1882.
49. Bramwell Booth, *Echoes and Memories*, p. 69.
50. E. W. Benson to R. T. Davidson, 25 Nov. 1882, A. C. Benson, *Life of Edward White Benson*, vol. I (1899) p. 540.
51. E. W. Benson to B. F. Westcott, 14 Dec. 1882, ibid., p. 543.
52. *The Times*, 11 Apr. 1883; Lambeth Palace Library: Benson Ms 7/98–9 W. Booth to E. W. Benson, 11 Apr. 1883; Benson Ms 7/148 J. F. Mackarness to E. W. Benson, 25 May 1883.
53. Lambeth Palace Library: Davidson Ms: H. Begbie to R. T. Davidson, 22 May 1914; R. T. Davidson to H. Begbie, 3 May 1914. But see his less than enthusiastic reaction to Begbie's draft: R. T. Davidson to Sir Frederick Macmillan, 8 Nov. 1919.
54. *Guardian*, 12 July 1882.
55. F. P. Cobbe, 'The Last Revival', *Contemporary Review*, 42 (1882) 188.
56. J. B. Lightfoot, *Primary Charge. Two Addresses to the Clergy of the Diocese of Durham, December 1882* (1882) p. 70.
57. Caroline Scott, *The Heavenly Witch. The Story of the Maréchale* (1981) pp. 73ff.
58. Lambeth Palace Library: Benson Ms. 100/120: S. Charlesworth to E. W. Benson, 9 Dec. 1890.
59. *The Times*, 19 Feb. 1883.
60. *Guardian*, 28 Feb. 1883.
61. *Spectator*, 24 Feb. 1883.
62. *The Times*, 2 Mar. 1883.
63. Ann Stafford, *The Age of Consent* (1964); Frank Mort, 'Purity, Feminism and the State: Sexuality and Moral Politics 1880–1914', in Mary Langan and Bill Schwarz, *Crises in the British State 1880–1930* (1985).
64. Victor Bailey, '*In Darkest England and the Way Out*. The Salvation Army, Social Reform and the Labour Movement, 1885–1910', *International Review of Social History* (1984); Robertson, 'The Salvation Army', p. 51.
65. D. W. Bebbington, *The Nonconformist Conscience* (1982) p. 30.
66. The most recent is the Marplan poll for the *Sunday Express* in Nov. 1986.
67. D. W. Bebbington, *The Nonconformist Conscience* (1982) p. 30.

I am grateful for assistance to: two archivists, Melanie Barber of Lambeth Palace Library and Major Jenty Fairbank of the Salvation Army International Archives and Research Centre, London; to Dr Victor Bailey of the University of Hull; and to members of the Church History Seminar, University of Cambridge, where a version of this paper was first presented.

10. THE IRISH PROBLEM   Alan O'Day

1. *Irishman*, 9 Mar. 1867.
2. Quoted in *Annual Register* (1868) pp. 3–4.
3. Memorandum, 12 Nov. 1898, Public Record Office (PRO), CAB 37/48/82.
4. Vernon Bogdanor, *Devolution* (Oxford, 1979) p. 8.
5. *Annual Register* (1899) p. 241.
6. Ibid. (1900) p. 251.
7. Nicholas Mansergh, *The Irish Question, 1840–1921*, 3rd edn (1975) pp. 126, 202.
8. F. S. L. Lyons, *Ireland Since the Famine* (1973) p. 3.
9. Quoted in C. H. D. Howard (ed.) *Joseph Chamberlain: A Political Memoir* (1953) p. 253.
10. Census of Ireland, 1881: General Report.
11. Mary Daly, *Dublin, The Deposed Capital* (Cork, 1984) p. 209.
12. L. J. McCaffrey, *Irish Federalism in the 1870s* (Philadelphia, 1961) p. 22; *The Tablet*, 25 June 1881.
13. Census of Ireland, 1881: General Report.
14. Census of Ireland, 1871: General Report.
15. Quoted in Bernard Holland, *The Life of Spencer Compton, Eighth Duke of Devonshire* (1911) I, p. 69.
16. Desmond Keenan, *The Catholic Church in Nineteenth-Century Ireland* (Dublin, 1983) p. 245.
17. Spencer to Gladstone, 7 June 1882, Gladstone Papers, British Library, Add. Ms. 44,309.
18. Spencer to A. Mundella, 5 Aug. 1882, Mundella Papers, University of Sheffield.
19. Churchill to Lord Carnarvon, 27 Aug. 1885, Carnarvon Papers, PRO 30/6/55.
20. G. O. Trevelyan to Gladstone, 25 May 1883, Add. Ms. 44,355.
21. John Morley, *Recollections* (1905) I, pp. 308–9.
22. Morley to Rosebery, 18 Sept. 1892, Rosebery Papers, National Library of Scotland, MS 10,046.
23. *Belfast Newsletter*, 16 May 1898.
24. Raymond Crotty, *Irish Agricultural Production* (Cork, 1966) p. 83.
25. *Nation*, 21 July 1877.
26. *Parliamentary Debates*, LIV (1898) 516–17.
27. Andrew Jones, *The Politics of Reform, 1884* (Cambridge, 1972) p. 127.
28. Charles Townshend, *Political Violence in Ireland* (Oxford, 1983) p. 64.
29. Mrs Campbell Praed, *Our Book of Memories* (1911) p. 33.

30. *The Times*, 22 Apr. 1891.

31. R. V. Comerford, 'Patriotism as Pastime: The Appeal of Fenianism in the Mid-1860s', *Irish Historical Studies*, XXII (1981) 239–50. Reprinted in Alan O'Day (ed.) *Responses to Irish Nationalism, 1865–1914* (1987).

32. A. J. Kettle to Isaac Butt, 5 Jan. 1875, I. Butt Papers, National Library of Ireland, MS 8697 (1); M. Henry to Butt, 19 Sept. 1875, MS 8697 (18).

33. Quoted in Townshend, *Political Violence in Ireland*, p. 118.

34. See Alan O'Day, *Parnell and the First Home Rule Episode* (Dublin, 1986).

35. Quoted in Mark Tierney, *Croke of Cashel* (Dublin, 1976) p. 255.

36. Joseph V. O'Brien, *William O'Brien and the Course of Irish Politics, 1881–1918* (Berkeley, 1976) p. 103.

37. David Thornley, *Isaac Butt and Home Rule* (1964) p. 246; J. P. McAlister to Butt, 5, 12, 16 July 1878, Butt Papers, MS 8700 (11, 19, 21).

38. Emmet Larkin, 'Economic Growth, Capital Investment, and the Roman Catholic Church in Nineteenth-Century Ireland', *American Historical Review*, LXXII (Apr. 1967) 852–84.

39. David Fitzpatrick, *Irish Emigration 1801–1921* (Dublin, 1984).

40. L. M. Cullen, *An Economic History of Ireland since 1660* (1972) pp. 167–80.

41. *Annual Register* (1896) p. 224.

42. G. O. Trevelyan to Earl Spencer, 16 June 1883, Spencer Papers.

11.   DID THE LATE VICTORIAN ECONOMY FAIL?   *Keith Burgess*

1. Martin J. Wiener, *English Culture and the Decline of the Industrial Spirit 1850–1980* (Cambridge, 1981).

2. Stephen Nicholas, 'Total Factor Productivity Growth and the Revision of post-1870 British Economic History', *Economic History Review*, 2nd series, XXXV, no. 1 (1982); Robert R. Locke, *The End of the Practical Man: Entrepreneurship and Higher Education in Germany, France and Great Britain, 1880–1940* (Greenwich, Connecticut, 1984).

3. Sidney Pollard, 'British and World Shipbuilding, 1890–1914: A Study in Comparative Costs', *Journal of Economic History*, XVII, no. 3 (1957).

4. P. L. Payne, *British Entrepreneurship in the Nineteenth Century* (1974).

5. Joseph A. Schumpeter, *Capitalism, Socialism and Democracy* (1943).

6. Bernard Elbaum and William Lazonick (eds) *The Decline of the British Economy* (Oxford, 1986).

7. Donald Coleman and Christine Macleod, 'Attitudes to New Techniques: British Businessman, 1800–1950', *Economic History Review*, 2nd series, XXXIX, no. 4 (1986) 605–9.

8. C. Knick Harley, 'British Industrialisation before 1841: Evidence of Slower Growth During the Industrial Revolution', *Journal of Economic History*, XLII, no. 2 (1982).

9. N. F. R. Crafts, *British Economic Growth during the Industrial Revolution* (Oxford, 1985) Table 3.2, p. 54.

10. Ibid.

11. Ibid., Table 3.6, pp. 62–3.

12. R. C. O. Matthews, C. H. Feinstein and J. C. Odling-Smee, *British Economic Growth 1856–1973* (Oxford, 1982).

13. Locke, *The End of the Practical Man*, is an exception.

14. C. H. Feinstein, R. C. O. Matthews and J. C. Odling-Smee, 'The Timing of the Climacteric and its Sectoral Incidence in the UK, 1873–1913', in C. P. Kindleberger and G. di Tella (eds) *Economics in the Long View* (1982) vol. 2, Table 8.3, p. 175.

15. Crafts, *British Economic Growth*, Table 8.3, p. 175.

16. Feinstein *et al.*, 'The Timing of the Climacteric', Table 8.3, p. 175.

17. Royal Commission on the Depression of Trade and Industry, 1886 (xxi), Cd. 4715, First Report, Appendix A, contains replies to a questionnaire from Chambers of Commerce. In the Second Report, 1886 (xxii), Cd. 4715-I, Appendix D, there are replies to a similar questionnaire from the trade unions, and a comparison of the two is instructive.

18. Mark Thomas, 'Accounting for Growth, 1870–1940: Stephen Nicholas and Total Factor Productivity'; and Stephen Nicholas, 'British Economic Performance and Total Factor Productivity Growth, 1870–1940', *Economic History Review*, 2nd series, xxxviii, no. 4 (1985).

19. Crafts, *British Economic Growth*, Table 8.1, p. 159, confirms this view.

20. Feinstein *et al.*, 'The Timing of the Climacteric', Table 8.3, p. 175.

21. Ibid., Table 8.4, pp. 178–80.

22. Jeffrey G. Williamson, *Did British Capitalism Breed Inequality?* (1985) Table 2.13, p. 30.

23. R. S. Neale, 'The Poverty of Positivism: from Standard of Living to Quality of Life, 1780–1850', in the same author's *Writing Marxist History. British Society, Economy and Culture since 1700* (Oxford, 1985).

24. British Library of Political & Economic Science: Webb Collection E (Trade Unions), Section A, vol. x.

25. James A. Schmiechen, *Sweated Industries and Sweated Labour. The London Clothing Trades, 1860–1914* (1984).

26. See, for example, Eric Hopkins, 'Small Town Aristocrats of Labour and their Standard of Living, 1840–1914', *Economic History Review*, 2nd series, xxviii, no. 2 (1975); A. A. Hall, 'Wages, Earnings and Real Earnings in Teeside: A Re-Assessment of the Ameliorist Interpretation of Living Standards in Britain, 1870–1914', *International Review of Social History*, xxvi, Pt. 2 (1981); Elizabeth Roberts, 'Working-Class Standards of Living in Three Lancashire Towns, 1890–1914', *International Review of Social History*, xxvii, Pt. 1 (1982).

27. Williamson, *Inequality*, Table 4.5, pp. 68–9.

28. Jeffrey G. Williamson, 'Earnings Inequality in Nineteenth Century Britain', *Journal of Economic History*, xl, no. 3 (1980).

29. D. J. Oddy, 'Working-Class Diets in late Nineteenth-Century Britain', *Economic History Review*, 2nd series, xxiii, no. 2 (1970).

30. Peter Mathias, 'Taxation and Industrialisation in Britain, 1700–1870', in his *The Transformation of England* (1979) p. 122.

31. Geoffrey Ingham, *Capitalism Divided? The City and Industry in British Social Development* (1984) p. 9.

32. Marcello de Cecco, *Money and Empire. The International Gold Standard, 1890–1914* (Oxford, 1974).

33. Royal Commission on the Depression of Trade and Industry, 1886 (XXI) First Report, Appendix A.

34. Mitchell Library, Glasgow: Minutes of Glasgow Chamber of Commerce, vol. 12, 1885–92, 103rd Annual Report, 18th Jan. 1886, 12 (ref. M/F 13657); Brooke Adams, 'The Golden Standard', *Fortnightly Review*, LVI (Aug. 1894).

35. David Blackbourn and Geoff Eley, *The Peculiarities of German History. Bourgeois Society and Politics in Nineteenth-Century Germany* (Oxford, 1984).

36. Minutes of Glasgow Chamber of Commerce, vol. 13, 1892–9, Annual General Meeting, 17th Jan. 1898.

37. William P. Kennedy, 'Notes on Economic Efficiency in Historical Perspective: the Case of Britain, 1870–1914', *Research in Economic History*, 9 (1984).

38. Locke, *The End of the Practical Man*. It is noteworthy that the problem here was as much one of 'demand' as of 'supply' in the development of British accountancy, since more sophisticated financial controls *were* developed in Britain in response to the needs of the railway companies during the late Victorian period. I am indebted for this point to Dr T. R. Gourvish.

39. de Cecco, *Money and Empire*; and Kennedy, 'Notes on Economic Efficiency'.

40. Barry J. Eichengreen, 'The Proximate Determinants of Domestic Investment in Victorian Britain', *Journal of Economic History*, XLII, no. 1 (1982), Figure 1.

41. British Library of Political & Economic Science: 1904 Tariff Reform Commission, evidence of T. O. Callender, Managing Director of Callender Cable & Construction Co. Ltd (ref. TC3 1/27).

42. Derek Fraser, *The Evolution of the British Welfare State* (1973), cited pp. 244–5.

43. Crafts, *British Economic Growth*, Table 3.6, pp. 62–3.

44. Williamson, *Inequality*, pp. 100–1.

45. Locke, *The End of the Practical Man*.

46. Paul L. Robertson, 'Employers and Engineering Education in Britain and the United States, 1890–1914', *Business History*, XXIII, no. 1 (1981).

47. 1904 Tariff Commission: see, for example, John McLaren of the Midland Engine Works, Leeds, makers of agricultural machinery, who was a keen advocate of technical education (ref. TC3 1/133).

48. Ibid., Lionel Brook Holliday of Read, Holliday & Sons Ltd, Huddersfield dye-makers (ref. TC3 1/320).

49. Ibid., Messrs A. & W. Flateau, London shoe manufacturers (ref. TC3 1/216).

50. Royal Commission on the Depression of Trade and Industry, 1886 (XXI), Second Report, Cd. 4715-I, evidence of J. W. Dixon, p. 253.

51. Crafts, *British Economic Growth*, pp. 160–3.

52. 1904 Tariff Commission: see, for example, the evidence of Bergtheil & Young Ltd, Engineers & Electric Power Specialists, London (ref. TC3 1/315).

53. Ingham, *Capitalism Divided?* See also John Turner (ed.) *Businessmen and Politics. Studies of Business Activity in British Politics 1900–1945* (1984), Chapter 1.

54. P. L. Payne, 'The Emergence of the Large-scale Company in Great Britain, 1870–1914', *Economic History Review*, 2nd series, xv, no. 3 (1967); Alfred A. Chandler, 'The Growth of the Transnational Firm in the United States and the United Kingdom: A Comparative Analysis', *Economic History Review*, 2nd series, xxxii, no. 3 (1980).

55. John Scott and Catherine Griff, *Directors of Industry. The British Corporate Network 1904–1976* (Oxford, 1984) pp. 49–50.

56. R. C. Michie, 'The London Stock Exchange and the British Securities Market, 1850–1914', *Economic History Review*, 2nd series, xxxviii, no. 1 (1985) Table 3.

57. C. H. Lee, 'Regional Growth and Structural Change in Victorian Britain', *Economic History Review*, 2nd series, xxxiv, no. 3 (1981).

58. Ibid., 451.

59. See, for example, M. W. Kirby, *Men of Business and Politics. The Rise and Fall of the Quaker Pease Dynasty of North-East England 1700–1943* (1984).

12. SCIENCE AND THE ANGLO-GERMAN ANTAGONISM   *P. Alter*

1. Lecture to the Literary and Philosophical Society in Newcastle, on 19 Nov. 1900. Printed under the title *National Life from the Standpoint of Science* (1901). A second edition appeared in 1905.

2. *Nature*, 71 (1904–5) 108.

3. Address to the constituent assembly of the British Science Guild (*The Times*, 31 Oct. 1905).

4. The term 'scientific community' here covers, apart from the scientists themselves, all those who publicly championed the interests of science in Britain. On the problems associated with this term, see W. O. Hagstrom *The Scientific Community* (New York and London, 1965).

5. H. Rose and S. Rose, *Science and Society* (Harmondsworth, 1971) p. 32.

6. G. L'E. Turner (ed.) 'Introduction', in *The Patronage of Science in the Nineteenth Century* (Leyden, 1976) p. 5.

7. D. S. L. Cardwell, *The Organisation of Science in England*, 2nd edn (1972).

8. J. B. Poole and K. Andrews (eds) *The Government of Science in Britain* (1972) p. 28.

9. Lockyer's address is printed in *Report of the Seventy-Third Meeting of the British Association for the Advancement of Science* (1904) pp. 3–28. Also in *Nature*, 68 (1903) 439–47, and in J. Norman Lockyer, *Education and National Progress. Essays and Addresses, 1870–1905* (1906) pp. 172–215. See also T. Mary Lockyer and Winifred L. Lockyer, *Life and Work of Sir Norman Lockyer* (1928) p. 186; A. J. Meadows, *Science and Controversy. A Biography of Sir Norman Lockyer* (Cambridge, Mass., 1972) p. 266.

10. *Report of the Seventy-Third Meeting of the British Association*, pp. 5–6.

11. Ibid., pp. 3–4 and 27–8.

12. For the terminology, see J. Ben-David, *Centers of Learning. Britain, France, Germany, United States* (New York, 1977), 'The Rise and Decline of

France as a Scientific Centre', *Minerva. A Review of Science, Learning and Policy*, 8 (1970) 160–79, and 'Scientific Growth: A Sociological View', *Minerva*, 2 (1964) 455–76; R. von Gizycki, 'Centre and Periphery in the International Scientific Community: Germany, France and Great Britain in the Nineteenth Century', *Minerva*, 11 (1973) 474–94.

13. A. O'Day (ed.) *The Edwardian Age: Conflict and Stability 1900–1914* (1979).

14. According to Richard B. Haldane at the Annual Meeting of the Chemical Society in 1905, *Nature*, 71 (1904–5) 589.

15. According to the president of the Chemical Society at the Annual Meeting of the Society in 1907, *Nature*, 76 (1907) 231.

16. *Nature*, 94 (1914–15) 547.

17. D. S. L. Cardwell, *Technology, Science and History* (1972) p. 192. See also G. Haines, *Essays on German Influence upon English Education and Science, 1850–1919* (Hamden, Conn., 1969) pp. 21, 60–7; G. Hollenberg, *Englisches Interesse am Kaiserreich. Die Attraktivität Preussen-Deutschlands für konservative und liberale Kreise in Großbritannien 1860–1914* (Wiesbaden, 1974); P. M. Kennedy, *The Rise of the Anglo-German Antagonism 1860–1914* (1980) pp. 103–23. Between 1849 and 1914, about 9000 British students were enrolled at German universities (Gizycki, 'Centre and Periphery', 483). Hollenberg (pp. 297–9) gives a list of British professors who had spent some time in Germany as students.

18. P. Alter, *The Reluctant Patron: Science and the State in Britain 1850–1920* (Leamington Spa, 1987) pp. 138–72; E. Pyatt, *The National Physical Laboratory. A History* (Bristol, 1983); A. R. Hall, *Science for Industry. A Short History of the Imperial College of Science and Technology and its Antecedents* (1982).

19. A. Geikie, 'Retrospect and Prospect', *Nature*, 104 (1919–20) 196.

20. 'The Kaiser-Wilhelm Society for the Promotion of Science', *Nature*, 86 (1911) 69.

21. See C. Trebilcock, 'War and the Failure of Industrial Mobilisation: 1899 and 1914', in J. M. Winter (ed.) *War and Economic Development. Essays in Memory of David Joslin* (Cambridge, 1975) pp. 148–50.

22. See G. R. Searle, *The Quest for National Efficiency. A Study in British Politics and British Political Thought, 1899–1914* (Oxford, 1971); B. Semmel, *Imperialism and Social Reform. English Social-Imperial Thought, 1895–1914* (Oxford, 1960); H. C. G. Matthew, *The Liberal Imperialists. The Ideas and Politics of a Post-Gladstonian Elite* (Oxford, 1973); E. J. T. Brennan (ed.) *Education for National Efficiency: The Contribution of Sidney and Beatrice Webb* (1975).

23. Eric J. Hobsbawm writes about this: 'There was, especially in the last years before the First World War, an atmosphere of uneasiness, or disorientation, of tension, which contradicts the journalistic impression of a stable *belle époque*. . . . They were the years when wisps of violence hung in the English air, symptoms of a crisis in economy and society which the self-confident opulence of the architecture of Ritz hotels, pro-consular palaces, West End theatres, department stores and office-blocks could not quite conceal', *Industry and Empire. An Economic History of Britain since 1750* (1973) pp. 162–3.

24. *Daily Mail*, 8 June 1901.
25. E. E. Williams, *Made in Germany* (1896) p. 1. See R. J. S. Hoffmann, *Great Britain and the German Trade Rivalry, 1875–1914* (1933, reprint New York, 1964); C. P. Kindleberger, 'Germany's Overtaking of England, 1806 to 1914', in his *Economic Response. Comparative Studies in Trade, Finance, and Growth* (Cambridge, Mass., 1978) pp. 185–236.
26. Aniline Dyes, CAB 37/66/63, 30 July 1903 (PRO).
27. See especially C. Wilson, 'Economy and Society in late Victorian Britain', *Economic History Review*, 18 (1965) 183–98; D. N. McCloskey, 'Did Victorian Britain Fail?', *Economic History Review*, 23 (1970) 446–59; A. L. Levine, *Industrial Retardation in Britain 1880–1914* (1967); S. B. Saul, *Industrialisation and De-Industrialisation? The Interaction of the German and British Economies before the First World War* (1980), D. H. Aldcroft and H. W. Richardson, *The British Economy 1870–1939* (1969); M. W. Kirby, *The Decline of British Economic Power since 1870* (1981) pp. 1–23; P. Warwick, 'Did Britain Change? An Inquiry into the Causes of National Decline', *Journal of Contemporary History*, 20 (1985) 99–113; R. Floud and D. McCloskey (eds) *The Economic History of Britain since 1700*, vol. 2, *1860 to the 1970s* (Cambridge, 1981).
28. D. H. Aldcroft, 'The Entrepreneur and the British Economy, 1870–1914', *Economic History Review*, 17 (1964–5) 113; D. C. Coleman, 'Gentlemen and Players', *Economic History Review*, 26 (1973) 92–116; D. N. McCloskey (ed.) *Essays on a Mature Economy: Britain after 1840* (1971); N. F. R. Crafts, *British Economic Growth during the Industrial Revolution* (Oxford, 1985) esp. Chapter 8: 'Some Legacies of the Early Start', pp. 155–77. See also M. J. Wiener, *English Culture and the Decline of the Industrial Spirit, 1850–1980* (Cambridge, 1981).
29. W. E. H. Lecky, *Democracy and Liberty*, vol. 1 (1896) p. 276.
30. M. Foster, 'The State and Scientific Research', *The Nineteenth Century and After*, 55 (1904) 742–3.
31. See Alter, *Reluctant Patron*, pp. 22–35, 138–77.
32. See instead C. E. McClelland, *State, Society, and University in Germany 1700–1914* (Cambridge, 1980).
33. O. MacDonagh, 'The Nineteenth-Century Revolution in Government: A Reappraisal', *Historical Journal*, 1 (1958) 52–67. See also F. Bédarida, 'L'Angleterre victorienne paradigme du laissez-faire? A propos d'une controverse', *Revue Historique*, 261 (1979) 79–98.
34. W. H. Brock, 'The Spectrum of Science Patronage', in Turner (ed.) *Patronage*, pp. 173–206.
35. Hansard, Parl. Deb., 4th Series, vol. 101, col. 800 (24 Jan. 1902).
36. *Nature*, 71 (1904–5) 107.
37. *Reports from those Universities and University Colleges in Great Britain which Participated in the Parliamentary Grant for University Colleges in the Year 1908–09*, Cd. 5246 (1910) p. iii.
38. Ibid., p. iv.
39. *Nature*, 100 (1917–18) 266.
40. R. Meldola, 'The Position and Prospects of Chemical Research in Great Britain', *Nature*, 76 (1907) 232.
41. R. MacLeod and E. K. MacLeod, 'The Social Relations of Science and

Technology 1914–1939', in C. M. Cipolla (ed.) *The Fontana Economic History of Europe: The Twentieth Century* (Glasgow, 1976) p. 306.

42. *Report on Chemical Instruction in Germany and the Growth and Present Condition of the German Chemical Industries* (Diplomatic and Consular Reports, Misc. Series), Cd. 430 (1901) p. 32.

43. 'Anniversary Meeting of the Royal Society', *Nature*, 67 (1902–3) 108.

44. *Nature*, 94 (1914–15) 292.

45. R. MacLeod, 'The Support of Victorian Science: The Endowment of Research Movement in Great Britain, 1868–1900', *Minerva*, 4 (1971) 228.

46. Meldola, 'Position and Prospects', 233.

47. A. H. Halsey, 'British Universities and Intellectual Life', in Halsey, J. E. Floud and C. A. Anderson (eds) *Education, Economy and Society* (New York, 1961), p. 507.

Notes on Contributors

PETER ALTER took his degrees at the University of Cologne and also studied at Corpus Christi College, Oxford. He is deputy director of the German Historical Institute, London, and Professor of Modern History at the University of Cologne. His publications have been in the area of Irish, British and German history and include *Die irische Nationalbewegung zwischen Parlament und Revolution, Nationalismus, The Reluctant Patron: Science and the State in Britain 1850–1920* and numerous articles.

KEITH BURGESS received his BA and MA from the University of California, Los Angeles, and a PhD from the University of Leeds. He is head of the History Department at the Roehampton Institute of Higher Education. His publications include *The Origins of British Industrial Relations, The Challenge of Labour: Shaping British Society 1850–1930* and numerous articles in journals and collected volumes. He is currently completing a social history of the eugenics movement.

M. J. DAUNTON received his BA from the University of Nottingham and PhD from the University of Kent. He is Reader in History at University College, London. His publications include *Coal Metropolis: Cardiff, 1870–1914, House and Home in the Victorian City: Working-class Housing, 1850–1914, Royal Mail: The Post Office since 1840,* (ed.) *Councillors and Tenants: Local Authority Housing in English Cities, 1919–1939* and numerous articles. He is currently preparing a social history of the City of London in the nineteenth century.

J. P. D. DUNBABIN studied at the University of Oxford. He is Official Fellow and Tutor in Politics and Modern History at St Edmund Hall, Oxford. His many publications include *Rural Discontent in Nineteenth Century Britain,* numerous articles in the *English Historical Review, Past and Present, Economic History Review, Historical Journal* and other journals and edited volumes. *The History of Oxford,* vol. 5 contains his 'College Estates and Wealth 1660–1815', and the forthcoming vol. 6 will have 'College and University Incomes and Endowments, 1815–1914'. He is currently completing *Make Do and Mend: A History of International Relations, 1945–80.*

JOHN GARRARD received his degrees from the Universities of Keele and Manchester. He is Lecturer in Politics and Contemporary History at the University of Salford. His publications include *The English and Immigration 1880–1914, Leadership and Power in Victorian Industrial Towns 1830–80,* (co. ed.) *The Middle Classes in Politics* and numerous articles.

T. R. GOURVISH received his degrees from the University of London (King's

College; LSE). He is Senior Lecturer in Economic and Social History and Dean of the School of Economic and Social Studies, University of East Anglia. His publications include *Mark Huish and the London & North Western Railway*, *Railways and the British Economy 1830–1914*, *British Railways 1948–73: A Business History* and numerous articles. Since 1979 he has been joint editor of *The Journal of Transport History*. He has just completed a business history of Steward & Patteson, the Norwich brewers.

PAUL HAYES received his degrees from the University of Oxford and also studied at the universities of Dijon, Marburg and Lausanne. He is Official Fellow in Modern History and Politics at Keble College, Oxford. His publications include *Quisling: The Career and Political Ideas of Vidkum Quisling, 1887–1945*, *Fascism*, two volumes in the Modern British Foreign Policy Series, *The Nineteenth Century, 1814–80* and *The Twentieth Century, 1880–1939*, and numerous articles. At present most of his research is into post-Bismarckian Germany and he is based for several months a year at the Max-Planck Institute for History in Gottingen.

STUART MEWS received his BA and MA from the University of Leeds and PhD from the University of Cambridge, where his thesis was awarded the Hulsean Prize. He is Lecturer in Religious Studies at the University of Lancaster. His publications include (ed.) *Religion and National Identity* and numerous articles. He is editor of *Religion*. Recently he has been a Visiting Research Fellow at St John's College, Oxford. Hs is completing a book on English religion in the years 1900–18.

ALAN O'DAY received his BA and MA from American universities and a PhD from the University of London. He is Senior Lecturer in History, The Polytechnic of North London. His publications include *The English Face of Irish Nationalism*, *Parnell and the First Home Rule Episode*, (ed.) *The Edwardian Age*, (co. ed.) *Terrorism in Ireland*, (co. ed.) *Ireland's Terrorist Dilemma*, (ed.) *Reactions to Irish Nationalism, 1865–1914* and several articles. He is a member of the panel preparing a study of ethnic minorities in modern Europe sponsored by the European Science Foundation.

ROLAND QUINAULT received his MA and DPhil from the University of Oxford and also studied at Columbia University. He is Senior Lecturer in History, The Polytechnic of North London. His publications include (co. ed.) *Popular Protest and Public Order* and numerous articles in the *English Historical Review*, *Historical Journal*, *Irish Historical Studies* and other periodicals and volumes. He is preparing a book on the politics of the Churchill family and investigating parliamentary reform in modern Britain.

PAT THANE received her degrees from the Universities of Oxford and London (LSE). She is Principal Lecturer in social history, Department of Social Science and Administration, Goldsmiths' College, London. Her publications include *The Foundations of the Welfare State*, (ed.) *Origins of British Social Policy*, (co. ed.) *The Power of the Past: Essays for Eric Hobsbawm*, (co. ed.) *Essays in Social*

History, vol. 2 and numerous articles. She is a member of the Council of the Economic History Society and of the committee of the Social History Society of Great Britain. Currently she is engaged in research on the history of women, of old age and of British financiers in the period 1880–1950.

Index

Kingsley, Mary, 191
Kinnaird, Lord, 219
Kipling, Rudyard, 89
Kitto, John F., 221
Kuwait, 163

labour, 9, 39, 47, 196–7:
  agricultural, 77–9, 113–14, 199,
  238; casual, 54, 67, 194; market,
  62, 200, 203; unrest, 1, 145, 257,
  259
Lagos, 163
Laing, Samuel, 99
laissez-faire, 11, 112, 125, 162, 238,
  273, 285
Lancashire, 7, 67, 94, 110, 122, 125,
  127–50
Lansdowne, Lord, 83, 165, 170
Larson, Margali S., 15
Laurier, Sir Wilfrid, 88
law, lawyers, 15, 19, 21–5 *passim*,
  30, 35, 115, 234
Law Society, 23, 25
Lawson, Wilfrid, 219
Lawton, J. E., 133
Lecky, W. E. H., 283
Lee, Henry, 139
Leeds, 41, 44–5, 57, 65
legislation: Apothecaries Act 1815,
  25–6; Artisans' and Labourers'
  Dwellings Improvement Act
  1875, 53–4; Burials Act 1880,
  125, 227; Contagious Diseases
  Acts 1864, 1868–9, 185–6;
  Criminal Law Amendment Act
  1885, 186; Dentists Act 1878, 21;
  Education Act 1870, 28–9, 50,
  75, 77, 79, 109; Education Act
  1902, 29; Housing Act 1890, 54;
  Irish Land Act 1903, 237–8;
  Land Law (Ireland) Act 1881,
  248; Land Transfer Act 1897, 25;
  Matrimonial Causes Act 1857,
  179; Medical Act 1858, 21, 26;
  Medical Act 1886, 26–7;
  Metropolis Management Act
  1855, 50–1; Naval Defence Act
  1889, 169; Poor Law Amendment

Act 1834, 95; Public Health Act
1858, 55; Public Health Act
1875, 55; Public Worship
Regulation Act 1874, 210;
Regulation of Railways Act 1868,
31; Small Holdings Act 1892, 78;
Solicitors Act 1888, 25; Supreme
Court of Judicature Act 1873, 25;
Town Planning Act 1909, 56;
Trade Boards Act 1909, 205;
Tramways Act 1870, 41; *see also*
electoral reform
Leicester, 58, 194
Letchworth, 56–7
Levant, 156–8, 166
Liberty and Property Defence
  League, 45
Lightfoot, Bishop, 221, 224–5
limited liability, 31, 264–5, 268
Lincolnshire (South), 94
Liverpool, 5, 37, 47, 82
Llandaff, 217
Llanfrothen, 125
Lloyd George, David, 49, 56, 125
local government, 5, 14, 40–2, 50,
  53, 74, 79, 89, 206–7, 233, 237,
  239; bureaucracy, 46; cost of, 43–
  4, 46–7, 50, 75; investment by, 5,
  40, 42–3, 45
Local Government Board, 55, 78
Lockyer, Sir Norman, 272, 274
London, 5, 6, 26, 37–40 *passim*, 50–
  1, 55, 56, 63–5 *passim*, 71–3, 89,
  116, 192, 211, 219, 224, 259, 286:
  the City, 6, 11, 64, 71–2, 162,
  261–9 *passim*; London County
  Council, 46, 51, 75, 110;
  Metropolitan Board of Works,
  50–1, 79
Lowe, Robert, 96, 111
Lucy, Henry, 90, 91
Luxembourg, 168
Lyons, F. S. L., 231–2, 242–3
Lyons Corner House, 66
Lyttleton, Alfred, 83

Maamtrasna incident, 241–2
Macarthur, Mary, 205